The Ultimate Guide to Planning Your Estate

The
Estate
Planning
Toolkit

The Ultimate Guide to Planning Your Estate

The
Estate
Planning
Toolkit

DANIEL SITARZ, ATTORNEY-AT-LAW

Nova Publishing Company
Small Business and Consumer Legal Books
Carbondale Illinois

ISBN 10: 1-892949-44-X
ISBN 13: 978-1-892949-44-8
Book w/CD-Rom   price: $39.95

Cataloging-in-Publication Data
      Sitarz, Dan, 1948-
      The Estate Planning Toolkit / by Daniel Sitarz -- 1st ed. --Carbondale, Ill.:
      Nova Publishing, c2008
           p. ; cm + CD-ROM (4.75")
      (Legal Toolkit Series) Includes index
      ISBN 978-1-892949-44-8
      At head of title: The Ultimate Guide to Planning Your Estate

      1. Estate planning--United States--Popular works. 2. Estate planning--United States--States--Popular works.
      3. Estate planning--United States--Forms. 4. Wills--United States--Popular works. 5. Wills--United States--Forms
      I. Title. II. Title: Ultimate Guide to Planning Your Estate III. Series
      KF750 .S5854 2008   346.7305/2-dc22   0806

Nova Publishing Company is dedicated to providing up-to-date and accurate legal information to the public. All Nova publications are periodically revised to contain the latest available legal information.

1st Edition; 1st Printing / June, 2008

DISCLAIMER

Nova Publishing Company   Distributed by:
Small Business and Consumer Legal Books and Software   National Book Network
1103 West College St.   4501 Forbes Blvd., Suite 200
Carbondale, IL 62901   Lanham, MD 20706
Tech Support: (800) 748-1175   Orders: (800) 462-6420 or
Editorial: (618)457-3521   www.novapublishing.com

Nova Publishing Company Green Business Policies

Nova Publishing Company is committed to preserving ancient forests and natural resources. Our company's policy is to print all of our books on recycled paper, with 100% post-consumer waste de-inked in a chlorine-free process. In addition, all Nova books are printed using soy-based inks. As a result, for the printing of this book, we have saved:

26.1 trees • 75,61 gallons of water • 4,428 kilowatt hours of electricity • 64.8 pounds of pollution

Nova Publishing Company is proud to be one of the first members of the Green Press Initiative, a nonprofit program dedicated to supporting publishers in their efforts to reduce their use of fiber obtained from endangered forests. Nova Publishing is also proud to be an initial signatory on the Book Industry Treatise on Responsible Paper Use. For more information, check out www.greenpressinitiative.org. In addition, Nova uses all compact fluorescent lighting; recycles all office paper products, aluminum and plastic beverage containers, and printer cartridges; uses 100% post-consumer fiber, process-chlorine-free, acid-free paper for 95% of in-house paper use; and, when possible, uses electronic equipment that is EPA Energy Star-certified. Nova's freight shipments are coordinated to minimize energy use whenever possible. Finally, all carbon emissions from Nova office energy use are offset by the purchase of wind-energy credits that are used to subsidize the building of wind turbines on the Rosebud Sioux Reservation in South Dakota (see www.nativeenergy.com).
We strongly encourage other publishers and all partners in publishing supply chains to adopt similar policies.

Table of Contents

CHAPTER 10: Changing a Living Trust 216

CHAPTER 11: Preparing a Living Will 223

CHAPTER 12: Preparing a Health Care Power of Attorney 236

List of Forms (in book and on CD)
All Forms on CD are in PDF and text format unless noted

Property Questionnaire
Beneficiary Questionnaire
Successor Trustee/Executor Duties Checklist
Successor Trustee/Executor Information Checklist
Will for Married Person with Children
Will for Single Person with Children
Will for Married Person with No Children
Will for Single Person with No Children
Codicil
Living Trust with Children's Trust
Living Trust without Children's Trust
Schedule of Assets of Living Trust
Schedule of Beneficiaries of Living Trust
Assignment to Living Trust
Registration of Living Trust
New York Notice of Assignment of Property to Living Trust
Affidavit of Assumption of Duties by Successor Trustee
Amendment to Living Trust
Revocation of Living Trust
Living Will and Directive to Physicians
Revocation of Living Will
Durable Health Care Power of Attorney and Appointment of Health Care Agent
    and Proxy
Durable Unlimited Power of Attorney for Financial Affairs-effective immediately
Durable Unlimited Power of Attorney for Financial Affairs-effective on disability
State-Specific Durable Powers of Attorney (PDF format only & on-CD only; certain
    states only: *Alaska, Arkansas, California, Colorado, Connecticut, District of Co-
    lumbia, Georgia, Illinois, Montana, Nebraska, New Hampshire, New Mexico, New
    York, North Carolina, Oklahoma, Pennsylvania, Rhode Island, Texas*)
Revocation of Durable Unlimited Power of Attorney for Financial Affairs
State-Specific Advance Health Care Directives (PDF format only & on CD only;
    available for all states)
Revocation of Advance Health Care Directive
Witness Affidavit of Oral Revocation of Advance Health Care Directive
Additional Information for Advance Health Care Directive
Designation of Primary Physician

Introduction to the Estate Planning Toolkit

This book is designed to assist its readers in understanding the general aspects of the law as it relates to estate planning and after-death distribution of property, and to assist its readers in the preparation of their own estate plans. However, the range of personal finances, property, and desires is infinite and one book cannot hope to cover all potential situations or contingencies. In situations involving complex personal or business property holdings, complicated or substantial financial investments, or unusual or highly-complex post-death distribution plans, readers are advised to seek additional competent legal advice. In addition, estate and inheritance tax laws and regulations are among the most complex laws in existence. Consequently, although a general overview of these laws is provided and the vast majority of people are exempt from Federal estate taxes, readers with very large estates (generally, over $1 million) or complex financial resources are encouraged to seek the assistance of a tax professional or attorney if they wish to limit or lessen the tax consequences of the transfer of any property.

Regardless of whether or not a lawyer is ultimately retained in certain situations, the legal information in this handbook will enable the reader to understand the framework of law in this country as it relates to estate planning. To try and make that task as easy as possible, technical legal jargon has been eliminated whenever possible and plain English used instead. When it is necessary to use a legal term which may be unfamiliar to most

> **⚡ Warning!**
>
> If the total value of your property is over $1 million, you should see a tax professional or tax attorney before using any of the estate planning tools in this book.

> **⊘ Definition:**
>
> ## Estate:
> All of your assets, both real estate and personal property. Essentially, every thing that you own.

> **⊘ Definition:**
>
> ## Beneficiary:
> Someone who benefits from or receives money or property, often through a will or trust.

> **⊘ Definition:**
>
> ## Probate:
> The court-supervised administration of a person's estate (generally based on the person's will or on statutory rules if there is no will).

people, it will be shown in *italics* and defined when first used. There is a glossary of most legal terms used in the process of estate planning at the end of this book. It will help in deciphering your current estate plan if it was prepared by an attorney using outdated technical legal language. Lawyers often caution people that such antiquated language is most important and that, of course, only they, the lawyers, can properly prepare and interpret legal documents using such language. Naturally, plain and easily-understood English is not only perfectly proper for use in all legal documents, but in most cases, leads to far less confusion on the part of later readers.

Chapter 1 of this guide will attempt to explain the usefulness and in many cases the necessity of a comprehensive estate plan. An estate plan can help insure that your property and money are passed on to the loved ones whom you desire and that you have made arrangements in advance for your health care in case of an emergency situation. Chapter 1 will also explain the legal effects of having an estate plan and the potential consequences of not having a plan.

In Chapter 2, guidelines are provided for planning the distribution of your estate. Your *estate* consists of all of your assets, both real estate and personal property. Estate planning tools, such as wills, living wills, living trusts and powers of attorneys are discussed. A step-by-step outline of the procedures to follow to prepare your own estate plan using this book is also provided. In addition, an estate planning chart provides a side-by side comparison of the various estate planning tools that are discussed in this book.

Chapter 3 provides a discussion of what property may be disposed of with your estate plan. It also provides a detailed Property Questionnaire that will allow you to assemble the necessary property and financial information that you will need in preparing your estate plan. This chapter also includes information on the inheritance and estate tax consequences of the transfer of property at death. Chapter 4 provides information on who may be a *beneficiary* (one who benefits or receives a gift through a will or trust). This chapter also explains the various forms your gifts may take and also provides a thorough Beneficiary Questionnaire for setting out your decisions on who should receive which of your assets.

Chapter 5 includes an overview of information relating to the *probate* (court administration) of your estate, information, and a checklist for use by your executor (or successor trustee, if you decide to utilize a living trust in your estate plan), and a final information sheet for your executor's use in locating your assets and administering your estate.

In Chapter 6, four pre-assembled wills are provided for use. The mechanics and legal requirements for actually preparing your will are set forth in Chapter 7. These requirements, although not at all difficult, must be followed precisely to insure that your will is acceptable as a valid legal document. Methods and instructions for safeguarding your will are also contained in this chapter. Chapter 8 contains information regarding when it may be prudent and how to accomplish any changes or alterations to your will at a later date.

If you should decide to include one in your estate plan, the necessary forms and instructions for preparing a *living trust* are provided in Chapter 9. A living trust is a document designed to avoid probate when distributing property upon one's death. Chapter 10 provides instructions for amending or revoking your living trust.

Chapter 11 provides an explanation and form for your preparation of a *living will*—a document directing that, if you are diagnosed as terminally ill or in a vegetative state, you desire that no extraordinary life support measures be instituted to artificially prolong your life.

In Chapter 12, instructions are provided for preparing a basic *health care power of attorney* form, a document that provides a person of your choosing with the legal authority to issue instructions to your physician in the event that you are unable to communicate.

Chapter 13 provides for creating a *durable power of attorney for financial affairs*, which is a type of general power of attorney that remains in effect even in the event of your incapacitation. Chapter 14 explains the use of an *advance health care directive*. State-specific forms for this are provided on the enclosed CD. Chapter 15 provides for selecting a primary physician in advance

---

⊘ Definition:

Living Will:
A legal document that directs how you would like artificial life support to be used if you are diagnosed as terminally ill or in a vegetative state.

⊘ Definition:

Living Trust:
A revocable trust that allows you to designate that your property pass directly to your chosen beneficiaries without passing through the probate process.

Ø Definition:

Advance Health Care Directive: Comprehensive form that contains a state-specific living will, health care power of attorney, primary physician designation and organ donation form.

of any health care emergencies and Chapter 16 provides instructions on preparing an Organ Donation form. The final chapter, Chapter 17, provides instructions for using a quitclaim deed if needed to complete your estate plan.

The Appendix contains a detailed listing of the individual state legal requirements relating to wills, living wills, trusts, and other estate planning issues for each of the 50 states and the District of Columbia. Finally, a glossary of legal terms most often encountered in estate planning is included.

As with many routine legal tasks, preparation of an estate plan is not as difficult as most people fear. With the proper information before them, most people will be able to prepare a legally-valid estate plan which specifically addresses their individual needs in a matter of a few hours. Read through this manual carefully, follow the step-by-step instructions, and be assured that your wishes will be safely contained in your own personalized estate plan.

☿ Toolkit Tip!

Check your home state's listing in the Appendix to see any specific state laws for your location.

Installation Instructions for Installing Forms-on-CD

Installation Instructions for PCs

1. Insert the enclosed CD in your computer.
2. The installation program will start automatically. Follow the onscreen dialogue and make your appropriate choices.
3. If the CD installation does not start automatically, click on START, then RUN, then BROWSE, and select your CD drive, and then select the file "Install.exe." Finally, click OK to run the installation program.
4. During the installation program, you will be prompted as to whether or not you wish to install the Adobe Acrobat Reader® program. This software program is necessary to view and fill in the PDF (potable document format) forms that are included on the Forms-on-CD. If you do not already have the Adobe Acrobat Reader® program installed on your hard drive, you will need to select the full installation that will install the program on your computer.

Installation Instructions for MACs®

1. Insert the enclosed CD in your computer.
2. Copy the folder "Forms for Macs" to your hard drive. All of the PDF and text-only forms are included in this folder.
3. If you do not already have the Adobe Acrobat Reader® program installed on your hard drive, you will need to download the version of this software that is appropriate for your particular MAC operating system from www.adobe.com. Note: The latest versions of the MAC operating system (OS-X) has PDF capabilities built into it.

☿ Toolkit Tip!

MAC ® users will need to download Adobe Acrobat Reader ® directly from *www.adobe.com*.

Instructions for Using Forms-on-CD

All of the forms that are included in this book have been provided on the Forms-on-CD for your use if you have access to a computer. If you have completed the Forms-on-CD installation program, all of the forms will have been copied to your computer's hard drive. By default, these files are installed in the C:\Estate Planning Toolkit\Forms folder which is created by the installation program. (Note for MAC users: see instructions above). Opening the Forms folder will provide you with access to folders for each of the topics corresponding to chapters in the book. Within each chapter, the forms are provided in two separate formats:

Text forms may be opened, prepared, and printed from within your own word processing program (such as Microsoft Word®, or WordPerfect®). The text forms all have the file extension: .txt. These forms are located in the TEXT FORMS folders supplied for each chapter's forms. You will use the forms in this format if you will be making changes to any of the text on the forms. Please page 18 for steps on how to access and use text forms.

PDF forms may be filled in on your computer screen and printed out on any printer. This particular format provides the most widely-used format for accessing computer files. Files in this format may be opened as images on your computer and printed out on any printer. The files in PDF format all have the file extension: .pdf. Although this format provides the easiest method for completing the forms, the forms in this format can not be altered (other than to fill in the information required on the blanks provided). To access the PDF forms, please see below. If you wish to alter the language in any of the forms, you will need to access the forms in their text-only versions. To access these text-only forms, please also see page 18.

☀Toolkit Tip!

Use the 'PDF' forms that are provided on the CD if you wish to simply fill in and print out the form that you select.

To Access PDF Forms

1. You must have already installed the Adobe Acrobat Reader® program to your computer's hard drive. This program is installed automatically by the installation program. (MAC users will need to install this program via www.adobe.com).

2. On your computer's desktop, you will find a shortcut icon labeled "Acrobat Reader®" Using your mouse, left double click on this icon. This will open the Acrobat Reader® program. When the Acrobat Reader® program is opened for the first time, you will need to accept the Licensing Agreement from Adobe in order to use this program. Click "Accept" when given the option to accept or decline the Agreement.

3. Once the Acrobat Reader® program is open on your computer, click on FILE (in the upper left-hand corner of the upper taskbar). Then click on OPEN in the drop down menu. Depending on which version of Windows or other operating system you are using, a box will open which will allow you to access files on your computer's hard drive. The files for estate planning forms are located on your computer's "C" drive, under the folder "Estate Planning Toolkit." In this folder, you will find a subfolder "Forms." (Note: if you installed the forms folder on a different drive, access the forms on that particular drive).

4. If you desire to work with one of the forms, you should then left double-click your mouse on the sub-folder: "Forms." A list of form topics (corresponding to the chapters in the book) will appear and you should then left double-click your mouse on the topic of your choice. This will open two

folders: one for text forms and one for PDF forms. Left double click your mouse on the PDF forms folder and a list of the PDF forms for that topic should appear. Left double click your mouse on the form of your choice. This will open the appropriate form within the Acrobat Reader® program.

To Fill in and Use PDF Forms

1. Once you have opened the appropriate form in the Acrobat Reader® program, filling in the form is a simple process. A 'hand tool' icon will be your cursor in the Acrobat Reader® program. Move the 'hand tool' cursor to the first blank space that will need to be completed on the form. A vertical line or "I-beam" should appear at the beginning of the first space on a form that you will need to fill in. You may then begin to type the necessary information in the space provided. When you have filled in the first blank space, hit the TAB key on your keyboard. This will move the 'hand' cursor to the next space which must be filled in. Please note that some of the spaces in the forms must be completed by hand, specifically the signature blanks.

2. Move through the form, completing each required space, and hitting TAB to move to the next space to be filled in. For details on the information required for each blank on the forms, please read the instructions in this book. When you have completed all of the fill-ins, you may print out the form on your computer's printer. (Please note: hitting TAB after the last fill-in will return you to the first page of the form.)

3. IMPORTANT NOTE: Unfortunately, the Adobe Acrobat Reader® program does NOT allow you to save the filled-in form to your computer's hard drive. You can only save the form in a printed version. For this reason, you should complete a form only when you have all of the information necessary to complete a form in one session. You may, of course, leave the Acrobat program open on your computer and leave a partially-completed form open in the program. However, if you close the file or if you close the Acrobat Reader® program, the filled-in information will be lost.

> **Toolkit Tip!**
>
> Filled-in PDF forms can be printed out but not saved in the Adobe Acrobat Reader® software program.

☀Toolkit Tip!

Use the 'text' forms that are provided on the CD if you wish to make changes to the form you select.

To Access and Complete Text Forms

For your convenience, all of the forms in this book (except certain state-specific forms) are also provided as text-only forms which may be altered and saved. To open and use any of the text forms:

1. First, open your preferred word processing program. Then click on FILE (in the upper left-hand corner of the upper taskbar). Then click on OPEN in the drop down menu. Depending on which version of Windows or other operating system you are using, a box will open which will allow you to access files on your computer's hard drive. The files for estate planning forms are located on your computer's "C" drive, under the folder "Estate Planning Toolkit." In this folder, you will find a sub-folder: "Forms."

2. If you desire to work with one of the forms, you should then left double-click your mouse on the sub-folder: "Forms." A list of form topics (corresponding to the chapters in the book) will appear and you should then left double-click your mouse on the topic of your choice. This will open two folders: one for text forms and one for PDF forms. Left double click your mouse on the text forms folder and a list of the text forms for that topic should appear. Left double click your mouse on the form of your choice. This will open the appropriate form within your word processing program.

3. You may now fill in the necessary information while the text-only file is open in your word processing program. You may need to adjust margins and/or line endings of the form to fit your particular word processing program. Note that there is an asterisk (*) in every location in these forms where information will need to be included. Replace each asterisk with the necessary information. When the form is complete, you may print out the completed form and you may save the completed form. If you wish to save the completed form, you should rename the form so that your hard drive will retain an unaltered version of the original form.

Technical Support

Please also note that Nova Publishing Company cannot provide legal advice regarding the effect or use of the forms in this book or on the CD. For questions about installing the Forms-on-CD and software, you may call Nova Technical Support at 1-800-748-1175 or access the Nova Publishing Website for support at www.novapublishing.com.

For any questions relating to Adobe Acrobat Reader®, please access Adobe Technical Support at www.adobe.com/support/main.html or you may search for assistance in the HELP area of Adobe Acrobat Reader® (located in approximately the center of the top line of the program's desktop).

Note regarding legal updates: Although estate planning laws are relatively stable and the information provided in this book is based on the most current state statutes, laws regarding estate planning are subject to constant change. In the Appendix of this book are provided internet addresses for each state's legislature and statutes. These sites may be accessed to check if any of the laws have changed since the publication of this book. In addition, the Nova Publishing website also provides legal updates for information that has changed since the publication of any Nova titles.

> ♀ Toolkit Tip!
>
> Check online at *www.nova publishing. com* for any updates to the legal information in the Appendix of this book.

Chapter 1

Why Do You Need an Estate Plan?

Your entire life has been spent accumulating possessions and wealth for your own comfort and the comfort of your loved ones. One of the purposes of this book is to assist you in the difficult task of showing these loved ones your continuing concern for their well-being after you are gone. Through the proper use of an estate plan, you have a once-in-a-lifetime opportunity to personally decide what will happen to your *estate* (your accumulated wealth and possessions) when you are gone. It is entirely your personal decision. Indeed, it is your legal privilege to make this decision. No one but you has the power to decide, prior to your death, how and to whom your property should be distributed on your demise. But to do so, you must take the initiative and overcome the understandable difficulty of these decisions. If you do not take the initiative and prepare your own estate plan, on your death an impersonal court will decide who will receive your wealth.

To actually sit down and decide how your property and possessions should be divided amongst your loved ones in the event of your own death is not an easy task. However, it is you alone who knows your wishes. The property and possessions that you own may be land, your home, your personal household furnishings, keepsakes, heirlooms, money, stocks, bonds, or any other

> ⊘ **Definition:**
>
> **Estate Plan:**
> A formal plan to handle both the distribution of your assets after your death and provide advance health care decisions for the possibility of being unable to communicate your decisions.

type of property. It may be worth many thousands of dollars or it may be worth far less. If you are like most people, you want to insure that it is passed on to the persons whom you choose. But again, if you are like most people, you have put off preparing an estate plan. Nearly 75 percent of Americans are without a valid will or any other formal estate planning tool. *Wills* and *living trusts*, written documents that provide for the distribution of your assets upon your death, are the main legal tools for the asset distribution portion of an estate plan. There are, however, many other tools that will be explained throughout this book.

The other main purpose of an estate plan is to plan, in advance, how you would like to confront possible health care issues that may arise, often unexpectedly, in the future. In recent years, a variety of legal tools have developed to allow you to make your health care wishes known to health care providers (and your family) in advance of any emergency medical situations. These range from *living wills* that inform health care providers of your wishes in terminal medical situations to *health care powers of attorney* that grant authority to another person to make medical decisions if you are incapacitated. There are also other tools that can assist your family and health care providers in emergency medical situations and that may be valuable parts of a comprehensive estate plan.

In some cases (for example, those situations involving extremely complicated business or personal financial holdings or the desire to create a complex trust arrangement), it is clearly advisable to consult an attorney for the preparation of your estate plan. However, in most circumstances and for most people, the details of an estate plan which can provide for the necessary protection of your assets are relatively routine and may safely be prepared without the added expense of consulting a lawyer.

> **⊘ Definition:**
> **Health Care Power of Attorney:**
> Allows you to grant authority to another person to make health care decisions for you if you are unable to communicate your wishes.

Reasons for Having an Estate Plan

There are many reasons why it is desirable to have an estate plan. Perhaps most important is to ensure that it is *you* who decides the important questions that an estate plan addresses: how your estate is distributed upon your death and how potential

☀️ Toolkit Tip!

Federal law (The Federal Patient Self-Determination Act) requires that all health care agencies and providers must honor valid living wills or other advance health care directives.

health issues are handled. With a comprehensive estate plan you can both be assured that those loved ones whom you wish to share in your bounty actually receive your gifts and that your wishes regarding health care will be followed in the event of any incapacitating medical situations. Let's look in depth at the reasons an estate plan is a valuable tool and the reasons for having one:

To Provide Advance Health Care Plans for Emergencies

No one really wants to contemplate situations in which they would be totally incapacitated and unable to communicate with others. Unfortunately, such situations can arise without warning. Proper planning can provide methods by which your wishes can still govern health care situations when you are unable to effectively make those wishes known to your family or health care providers. Through the use of various estate planning tools, such as a living will or health care power of attorney, you can, in advance of any emergency, provide a legal statement of your wishes to guide your health care.

To Avoid the State Deciding Who Will Receive Your Property

⚡ Warning!

If you do not prepare a valid will or living trust or use some other type of estate planning, the state will decide which of your relatives will receive your property on your death.

What happens to your property and possessions if you do not have a valid estate plan that deals with post-death distribution of your property? And what happens if the legal documents that you used are found to be invalid by the probate court because they were not signed or witnessed properly? For most people, a will is the legal tool used to plan the distribution of their assets upon their deaths. Law books are filled with many unfortunate cases in which, because of the lack of a formal and valid will, the true desires and wishes of a person as to who should inherit their property have been frustrated. If there is no valid will to use for direction, a probate judge must give a person's property to either the spouse, children, or the closest blood relatives of the deceased person. This result is required even in situations where it is perfectly clear that the deceased person did not, under any circumstances, want those relatives to inherit the property. Although the probate judge is required to interpret a will to best satisfy what appears to be the written intentions of the person who signed it, the judge must first have before him a valid will. To be valid, the document must, generally, have been signed and witnessed in a formal manner and prepared in such a way as to satisfy certain legal requirements. These requirements are strictly enforced to ensure that the document presented to a probate court is, indeed, the real and valid will of the deceased person whose property is to be divided.

Without such a valid will (or possibly a valid living trust) before him or her, a judge must rely on a legislative scheme that has been devised to provide for an orderly distribution of property in all cases where there is no valid will or other post-death distribution plan. This scheme is present as law, in one form or another, in all 50 states and is generally referred to as *intestate distribution*.

The terms of state intestate distribution plans are very complex in most states. In general, a person's spouse is first in line to receive the property when there is no will at death. Most states provide that the spouse and children will either share the entire estate or the surviving spouse will take it all in the hopes that the spouse will share it with the children. Generally, the spouse will receive one-half and the children will receive one-half. In many states, if a person dies without a valid will and is survived by a spouse but not by any children, the spouse will inherit the entire estate and the surviving parents, brothers, sisters, and any other blood relatives of the deceased will be entitled to nothing.

If there is no surviving spouse or children, the blood relatives of the deceased will receive the estate. If there are several persons within the next closest relationship level (for example, parents, brothers, or sisters) who are alive upon the death of the person, then these relatives will receive all of the person's property or share it equally with all the others alive who are in a similar relationship level. Once a level of blood relationship is found in which there is at least one living person, all persons who are more distantly related inherit nothing.

In addition, these legislative distribution plans are set up on the assumption that family members are the only parties that a deceased person would wish to have inherit his or her property. Thus, without a will or living trust, it is impossible to leave any

---

⊘ Definition:

Intestate Distribution: A legislative design in all states that provides a plan outlining which blood relatives will receive what portions of the property of a person that dies without a will or other formal estate plan.

> **⊘ Definition:**
>
> **Escheat:**
> A legislative policy that allows the state to confiscate the property of a person that dies without a will or other formal estate plan and has no blood relatives that can be found.

gifts to close friends, in-laws, relatives more distant than your closest living relatives, charities, or organizations of any type. If there is no will (or living trust) and no blood relatives are alive, the state confiscates all of a person's property under a legal doctrine entitled *escheat*.

As an example of a typical legislative intestate distribution scheme, the following is a general representative outline of the various levels of distribution that are set up in many states. Keep in mind, however, that this example is only an illustration of the method that states may use and is not intended to be used in determining how your own estate would be divided. Check the listing in the Appendix for your own state's intestate distribution plan for specific details:

- If a spouse and children born of the spouse are surviving: $50,000.00 and one-half of the balance of the estate will go to the spouse and one-half of the balance of the estate will go to the children in equal shares. If one of the children has *predeceased* (died before) the parent and leaves surviving children (grandchildren of the deceased parent), then the grandchildren will split the deceased child's share equally.

- If a spouse and children not born of the spouse are surviving: one-half of the balance of the estate will go to the spouse and one-half of the balance of the estate will go to the children equally. If one of the children has predeceased the parent and leaves surviving children (grandchildren of the deceased parent), then the grandchildren will split the deceased child's share equally.

- If a spouse is surviving, but no children or parents of the deceased are surviving: All of the estate will go to the spouse.

- If a spouse and one or both parents are surviving, but no children are surviving: $50,000.00 and one-half of the balance of the estate will go to the spouse and one-half of the balance of the estate will go to the parents equally. If only one parent is surviving, that parent gets the entire one-half share of the estate.

- If there are children of the deceased surviving, but no spouse is surviving: All of the estate goes to the children. If one of the children has predeceased the parent and leaves surviving children (grandchildren of the deceased parent), then the grandchildren will split the deceased child's share equally.

- If one or both parents are surviving, but no spouse or children are surviving: All of the estate will go to the parents equally, or the entire estate will go to the surviving parent.

- If there is no spouse surviving, or no children or parents are surviving: All of the estate will go to brothers and sisters in equal shares. If a brother or sister has predeceased the deceased sibling and has left surviving children, those children will split the deceased brother or sister's share equally.

- If there is no spouse, no children, no parents, and no brothers and sisters or their children surviving: one-half of the estate will go to the maternal grandparents and one-half will go to the paternal grandparents. If the grandparents on either side have predeceased the decedent, the grandparent's children will split their share.

- If there is no spouse, no children, no parents, no brothers and sisters or their children, and no grandparents or their children surviving: The estate will pass to the surviving members of the closest level of blood relatives: aunts, uncles, nephews, nieces, great-grandparents, great uncles, great aunts, first cousins, great-great grandparents, second cousins, etc.

- If there are no surviving kin: The estate will be claimed by the state under the doctrine of *escheat*.

Many disastrous consequences can result from having your property distributed according to a standardized state plan. Take, for example, a situation in which a person and his or her spouse

> **☼ Toolkit Tip!**
>
> Many states provide that a surviving spouse will receive most or all of a deceased person's property if there was no valid will or other estate plan to distribute the property. Check the Appendix for your state's rules.

die from injuries sustained in a single accident, but one spouse survives a few hours longer. If there is no will, the result in this scenario is that the property of the first spouse to die passes to the spouse who survives. A few hours later, upon the death of the surviving spouse, the property automatically passes only to the relatives of the spouse who survived the longest. The relatives of the first spouse to die can inherit nothing at all. This, obviously would not normally be the desired consequence. Under the typical state scheme, luck and chance play a large role in deciding who is to inherit property.

Each state has a complicated and often different method for deciding which particular family members will take property when there is no will or other estate plan. However, the results are often far from the desires of how the person actually wished to have the property distributed. Obviously, under this type of state distribution of your property, the individual circumstances of your family are not taken into consideration at all. Neither are any intentions that you may have had, regardless of how strongly you may have expressed them during your lifetime. The only way to avoid having the state decide who is to receive your property is to have prepared a legally-valid estate plan. If you die without a valid will or living trust, the state essentially writes one for you on its own terms.

To Avoid the Delays and Expense of Probate

⊘ Definition:

Payable-on-Death Account: A type of bank account that allows you to name a beneficiary who will become the immediate owner of your account upon your death.

Many of the options available in planning for the distribution of your estate after your death also allow for that property to be distributed to your beneficiaries without going through the process of probate. *Probate* is the legal process of proving the validity of a will (if there is one) and the subsequent court supervision of the distribution of the assets of the deceased. Through the use of a living will, payable-on-death (may also be called 'transfer-on-death) bank accounts, joint tenancy and other estate planning tools, most (and perhaps all) of a person's assets can be distributed to beneficiaries outside the probate process. This has the potential of greatly lowering both the costs of distribution and the time involved in the distribution. Nearly all states have enacted simplified probate procedures in recent years that also are less expensive and take less time than traditional probate.

To Save Money on the Distribution of Your Estate

In addition to avoiding probate and its attendant expenses, a thoughtful estate plan can also save additional expenses by providing trusted people to administer your estate after your death. As noted in the next sections, you have the ability to appoint trusted and reliable people to distribute your property on your death, act as trustee for any children's trust that you may chose to set up, and act as guardian of your children (although this is usually your spouse). This will generally prevent the posting of bond by your chosen representatives as well as avoid the fees that are associated with having your estate hire professionals to handle these tasks. The more money that is saved for your estate means that more of your wealth can be passed on to your chosen beneficiaries.

To Appoint Someone to Administer Your Property

Another very important reason for having an estate plan is the ability to appoint an executor or successor trustee of your own choice. An *executor* is your personal representative for seeing that your wishes, as contained in your *will*, are carried out after your death and that your taxes and debts are paid. An executor also collects and inventories all of your property and is in charge of seeing that it is distributed according to your wishes as expressed in your will. A *successor trustee* handles most of the same duties under the terms of a *living trust* if you choose to distribute some of your property in this manner.

Typically, a spouse, brother, sister, other close family member, or trusted friend is chosen to act as executor/successor trustee. However, your executor/successor trustee can be any responsible adult whom you would feel confident having this duty. The executor/successor trustee can even be a local bank or trust company. In that case, of course, there will be an often substantial fee charged to your estate for the completion of these generally routine duties by the corporate executor/successor trustee. If you choose an individual, he or she should be a resident of your home state. The wills or living trusts in this book will enable you to appoint your executor/successor trustee and an alternate

⊘ Definition:

Executor:
The person that you appoint in your will to handle the distribution of your property after your death.

⊘ Definition:

Successor Trustee:
Similar to an *executor,* this is the person that you appoint in your living trust who will handle the distribution of your property after your death. Since you are the original trustee, this person will be the 'successor' trustee.

executor/successor trustee so that in the event your first choice cannot perform, it is still your personal choice as to who will administer your will or living trust.

If you do not have a will or living trust or do not choose an executor/successor trustee in your will, the probate court judge will appoint someone to administer the distribution of your property. Often it will be a local attorney, court official, or bank officer who may not know you or your beneficiaries at all. Your estate will then be distributed by a stranger who will charge your estate a hefty fee for the collection and distribution of your assets.

By appointing your own executor/successor trustee, you are also able to waive the posting of a bond by your executor/successor trustee and, most often, a family member executor/successor trustee will not accept a fee for serving. This will allow more of your assets to reach your beneficiaries, rather than paying for the expenses of administration of your estate.

To Appoint a Guardian for Your Minor Children

For those with minor children, the appointment of a guardian for any children is another very important item which may be accomplished, in most states, only through the use of a will. (Note: a child's guardian can not generally be appointed in a living trust.) A *guardian "of the person,"* as this type of guardian is usually referred to, is responsible for the actual care, custody, and upbringing of a child. If your spouse is alive, he or she would generally be appointed as guardian in any event, with or without a will. However, there is the possibility that you both will be killed in a single accident or catastrophe. Also, if you are a single parent, you will need to designate a choice for guardian. Without a will for direction, a probate judge has little guidance in choosing the person whom you feel would be the best alternative for caring for your children. With a will, however, you can select a guardian for just such an eventuality.

To Appoint Someone to Administer a Minor Child's Property

You can also have such a guardian administer the property or money that you leave to your children (a *guardian "of the property*"), or you may set up a trust and appoint a trustee to administer your children's inheritance until a time when you feel that they will be able to handle their own affairs. A *trust* consists of assets that are managed and distributed by a *trustee* to benefit one or more *beneficiaries*. Instructions to provide for these alternatives are simply stated in a will or living trust, but are more difficult to accomplish without one. If such instruction is not provided for in a will or living trust, and a minor child is left money or property by way of the state intestate succession laws, the courts will generally decide who should administer the property. Such court-supervised guardianship of the property or money will automatically end at the child's reaching the legal age of majority in the state (often 18 years of age). At this age, without a will to direct otherwise, the child will receive full control over the property and/or money. This may not be the most prudent result, as many 18 year-olds are not capable of managing property or large sums of money. With a will or living trust, it is easy to arrange for the property or money to be held in trust and used to benefit the child until a later age, perhaps 21, 25, or even 30 years of age.

> ⊘ **Definition:**
> **Guardian of the Property:** A person who is appointed to handle only the assets and property of another person, most often of a minor child.

To Disinherit a Child or Other Relative

Disinheritance of a child or other relative whom you feel is not deserving of your property, or has no need of your property, is also something that can be accomplished only through the use of a will or living trust. Although the total disinheritance of a spouse is not possible under the laws of any state, any other relative may, generally, be cut off without a penny from your estate through the use of a will. (Note: in Louisiana, children may only be disinherited in certain circumstances).

To Accomplish Other Results

Many other things may be accomplished only through the use of an estate plan. You can forgive a debt that is owed to you in your will. You can revoke any other previous wills or living trusts. You can provide instructions for organ donations, the disposition of your body, and burial, although it is generally wise to also leave these instructions with your executor/successor trustee on a sepa-

☼ Toolkit Tip!

Regardless of how you plan for the eventual distribution of your estate, the use of a basic will is *always* recommended.

rate sheet. Additionally, the proper use of an estate plan normally lessens the expenses of probate, since the disposition of all of your property has been planned in advance, by you.

Even if you have used the various estate planning tools outlined in the next chapter to attempt to have your estate avoid probate, a will is always still highly recommended. There may be assets that you have neglected, forgotten about, or that may not be uncovered until your death. If you have used a trust, joint property agreements, and other estate planning tools, these unknown or forgotten assets may wind up passing to your heirs as intestate property and causing probate proceedings to be instituted. Through the use of a simple will, you can avoid this possibility.

Although it can be fairly simple and straightforward, an estate plan is an important tool that can accomplish many tasks. The proper use of an estate plan can eliminate much confusion for those left behind. Since it provides a clear and legal record of your wishes, it can also prevent feuding and squabbles among your family members and confusion among health care providers about what your desires actually were. Perhaps most importantly, it can make your last wishes come true.

Chapter 2

Developing Your Own Personal Estate Plan

Your estate consists of everything that you own, whether it is real estate or personal property. Your *estate plan* is the total comprehensive plan that you use to (1) distribute your estate upon your death, and (2) provide advance plans for your medical care in the event that you become incapacitated. To develop a personalized estate plan, you will first need to know what can and cannot be accomplished using the various tools available in estate planning. There are many different methods that can be used to distribute your property after you die: wills, trusts, life insurance, joint ownership, and many others. There are also various documents that can be used to provide advance instructions for your medical care. There are also some general qualifications for being able to develop your own estate plan. Below is a look at these basic qualifications and an overview of the different tools that you may use to develop your estate plan:

Qualifications for Having an Estate Plan

Are you legally qualified to have an estate plan? In general, if you are over 18 years of age and of "sound mind," you will qualify. There are a few states that have different minimum ages for signing a will or other documents, some allowing wills by children as young as 14. For the specific age requirements, check your own state's age requirements in the Appendix.

> **☼Toolkit Tip!**
>
> As the recent tragic case of Terry Schiavo indicates, even young adults should have an advance health care plan in place, such as a living will or advance health care directive.

⌀ **Definition:**

Sound Mind:
A person is assumed to have a 'sound mind' if they are aware of what they own, who it is they wish to have their property, and what type of document they are signing.

Estate plan legal documents are governed by state law and all states have slightly differing laws. An outline of each state's laws relating to estate planning is included in the Appendix of this book. It is also important to understand that laws of different states may apply to your estate plan. For example, the laws of the state in which you have your principal residence will be used to decide the validity of your will as to any personal property and real estate located in that state. However, if any real estate outside of your home state is mentioned in the will, then the laws of the state in which that real estate is found will govern the disposition of that particular real estate. Thus, if you own property outside of the state where you live, when you check the Appendix for information concerning specific state laws, be certain to check both your own state's laws and those of the state in which your other property is located.

The requirement to have a "sound mind" refers to the ability to understand the following:

- You are signing a will, or other legal document
- You know who your beneficiaries are
- You understand the nature and extent of your assets

⌀ **Definition:**

Undue Influence & Fraud:
These terms refer to any efforts to deceive, coerce, trick, or force someone to sign a will that is not what they personally wish to have their will state.

Having a "sound mind" refers only to the moment when you actually *execute* (or sign) the will or other legal document. A person who is suffering from a mental illness or uses drugs or alcohol, or even a person who is senile may legally sign a will or trust. This is acceptable as long as the legal document is signed and understood during a period when the person is lucid and has sufficient mental ability to understand the extent of his or her property, who is to receive that property, and exactly what type of document is being signed. The fact that a person has a physical incapacity makes no difference in his or her right to sign a legal document for their estate plan. Regardless of whether a person is blind, deaf, cannot speak, is very weak physically, or is illiterate; as long as he or she understands what he or she is doing and is signing, the "sound mind" requirement is met.

Related to the requirement that the person signing a legal document have a "sound mind" at the time of signing the document is the requirement that the document be signed without any undue influence, fraud, or domination by others. In other words, the document must be freely signed and reflect the wishes of the person signing it for it to be legally valid. You do not *ever* have to sign any document that is not exactly what you desire. Do not let anyone coerce or force you to sign any legal document that does not accurately reflect your own personal wishes. If you are in a situation of this nature, it is highly recommended that you immediately seek the assistance of a competent lawyer.

The various estate planning tools outlined below may be used separately or together to achieve a very wide variety of ends. For example, you may wish to own your home and car as joint tenants with your spouse. This will remove those assets from probate and will also provide that your spouse will immediately become sole owner of these assets upon your death. You may then wish to place your brokerage account into a living trust that distributes the assets to your spouse and other family members upon your death. The use of a living trust will also prevent these assets from being processed through a probate court. Your life insurance policy may also be used to pass assets to your chosen beneficiaries without them going through probate. Finally, you may choose to use a will to pass various items of personal property to your beneficiaries, even though this will generally require probate. Most states have simplified probate rules that apply to small amounts of property (although these may often be for property amounts of even up to $100,000.00 or more). Please see the Chapter 5 and the Appendix for more information on simplified probate procedures and rules.

In the area of health care, you may choose to use a living will to put your wishes in writing regarding the extent of medical care that you would like at the end of your life. You may also wish to designate a trusted person to have the authority to make medical decisions for you in the event of your incapacitation and inability to communicate your wishes. You can also pre-designate your choice as your primary physician and you may wish to make organ donations to save lives after your own death. Thus, by using a combination of the estate planning tools, you will be able to accomplish many goals and be assured that your property will pass to those whom you choose and that your health care will be handled in the manner that you, yourself, have chosen.

⚡ Warning!

If anyone attempts to make you sign a will that is not exactly what you desire, you should refuse to sign and immediately contact a competent attorney.

💡 Toolkit Tip!

Generally, the only property that will need to be probated is property that passes to others via either a will or by intestate distribution (if no will or other estate planning device is present).

Estate Planning Tools

The use of a will is, by far, the most popular and widespread legal tool for planning for the distribution of your estate. As explained in Chapter 1, through the use of a will you can accomplish the planned distribution of your estate property and many other goals. However, there may be other objectives in your planning that cannot be accomplished solely through the use of a will. Other estate planning documents may be necessary to achieve all of your goals. There are four basic reasons that other estate planning tools may be useful in certain situations: distributing property, avoidance of probate, reducing taxes, and healthcare considerations. Some tools can accomplish multiple purposes, for example, a living trust both provides for the distribution of your property on death and prevents that property from having to go through probate.

Distribution of Property on Death

Several estate planning tools are useful for the distribution of property on your death. A last will and testament (more commonly referred to as simply a *will*) is often the cornerstone of any comprehensive arrangement to plan for the distribution of your property upon your death. A living trust may also be used for this purpose, but its main purpose is for the avoidance of probate and, thus, is listed under that heading. Similarly, joint tenancies, payable-on-death accounts, and life insurance may be used to pass property to others upon death, but they are useful as probate avoidance tools and are listed under that heading.

Last Will and Testament:

A *will* is a legal document that, when accepted by the probate court, is proof of an intent to transfer property to the person(s) or organization(s) named in the will upon the death of the maker of the will. The maker of the will is known as the *testator*. A will is effective for the transfer of property that is owned by the testator on the date of his or her death. A will can be changed, modified, or revoked at any time by the testator prior to death.

⊘ Definition:

Testator:

A person who makes and signs a will (technically known as a 'last will and testament'.

It is equally important to understand that for a will to be valid, it must generally be prepared, witnessed, and signed according to certain technical legal procedures. Although a will is perfectly valid if it is written in plain English and does not use technical legal language, it *must* be prepared, witnessed, and signed in the manner outlined in this book. This cannot be overemphasized. You cannot take any shortcuts when following the instructions as they relate to the procedures necessary for completing and signing your will. These procedures are not at all difficult and consist generally of carefully typing (or printing on a computer) your will in the manner outlined later, signing it in the manner specified, and having three witnesses and a notary public also sign the document. (Although not a legal requirement, the notarization of your will can aid in its proof in court later, if necessary).

> ### ⚡ Warning!
> For your will to be valid, it *must* be signed and witnessed by at least two witnesses. (As an additional precaution, the wills in this book require three witnesses).

In the past, it was possible to simply write down your wishes, sign the paper, and be confident that your wishes would be followed upon your death. Unfortunately, this is, in most cases, no longer possible. *Holographic* (or handwritten and unwitnessed) wills are no longer accepted as valid in most jurisdictions. *Nuncupative* (or oral) wills are also not admissible in most probate courts to prove a person's intent to dispose of property on death. For this reason, a valid, typewritten (or computer printed) will that is prepared, signed, and witnessed according to formal legal requirements is necessary. This type of will is now essentially the only secure method to ensure the desired disposition of your property, possessions, and money after your death and to assure that your loved ones are taken care of according to your final wishes.

To prepare a will, please read the chapters on property (Chapter 3), beneficiaries (Chapter 4) and probate (Chapter 5). Then follow the instructions in Chapters 6 and 7 to select and prepare your own will.

Avoiding Probate

For many people, the desire to avoid having their property be subject to probate proceedings is a main consideration for their estate plan. Although in some situations, the probate process has been abused, there are valid reasons for allowing your property to be handled through probate. It allows for an examination of the validity of your will. It provides a process by which the improper distribution of your assets is guarded against. Having your property distributed through a probate process also puts a definite limit on the length of time that a creditor can file a claim against your estate.

One of the main drawbacks of probate is that it can delay the distribution of your property while the probate process continues. The probate of an estate can take, generally, from four to 18 months, and sometimes much longer. Additionally, probate costs can be substantial. Court costs, appraisal fees, lawyer's fees, and accounting bills can all cut deeply into the amount of property and funds that will eventually be distributed to your beneficiaries. However, for small estates (generally, under $100,000.00) most states have simplified probate procedures that can be handled without lawyers and can substantially reduce these costs. The probate process itself is explained in more detail in Chapter 5.

There are various methods for having property pass to others without going through the probate process. The five most important are as follows:

⌀ Definition:

Joint Tenants with Right of Survivorship:
Property ownership in which two or more persons jointly own property and the surviving owner(s) will automatically own any deceased owner's share of the property.

Joint Tenancy with Right of Survivorship:

Upon one owner's death, any property (either real estate or personal property) held as *joint tenants with right of survivorship* passes automatically to the surviving owner without probate or court intervention of any kind. Under the laws of most states, the description of ownership on the deed or other title document must specifically state that the property is being held by the owners as "joint tenants with right of survivorship," often abbreviated as "JTWROS". If not, the property is usually presumed to be held as *tenants-in-common*, which means that each owner owns a certain specific share of the property that they may leave by way of a will or other estate-planning device. Some states have another class of property known as *tenancy-by-the-entirety* which is, essentially, a joint tenancy specifically for spouses. Please see the Appendix to see if your state has this type of property ownership. Note also that a few community property states allow for community property to be held with a right of survivorship. See the Appendix to see if your state has this option.

If property is held as joint tenants with right of survivorship (or if held in a tenancy-by-the-entireties), when one owner dies, the remaining owner automatically become the owner of the deceased owner's share. For example, if a husband and wife own their home as JTWROS, when one spouse dies, the other spouse becomes the sole owner of the property. This happens automatically upon the death of the other spouse. No court or lawyer is needed for the shift in ownership to take place. It is often a good idea to place a copy of the death certificate of the deceased owner into the county records to verify that the surviving owner is now the sole owner of JTWROS property. (Note that it is possible to have a joint tenancy involving more that two joint owners, in which case any surviving owners would jointly own the deceased owner's share).

Property held in this type of ownership does not go through probate. This type of ownership is most often used for real estate, vehicles, bank accounts, brokerage accounts, and similar properties. Nor is it necessary to provide for beneficiaries, as the surviving owner is actually the beneficiary. However, consideration must be given for a situation where both joint tenants die simultaneously. For financial accounts, provisions for alternative beneficiaries (in the event of the death of both tenants) may be arranged with the financial institution in question. For other personal property or real estate, the property may pass under the terms of a will or by intestate succession if both joint tenants die simultaneously. Keep in mind that if you set up a joint bank account, each joint owner will have total access to the account at all times, including the ability to withdraw all funds. In certain situations, it may be a better idea to set up a "payable-on-death" bank account (explained below) that will pass the funds of the account to another person on the account holder's death, but does not allow any access or control of the account by any other person during the account holder's lifetime.

Another consideration is that creditors can not go after a non-debtor joint tenant's interest in a piece of property. However, a court may require that the property be sold to satisfy the debtor joint tenant's creditors.

Three other considerations are important when considering the use of joint tenancies. First, once property is placed into a joint

---

Ø **Definition:**

Tenants-in-Common: Property ownership in which two or more persons jointly own property, but each owner owns their share in full (and may, thus, leave their share of the property to others through a will or trust).

Ø **Definition:**

Tenancy-by-the-Entireties: Ownership of property identical to joint tenants with right of survivorship, but only between a married couple.

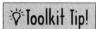
tenancy with another, you may not remove the other person from ownership without their permission (but you may end the joint tenancy. See the following paragraph). Placing property into joint tenancy ownership is irrevocable; each joint tenant has a permanent right to one half of the property unless they agree to give their share of the property back to the original owner. So be certain that you actually desire this type of ownership before signing any documents that create this type of ownership.

Second, and related to the last point, is that, in most states, any joint tenant can end a joint tenancy and transform the tenancy into a tenancy-in-common without the consent or permission of the other joint tenant. This effectively ends the right of survivorship aspect of the joint tenancy. Some states require a court hearing to separate the property into equal halves while, in other states, a joint tenant can create a tenancy-in-common without court intervention. Once the property is held as tenants-in-common, each owner is then legally able to sell their share without the other's permission. A tenant in common may also be able to force the sale of a property and have a court divide the proceeds of the sale. For this reason, you should be absolutely certain that you trust the person with whom you will share any joint tenancy.

A final consideration about joint tenancies is that the language required to create them is not universal for all states. Some state allow the creation with the simple language "as joint tenants," while others require that the phrase "with right of survivorship" be mentioned. Others allow the abbreviation JTWROS to be used and sometimes (such as in South Carolina) it must be stated that the tenancy is specifically not a tenancy-in-common (such as "joint tenants with right of survivorship and not as tenants-in-common"). For this reason, you should check locally with a real estate professional or attorney for the language required in your jurisdiction. In addition, community property has similar characteristics to joint tenancies and, several community property states specifically allow for community property with a right of survivorship. More information on property ownership is provided in Chapter 3 and, for each state, in the Appendix of this book.

There are various ways to place property in a joint tenancy. If the property is real estate, you will need to prepare a new deed that declares that the owners are joint tenants. If the present owners are tenants-in-common, you would transfer ownership from the parties as tenants-in-common to the same parties as joint tenants (using the correct language in your jurisdiction). A quitclaim deed may be used for this purpose and this form and instructions on its preparation are included in Chapter 17. If the property is real estate but is held currently by a sole owner, the quitclaim deed would transfer property from the sole owner to the new joint tenants (again being certain to use the correct language in your jurisdiction). If your wish is to place personal property into a joint tenancy and the property has a title document (such as for a car), you would need to apply for a new title placing the ownership of the property into the names of the new joint tenants. If the personal property does not have a document of title (such as personal belongings), you may simply declare that the property is held as joint tenants in a simple signed statement and have that statement notarized. This will effectively take that property out of probate. Such a statement need not be recorded with any authority, but should be kept in a safe and secure place with your other important documents. You should also be certain that your chosen executor or successor trustee be made aware of such an agreement.

Living or Revocable Trusts:

An increasingly popular estate planning tool, *living* or *revocable* trusts can also be effectively used to avoid probate. There are many reasons why it is desirable to have a living trust. One of the most important is that through the proper use of a living trust most or all of the expense and delay of probate is avoided. This type of document generally provides that all or most of a person's property be transferred to trust ownership. The owner of the property generally retains full control and management of the trust as *trustee*. In the trust document, *beneficiaries* are chosen, much the same as in a will. (Note: generally, the creator of the trust will be the beneficiary of the trust during his or her lifetime). The terms of the trust can actually parallel the terms of a will. The difference is that, upon the death of the creator (*grantor*) of the trust, all of the property that has been transferred to trust ownership passes immediately and automatically to the beneficiaries without any court intervention or supervision.

🔅Toolkit Tip!

The easiest way to add another person to the ownership of real estate is by use of a quitclaim deed. See Chapter 17.

⊘ Definition:

Grantor:
The person who creates a trust *or* who owns and is transferring ownership of real estate by deed.

☀ Toolkit Tip!

A unique aspect of a 'living' trust is that the grantor, original trustee, and original beneficiary are all, generally, the person that creates the trust.

The owner of the property retains full control over the property until death and the creator of the trust can terminate this type of trust at any time prior to death. However, there are increased paperwork requirements in setting up and operating a trust. The trust itself must be prepared and all of your property ownership (stocks, bonds, bank accounts, real estate deeds, car titles, etc.) actually transferred to the trust. A living trust may be used in conjunction with a will and other estate planning tools to avoid probate or to reduce the amount of the probated estate so that it will qualify for a state's simplified probate rules. Simplified probate procedures are discussed in Chapter 5 and in the Appendix. Details regarding a living trust are contained in the Appendix and the procedures for setting up a living trust are provided in Chapter 9.

Life Insurance:

⚡ Warning!

If you hope to use life insurance as your main estate planning tool, you will need to consult a professional who is knowledgeable in both life insurance and estate planning.

Another common method of passing funds to a person upon death while avoiding probate is through the use of life insurance. By making the premium payments throughout your life, you are accumulating assets for distribution on your death. The life insurance benefits are paid directly to your chosen beneficiaries without probate court intervention. An advantage to life insurance is that the beneficiary will receive the cash proceeds relatively quickly after the death of the insured person. There are many types of life insurance that may be appropriate in different situations. For example, you may use separate life insurance policies to provide for children of different marriages. For more information on insurance, you are advised to consult an insurance professional.

Retirement Accounts and/or Pension Plans:

Many people have accumulated retirement benefits from an employer during their lifetime. Generally, most retirement or pension plans will pay benefits to a chosen beneficiary if the covered person dies before retirement age. In addition, most plans provide for benefit choices that will pay continuing benefits to another beneficiary upon the death of the original retiree. In most cases, state laws require that at least a portion of retirement benefits be paid to a spouse upon the death of a retiree.

In addition, IRAs (Individual Retirement Accounts) provide for the naming of beneficiaries. Upon the death of the owner of the IRA, the beneficiary will immediately have access to the funds in the IRA without having to go through probate. If you have a retirement or pension plan, you should contact the company or financial institution that holds the assets for an explanation of what will take place upon your death. In general, if the plan has named beneficiaries, the assets will pass to them on your death without probate. If you have assets in an IRA or other government plan (such as a Roth IRA or 401(k), you should also contact the financial institution that holds those assets for an explanation of post-death distribution.

> **⚡ Warning!**
>
> You should contact the plan adminis-trator of your retirement account or pension plan for information regarding the details of the plan's distri-bution upon your death.

Payable-on-Death Bank Accounts:

This type of property ownership consists of a bank account held in trust for a named beneficiary. It may also be referred to as a *Totten* trust or a *Bank* trust account. It is a very simple method for providing that the assets in a bank account are immediately accessible to a beneficiary upon your death without the beneficiary having any control over the account during your life, as is the case with a joint bank account. This trust-type bank account allows for the property to be transferred without probate and is very simple to set up. Bear in mind that this type of account will not allow any access by others in the event of your incapacitation. For that possibility, you may wish to set up a *durable power of attorney,* that will provide for a trusted person to be able to handle your financial affairs if you are unable to handle them yourself (see below and Chapter 13 for more information on durable powers of attorney).

Any type of bank account, whether checking, savings, money market, or even certificates of deposit, may, generally, be designated as a payable-on-death account by filling out simple forms at your financial institution. Brokerage and mutual fund accounts, individual stocks and bonds may also often be set up as payable-on-death. You will need to check with the account holder or financial institution for the correct paperwork to set up this type of account.

Note: A few states (California, Connecticut, Kansas, Missouri, and Ohio) allow you to register the title to vehicles with a *transfer-on-*

death title that provides that the vehicle title automatically shifts to the chosen beneficiary upon the death of the owner. If you live in one of these states, contact your state department of motor vehicles for more information. Finally, a few states have accepted *beneficiary deeds* which are, in effect, transfer-on-death deeds. These deeds provide that the property will pass directly to the named beneficiary on the death of the property owner. Generally, unlike typical deeds, you can revoke this type of deed anytime before your death. If you live in the states of Arizona, Arkansas, Colorado, Kansas, Missouri, Nevada, New Mexico, Ohio or Wisconsin, and wish to use this type of deed, you should contact an attorney familiar with this type of estate planning tool.

Gifts to Minors:

> **☀ Toolkit Tip!**
>
> If you wish to set up a bank account for a minor that the minor will own on reaching adulthood, please contact the bank or financial institution you wish to use.

All states, except South Carolina and Vermont, have enacted either the Uniform Gifts to Minors Act or the Uniform Transfers to Minors Act. These acts of legislation provide a standardized method to transfer assets to children under the age of majority in your state. You may set up a bank account under these acts that hold assets until the child is of legal age. Upon reaching the age of majority (generally 18 to 21, but in a few states this can be up to age 25), the child then has full access to the funds that are held in the account. This may not always be a good idea for large amounts of money, as many 18-year olds don't have the wisdom to manage their own affairs. You may prefer to set up a children's trust using a will or living trust. This will allow you to set the age when you think your children will be mature enough to handle their inheritance. If you wish to set up an account for a minor under either of these legislative acts, please contact your local bank or other financial institution.

Reducing Taxes

After distributing your property and avoiding probate, the third major use for estate planning tools is to attempt to lessen or completely avoid the payment of any taxes on the transfer of property upon death. Upon death, the transfer of property may be subject to federal estate taxes, state estate taxes, and state inheritance taxes. However, much of the taxation of estates (most importantly, federal taxation) does not become a factor unless your estate is valued at over $2 million. Thus, for the vast majority of people, the need to pursue complicated tax avoidance estate plans is unnecessary. For reference, however, details regarding taxation of estates are provided in Chapter 3. In addition, the Appendix contains information regarding each individual state's laws on gift, inheritance, and estate taxation. The complexity of tax laws and of the methods to avoid taxes through estate planning is beyond the scope of this book. If your estate is over $2 million, it may be wise to seek the assistance of a tax professional and/or an attorney skilled in estate planning and tax avoidance.

Healthcare Concerns

The final purpose of estate planning is a relatively new concern. Recent advances in medical technology have allowed modern medicine, in many cases, to significantly extend the lives of many people. In addition, many people have become aware of the possibility of their lives being continued indefinitely through technological life support procedures. Finally, there may be a need for someone to handle a person's financial affairs in the event that the person is unable, because of medical conditions, to handle their own affairs. Several legal documents have been developed to deal with these and other health care concerns.

Living Will:

A *living will* is a document that can be used to state your desire that extraordinary life support means not be used to artificially prolong your life in the event that you are stricken with a terminal disease or injury. Its' use has been recognized in all states in recent years. The purpose of a living will is to provide doctors and other health care workers with clear directions regarding how you would like your medical care handled toward the end of your life. A living will makes it possible for you to specify, in advance, exactly what your preferences are regarding the use of life-sustaining medical procedures if you are ever in a terminal medical condition or in a vegetative state, and are unable to give such directions yourself. The Appendix provides information regarding the recognition of living wills in each state. For detailed information on preparing a living will, please see Chapter 11.

> **☀️Toolkit Tip!**
> A living will and/or health care power of attorney will *not* come into effect if you are able to communicate your own health care decisions, even if only by blinking or some other non-verbal communication.

Health Care Power of Attorney:

This relatively new legal document has been developed to allow a person to appoint another person to make health care decisions on one's behalf, in the event that he or she becomes incapacitated or incompetent. Generally, a *health care power of attorney* will only take effect upon a person becoming unable to manage his or her own affairs, and only after this incapacitation has been certified by an attending physician. The person appointed will then have the authority to view your medical records, consult with your doctors and make any required decisions regarding your health care. This document may be carefully tailored to fit your needs and concerns and can be used in conjunction with a living will. It can be a valuable tool for dealing with difficult healthcare situations. For instructions and forms for preparing a health care power of attorney and a revocation of health care power of attorney, please refer to Chapter 12.

Durable Power of Attorney for Financial Affairs:

Situations may arise when you are unable to handle your own financial affairs due to an incapacitating illness or accident. For those situations, a durable power of attorney for financial affairs has been developed to give authority to another person to take care of your financial affairs. *Durable* refers to the fact that the authority that you give to another will be in effect even if you are incapacitated. Such a document provides another person that you appoint with the same powers and authority that you, yourself, have over your property. Your appointed person can sign checks, pay bills, sign contracts, and handle all of your affairs on your behalf. In general, there are two types of durable powers of attorney: one that is immediately in effect and that will *remain* in effect in the event of your incapacitation, and another that *only* goes into effect if you become incapacitated. For information on preparing these two types of durable powers of attorney for financial affairs, please see Chapter 13.

Advance Health Care Directive:

An Advance Health Care Directive is a legal document that may be used in any state that allows you to provide written di-

---

☀ Toolkit Tip!

A durable power of attorney for financial affairs may be set up to 1) take effect immediately and remain in effect if you become incapacitated, or 2) go into effect only if you become incapacitated. Both types are provided in Chapter 13.

rections relating to your future health care should you become incapacitated and unable to speak for yourself. Advance Health Care Directives give you a direct voice in medical decisions in situations when you cannot make those decisions yourself. Your Advance Health Care Directive will not be used as long as you are able to express your own decisions. You can always accept or refuse medical treatment and you always have the legal right to revoke your Advance Health Care Directive at any time.

State-specific Advance Health Care Directives are provided on the CD that accompanies this book. However, you may wish to prepare individual version of the separate forms that comprise an Advance Health Care Directive. For instructions, please see Chapter 14. The Advance Health Care Directives that are provided with this book contain four separate sections, each dealing with different aspects of potential situations that may arise during a possible period of incapacitation:

- Living Will
- Selection of Health Care Agent
- Designation of Primary Physician
- Organ Donation

Designation of Primary Physician:

Through the use of this document, you will be able to designate your choice for your primary physician in the event you are unable to communicate your wishes after an accident or during an illness. Although your family may know your personal doctor, it may still be a good idea to put this choice in writing so that there is no question regarding who your choice for a doctor may be. Instructions for preparing this form are in Chapter 15.

Organ Donation:

Finally, you may wish that your vital organs or, indeed, your entire body be used after your death for various medical purposes. Every year, many lives are saved and much medical research is enhanced by organ donations. All states allow for you to personally declare your desires regarding the use of your body and/or organs after death. The details of providing for this important consideration are included in Chapter 16.

> ### ⚘ Toolkit Tip!
>
> This book provides two separate methods for preparing advance health care directives: 1) by preparing a state-specific comprehensive form, or 2) by preparing each individual part of the directive as a separate form.

Steps in Preparing Your Estate Plan

There are several steps that must be followed to properly prepare your estate plan using this book. None of them are very difficult or overly complicated. However, they must be done carefully in order to effectively accomplish what you set out to do: be assured that your property is left to those loved ones whom you choose and that your health care is provided according to your wishes. What follows is a brief outline of the necessary steps which must be followed to prepare an estate plan with this book. You will probably refer back to this chapter several times in the course of preparing your own estate plan to be certain that you are on the right track and have not left out any steps.

> ## ⚡ Warning!
>
> If you believe that your situation warrants additional estate planning or if you are confused about how to set up your estate plan, you will need to consult an experienced financial planner, tax professional or attorney.

1. Read through this entire book. You are advised to read carefully through this entire book before you actually begin preparing your own estate plan. By doing this you will gain an overview of the entire process and will have a much better idea of where you are heading before you actually begin the preparation of your estate plan.

2. Fill in the Property Questionnaire contained in Chapter 3 and the Beneficiary Questionnaire in Chapter 4. These questionnaires are designed to compile all of the necessary personal information for your estate planning. Information regarding your personal and business assets, percentages of ownership of these assets, marital relationship, names and addresses of relatives, and many other items will be gathered together in these questionnaires for your use. As you fill in these questionnaires, you will be making the actual decisions regarding distribution of your assets. In addition, in Chapter 5, you will fill out an Executor/Successor Trustee Information Checklist which will provide important data for use by your chosen executor or successor trustee.

3. Review your own state's legal requirements as contained in the Appendix. The Appendix contains a concise listing of the laws relating to wills, trusts, living wills, and other estate planning considerations in every state. Although the standard legal documents used in this book will alleviate most of the concerns raised by these legal requirements, some

of your own state's requirements may affect how you decide to prepare your own estate plan.

4. Use the Estate Planning Chart at the end of this chapter to review the uses of each of the various estate planning tools. This chart will help you decide which documents to use and how you will actually set up your estate plan.

5. Make photocopies or print out copies of all of those portions of the legal documents that will be included in your own estate plan. These copies will be your estate plan preparation worksheets. After you have done this, fill in the appropriate information on the copies using your Property and Beneficiary Questionnaires or other information.

6. Prepare a clean original of each of your estate planning documents as explained in each relevant chapter. With your filled-in worksheets before you, this should be a relatively easy task.

> ⚡ **Warning!**
>
> *Do not* make any erasures or corrections on your final estate plan documents. In most cases, this will invalidate the document. If necessary, you will need to retype or reprint the documents to correct any errors.

7. Proofread all of your estate planning documents very carefully to be certain that they are exactly what you want. If there are any typographical errors or if you want to change some provision, no matter how slight, you *must* retype or reprint that page of your documents. *Do not* make any corrections on the final versions of the documents themselves.

8. If any of the documents that you will use in your estate plan require the use of witnesses or notarization, assemble your witnesses and notary public and formally sign your documents. This is known as the *execution* of your documents and for wills must be done very carefully following the details contained in Chapter 7.

9. Make photocopies of your original signed estate planning documents and give them to the persons who may need such copies, for example: the executor whom you have named in your will, your chosen health care attorney-in-fact, your primary physician, or other persons. You may also wish to give the executor or successor trustee a copy of the Executor/Successor Trustee Information List from Chapter 5. Store the original of your estate planning documents in

a safe place but one that is readily accessible to others in case of an emergency situation.

10. Review your estate plan periodically and prepare new estate planning documents if your situation changes.

That's all there is to it. Actually, that may sound like a lot of work and bother, but realize that you would have to follow many of the same steps even if a lawyer were to prepare your estate plan. However, in that case, you would give him or her all of the information and he or she would simply prepare the legal documents in much the same fashion that you will use in this book. The difference, of course, is that you must pay an often exorbitant price to have this done by a lawyer. Additionally, by preparing your plan yourself and doing so at your own pace, you are certain to take more care and give more thought to the entire process than if you have someone else prepare it for you.

Estate Planning Quick Checklist

- ❏ Read this entire book first
- ❏ Fill in the Property and Beneficiary Questionnaires
- ❏ Review your state's legal requirements
- ❏ Choose the appropriate estate planning documents using the chart which follows
- ❏ Make a rough-draft version of your estate planning documents and fill them in
- ❏ Type or print out an original of your estate planning documents
- ❏ Carefully proofread your estate planning documents
- ❏ Assemble the witnesses and notary public and sign your documents
- ❏ Give copies of documents to the appropriate persons and store originals safely
- ❏ Review your estate plan periodically and make any changes as necessary

Estate Planning Chart

On the next two pages is an Estate Planning Chart to give you a quick overview of the types of estate planning tools that are available and what their purposes are. Also the advantages and disadvantages of each type of planning method is explained. Use this chart to decide which estate planning documents or tools that you will need to prepare. The last column in this chart is for your own use. If you decide to use each type of planning tool, check the box in the last column and then, if necessary, go to the appropriate chapter in this book to find the details needed to prepare the document selected.

The Estate Planning Toolkit

Estate Planning Method or Tool	Property Distribution	Probate Avoidance	Health Care Usage	Advantages	Disadvantages	Use in Your Plan?
Will	Yes	No, except for small estates	No	Can be simple and easy; good for setting up trust and/or guardianship for children	Must be witnessed; Will must generally be probated (except for small estates in some states)	
Joint Tenancy (with right of survivorship)	Yes	Yes	No	Easy to create (Generally, with quitclaim deed)	Possible danger if other joint tenant is not trustworthy	
Community Property	Yes	Yes	No	Easy to create (automatic between spouses in community property states, except Alaska)	Only available in a few states (Alaska, Arizona, California, Idaho, Louisiana, Nevada, New Mexico, Texas, Washington, Wisconsin) See Appendix	
Living Trust	Yes	Yes	No	Retain complete control if capable and allow for management if incapacitated; can use to set up trust for children	More paperwork to set up and more on-going maintenance than a will. Cannot be used to select guardian for children	
Payable-on-Death Accounts	Yes	Yes	No	Easy to create, retain complete control during life	Only for certain bank or financial accounts	
Life Insurance and/or pension plans	Yes	Yes	No	Easy to set up; can provide immediate cash to beneficiaries	May be expensive; may be restrictions in policy or plan	

Estate Planning Method or Tool	Property Distribution	Probate Avoidance	Health Care Usage	Advantages	Disadvantages	Use in Your Plan?
Advance Health Care Directive	No	No	Yes	Comprehensive document that includes living will, health care power of attorney, designation of primary physician, and organ donation	See each individual type of document (below) for individual disadvantages. Does not include a financial power of attorney	
Living Will	No	No	Yes	Can use to make advance health care decisions	Difficult to consider all potential health care situations	
Health Care Power of Attorney	No	No	Yes	Can choose a person to make health care decisions for you if you are incapacitated	Person chosen must be reliable; difficult to set out detailed instructions for person chosen	
Durable Power of Attorney for Financial Affairs	No	No	Yes	Can choose a person to handle financial affairs	Person chosen must be reliable and trustworthy	
Designation of Primary Physician	No	No	Yes	Can choose a doctor for primary medical situations	Not useful for choice of medical specialists	
Organ Donation	No	No	Yes	Can decide which, if any, organs and what purposes for use	Must coordinate with donation clause in will and/or driver's license	
Quitclaim Deed	Yes	Yes	No	Allows transfer of property prior to death of owner	Will make the recipient an immediate owner	

51

Chapter 3

Property and Taxation Information

The methods and manners of disposition of your property using an estate plan are discussed in this chapter. Your estate consists of different types of property. They may be personal property, real estate, "community" property, stocks, bonds, cash, heirlooms, or keepsakes. Regardless of the type of property you own, there are certain general rules that must be kept in mind as you prepare your estate plan.

Later in this chapter, there is also a discussion of federal and state estate, inheritance and income taxes as they relate to estate plans. Recent changes in federal law have made the tax consequences of estate planning relevant mainly for people whose estates are valued at $2 million or more.

In addition, in this chapter you will also prepare an inventory of all of your assets and liabilities. This will allow you to have before you a complete listing of all of the property that you own as you begin to consider which beneficiaries should receive which property in your estate plan.

What Property May be Disposed of With Your Estate Plan?

In general, you may dispose of any property that you own at the time of your death. This simple fact, however, contains certain factors which require further explanation. There are forms of property which you may "own," but which may not be transferred by way of a living trust or will. In addition, you may own only a percentage or share of certain other property. In such situations, only that share or percentage which you actually own may be left to others via your estate plan. Finally, there are types of property ownership which are automatically transferred to another party at your death, regardless of the presence of a will or trust in your estate plan.

In the first category of property which cannot be transferred by will or trust are properties that have a designated beneficiary outside of the provisions of your will or living trust. These types of properties include:

- Life insurance policies
- Retirement plans
- IRAs and KEOGHs
- Pension plans
- Trust bank accounts
- Payable-on-death bank accounts
- U.S. Savings Bonds, with payable-on-death beneficiaries

In general, if there is already a valid determination of who will receive the property upon your death (as there is, for example, in the choice of a life insurance beneficiary), you may not alter this choice of beneficiary through the use of your will or trust. If you wish to alter your choice of beneficiary in any of these cases, you must alter the choice directly with the holder of the particular property (for instance, the life insurance company, bank, or pension plan). Note also that property that is included in a living trust may not be left by will, since it already (presumably) has a named beneficiary under the terms of the living trust. In a similar vein, property that is already promised to another under a contract cannot be left to another by will.

The next category of property that may have certain restrictions regarding its transfer by will or trust is property in which you may only own a certain share or percentage. Examples of this might be a partnership interest in a company or jointly-held property. Using a will or trust, you may only leave that percentage or fraction of the ownership of the property that is actually

> **♡ Toolkit Tip!**
>
> Property that already has a designated beneficiary (such as life insurance or IRAs) can *not* be left by will or living trust. The property will be passed to the person or persons who were named as beneficiaries for that particular property.

yours. For business interests, it is generally advisable to pass the interest that you own to a beneficiary intact. The forced sale of the share of a business for estate distribution purposes often results in a lower value being placed on the share. Of course, certain partnership and other business ownership agreements require the sale of a partner's or owner's interest upon death. These buy-out provisions will be contained in any ownership or partnership documents that you may have. Review such documentation carefully to determine both the exact share of your ownership and any post-death arrangements that are specified in the business documents. If your business situation is complex or if you are unsure of how your estate plan will impact your business upon your death, you should consult an attorney knowledgeable in business matters.

The ownership rights and shares of property owned jointly must also be considered. This is discussed below under common-law property states, although most joint ownership laws also apply in community property states as well. Another example of property in which only a certain share is actually able to be transferred by will or trust is a spouse's share of marital property in states that follow community property designation of certain jointly-owned property. The following is a discussion of the basic property law rules in both community property and common-law property states. The rules regarding community property only apply to married persons in those states that follow this type of property designation. If you are single, please disregard this section and use the common-law property states rules below to determine your ownership rights.

Note for residents of Louisiana: Louisiana law is derived from French law and has slightly differing rules. Differences in Louisiana law will be highlighted in the text when applicable, but please check the Appendix listing for details of Louisiana laws relating to estate planning issues.

Community Property States

Several states, mostly in the western United States, follow the community property type of marital property system. Please refer to the Appendix to see if your state has this type of system.

The system itself is derived from ancient Spanish law. It is a relatively simple concept. All property owned by either spouse during a marriage is divided into two types: separate property and community property.

Separate property consists of all property considered owned entirely by one spouse. Separate property, essentially, is all property owned by the spouse prior to the marriage and kept separate during the marriage; and all property received individually by the spouse by gift or inheritance during the marriage. All other property is considered community property. In other words, all property acquired during the marriage by either spouse, unless by gift or inheritance, is community property. Community property is considered to be owned in equal shares by each spouse, regardless of whose efforts actually went into acquiring the property. (Major exceptions to this general rule are Social Security and Railroad retirement benefits, which are considered to be separate property by federal law).

Specifically, separate property generally consists of:

- All property owned by a spouse prior to a marriage (if kept separate)
- All property a spouse receives by gift or inheritance during a marriage (if kept separate)
- All income derived from separate property (if kept separate). Note: in Texas and Idaho, income from separate property is considered community property

Community property generally consists of:

- All property acquired by either spouse during the course of a marriage, unless it is separate property (thus it is community property unless it is acquired by gift or inheritance or is income from separate property)
- All pensions and retirement benefits earned during a marriage (except Social Security and Railroad retirement benefits)
- All employment income of either spouse acquired during the marriage
- All separate property which is mixed or co-mingled with community property during the marriage

⌀ Definition:

Community Property:
The property acquired by either spouse during the marriage, other than by gift or inheritance. Each spouse owns half-interest in community property.

⌀ Definition:

Separate Property:
Generally, all property owned by the spouse prior to the marriage and kept separate during the marriage; and all property received individually by the spouse by gift or inheritance during the marriage.

Thus, if you are a married resident of a community property state, the property that you may dispose of by will or living trust consists of all of your separate property and one-half of your jointly-owned marital community property. The other half of the community property automatically becomes your spouse's sole property upon your death. A spouse in a community property state may disinherit the other spouse from receiving any of their separate property. However, a surviving spouse will still receive the deceased spouse's share of marital property. In addition, residents of most community property states may also generally own property jointly as tenant-in-common or as joint tenants. These forms of ownership are discussed below.

Common-Law Property States

Residents of all other states are governed by a common-law property system, which was derived from English law. Under this system, there is no rule that gives fifty percent ownership of the property acquired during marriage to each spouse.

In common-law states, the property that you may dispose of with your will or living trust consists of all the property held by title in your name, any property that you have earned or purchased with your own money, and any property that you may have been given as a gift or have inherited, either before or during your marriage.

If your name alone is on a title document in these states (for instance, a deed or automobile title), then you own the property solely. If your name and your spouse's name is on the document, you both generally own the property as tenants-in-common, unless the title specifically states that your ownership is to be as joint tenants with right of survivorship, or if your state allows, as a tenancy-by-the-entireties (a form of joint tenancy between married persons). There is an important difference between these types of joint ownership: namely, survivorship. (Note: a few common law states provide that when spouses acquire property jointly, the property is assumed to be held as joint tenants).

With property owned as tenants-in-common, the percentage or fraction that each tenant-in-common owns is property that may be disposed of under a will or trust. If the property is held as joint tenants with right of survivorship or as tenants-by-the entireties, the survivor automatically receives the deceased party's share. Thus, in your will or trust, you may not dispose of any property held in joint tenancy or tenancy-by-the entirety since it already has an automatic legal disposition upon your death. For example: if two persons own a parcel of real estate as equal tenants-in-common, each person may leave a one-half interest in the property to the beneficiary of their choice by their will or living trust. By contrast, if the property is owned as joint tenants with right of survivorship, the one-half interest that a person owns will automatically become the surviving owner's property upon death.

In common-law states, you may dispose of any property that has your name on the title in whatever share that the title gives you, unless the title is held specifically as joint tenants with right of survivorship or tenants-by-the entireties. You may also dispose of any property that you earned or purchased with your own money, and any property that you have been given as a gift or have inherited. If you are married, however, there is a further restriction on your right to dispose of property by will or trust.

All common-law states protect spouses from total disinheritance by providing a statutory scheme under which a spouse may choose to take a minimum share of the deceased spouse's estate, regardless of what the deceased spouse's will or living trust states. This effectively prevents any spouse from being entirely disinherited through the use of the common law rules of property: name on the title equals ownership of property.

In most states, the spouse has a right to a one-third share of the deceased spouse's estate, regardless of what the deceased spouse's will or living trust states. However, all states are slightly different in how they apply this type of law and some allow a spouse to take as much as one-half of the estate. Please check your particular state's laws on this aspect in the Appendix. The effect of these statutory provisions is to make it impossible to disinherit a spouse entirely in common law states (recall that you can't really disinherit a spouse in community property states either as the spouse has a legal right to one-half of the marital property in such states). If you choose to leave nothing to your

> **☼ Toolkit Tip!**
>
> In most states, the spouse has a right to a one-third share of the deceased spouse's estate, regardless of what the deceased spouse's will or living trust states.

> **☼ Toolkit Tip!**
>
> The details of each state's spousal statutory share are outlined in the Appendix under the listing "Spouses Right to Property Regardless of Will."

> **⊘ Definition:**
>
> **Tenants-in-Common:** Property ownership in which two or more persons jointly own property, but each owner owns their share in full (and may, thus, leave their share of the property to others through a will or trust).

spouse under your will or by other means (such as life insurance or joint tenancies), he or she may take it anyway, generally from any property that you tried to leave to others. The details of each state's spousal statutory share are outlined in the Appendix under the listing "Spouses Right to Property Regardless of Will."

You may, however, disinherit anyone else, even your children (except in the state of Louisiana in certain circumstances). To disinherit children, you will need to specifically name them in your will or living trust in order to effectively disinherit them. For anyone else, merely leaving them out of your estate plan effectively disinherits them.

Some states also allow a certain family allowance and/or homestead allowance to the spouse or children to insure that they are not abruptly cut off from their support by any terms of a will or living trust. These allowances are generally of short duration for relatively minor amounts of money and differ greatly from state to state. Thus, the property that you may dispose of by will or living trust is as follows:

- In community property states: For married couples, all separate property (property that was brought into a marriage and held separately, or obtained by gift or inheritance during the marriage) and one-half of the community property (all other property acquired during the marriage by either spouse). If you are single, follow the common-law state rules below.

- In common-law states: Your share of all property where your name is on the title document, unless the property is held as joint tenants or tenants-by-the-entireties. Also your share of all other property that you own, earned, or purchased in your own name. An exception to this is property for which a beneficiary has already been chosen by the terms of the ownership of the property itself (for example: life insurance or payable-on-death bank accounts). In addition, please check the Appendix for information relating to the spouse's minimum statutory share of an estate in your state.

Finally, if you live in a common-law state, but own property in a community property state, your estate will be probated in the state in which you reside (the common-law state). Generally, probate courts will treat out-of-state property in the same manner that it would be treated in the state where it is located. Thus, the common-law state probate court will, generally, treat the community property state asset as if it were a community property asset. The same would hold true if you live in a community property state, but own property in a common-law state. The community property state probate court would generally treat the common-law state asset as common-law property. If you are in this situation, however, it may be a good idea to consult with an attorney to be certain about how your property will be treated by different states.

> **♀Toolkit Tip!**
>
> Property held as joint tenants with right of survivorship or as tenants-by-the entireties will pass directly to the surviving owner, without having to go through the probate process.

Federal and State Taxes Relating to Estates

Various taxes may apply to property transfers upon death. In general, there are two main type of taxes: estate taxes and inheritance taxes. An estate tax is a government tax on the privilege of being allowed to transfer property to others upon your death. This tax is assessed against the estate itself and is paid out of the estate before the assets are distributed to the beneficiaries. An inheritance tax is a tax on property received and is paid by the person who has actually inherited the property. The federal government assesses an estate tax. Various states impose additional estate taxes and inheritance taxes. Additionally, the federal government and a few states apply a gift tax on property transfers during a person's life. There are a number of states that do not impose any estate, inheritance, or gift taxes. Basic information regarding each state's tax situation is provided in the Appendix under the listing "State Gift, Estate or Inheritance Taxes".

Federal Estate Taxes

With regard to federal estate taxes, recent changes in the federal Income Tax Code, as it relates to estate taxes, have released an estimated 97 percent of the American public from any federal estate tax liability on their death. The current Internal Revenue

Service rules provide for the equivalent of an exemption from all estate tax for the first $2 million of a person's assets. If you are married, both you and your spouse are entitled to separate $2 million exemptions. The current $2 million figure is scheduled to increase in stages over the next few years: up to $3.5 million in 2009. In 2010, the estate tax is scheduled to be repealed altogether, although only for one year. Congress will undoubtedly tinker with the federal estate tax again as we approach 2010.

In addition, all of the value of a person's estate that is left to a spouse who is a U.S. citizen (or to a tax-exempt charity) is exempt from any federal estate tax. Even if your particular assets are over this minimum exemption, there are still methods to lessen or eliminate your tax liability. One such method for couples is referred to as an AB trust. A QDOT trust may be used to leave property to a non-citizen spouse. These methods, however, are beyond the scope of this book. Note also that the $2-million exemption includes any substantial gifts that you have made during your lifetime. See the discussion of gift taxes below. From a planning standpoint, the changes in the federal estate tax have virtually eliminated any consideration of tax consequences from the preparation of a estate plan for most Americans. However, if your assets (or your joint assets, if married) total over approximately $2 million, it is recommended that you consult a tax professional prior to preparing your estate plan. The estate tax rate for assets over the $2 million limit is very high: 45% of all taxable assets for the tax years from 2007 to 2009.

State Estate Taxes

State estate taxes are, as a rule, also very minimal or even non-existent until the value of your estate is over $2 million. Most state's estate tax laws were previously tied directly to the federal estate tax regulations and allowed for the same level of exemption equivalent from state estate taxes on death if the estate property totaled under the federal exemption level. This changed in 2006 and now some states may impose an additional level of estate tax. However, unless your estate is very large, any such state estate taxes will be minimal. The details of each state's estate tax situation are outlined in the Appendix. If your estate is large (over $2 million), you are urged to consult a tax professional for assistance in lessening the potential estate tax bite on your estate.

State Inheritance Taxes

Estate taxes are levied on the estate itself, prior to its distribution to any beneficiaries. Inheritance taxes, on the other hand, are taxes levied on the person that actually inherits property. There is no federal inheritance tax and less than half of the states impose an inheritance tax on the receipt of property resulting from someone's death. There are generally relatively high exemptions allowed and the inheritance taxes are usually scaled such that spouses, children, and close relatives pay much lower rates than more distant relatives or unrelated persons. If your estate is over $2 million, you are advised to consult with a tax planning specialist prior to preparing your estate plan.

Federal Gift Tax

Besides estate and inheritance taxes, the federal gift tax may also apply to distributions under your estate plan. This tax is levied on the giver of the gift, not on the recipient. Its purpose is to prevent people from avoiding the federal estate tax by giving away large amounts of property during their lifetimes. From 2006 through 2010, the lifetime federal gift tax exemption is $1 million. You are also allowed under current rules to give a gift of up to $12,000.00 to an individual each year without incurring any gift tax. The amount of gifts over this yearly minimum exclusion is the amount that is subject to the federal gift tax. However, you do not actually pay the federal gift tax when you make a large gift. The amount of the gift that is subject to the gift tax is deducted from the amount of your personal exemption from the federal estate tax. For example, if in tax year 2008, you make a gift to your daughter of $62,000.00, the first $12,000.00 is exempt from any gift tax and the additional $50,000.00 (the amount that is subject to a gift tax) is deducted from your estate tax exemption ($2 million minus $50,000.00), leaving an estate tax exemption of $1,950,000.00. Two final notes regarding gift taxes: First, any gifts between spouses are totally exempt from any gift taxes (unless one spouse is not an American citizen, in

> ⚡ **Warning!**
>
> From 2006 through 2010, the lifetime federal gift tax exemption is $1 million. You are also allowed under current rules to give a gift of up to $12,000.00 to an individual each year without incurring any gift tax.

Toolkit Tip!

Under current federal law, there is no income or capital gains tax on inherited property.

which case the exclusion amount is $117,000.00, rather than the $12,000.00 limit that applies to all other gifts). Finally, any gifts that are made directly to a school or health care provider to pay for educational or health care expenses, and any gifts that are made to tax-exempt charities are exempt from the federal gift tax. As with all situations where an estate is large enough for tax consequences to be important, you are advised to seek additional professional assistance if you anticipate making gifts of over $12,000.00 per year to any individual.

Income Tax on Inheritances

Under current federal law, there are no income or capital gains taxes on inherited property. Inherited property is valued at its "fair market value" at the time of death of the property's owner. Thus, any increase in the value of the property during the life of the deceased owner escapes any capital gains tax. This can provide a substantial tax savings for the recipient of an inheritance of property that has increased in value during the life of the owner. (Note that this tax rule is scheduled to change in 2010). Any income that the inherited property earns after the inheritance will be subject to income tax, however.

Property Questionnaire Instructions

Before you begin to actually prepare your estate plan, you must understand what your assets are, who your beneficiaries are to be, and what your personal desires are as to how those assets should be distributed among your beneficiaries. Since you may only give away property that you actually own, before you prepare your plan it is helpful to gather all of the information regarding your personal financial situation together in one place. The following Property Questionnaire will assist you in that task. Determining who your dependents are, what their financial circumstances are, what gifts you wish to leave them, and whether you wish to make other persons or organizations beneficiaries under your estate plan are questions that will be answered as you complete the Beneficiary Questionnaire in Chapter 4.

Together, these two questionnaires should provide you with all of the necessary information to make the actual preparation of your estate plan a relatively easy task. In addition, the actual process of filling out these questions will gently force you to think about and make the important decisions that must be made in the planning and preparation of your estate plan. When you have finished completing this Questionnaire, have it in front of you as you complete your estate plan using the rest of this book. It may also be prudent to leave a photocopy of these question-naires with the original of your will and/or living trust and provide a copy to your executor (and/or successor trustee), in order to provide a readily-accessible inventory of your assets and list of your beneficiaries for use by your executor (and/or successor trustee) in managing your estate.

Please note that copies of both the Property Questionnaire and the Beneficiary Questionnaire are included on the Forms-on-CD as text forms that may be filled in on your computer or as PDF forms that may be printed out and filled in by hand.

> **Toolkit Tip!**
>
> When you have finished completing this Question-naire, have it in front of you as you complete your estate plan using the rest of this book.

What Are Your Assets?

Cash and Bank Accounts

Individual accounts can be left by will or living trust; joint tenancy and payable-on-death accounts cannot.

Checking Account .... $ _____
Bank _____
Account number _____
Name(s) on account _____

Checking Account .... $ _____
Bank _____
Account number _____
Name(s) on account _____

Savings Account .... $ _____
Bank _____
Account number _____
Name(s) on account _____

Savings Account .... $ _____
Bank _____
Account number _____
Name(s) on account _____

Certificate of Deposit .... $ _____
Held by _____
Expiration date _____
Name(s) on account _____

Other Account .... $ _____
Bank _____
Account number _____
Name(s) on account _____

Total Cash and Bank Accounts .... (A) $ _____

Insurance and Annuity Contracts

Life insurance benefits cannot be left by will or living trust.

Ordinary Life .... $ _____
Company _____
Policy number _____
Beneficiary _____
Address _____

Ordinary Life .... $ _____
Company _____
Policy number _____
Beneficiary _____
Address _____

Endowment .... $ _____
Company _____
Policy number _____
Beneficiary _____
Address _____

Term Life .... $ _____
Company _____
Policy number _____
Beneficiary _____
Address _____

Term Life .... $ _____
Company _____
Policy number _____
Beneficiary _____
Address _____

Annuity Contract .... $ _____
Company _____
Policy number _____
Beneficiary _____
Address _____

Total Insurance and Annuity Contracts .... (B) $ _____

Accounts and Notes Receivable

Debts payable to you may be left by will or living trust.

Accounts Receivable .... $ _____
Due from _____
Address _____

Accounts Receivable .... $ _____
Due from _____
Address _____

Accounts Receivable .... $ _____
Due from _____
Address _____

Notes Receivable .... $ _____
Due from _____
Address _____

Notes Receivable .... $ _____
Due from _____
Address _____

Notes Receivable .... $ _____
Due from _____
Address _____

Other Debts .... $ _____
Due from _____
Address _____

Other Debts .... $ _____
Due from _____
Address _____

Other Debts .... $ _____
Due from _____
Address _____

Total Accounts and Notes Receivable .... (C) $ _____

Stocks and Mutual Funds

Ownership of individually-held stock and mutual funds may be left by will or living trust.

Company _____
CUSIP or certificate number _____
Number and type of shares _____
Value $ _____

Company _____
CUSIP or certificate number _____
Number and type of shares _____
Value $ _____

Company _____
CUSIP or certificate number _____
Number and type of shares _____
Value $ _____

Company _____
CUSIP or certificate number _____
Number and type of shares _____
Value $ _____

Company _____
CUSIP or certificate number _____
Number and type of shares _____
Value $ _____

Company _____
CUSIP or certificate number _____
Number and type of shares _____
Value $ _____

Company _____
CUSIP or certificate number _____
Number and type of shares _____
Value $ _____

Total Stocks and Mutual Funds .... (D) $ _____

Bonds and Mutual Bond Funds

Ownership of individually-held bonds or mutual bond funds may be left by will or living trust.

Company or Fund _____
CUSIP or certificate number _____
Number and type of shares _____
Value $ _____

Company or Fund_____
CUSIP or certificate number _____
Number and type of shares _____
Value $ _____

Company or Fund_____
CUSIP or certificate number _____
Number and type of shares _____
Value $ _____

Company or Fund _____
CUSIP or certificate number _____
Number and type of shares _____
Value $ _____

Company or Fund_____
CUSIP or certificate number _____
Number and type of shares _____
Value $ _____

Company or Fund _____
CUSIP or certificate number _____
Number and type of shares _____
Value $ _____

Company or Fund _____
CUSIP or certificate number _____
Number and type of shares _____
Value $ _____

Total Bonds and Mutual Bond Funds .... (E) $ _____

Business Interest

Ownership of business interests may generally be left by will or living trust, but you are advised to seek legal assistance for leaving partnership, LLC, or close corporation interests under your estate plan.

Individual Proprietorship
Name _____
Location _____
Type of business _____
Your net value $ _____

Individual Proprietorship
Name _____
Location _____
Type of business _____
Your net value $ _____

Interest in Partnership
Name _____
Location _____
Type of business _____
Gross value $ _____ Percentage interest _____%
Your net value $ _____

Interest in Partnership
Name _____
Location _____
Type of business _____
Gross value $ _____ Percentage interest _____%
Your net value $ _____

Closely-held Corporation Interest
Name _____
Location _____
Type of business _____
Gross value $ _____ Percentage of shares held _____%
Your net value $ _____

Total Business Interests .... (F) $ _____

Real Estate

Property owned individually or as tenants-in-common may be left by will or living trust. Property held in joint tenancy or tenancy-by-the-entirety may not.

Personal Residence
Location _____
Value $ _____
How is property held (joint tenants, tenancy-in-common, etc.)? _____
What is your percent? _____%
Value of your share $ _____

Vacation Home
Location _____
Value $ _____
How is property held (joint tenants, tenancy-in-common, etc.)? _____
What is your percent? _____%
Value of your share $ _____

Vacant Land
Location _____
Value $ _____
How is property held (joint tenants, tenancy-in-common, etc.)? _____
What is your percent? _____%
Value of your share $ _____

Income Property
Location _____
Value $ _____
How is property held (joint tenants, tenancy-in-common, etc.)? _____
What is your percent? _____%
Value of your share $ _____

Other Property
Location _____
Value $ _____
How is property held (joint tenants, tenancy-in-common, etc.)? _____
What is your percent? _____%
Value of your share $ _____

Total Real Estate .... (G) $ _____

Personal Property

Personal property owned individually or as a tenant-in-common may be left by will or trust.

Car .... $ _____
Description _____
_____

Car .... $ _____
Description_____
_____

Boat .... $ _____
Description_____
_____

Other Vehicle .... $ _____
Description_____
_____

Furniture .... $ _____
Description _____
_____

Furniture .... $ _____
Description _____
_____

Appliance .... $ _____
Description _____
_____

Jewelry and Furs .... $ _____
Description _____
_____

Music System .... $ _____
Description _____
_____

Artwork .... $ _____
Description _____
_____

Other .... $ _____
Description _____
_____

Other .... $ _____
Description _____
_____

Total Personal Property .... (H) $ _____

Miscellaneous Assets

Personal property owned individually or as a tenant-in-common may be left by will or trust.

Royalties .... $ _____
Description _____
_____

Royalties .... $ _____
Description _____
_____

Patents .... $ _____
Description _____
_____

Copyrights .... $ _____
Description _____
_____

Heirlooms .... $ _____
Description _____
_____

Heirlooms .... $ _____
Description _____
_____

Heirlooms .... $ _____
Description _____
_____

Heirlooms .... $ _____
Description _____
_____

Other .... $ _____
Description _____
_____

Other .... $ _____
Description _____
_____

Other .... $ _____
Description _____
_____

Total Miscellaneous Assets .... (I) $ _____

Employee Benefit and Pension/Profit-sharing Plans

Retirement benefits cannot generally be left by will or living trust.

Company _____
Plan type _____

Net value .... $ _____

Company _____
Plan type _____

Net value .... $ _____

Company _____
Plan type _____

Net value .... $ _____

Company _____
Plan type _____

Net value .... $ _____

Company _____
Plan type _____

Net value .... $ _____

Total Employee Benefit and Pension/Profit-sharing Plans .... (J) $ _____

Total Assets

Insert totals from previous pages.

Cash and Bank Accounts Total .... (A) $ _____
Insurance and Annuity Contracts Total .... (B) $ _____
Accounts and Notes Receivable Total .... (C) $ _____
Stocks and Mutual Funds Total .... (D) $ _____

Bonds and Mutual Bonds Fund Total .... (E) $ _____
Business Interests Total .... (F) $ _____
Real Estate Total .... (G) $ _____
Personal Property Total .... (H) $ _____
Miscellaneous Assets Total .... (I) $ _____
Employee Benefit and Pension/Profit-sharing Plans Total .... (J) $ _____

Total Assets .... (1) $ _____

What Are Your Liabilities?

Notes and Loans Payable

Payable to _____
Address _____
Term _____
Interest rate _____

Amount due .... $ _____

Payable to _____
Address _____
Term _____
Interest rate _____

Amount due .... $ _____

Payable to _____
Address _____
Term _____
Interest rate _____

Amount due .... $ _____

Total Notes and Loans Payable .... (K) $ _____

Accounts Payable

Payable to _____
Address _____
Term _____
Interest rate _____

Amount due .... $ _____

Payable to _____
Address _____
Term _____
Interest rate _____

Amount due .... $ _____

Payable to _____
Address _____
Term _____
Interest rate _____

Amount due .... $ _____

Payable to _____
Address _____
Term _____
Interest rate _____

Amount due .... $ _____

Payable to _____
Address _____
Term _____
Interest rate _____

Amount due .... $ _____

Total Accounts Payable .... (L) $ _____

Mortgages Payable

Property Location _____
Payable to _____
Address _____
Term _____
Interest rate _____

Amount due .... $ _____

Property Location _____
Payable to _____
Address _____
Term _____
Interest rate _____

Amount due .... $ _____

Property Location _____
Payable to _____
Address _____
Term _____
Interest rate _____

Amount due .... $ _____

Property Location _____
Payable to _____
Address _____
Term _____
Interest rate _____

Amount due .... $ _____

Total Mortgages Payable .... (M) $ _____

Taxes Payable

Federal Income Taxes .... $ _____
State Income Taxes .... $ _____
Personal Property Taxes .... $ _____
Real Estate Taxes .... $ _____
Payroll Taxes .... $ _____
Other Taxes .... $ _____
Other Taxes .... $ _____
Other Taxes .... $ _____

Total Taxes Payable .... (N) $ _____

Credit Card Accounts Payable

Credit Card Company _____
Credit card account number _____
Address _____
Interest rate _____

Amount due .... $ _____

Credit Card Company _____
Credit card account number _____
Address _____
Interest rate _____

Amount due .... $ _____

Credit Card Company _____
Credit card account number _____
Address _____
Interest rate _____

Amount due .... $ _____

Total Credit Card Accounts Payable .... (O) $ _____

Miscellaneous Liabilities Payable

To Whom Due _____
Address _____
Term _____
Interest rate _____

Amount due .... $ _____

To Whom Due _____
Address _____
Term _____
Interest rate _____

Amount due .... $ _____

To Whom Due _____
Address _____
Term _____
Interest rate _____

Amount due .... $ _____

To Whom Due _____
Address _____
Term _____
Interest rate _____

Amount due .... $ _____

To Whom Due _____
Address _____
Term _____
Interest rate _____

Amount due .... $ _____

Total Miscellaneous Liabilities Payable .... (P) $ _____

Total Liabilities

Insert totals from previous pages

Notes and Loans Payable Total .... (K) $ _____
Accounts Payable Total .... (L) $ _____
Mortgages Payable Total .... (M) $ _____
Taxes Payable Total .... (N) $ _____
Credit Card Accounts Payable Total .... (O) $ _____
Miscellaneous Liabilities Payable Total .... (P) $ _____

Total Liabilities .... (2) $ _____

Net Worth of Your Estate

Total Assets (from Page 74) .... (1) $ _____
Minus (-) Total Liabilities (from above) .... (2) $ _____

Equals (=) Your Total Net Worth .... $ _____

79

Chapter 4

Beneficiary and Gift Information

In this chapter you will determine both whom you would like your beneficiaries to be and what specific property you will leave each beneficiary under your estate plan. First, there is a brief discussion regarding who may be a beneficiary. Next, there is an explanation of the various methods that you may use to leave gifts to your beneficiaries. Finally, there is a Beneficiary Questionnaire that you will use to actually make the decisions regarding which beneficiaries will receive which property.

Who May Be a Beneficiary?

Any person or organization who receives property under a will or trust is termed a beneficiary. Just as there are certain requirements that the person signing the will or trust must meet, there are certain requirements relating to who may receive property under a will. These generally, however, are in the form of negative requirements. Stated in another way, this means that any person or organization may receive property under a will or living trust unless they fall into certain narrow categories of disqualification.

Besides these few exceptions noted below, any person or organization you choose may receive property under your will or living trust. This includes any family members, the named executor (or

 Definition:

Beneficiary:
Any person or organization who receives property under a will or trust is termed a beneficiary

successor trustee), illegitimate children (if named specifically), corporations, charities (but see below on possible restrictions), creditors, debtors, friends, acquaintances, or even strangers. The few categories of disqualified beneficiaries are as follows:

Toolkit Tip!

Besides a few exceptions that are noted in this chapter, any person or organization you choose may receive property under your will or living trust.

- An attorney who drafts the will or living trust is generally assumed to have used undue influence if he or she is made a beneficiary.
- Many states disqualify any witnesses to the signing (execution) of the will. Check the Appendix to see if your state has this restriction. However, to be safe, it is recommended that none of your witnesses be beneficiaries under your will or living trust.
- A person who murders a testator is universally disqualified from receiving any property under the murdered person's will (even if they are named as a beneficiary).
- An unincorporated association is typically not allowed to receive property under a will or living trust. This particular disqualification stems from the fact that such associations generally have no legal right to hold property.

A few states also have restrictions on the right to leave property to charitable organizations and churches. These restrictions are usually in two forms: a time limit prior to death when changes to a will that leave large amounts of money or property to a charitable organization are disallowed or a percentage limit on the amount of a person's estate that may be left to a charitable organization (often a limit of 50 percent). The reasoning behind this rule is to prevent abuse of a dying person's desire to be forgiven. There have been, in the past, unscrupulous individuals or organizations who have obtained last-minute changes in a will in an attempt to have the bulk of a person's estate left to them or their group. If you intend to leave large sums of money or property to a charitable organization or church, please consult an attorney for further assistance to see if there are any restrictions of this type in force in your state.

Under this same category as to who may be a beneficiary under your will or living trust are several points related to marriage, divorce, and children. First and foremost, you are advised to review your estate plan periodically and make any necessary changes as your marital or family situation may dictate. If you are divorced, married, remarried, or widowed, or adopt or have a child, there may be unforeseen consequences based on the way you have prepared your estate plan. Each state has differing laws on the effect of marriage and divorce on a person's will. In some states, divorce entirely revokes a will as it pertains to the divorced spouse. In other states, divorce has no effect and your divorced spouse may inherit your estate if you do not change your will. Marriage and the birth of children are also treated somewhat differently by each state. You are advised to review the Appendix as it relates to these aspects of your life and prepare your estate plan accordingly.

Your estate plan should be prepared with regard to how your life is presently arranged. It should, however, always be reviewed and updated each time there is a substantial change in your life.

What Type of Gifts May You Make?

There are various standard terms and phrases that may be employed when making gifts under your estate plan. The wills and living trusts that are used in this book incorporate these standard terms. Using these standard phrases, you may make a gift of any property that you will own at your death to any beneficiary whom you choose (remembering the few disqualified types of beneficiaries).

A few types of gifts are possible but are not addressed in the wills or living trusts that may be prepared using this book. Simple shared gifts (for example: I give all my property to my children, Alice, Bill, and Carl, in equal shares) are possible using this book. However, any complex shared gift arrangements will require the assistance of an attorney. In addition, you may impose simple conditions on any gifts in wills or living trusts prepared using this book. However, complex conditional gifts that impose detailed requirements that the beneficiary must comply with in order to receive the gift are also beyond the scope of this book. Finally, although it is possible to leave any gifts through your estate plan in many types of trusts, a living trust and a simple trust for leaving gifts to children are the only trusts available in estate plans

☀ Toolkit Tip!

The wills and trusts in this book allow you to leave gifts to minors 'in trust', that is to be held in a separate 'children's trust' until the child reaches an acceptable age to handle the gift on their own.

prepared using this book. If you desire to leave property in trust to an adult or in a complex trust arrangement, you are advised to seek professional legal advice.

The terms that you use to make a gift can be any that you desire, as long as the gift is made in a clear and understandable manner. Someone reading the document at a later date, perhaps even a stranger appointed by a court, must be able to determine exactly what property you intended to be a gift and exactly who it is you intended to receive it. If you follow the few rules that follow regarding how to identify your gifts and beneficiaries, your intentions will be clear to whomever may need to interpret your estate plan documents in the future:

> Always describe the property in as detailed and clear a manner as possible. For example: do not simply state "my car;" instead state "my 2002 Honda Accord Sedan, Serial #123456789." Describe exactly what it is you wish for each beneficiary to receive. You may make any type of gift that you wish, either a cash gift, a gift of a specific piece of personal property or real estate, or a specific share of your total estate. If you wish to give some of your estate in the form of portions of the total, it is recommended to use fractional portions. For example, if you wish to leave your estate in equal shares to two persons, use "I give one-half of my total estate to …" for each party.

> In your description of the property, you should be as specific and precise as possible. For land, it is suggested that you use the description exactly as shown on the deed to the property. For personal property, be certain that your description clearly differentiates your gift from any other property.

> Always describe the beneficiaries in as precise and clear a manner as is possible. For example: do not simply state "my son;" instead state "my son, Robert Edward Smith, of Houston Texas." This is particularly important if the beneficiary is an adopted child.

> Never provide a gift to a group or class of people without specifically stating their individual names. For example: do not simply state "my sisters;" instead state "my sister Kath-

Toolkit Tip!

If a gift under a will or living trust is real estate, you should always describe the property using the exact legal description as shown on the deed to the property.

erine Mary Jones, and my sister Elizabeth Anne Jones, and my sister Annette Josephine Jones."

You may put simple conditions on the gift if they are reasonable and not immoral or illegal. For example: you may say "This gift is to be used to purchase daycare equipment for the church nursery;" but you may not say "I give this gift to my sister only if she divorces her deadbeat husband Ralph Edwards."

> ## ⊘ Definition:
>
> ### Residuary Clause:
> A clause in a will or living trust that provides for the disposition of any property not already provided for elsewhere in the will or trust.

You should always provide for an alternate beneficiary for the purpose of allowing you to designate someone to receive the gift if your first choice to receive the gift dies before you do (or, in the case of an organization chosen as primary beneficiary, is no longer in business). Your choice for alternate beneficiary may be one or more persons or an organization. In addition, you may delete the alternate beneficiary choice and substitute the words "the residue" instead. The result of this change will be that if your primary beneficiary dies before you do, your gift will pass under your residuary clause, which is discussed next.

Although not a technical legal requirement, a residuary clause should be included in every will (and living trust) in this book. With this clause, you will choose the person, persons, or organization to receive anything not covered by other clauses of your will or living trust. Even if you feel that you have given away everything that you own under other clauses of your will or living trust, this can be a very important clause.

If, for any reason, any other gifts under your will or living trust are not able to be completed, this clause takes effect. For example, if a beneficiary refuses to accept your gift or the chosen beneficiary has died and no alternate was selected or both the beneficiary and alternate have died, the gift will be returned to your estate and would pass under the "residuary clause." If there is no "residuary clause" included in your will, any property not disposed of under your will is treated as though you did not have a will and could potentially be forfeited to the state. Note that if there is no residuary clause in your living trust, any property not disposed of under your living trust will then be disposed of under the terms of your will, if you have one.

A survivorship clause also should be included in every will and living trust. This provides for a period of survival for any beneficiary. For wills and living trusts prepared using this book, the period is set at 30 days. The practical effect of this is to be certain that your property passes under your will (or living trust) and not that of a beneficiary who dies shortly after receiving your gift.

Without this clause in your will or trust, it would be possible that property would momentarily pass to a beneficiary under your will or trust. When that person dies (possibly immediately if a result of a common accident or disaster), your property could wind up being left to the person whom your beneficiary designated, rather than to your alternate beneficiary.

To disinherit anyone from receiving property under your will, you should specifically name the person to be disinherited, rather than rely upon simply not mentioning them in your will. To disinherit children and grandchildren of deceased children, they must be mentioned specifically. In the case of children born after a will is executed and of spouses of a marriage that takes place after a will is executed, there are differing provisions in many states as to the effect of their not being mentioned in a will.

Please also note that although one may choose to leave nothing to a spouse in a will, all states provide rules that allow a spouse the right to a certain share of the other spouse's property on death. Refer back to the chapter on Property and Taxation Information for more details. Please also see the Appendix for information regarding the laws in your particular state. The safest method of disinheritance, however, is to specifically mention anyone to be disinherited. Be sure to clearly identify the person being disinherited by full name. (Also note, in Louisiana, in order to disinherit children or grandchildren, specific and just reasons must be stated in the will). Another legal method to achieve approximately the same result as disinheritance is to leave the person a very

> ⦿ **Definition:**
>
> ## Survivorship Clause:
>
> A clause in a will or living trust that provides that any beneficiary must survive the deceased person by a certain time limit. Documents in this book set this time limit at 30 days.

small amount (at least $1.00) as a gift in your will. Also, be sure to review your estate plan each time there is a change in your family circumstances. Please see Chapter 8 for a discussion regarding changing your will.

Finally, property may be left to your children in trust using the children's trust that is included in the appropriate wills and living trusts in this book. Please refer to the discussion of the children's trust in the chapters relating to wills and living trusts.

If you state your gifts simply, clearly, and accurately, you can be assured that they will be able to be carried out after your death regardless of who may be required to interpret the language in your will or living trust.

The beneficiary questionnaire on the following pages will help you determine who you wish to leave gifts and what those gifts may be. It will also help you to determine which assets and beneficiaries will be dealt with using various documents in your estate plan, under the listing "Methods by which you will transfer gift," for example by will or living trust or some other method, such as a lifetime gift, payable-on-death designation, quitclaim deed, or other estate planning tool. Recall also that this questionnaire is available on the Forms-on-CD.

Beneficiary Questionnaire

Who Will Receive Your Assets?
Spouse

Spouse _____
Maiden name _____
Date of marriage _____
Date of birth_____
Address _____
Amount, specific items, or share of estate that you desire to leave _____
_____
_____
_____

Alternate beneficiary _____
Method by which you will transfer gift _____

Children

Child _____
Date of birth _____
Address _____
_____
_____
Spouse's name (if any) _____
Amount, specific items, or share of estate that you desire to leave _____
_____
_____

Alternate beneficiary _____
Method by which you will transfer gift _____

Child _____

Date of birth _____

Address _____

_____

_____

Spouse's name (if any) _____

Amount, specific items, or share of estate that you desire to leave _____

_____

_____

Alternate beneficiary _____

Method by which you will transfer gift _____

Child _____

Date of birth _____

Address _____

_____

_____

Spouse's name (if any) _____

Amount, specific items, or share of estate that you desire to leave _____

_____

_____

Alternate beneficiary _____

Method by which you will transfer gift _____

Child _____

Date of birth _____

Address _____

_____

_____

Spouse's name (if any) _____

Amount, specific items, or share of estate that you desire to leave _____

_____

_____

Alternate beneficiary _____

Method by which you will transfer gift _____

Grandchildren

Grandchild _____
Date of birth _____
Address _____
_____
_____

Spouse's name (if any) _____
Amount, specific items, or share of estate that you desire to leave _____
_____
_____

Alternate beneficiary _____
Method by which you will transfer gift _____

Grandchild _____
Date of birth _____
Address _____
_____
_____

Spouse's name (if any) _____
Amount, specific items, or share of estate that you desire to leave _____
_____
_____

Alternate beneficiary _____
Method by which you will transfer gift _____

Grandchild _____
Date of birth _____
Address _____
_____
_____

Spouse's name (if any) _____
Amount, specific items, or share of estate that you desire to leave _____
_____
_____

Alternate beneficiary _____
Method by which you will transfer gift _____

Grandchild _____
Date of birth _____
Address _____
_____
_____
Spouse's name (if any) _____
Amount, specific items, or share of estate that you desire to leave _____
_____
_____
Alternate beneficiary _____
Method by which you will transfer gift _____

Parents

Parent _____
Date of birth _____
Address _____
_____
_____
Spouse's name (if any) _____
Amount, specific items, or share of estate that you desire to leave _____
_____
_____
Alternate beneficiary _____
Method by which you will transfer gift _____

Parent _____
Date of birth _____
Address _____
_____
_____
Spouse's name (if any) _____
Amount, specific items, or share of estate that you desire to leave _____
_____
_____
Alternate beneficiary _____
Method by which you will transfer gift _____

Siblings

Sibling _____
Date of birth _____
Address _____
_____
_____

Spouse's name (if any) _____
Amount, specific items, or share of estate that you desire to leave _____
_____
_____

Alternate beneficiary _____
Method by which you will transfer gift _____

Sibling _____
Date of birth _____
Address _____
_____
_____

Spouse's name (if any) _____
Amount, specific items, or share of estate that you desire to leave _____
_____
_____

Alternate beneficiary _____
Method by which you will transfer gift _____

Sibling _____
Date of birth _____
Address _____
_____
_____

Spouse's name (if any) _____
Amount, specific items, or share of estate that you desire to leave _____
_____
_____

Alternate beneficiary _____
Method by which you will transfer gift _____

Other Dependents

Other Dependent _____

Date of birth _____

Address _____

_____

_____

Spouse's name (if any) _____

Amount, specific items, or share of estate that you desire to leave _____

_____

_____

Alternate beneficiary _____

Method by which you will transfer gift _____

Other Dependent _____

Date of birth _____

Address _____

_____

_____

Spouse's name (if any) _____

Amount, specific items, or share of estate that you desire to leave _____

_____

_____

Alternate beneficiary _____

Method by which you will transfer gift _____

Other Dependent _____

Date of birth _____

Address _____

_____

_____

Spouse's name (if any) _____

Amount, specific items, or share of estate that you desire to leave _____

_____

_____

Alternate beneficiary _____

Method by which you will transfer gift _____

Are There Any Other Relatives, Friends, or Organizations to Whom You Wish to Leave Gifts?

Name _____
Relationship _____
Address _____

_____

_____
Spouse's name (if any) _____
Amount, specific items, or share of estate that you desire to leave _____

_____

_____

_____
Alternate beneficiary _____
Method by which you will transfer gift _____

Name _____
Relationship _____
Address _____

_____

_____
Spouse's name (if any) _____
Amount, specific items, or share of estate that you desire to leave _____

_____

_____

_____
Alternate beneficiary _____
Method by which you will transfer gift _____

Name _____
Relationship _____
Address _____

_____

Spouse's name (if any) _____
Amount, specific items, or share of estate that you desire to leave _____

_____

_____

Alternate beneficiary _____
Method by which you will transfer gift _____

Name _____
Relationship _____
Address _____

_____

Spouse's name (if any) _____
Amount, specific items, or share of estate that you desire to leave _____

_____

_____

Alternate beneficiary _____
Method by which you will transfer gift _____

Name _____
Relationship _____
Address _____

_____

Spouse's name (if any) _____
Amount, specific items, or share of estate that you desire to leave _____

_____

_____

Alternate beneficiary _____
Method by which you will transfer gift _____

Are There Any Persons Whom You Wish to Specifically Leave Out of Your Will and/or Living Trust (Disinherit)?

Name _____

Relationship _____

Address _____

_____

Spouse's name (if any) _____

Reason for disinheritance _____

_____

_____

Name _____

Relationship _____

Address _____

_____

Spouse's name (if any) _____

Reason for disinheritance _____

_____

_____

Name _____

Relationship _____

Address _____

_____

Spouse's name (if any) _____

Reason for disinheritance _____

_____

_____

Chapter 5

Probate and Successor Trustee/Executor Information

In this chapter, various information relating to the probate process is provided. In addition, information relating to the executor of your will (or successor trustee of your living trust) is also outlined. For a living trust, you will need to select someone to distribute your trust assets to your chosen beneficiaries after your death. This person is referred to as your *successor trustee*. For a will, the person appointed in the will to administer your estate upon your death is referred to an *executor*. (Note that in some states an executor is referred to as a *personal representative*). Before actually setting up your estate plan, an overview of how the legal system operates after a person's death may be useful to keep in mind. The system of court administration of the estates of deceased parties is generally entitled *probate*. How to avoid the probate court was the subject of one of the first self-help law books to challenge the legal establishment's monopoly on law. Probate, however, despite what many lawyers would have you believe, is not all that mysterious a matter.

Overview of a Typical Probate Proceeding

If the bulk of your assets is placed in a living trust, your chosen successor trustee is authorized by the terms of the trust to distribute the assets to the chosen beneficiaries upon your death without notice to any court and without any court supervision.

Toolkit Tip!

Although the use of a living trust will avoid probate, you should always also have a valid will to handle any property that you may have overlooked, or property that you may receive after you prepared your living trust.

Additionally, if you have assets that have chosen beneficiaries, such as a life insurance policy or a payable-on-death bank account, the beneficiary will automatically become the owner of the property upon your death (although the beneficiary will have to provide the holder of the assets with proof of the death). Finally, if you have assets that are held as joint tenants with survivorship or community property assets in a community property state, those assets will automatically become the property of the joint owner or spouse upon your death. These situations all take place outside of a probate proceeding.

If, however, there is a will, upon a person's death, in most states there is a general sequence of events which takes place. First, if there is a will, the *executor* appointed in the will (who, hopefully, has been notified of her or his duties in advance) locates the will and files it with the proper authority. If necessary, the executor arranges for the funeral and burial. If the estate is complicated or very large, it may be prudent for the executor to hire a lawyer to handle the probate proceeding. Upon presenting the will to the probate court, the will is *proved*, which means that it is determined whether or not the document presented is actually the deceased's will. This may be done in most states with a *self-proving affidavit* that is prepared and notarized at the time your will is signed. The wills in this book are designed to be self-proving when completed and signed as indicated.

Upon proof that the will is valid, the executor is officially given legal authority to gather together all of the estate's property. This authority for the executor to administer the estate is generally referred to as *letters testamentary*. The probate court also officially appoints any trustees and also the parties who are designated as guardians of any minor children.

If no executor was chosen in the will, or if the one chosen cannot serve, the probate court will appoint one. The order of preference for appointment is commonly as follows: surviving spouse, next of kin, and then a person having an interest in the estate or claims against the estate.

If the will is shown to be invalid, or if there is no will, the same sequence of events generally is followed. When a person dies without a will this is referred to as dying *intestate*. However, in

♀ Toolkit Tip!

All wills prepared using this book contain a 'self-proving affidavit' that will, generally, allow for the will to be 'proved' in probate without the need to call the witnesses to court to testify.

97

this case, the party appointed to administer the estate is usually titled an *administrator* of the estate rather than an executor. The court orders granting authority to an administrator are generally referred to as *letters of administration*. The probate court will then use state law to determine how a person's assets are distributed. Please refer to the discussion in the first chapter of this book regarding intestacy and also check the Appendix for details regarding how your particular state handles distribution of estates of intestate persons.

After the executor or administrator is given authority, he or she handles the collection of assets, management of the estate, and payment of any debts and taxes until such time as all creditors' claims have been satisfied and other business of the estate completed. An inventory of all of the assets is typically the first official act of an executor. Creditors, by the way, only have a certain time period in which to make a claim against an estate. The same holds true for any *contests* (challenging the validity) of the will. Contesting a will is a fairly rare occurrence and is most difficult if the will was properly prepared and signed by a competent, sane adult.

The executor generally will also be empowered under state law to provide an allowance for the surviving spouse and children until such time as all affairs of the deceased person are completed and the estate is closed.

Upon completion of all business and payment of all outstanding charges against the estate, an accounting and inventory of the estate's assets are then presented to the probate court by the executor. At this time, if everything appears to be in order, the executor is generally empowered to distribute all of the remaining property to the persons or organizations named in the will and probate is officially closed. The entire probate process generally takes from four to 12 months to complete. The distribution of your property and money is usually handled solely by the executor (possibly with a lawyer's help to be certain that all legal requirements are fulfilled). Normally, this is done without further court approval of the disbursement.

Simplified Probate Procedures

� Toolkit Tip!

Check the Appendix of this book for the details of any simplified probate procedures in your own state.

Although, in the past, probate used to be a very expensive and time-consuming process, all states (except Georgia and Louisiana) now provide various methods for streamlined and simplified probate procedures for smaller estates. These simplified procedures generally take two forms: probate methods that consist of using affidavits to complete all of the distribution of an estate's assets and/or procedures that greatly simplify the probate process. These probate simplification procedures are generally available for estates that have limited assets, although in some states the cut-off amounts can be as high as several hundred thousand dollars. These simplified probate procedures have, in some cases, made estate planning issues for the sole purpose of probate avoidance somewhat less important. You may wish, however, to use your state's maximum limits for simplified probate to plan your estate in such a way as to make certain that you have removed enough property from probate to qualify for use of the simplified probate procedures for the remaining property. For example, let's say you have an estate consisting of a $200,000.00 home, $50,000.00 in a bank account, a $10,000.00 car, and $15,000.00 in personal property for a total estate of $275,000.00. This amount is over the simplified probate cutoff level for nearly all states. But you could put your home into a living trust and change your bank account to a payable-on-death account, leaving only $25,000.00 in property that is subject to probate, which you could then leave to your beneficiaries by way of a will. This amount of property left by will would then qualify for simplified probate procedures in most states. Please check the Appendix for an explanation of the simplified probate procedures in your state.

Choosing a Successor Trustee or Executor

Your choice of who should be your successor trustee or executor is a personal decision. A spouse, sibling, or other trusted party is usually chosen to act as successor trustee/executor, although a bank officer, accountant, or attorney can also be chosen. The person chosen should be someone you trust and whom you feel can handle or at least efficiently delegate the complicated tasks of making an inventory of all of your property and distributing it to your chosen beneficiaries. The person chosen should, generally, be a resident of the state in which you currently reside (See warning box below left). In addition, all states require that successor trustee/executors be competent, of legal age (generally, over 18) and a citizen of the United States. Although it is possible, it is generally not wise to appoint two or more persons as co-successor trustee/executors. It is preferable to appoint your first choice as primary successor trustee/executor and the other person as alternate successor trustee/executor. Note that if you will be using both a will and a living trust in your estate plan, you may select different people to serve as executor and successor trustee. It may, however, be more prudent to select the same person to act in each capacity in order to simplify the coordination of the distribution of your estate's assets. If you do choose to select different people to serve in these roles, you will need to specify which person you expect to handle the non-legal duties (these duties are outlined later in this chapter) that a successor trustee/executor may be expected to carry out. Generally, it is the executor of an estate that handles these various duties, but there is no legal requirement that would prevent a successor trustee from being requested to handle these duties.

In your will or living trust, you will grant the successor trustee/executor broad powers to manage your estate and will also provide that he or she is not required to post a bond in order to be appointed to serve as successor trustee/executor. This provision can save your estate considerable money, depending upon the estate's size. The fees for executor bonds are based upon the size of the estate and can amount to hundreds of dollars for every year that your estate is being managed. By waiving this bond requirement, these potential bond fees can be eliminated and the money saved can be passed on to your beneficiaries.

You should discuss your choice with the person chosen to be certain that he or she is willing to act as successor trustee/executor. In addition, it is wise to provide your successor trustee/executor, in advance, with a copy of your will, living trust, living will and any other estate planning documents; a copy of any organ-donation desires, a copy of your property and beneficiary questionnaires, and a copy of the information contained in this chapter.

Successor Trustee/Executor Duties Checklist Instructions

Provided on the following pages is a checklist of items that your successor trustee/executor may have to deal with after your death. Although this list is extensive, there may be other personal tasks that are not included. Scanning this list can give you an idea of the scope and range of the successor trustee/executor's duties. You can provide invaluable assistance to your successor trustee/executor by being aware of his or her duties and providing the successor trustee/executor with information to help him or her complete them. This checklist is divided into immediate and first-month time periods. These time periods are approximations and many of the duties may be required to be performed either before or after the exact time specified. Also included in the checklist are a number of financial duties. These duties cannot be delegated (except to an attorney or accountant specifically hired by the executor for that purpose). Following this list, a section is provided for listing such information for your successor trustee/executor. Please note that these checklists are included on the Forms-on-CD.

> **🔆 Toolkit Tip!**
> You should always discuss your choice with the person chosen to be certain that he or she is willing to act as successor trustee or executor.

Successor Truestee/Executor Duties Checklist

Immediate Duties

☐ Contact mortuary or funeral home regarding services

☐ Contact cemetery regarding burial or cremation

☐ Contact local newspaper with obituary information

☐ Contact relatives and close friends

☐ Contact employer and business associates

☐ Contact lawyer and accountant

☐ Arrange for Pallbearers

☐ Contact guardians or trustees named in will

☐ Arrange for immediate care of decedent's minor children

☐ Arrange for living expenses for decedent's spouse

☐ Contact veteran's organizations

Duties within First Month

☐ Contact insurance agent and report death

☐ Contact general insurance agent

☐ Contact medical and health insurance companies

☐ Contact Medicare

☐ Contact employer regarding pensions and death benefits

☐ Contact unions regarding pensions and death benefits

☐ Contact military regarding pensions and death benefits

☐ Contact Social Security Administration

☐ Obtain death certificates from attending physician

☐ Contact IRA or KEOGH account trustees

☐ Contact county recorder

☐ Contact post office

☐ Contact department of motor vehicles

☐ Arrange for management of business or real estate holdings

☐ Review all of decedent's records and legal documents

☐ Contact gas, telephone, cable, electric, trash and water companies

☐ Contact newspaper and magazine subscription departments

☐ Contact credit card companies

Financial Duties
Cannot be delegated

☐ Begin inventory of assets

☐ Arrange for appraisal of assets

☐ Begin collection of assets

☐ Contact banks, savings and loans, and credit unions

☐ Contact mortgage companies

☐ Contact stockbroker and investment counselor

☐ Open bank accounts for estate

☐ Open decedent's safe deposit box

The Estate Planning Toolkit

☐ File the will with probate court (Executor duty only)

☐ Inventory all estate assets

☐ Collect all monies and property due to decedent

☐ Pay all taxes due and file all necessary tax returns

☐ Provide notice to all creditors of the time limit for claims

☐ Pay all debts and expenses of decedent, including funeral expenses

☐ Arrange for sale of estate assets, if necessary

☐ Distribute all remaining assets according to will

☐ Submit final accounting and receipts to probate court

☐ Close estate books and affairs

Successor Trustee/Executor Information List Instructions

The following listing will provide your successor trustee/executor with valuable information that will make performing his or her difficult task much easier. Included in this questionnaire is information relating to the location of your records, any funeral or burial arrangements that you have made, lists of important persons, businesses, or organizations whom the successor trustee/executor will need to contact after your death, and information that will assist your successor trustee/executor in preparing any obituary listing. It may be very difficult to confront your own mortality and the need for this information. Please take the time to provide this valuable record of information for your successor trustee/executor. After your death, he or she may be under tremendous emotional stress and this information will help him or her perform the successor trustee/executor's necessary duties with the least difficulty. You will probably wish to give this information list and a copy of your will and/or living trust to the person whom you have chosen as your successor trustee/executor. Please note that a copy of this information checklist is included on the Forms-on-CD.

Note: You may also wish to leave a letter for your executor or successor trustee that explains any of your reasons for particular actions that you have taken in preparing your will, trust, or other estate planning devices. This letter will have no legal effect, but may go a long way in providing your beneficiaries with clear reasons why certain actions were taken, such as why (or why not) some gifts were made, or why there may be differences in the amounts or types of property that were left to siblings. A letter of this type may also be a good place to express your sentiments regarding friends or family. You may also wish to use such a letter to leave instructions for the care of pets.

Successor Trustee/Executor Information List

Location of Records

Original of will _____

Original of codicil _____

Trust documents _____

Safe deposit box and key _____

Bankbook and savings passbook _____

Treasury bills and certificates of deposit _____

_____

_____

Social Security records _____

Real estate deeds and mortgage documents _____

Veteran's information _____

Stock certificates and bonds _____

_____

_____

Promissory notes and loan documents _____

_____

Business records _____

Partnership records _____

Corporation records _____

Automobile titles _____

Income tax records _____

Credit card records _____

Birth certificate _____

Warranties _____

_____

_____

Other important papers _____

_____

_____

_____

_____

_____

_____

_____

_____

Funeral or Cremation Arrangements

Name of mortuary, funeral home, or crematorium _____
_____
Name of person contacted _____
Phone _____
Address _____
_____
Arrangements made _____
_____
_____
_____
_____
_____
_____

Name of cemetery _____
Name of person contacted _____
Phone _____
Address _____
_____
Arrangements made _____
_____
_____
_____
_____
_____
_____

Location of memorial or church service _____
_____
Name of person contacted _____
Phone _____
Address _____
_____
Arrangements made _____
_____
_____
_____

Persons, Businesses, and Organizations to Contact

Clergy _____

Address _____

City, State, Zip _____

Phone _____

Lawyer _____

Address _____

City, State, Zip _____

Phone _____

Accountant _____

Address _____

City, State, Zip _____

Phone _____

IRA or Keogh account trustee _____

Address _____

City, State, Zip _____

Phone _____

Stockbroker _____

Address _____

City, State, Zip _____

Phone _____

Investment counselor _____

Address _____

City, State, Zip _____

Phone _____

Life insurance agent _____

Address _____

City, State, Zip _____

Phone _____

General insurance agent _____

Address _____

City, State, Zip _____

Phone _____

Medical insurance agent _____
Address _____
City, State, Zip _____
Phone _____

Health insurance agent _____
Address _____
City, State, Zip _____
Phone _____

Physician _____
Address _____
City, State, Zip _____
Phone _____

Dentist _____
Address _____
City, State, Zip _____
Phone _____

Employer _____
Address _____
City, State, Zip _____
Phone _____

Employer _____
Address _____
City, State, Zip _____
Phone _____

Business associate _____
Address _____
City, State, Zip _____
Phone _____

Business associate _____
Address _____
City, State, Zip _____
Phone _____

Union representative _____
Address _____
City, State, Zip _____
Phone _____

Guardian named in will _____
Address _____
City, State, Zip _____
Phone _____

Guardian named in will _____
Address _____
City, State, Zip _____
Phone _____

Trustee named in will or trust _____
Address _____
City, State, Zip _____
Phone _____

Trustee named in will or trust _____
Address _____
City, State, Zip _____
Phone _____

Military unit _____
Address _____
City, State, Zip _____
Phone _____

Veteran's organization _____
Address _____
City, State, Zip _____
Phone _____

Bank, savings and loan, or credit union _____
Address _____
City, State, Zip _____
Phone _____

Bank, savings and loan, or credit union _____
Address _____
City, State, Zip _____
Phone _____

Mortgage company _____
Address _____
City, State, Zip _____
Phone _____

Utility _____
Address _____
City, State, Zip _____
Phone _____

Utility _____
Address _____
City, State, Zip _____
Phone _____

Utility _____
Address _____
City, State, Zip _____
Phone _____

Newspaper _____
Address _____
City, State, Zip _____
Phone _____

Magazine _____
Address _____
City, State, Zip _____
Phone _____

Credit card company _____
Address _____
City, State, Zip _____
Phone _____

Credit card company _____
Address _____
City, State, Zip _____
Phone _____

Credit card company _____
Address _____
City, State, Zip _____
Phone _____

Relatives to Contact

Relative name _____
Address _____
City, State, Zip _____
Phone _____

Relative name _____
Address _____
City, State, Zip _____
Phone _____

Relative name _____
Address _____
City, State, Zip _____
Phone _____

Relative name _____
Address _____
City, State, Zlp _____
Phone _____

Relative name _____
Address _____
City, State, Zip _____
Phone _____

Relative name _____
Address _____
City, State, Zip _____
Phone _____

Relative name _____
Address _____
City, State, Zip _____
Phone _____

Relative name _____
Address _____
City, State, Zip _____
Phone _____

Friends to Contact

Friend name _____
Address _____
City, State, Zip _____
Phone _____

Friend name _____
Address _____
City, State, Zip _____
Phone _____

Friend name _____
Address _____
City, State, Zip _____
Phone _____

Friend name _____
Address _____
City, State, Zip _____
Phone _____

Friend name _____
Address _____
City, State, Zip _____
Phone _____

Friend name _____
Address _____
City, State, Zip _____
Phone _____

Friend name _____
Address_____
City, State, Zip_____
Phone _____

Friend name _____
Address_____
City, State, Zip
Phone _____

Newspaper Obituary Information

Newspaper _____
Address _____
City, State, Zip _____
Phone _____

Newspaper _____
Address _____
City, State, Zip _____
Phone _____

Your Name _____
Date of birth _____
Place of birth _____
Current residence _____
_____

Former residence _____
_____
_____

Occupation _____
_____
_____

Education _____
_____
_____

Military service _____

_____

Club, union, civic, or fraternal organizations _____

_____

_____

Special achievements _____

_____

_____

_____

_____

_____

_____

Survivors _____

_____

_____

_____

_____

_____

_____

_____

Date of death _____
Place of service _____

_____

Date of service _____
Time of service _____

Memorial contribution preference _____

_____

_____

_____

Chapter 6

Selecting a Will

In this chapter,

there are four separate wills that have been prepared for the purpose of allowing persons whose situations fall into certain standard formats to prepare their wills quickly and easily on pre-assembled forms. Generally, the wills are for a single person with or without children and for a married person with or without children. Please read the description prior to each will to be certain that the will you choose is appropriate for your particular situation. Please note that each of the wills in this book is intended to be a *self-proving* will. This means that the signatures of the witnesses and the *testator* (the person whose will it is) will be verified by a notary public and thus, the witnesses' testimony will not be needed in probate court at a later date in order to authenticate their signatures.

Instructions for Selecting Your Will

These pre-assembled will forms are intended to be used as simplified worksheets for preparing your own personal will. The forms should be filled-in by hand and then retyped or printed out according to the following instructions and the instructions contained in Chapter 7. These pre-assembled wills are not intended to be filled-in and used "as is" as an original will. Such use would most likely result in an invalid will. The forms *must* be either retyped or completed on a computer and printed out. Be certain to carefully follow all of the instructions for use of these forms. They are not difficult to fill out, but must be prepared

♀ Toolkit Tip!

Be sure to check your state's listing in the appendix for details about the laws regarding wills for your specific state.

properly to be legally valid. In order to prepare any of the wills in this chapter, you should follow these simple steps:

1. Carefully read through all of the clauses in the blank pre-assembled will to determine if the clauses provided are suitable in your situation. Choose the will that is most appropriate. Make a photocopy or print out a copy of the will that you select to use as a worksheet . If you wish, you may use this book itself as a worksheet (unless it is a library book!).

2. Using your Property and Beneficiary Questionnaires, fill in the appropriate information where necessary on these forms.

3. After you have filled in all of the appropriate information, carefully reread your entire will. Be certain that it contains all of the correct information that you desire. Then, starting at the beginning of the will, cross out all of the words and phrases in the pre-assembled will that do not apply in your situation.

4. When you have completed all of your will clauses, turn to Chapter 7 for instructions on the final preparation of your will.

As you fill in the information for each clause, keep in mind the following instructions:

Title Clause: The title clause is mandatory for all wills and must be included. Fill in the name blank with your full legal name. If you have been known by more than one name, use your principal name.

Identification Clause: The identification clause is mandatory and must be included in all wills. In the first blank, include any other names that you are known by. Do this by adding the phrase: "also known as" after your principal full name. For example:

John James Smith, also known as Jimmy John Smith.

In the spaces provided for your residence, use the location of your principal residence; that is, the place where you currently live permanently.

⚡ Warning!

The will forms in the book are only intended as worksheets. You must either retype your will or prepare your will using the text or PDF forms that are supplied on the enclosed CD.

⚡ Warning!

Residents of Louisiana: The will forms in this book are not valid for use in the State of Louisiana. You will need to see a Louisiana attorney to prepare a will valid in your state.

> **⚬Toolkit Tip!**
>
> Be sure to clearly identify the beneficiary and alternate beneficiary by full name. You can also name joint beneficiaries, such as several children, if you choose.

Marital Status Clause: Each of the pre-assembled wills in this chapter is either for a married or single person. Select the proper will and if you are married, fill in the appropriate information. If you have previously been married, please add and complete the following sentence:

I was previously married to [name of your former spouse], and that marriage ended by [select either death, divorce, or annulment].

Identification of Children Clause: This clause will only be present in the pre-assembled wills that relate to children. In this clause, you should specifically identify all of your children, indicating their full names, current addresses, and dates of birth. Cross out those spaces that are not used.

Identification of Grandchildren Clause: This clause will only be used in the two pre-assembled wills that relate to grandchildren. If you do not have grandchildren, cross out this entire clause. If you do have grandchildren, you should specifically identify all of your grandchildren in this clause, indicating their full names, current addresses, and dates of birth. Cross out those spaces that are not used.

Specific Gifts Clause: For making specific gifts, use as many of the "I give ..." paragraphs as is necessary to complete your chosen gifts. In these paragraphs, you may make any type of gift that you wish; either a cash gift, a gift of a specific piece of personal property or real estate, or a specific share of your total estate. If you wish to give some of your estate in the form of portions of the total, it is recommended to use fractional portions. For example, if you wish to leave your estate in equal shares to two persons, use "I give one-half of my total estate to..." for each party. Although none of the wills in this chapter contain a specific clause that states that you give one person your entire estate, you may make such a gift using this clause by simply stating:

"I give my entire estate to...."

Be sure that you do not attempt to give any other gifts. However, you should still include the residuary clause in your will, which is explained on the next page.

In your description of the property, you should be as specific and precise as possible. For land, it is suggested that you use the description exactly as shown on the deed to the property. For personal property, be certain that your description clearly differentiates your gift from any other property. For example: "I give my blue velvet coat which was a gift from my brother John to...." Use serial numbers, colors, or any other descriptive words to clearly indicate the exact nature of the gift. For cash gifts, specifically indicate the amount of the gift. For gifts of securities, state the amount of shares and the name of the company. You may add simple conditions to the gifts that you make, if you desire. For example, you may state "I give $1,000.00 to the Centerville Church for use in purchasing a new roof for the church." Complex conditions, however, are not possible in this clause, and immoral or illegal conditions are not acceptable.

Be sure to clearly identify the beneficiary and alternate beneficiary by full name. You can also name joint beneficiaries, such as several children, if you choose. The space provided for an identification of the relationship of the beneficiary can simply be a descriptive phrase like "my wife," "my brother-in-law," or "my best friend." It does not mean that the beneficiary must be related to you personally.

> **Toolkit Tip!**
> Use your property and beneficiary questionnaires to easily complete the gift portions of your will.

The choice of alternate beneficiary is for the purpose of allowing you to designate someone to receive the gift if your first choice to receive the gift dies before you do (or, in the case of an organization chosen as primary beneficiary, is no longer in business). In this or any of the other gift clauses, your choice for alternate beneficiary may be one or more persons or an organization. It is recommended to always specifically name your beneficiary(ies), rather than using a description only, such as "my children." In addition, you may delete the alternate beneficiary choice and substitute the words "the residue" instead. The result of this change will be that if your primary beneficiary dies before you do, your gift will pass under your residuary clause, which is discussed below. If additional gifts are desired, simply photocopy an additional page to use as a worksheet.

Residuary Clause: Although not a technical legal requirement, it is strongly recommended that you include the residuary clause in every will. With this clause, you will choose the person(s) or organization(s) to receive anything not covered by other clauses of your will. Even if you feel that you have given away everything that you own under other clauses of your will, this can be a very important clause.

If, for any reason, any gifts under your will are not able to be completed, this clause goes into effect. For example, if a beneficiary refuses to accept your gift, the chosen beneficiary has died and no alternate was selected, or both the beneficiary and alternate has died, the gift is put back into your estate and would *pass under* (be distributed under the terms of) the residuary clause. If there is no residuary clause included in your will, any property not disposed of under your will is treated as though you did not have a will and could potentially be forfeited to the state. To avoid this, it is strongly recommended that you make this clause mandatory in your will.

In addition, you may use this clause to give all of your estate (except your specific gifts) to one or more persons. For example: you make specific gifts of $1,000.00 to a sister and a car to a friend. By then naming your spouse as the residuary clause beneficiary, you will have gifted everything in your estate to your spouse—except the $1,000.00 and the car. You could then name your children, in equal shares, as the alternate residuary beneficiaries. In this manner, if your spouse were to die first, your children would then equally share your entire estate—except the $1,000.00 and the car.

As with naming the beneficiary under any other clause, you should always be sure to clearly identify the beneficiary by full name and a description of their relationship to you (need not be a relative).

Survivorship Clause: This clause is included in every will. This clause provides for two possibilities. First, it provides for a required period of survival for any beneficiary to receive a gift under your will. The practical effect of this is to be certain that your property passes under your will and not under that of a beneficiary who dies shortly after receiving your gift. The second portion of this clause provides for a determination of how your property should pass in the eventuality that both you and a beneficiary (most likely your spouse) should die in a manner that makes it impossible to determine who died first.

Without this clause in your will, it would be possible that property could momentarily pass to a beneficiary under your will. When that person dies (possibly immediately if a result of a common accident or disaster), your property could wind up being left to the person whom your beneficiary designated, rather than to your alternate beneficiary.

If you and your spouse are both preparing wills, it is a good idea to be certain that each of your wills contains identical survivorship clauses. If you are each other's primary beneficiary, it is also wise to attempt to coordinate who your alternate beneficiaries may be in the event of simultaneous deaths.

Executor Clause: The executor clause must be included in every will. With this clause, you will make your choice of executor, the person who will administer and distribute your estate, and an alternate choice if your first choice is unable to serve. A spouse, sibling, or other trusted party is usually chosen to act as executor. The person chosen should be a resident of the state in which you currently reside. Please refer to Chapter 5 for more information on executors.

> ☀ **Toolkit Tip!**
>
> The wills in this book allow your executor to seek independent administration of your estate. Where allowed by state law, this enables your executor to manage your estate with minimal court supervision.

Note that you allow your executor to seek independent administration of your estate. Where allowed by state law, this enables your executor to manage your estate with minimal court supervision and can save your estate extensive court costs and legal fees. Additionally, you grant the executor broad powers to manage your estate and also provide that he or she not be required to post a bond in order to be appointed to serve as executor.

Be sure to clearly identify the executor and alternate executor by full name. The space provided for an identification of the relationship of the executor can simply be a descriptive phrase like "my wife," "my brother-in-law," or "my best friend." It does not mean that the executor must be related to you personally.

Child Guardianship Clause: This clause will only be present in the pre-assembled wills that relate to children. With this clause you may designate your choice as to whom you wish to care for any of your minor children after you are gone. If none of your children are minors, you may delete this clause.

> **⚡ Warning!**
>
> Your choice for a child's guardian should be a trusted person whom you feel would provide the best care for your children in your absence. Be aware, however, that the court is guided, but not bound, by this particular choice in your will.

Who you choose to be the guardian of your children is an important matter. If you are married, your spouse is generally appointed by the probate or family court, regardless of your designation in a will. However, even if you are married, it is a good idea to choose your spouse as first choice and then provide a second choice. This will cover the contingency in which both you and your spouse die in a single accident.

Your choice should obviously be a trusted person whom you feel would provide the best care for your children in your absence. Be aware, however, that the court is guided, but not bound, by this particular choice in your will. The court's decision in appointing a child's guardian is based upon what would be in the best interests of the child. In most situations, however, a parent's choice as to who should be their child's guardian is almost universally followed by the courts. Additionally, you grant the guardian broad power to care for and manage your children's property and also provide that the appointed guardian not be required to post a bond in order to be appointed.

Be sure to clearly identify the guardian and alternate guardian by full name. The space provided for an identification of the relationship of the guardian can simply be a descriptive phrase like "my wife," "my brother-in-law," or "my best friend." It does not mean that the guardian must be related to you personally.

Children's Trust Fund Clause: This clause will only be present in the pre-assembled wills that relate to children. It is with this clause that you may set up a trust fund for any gifts you have made to your minor children. You also may delay the time when they will actually have unrestricted control over your gift. It is not recommended, however, to attempt to delay receipt of control beyond the age of 30. If you have left assets to more than one child, this clause provides that individual trusts be set up for each child. If none of your children are minors, you may delete this clause.

The choice for trustee under a children's trust should generally be the same person whom you have chosen to be the children's guardian. This is not, however, a requirement. The choice of trustee is generally a spouse if alive, with the alternate being a trusted friend or family member. Be sure to clearly identify the trustee and alternate trustee by full name. The space provided for an identification of the relationship of the trustee can simply be a descriptive phrase like "my wife," "my brother-in-law," or "my best friend." It does not mean that the trustee must be related to you personally.

The terms of the trust provide that the trustee may distribute any or all of the income or principal to the children as he or she deems necessary to provide for the children's health, support, and education. The trust will terminate when either the specific age is reached, all of the money is spent prior to that age, or the child dies prematurely. Upon termination, any remaining trust funds will be distributed to the child (beneficiary) if surviving; if not surviving, to the heirs of the beneficiary (if any); or if there are no heirs of the beneficiary, to the residue of your estate. Additionally, you grant the trustee broad power to manage the trust and also provide that he or she not be required to post a bond in order to be appointed.

Organ Donation Clause: The use of this clause is optional. If you do not wish to make any organ donations, simply delete this clause. If you choose not to use this clause, you may delete it from your will. Use this clause to provide for any use of your body after death. You may, if you so desire, limit your donation to certain parts; for example, your eyes. If so desired, simply delete "any of my body parts and/or organs" from the following provision and insert your chosen donation. A copy of your will or instructions regarding this donation should be kept in a place that is readily-accessible by your executor and spouse. Please note that Chapter 14 contains a separate organ donation form that you may wish to complete. Be sure that if you use a will clause for organ donation and a separate document that the terms of each are identical.

Funeral Arrangements Clause: The use of this clause is optional. If you choose not to use this clause, you may delete it from your will. Use this clause to make known your wishes as to funeral and burial arrangements. Since it may be difficult to

> **Toolkit Tip!**
>
> The use of the organ donation clause is optional. If you choose not to use this clause, you may delete it from your will. Use this clause to provide for any use of your body after death.

obtain your will quickly in an emergency, it is also a good idea to leave information regarding these desires with your executor, your spouse, a close friend, or a relative.

⚡ Warning!

Do *not* prepare or sign your will until you carefully follow the instructions contained in Chapter 7.

Signature, Witness, and Notary Clauses: The signature lines and final paragraph of this clause must be included in your will. You will fill in the number of pages and the appropriate dates where indicated after you have properly typed or printed out your will. The use of the notary acknowledgment, although not a strict legal necessity, is strongly recommended. This allows the will to become "self-proving" and the witnesses need not be called upon to testify in court at a later date (after your death) that they, indeed, signed the will as witnesses. Although a few states have not enacted legislation to allow for the use of this type of sworn and acknowledged testimony to be used in court, the current trend is to allow for its use in probate courts. This saves time, money, and trouble in having your will admitted to probate when necessary.

The actual preparation and signing of your will by both you and your witnesses will be explained in Chapter 7. Do *not* prepare or sign your will until you carefully follow the instructions contained in that chapter.

Instructions for Will for Married Person with Children (Using Children's Trust)

This will is appropriate for use by a married person with one or more children. There are also provisions in this will for use if the parent has minor children and desires to place the property and assets that may be left to the children into a trust fund. In addition, this will allows a parent to choose a person to act as guardian for any minor children. In most cases, a married person may desire to choose the other spouse as both trustee and guardian for any of their children, although this is not a legal requirement. If the parent has no minor children, the will clauses relating to the children's trust and to guardianship of the children may be deleted. Each spouse/parent must prepare his or her own will. Do not attempt to prepare a joint will for both you and your spouse together.

This will contains the following standard clauses:

- Title Clause
- Identification Clause
- Marital Status Clause
- Children Identification Clause
- Grandchildren Identification Clause
- Specific Gifts Clause
- Residuary Clause
- Survivorship Clause
- Executor Clause
- Guardianship Clause
- Children's Trust Fund Clause
- Organ Donation Clause
- Funeral Arrangements Clause
- Signature and Witness Clause

Fill in each of the appropriate blanks in this will using the information that you included in your Property and Beneficiary Questionnaires. Cross out any information that is not appropriate to your situation. The necessary information to be filled-in is noted below and should be written into the place where the corresponding number appears in the following will form.

①   Full name of testator
②   Full name of testator (and any other names that you are known by)
③   Full address of testator

④   Spouse's full name (insert information on previous marriage, if necessary [see earlier instructions on this point])

⑤ Number of children
⑥ Child's name (repeat for each child)
⑦ Child's address (repeat for each child)
⑧ Child's date of birth (repeat for each child)

⑨ Number of grandchildren (if applicable)
⑩ Grandchild's name (repeat for each grandchild)
⑪ Grandchild's address (repeat for each grandchild)
⑫ Grandchild's date of birth (repeat for each grandchild)

⑬ Complete description of specific gift (repeat for each specific gift)
⑭ Full name of beneficiary (repeat for each specific gift)
⑮ Relationship of beneficiary to testator (repeat for each specific gift)
⑯ Full name of alternate beneficiary (repeat for each specific gift)
⑰ Relationship of alternate beneficiary to testator (repeat for each specific gift)

⑱ Full name of residual beneficiary
⑲ Relationship of residual beneficiary to testator
⑳ Full name of alternate residual beneficiary
㉑ Relationship of alternate residual beneficiary to testator

㉒ Full name of executor
㉓ Relationship of executor to testator
㉔ Full address of executor
㉕ Full name of alternate executor
㉖ Relationship of alternate executor to testator
㉗ Full address of alternate executor

㉘ Full name of guardian of children
㉙ Relationship of guardian of children to testator
㉚ Full address of guardian of children
㉛ Full name of alternate guardian of children
㉜ Relationship of alternate guardian of children to testator
㉝ Full address of alternate guardian of children

㉞ Children's age to be subject to children's trust
㉟ Children's age for end of children's trust (21, 25, or 30 years old or other age)
㊱ Full name of trustee of children's trust
㊲ Relationship of trustee of children's trust to testator
㊳ Full address of trustee of children's trust
㊴ Full name of alternate trustee of children's trust
㊵ Relationship of alternate trustee of children's trust to testator

126

㊶   Full address of alternate trustee of children's trust

㊷   Name of funeral home
㊸   Address of funeral home
㊹   Name of cemetery
㊺   Address of cemetery

    Number of total pages of will (fill in when will is typed or printed)
    Date of signing of will (DO NOT FILL IN YET)
    Signature of testator (DO NOT FILL IN YET)
    Printed name of testator
    Date of witnessing of will (DO NOT FILL IN YET)
    Signature of witness (repeat for each witness) [DO NOT FILL IN YET]
    Printed name of witness (repeat for each witness) [DO NOT FILL IN YET]
    Address of witness (repeat for each witness) [DO NOT FILL IN YET]

㊻   Notary Acknowledgment (to be filled in by Notary Public)

Will for Married Person with Children (Using Children's Trust)

Last Will and Testament of ①

I, ② ,
whose address is ③ ,
declare that this is my Last Will and Testament and I revoke all previous wills.

I am married to ④ .

I have ⑤ child(ren) living. His/Her/Their name(s), address(es), and date(s) of birth is/are as follows:
⑥
⑦
⑧

⑥
⑦
⑧

⑥
⑦
⑧

I have ⑨ grandchild(ren) living. His/Her/Their name(s), address(es), and date(s) of birth is/are as follows:
⑩
⑪
⑫

⑩
⑪
⑫

⑩
⑪
⑫

Page ___ of ___ pages   Testator's initials _____

I make the following specific gifts:
I give ⑬ ,
to ⑭ ,
my ⑮ ,
or if not surviving, then to ⑯ ,
my ⑰ .

I give ⑬ ,
to ⑭ ,
my ⑮ ,
or if not surviving, then to ⑯ ,
my ⑰ .

I give ⑬ ,
to ⑭ ,
my ⑮ ,
or if not surviving, then to ⑯ ,
my ⑰ .

I give ⑬ ,
to ⑭ ,
my ⑮ ,
or if not surviving, then to ⑯ ,
my ⑰ .

I give ⑬ ,
to ⑭ ,
my ⑮ ,
or if not surviving, then to ⑯ ,
my ⑰ .

I give ⑬ ,
to ⑭ ,
my ⑮ ,
or if not surviving, then to ⑯ ,
my ⑰ .

Page ___ of ___ pages

Testator's initials _____

I give all the rest of my property, whether real or personal, wherever located,
to ⑱ ,
my ⑲ ,
or if not surviving, to ⑳ ,
my ㉑ .

All beneficiaries named in this will must survive me by thirty (30) days to receive any gift under this will. If any beneficiary and I should die simultaneously, I shall be conclusively presumed to have survived that beneficiary for purposes of this will.

I appoint ㉒ ,
my ㉓ ,
of ㉔ ,
as Executor, to serve without bond. If not surviving or otherwise unable to serve,
I appoint ㉕ ,
my ㉖ ,
of ㉗ ,
as Alternate Executor, also to serve without bond. In addition to any powers, authority, and discretion granted by law, I grant such Executor or Alternate Executor any and all powers to perform any acts, in his/her sole discretion and without court approval, for the management and distribution of my estate, including independent administration of my estate.

If a Guardian is needed for any of my minor child(ren),
I appoint ㉘ ,
my ㉙ ,
of ㉚ ,
as Guardian of the person and property of any of my minor child(ren), to serve without bond. If not surviving, or unable to serve,
I appoint ㉛ ,
my ㉜ ,
of ㉝ ,
as Alternate Guardian, also to serve without bond. In addition to any powers, authority, and discretion granted by law, I grant such Guardian or Alternate Guardian any and all powers to perform any acts, in his/her sole discretion and without court approval, for the management and distribution of the property of any of my minor child(ren).

If any of my child(ren) are under ㉞ years of age, upon my death, I direct that any property that I give each child under this will be held in an individual trust for each child(ren), under the following terms, until each shall reach ㉟ years of age.

Page ___ of ___ pages   Testator's initials _____

In addition, I appoint ㊱ ,
my ㊲ ,
of ㊳ ,
as trustee of any and all required trusts, to serve without bond. If not surviving, or otherwise unable to serve, then I appoint �39 ,
my �40 ,
of �41 ,
as Alternate Trustee, also to serve without bond. In addition to all powers, authority, and discretion granted by law, I grant such trustee or alternate trustee full power to perform any act, in his/her sole discretion and without court approval, to distribute and manage the assets of any such trust.

In the trustee's sole discretion, the trustee may distribute any or all of the principal, income, or both, of any such trust as deemed necessary for the beneficiary's health, support, welfare, and education. Any income not distributed shall be added to the trust principal.

Any such trust shall terminate when the beneficiary reaches the required age, when the beneficiary dies prior to reaching the required age, or when all trust funds have been distributed. Upon termination, any remaining undistributed principal and income shall pass to the beneficiary; or if not surviving, to the beneficiary's heirs; or if none, to the residue of my estate.

I also declare that, pursuant to the Uniform Anatomical Gift Act, I donate any of my body parts and/or organs to any medical institution willing to accept and use them, and I direct my executor to carry out such donation.

Funeral arrangements have been made with the ㊷ ,
of ㊸ ,
for burial at ㊹ ,
located in ㊺ ,
and I direct my Executor to carry out such arrangements.

I publish and sign this Last Will and Testament, consisting of _____ typewritten pages,
on _____ , and declare that I do so freely, for the purposes expressed, under no constraint or undue influence, and that I am of sound mind and of legal age.

_____
Signature of Testator

_____
Printed Name of Testator

Page ___ of ___ pages

Testator's initials _____

We, the undersigned, being first sworn on oath and under penalty of perjury, state that:

On _____ , in the presence of all of us, the above-named Testator published and signed this Last Will and Testament, and then at Testator's request, and in Testator's presence, and in each other's presence, we all signed below as witnesses, and we declare that, to the best of our knowledge, the Testator signed this instrument freely, under no constraint or undue influence, and is of sound mind and legal age.

_____   _____
Signature of Witness   Signature of Witness

_____   _____
Printed Name of Witness   Printed Name of Witness

_____   _____
Address of Witness   Address of Witness

_____
Signature of Witness

_____
Printed Name of Witness

_____
Address of Witness

Notary Acknowledgment
State of _____
County of _____

On _____ , _____ the testator, and
_____ , _____ , and
_____ , the witnesses, personally came before me and, being duly sworn, did state that they are the persons described in the above document and that they signed the above document in my presence as a free and voluntary act for the purposes stated.

_____
Signature of Notary Public
Notary Public, In and for the County of _____ State of _____
My commission expires: _____   Notary Seal

Instructions for Will for Single Person with Children (Using Children's Trust)

This will is appropriate for use by a single person with one or more children. There are also provisions in this will for use if the parent has minor children and desires to place the property and assets that may be left to the children into a trust fund. In addition, this will allows a parent to choose a person to act as guardian for any minor children. In most cases, a parent may desire to choose the other parent as both trustee and guardian for any of their children, although this is not a legal requirement and may not be the best solution if the parents are divorced. If the parent has no minor children, the will clauses relating to the children's trust and to guardianship of the children may be deleted.

This will contains the following standard clauses:

- Title Clause
- Identification Clause
- Marital Status Clause
- Children Identification Clause
- Grandchildren Identification Clause
- Specific Gifts Clause
- Residuary Clause
- Survivorship Clause
- Executor Clause
- Guardianship Clause
- Children's Trust Fund Clause
- Organ Donation Clause
- Funeral Arrangements Clause
- Signature and Witness Clause

Fill in each of the appropriate blanks in this will using the information that you included in your Property and Beneficiary Questionnaires. Cross out any information that is not appropriate to your situation. The necessary information to be filled-in is noted below and should be written into the place where the corresponding number appears in the following will form.

①   Full name of testator
②   Full name of testator (and any other names that you are known by)
③   Full address of testator

(Insert information on previous marriage, if necessary [see earlier instructions])

④ Number of children
⑤ Child's name (repeat for each child)
⑥ Child's address (repeat for each child)
⑦ Child's date of birth (repeat for each child)

⑧ Number of grandchildren (if applicable)
⑨ Grandchild's name (repeat for each grandchild)
⑩ Grandchild's address (repeat for each grandchild)
⑪ Grandchild's date of birth (repeat for each grandchild)

⑫ Complete description of specific gift (repeat for each specific gift)
⑬ Full name of beneficiary (repeat for each specific gift)
⑭ Relationship of beneficiary to testator (repeat for each specific gift)
⑮ Full name of alternate beneficiary (repeat for each specific gift)
⑯ Relationship of alternate beneficiary to testator (repeat for each specific gift)

⑰ Full name of residual beneficiary
⑱ Relationship of residual beneficiary to testator
⑲ Full name of alternate residual beneficiary
⑳ Relationship of alternate residual beneficiary to testator

㉑ Full name of executor
㉒ Relationship of executor to testator
㉓ Full address of executor
㉔ Full name of alternate executor
㉕ Relationship of alternate executor to testator
㉖ Full address of alternate executor

㉗ Full name of guardian of children
㉘ Relationship of guardian of children to testator
㉙ Full address of guardian of children
㉚ Full name of alternate guardian of children
㉛ Relationship of alternate guardian of children to testator
㉜ Full address of alternate guardian of children

㉝ Children's age to be subject to children's trust
㉞ Children's age for end of children's trust (21, 25, or 30 years old or other age)
㉟ Full name of trustee of children's trust
㊱ Relationship of trustee of children's trust to testator
㊲ Full address of trustee of children's trust
㊳ Full name of alternate trustee of children's trust
㊴ Relationship of alternate trustee of children's trust to testator

4. Number of children
5. Child's name (repeat for each child)
6. Child's address (repeat for each child)
7. Child's date of birth (repeat for each child)

8. Number of grandchildren (if applicable)
9. Grandchild's name (repeat for each grandchild)
10. Grandchild's address (repeat for each grandchild)
11. Grandchild's date of birth (repeat for each grandchild)

12. Complete description of specific gift (repeat for each specific gift)
13. Full name of beneficiary (repeat for each specific gift)
14. Relationship of beneficiary to testator (repeat for each specific gift)
15. Full name of alternate beneficiary (repeat for each specific gift)
16. Relationship of alternate beneficiary to testator (repeat for each specific gift)

17. Full name of residual beneficiary
18. Relationship of residual beneficiary to testator
19. Full name of alternate residual beneficiary
20. Relationship of alternate residual beneficiary to testator

21. Full name of executor
22. Relationship of executor to testator
23. Full address of executor
24. Full name of alternate executor
25. Relationship of alternate executor to testator
26. Full address of alternate executor

27. Full name of guardian of children
28. Relationship of guardian of children to testator
29. Full address of guardian of children
30. Full name of alternate guardian of children
31. Relationship of alternate guardian of children to testator
32. Full address of alternate guardian of children

33. Children's age to be subject to children's trust
34. Children's age for end of children's trust (21, 25, or 30 years old or other age)
35. Full name of trustee of children's trust
36. Relationship of trustee of children's trust to testator
37. Full address of trustee of children's trust
38. Full name of alternate trustee of children's trust
39. Relationship of alternate trustee of children's trust to testator

Instructions for Will for Single Person with Children (Using Children's Trust)

This will is appropriate for use by a single person with one or more children. There are also provisions in this will for use if the parent has minor children and desires to place the property and assets that may be left to the children into a trust fund. In addition, this will allows a parent to choose a person to act as guardian for any minor children. In most cases, a parent may desire to choose the other parent as both trustee and guardian for any of their children, although this is not a legal requirement and may not be the best solution if the parents are divorced. If the parent has no minor children, the will clauses relating to the children's trust and to guardianship of the children may be deleted.

This will contains the following standard clauses:

- Title Clause
- Identification Clause
- Marital Status Clause
- Children Identification Clause
- Grandchildren Identification Clause
- Specific Gifts Clause
- Residuary Clause
- Survivorship Clause
- Executor Clause
- Guardianship Clause
- Children's Trust Fund Clause
- Organ Donation Clause
- Funeral Arrangements Clause
- Signature and Witness Clause

Fill in each of the appropriate blanks in this will using the information that you included in your Property and Beneficiary Questionnaires. Cross out any information that is not appropriate to your situation. The necessary information to be filled-in is noted below and should be written into the place where the corresponding number appears in the following will form.

① Full name of testator
② Full name of testator (and any other names that you are known by)
③ Full address of testator

(Insert information on previous marriage, if necessary [see earlier instructions])

㊵   Full address of alternate trustee of children's trust
㊶   Name of funeral home
㊷   Address of funeral home
㊸   Name of cemetery
㊹   Address of cemetery

Number of total pages of will (fill in when will is typed or printed)
Date of signing of will (DO NOT FILL IN YET)
Signature of testator (DO NOT FILL IN YET)
Printed name of testator
Date of witnessing of will (DO NOT FILL IN YET)
Signature of witness (repeat for each witness) [DO NOT FILL IN YET]
Printed name of witness (repeat for each witness) [DO NOT FILL IN YET]
Address of witness (repeat for each witness) [DO NOT FILL IN YET]

㊺   Notary Acknowledgment (to be filled in by Notary Public)

Will for Single Person with Children (Using Children's Trust)

Last Will and Testament of ①

I, ② ,
whose address is ③ ,
declare that this is my Last Will and Testament and I revoke all previous wills.

I am not currently married.

I have ④ child(ren) living. His/Her/Their name(s), address(es), and date(s) of birth is/are as follows:
⑤
⑥
⑦

⑤
⑥
⑦

⑤
⑥
⑦

I have ⑧ grandchild(ren) living. His/Her/Their name(s), address(es), and date(s) of birth is/are as follows:
⑨
⑩
⑪

⑨
⑩
⑪

⑨
⑩
⑪

Page ___ of ___ pages   Testator's initials _____

I make the following specific gifts:

I give ⑫ ,
to ⑬ ,
my ⑭ ,
or if not surviving, then to ⑮ ,
my ⑯ .

I give ⑫ ,
to ⑬ ,
my ⑭ ,
or if not surviving, then to ⑮ ,
my ⑯ .

I give ⑫ ,
to ⑬ ,
my ⑭ ,
or if not surviving, then to ⑮ ,
my ⑯ .

I give ⑫ ,
to ⑬ ,
my ⑭ ,
or if not surviving, then to ⑮ ,
my ⑯ .

I give ⑫ ,
to ⑬ ,
my ⑭ ,
or if not surviving, then to ⑮ ,
my ⑯ .

I give ⑫ ,
to ⑬ ,
my ⑭ ,
or if not surviving, then to ⑮ ,
my ⑯ .

I give ⑫ ,
to ⑬ ,
my ⑭ ,
or if not surviving, then to ⑮ ,
my ⑯ .

Page ___ of ___ pages   Testator's initials _____

I give all the rest of my property, whether real or personal, wherever located,
to ⑰ ,
my ⑱ ,
or if not surviving, to ⑲ ,
my ⑳ .

All beneficiaries named in this will must survive me by thirty (30) days to receive any gift under this will. If any beneficiary and I should die simultaneously, I shall be conclusively presumed to have survived that beneficiary for purposes of this will.

I appoint ㉑ ,
my ㉒ ,
of ㉓ ,
as Executor, to serve without bond. If not surviving or otherwise unable to serve,
I appoint ㉔ ,
my ㉕ ,
of ㉖ ,
as Alternate Executor, also to serve without bond. In addition to any powers, authority, and discretion granted by law, I grant such Executor or Alternate Executor any and all powers to perform any acts, in his or her sole discretion and without court approval, for the management and distribution of my estate, including independent administration of my estate.

If a Guardian is needed for any of my minor child(ren),
I appoint ㉗ ,
my ㉘ ,
of ㉙ ,
as Guardian of the person and property of any of my minor child(ren), to serve without bond. If not surviving, or unable to serve,
I appoint ㉚ ,
my ㉛ ,
of ㉜ ,
as Alternate Guardian, also to serve without bond. In addition to any powers, authority, and discretion granted by law, I grant such Guardian or Alternate Guardian any and all powers to perform any acts, in his/her sole discretion and without court approval, for the management and distribution of the property of any of my minor child(ren).

If any of my child(ren) are under ㉝ years of age, upon my death, I direct that any property that I give each child under this will be held in an individual trust for each child(ren), under the following terms, until each shall reach ㉞ years of age.

Page ___ of ___ pages   Testator's initials _____

In addition, I appoint ㉟ ,
my ㊱ ,
of ㊲ ,
as trustee of any and all required trusts, to serve without bond. If not surviving, or otherwise unable to serve, then I appoint ㊳ ,
my ㊴ ,
of ㊵ ,
as Alternate Trustee, also to serve without bond. In addition to all powers, authority, and discretion granted by law, I grant such trustee or alternate trustee full power to perform any act, in his/her sole discretion and without court approval, to distribute and manage the assets of any such trust.

In the trustee's sole discretion, the trustee may distribute any or all of the principal, income, or both, of any such trust as deemed necessary for the beneficiary's health, support, welfare, and education. Any income not distributed shall be added to the trust principal.

Any such trust shall terminate when the beneficiary reaches the required age, when the beneficiary dies prior to reaching the required age, or when all trust funds have been distributed. Upon termination, any remaining undistributed principal and income shall pass to the beneficiary; or if not surviving, to the beneficiary's heirs; or if none, to the residue of my estate.

I also declare that, pursuant to the Uniform Anatomical Gift Act, I donate any of my body parts and/or organs to any medical institution willing to accept and use them, and I direct my executor to carry out such donation.

Funeral arrangements have been made with the ㊶ ,
of ㊷ ,
for burial at ㊸ ,
located in ㊹ ,
and I direct my Executor to carry out such arrangements.

I publish and sign this Last Will and Testament, consisting of _____ typewritten pages, on _____ , and declare that I do so freely, for the purposes expressed, under no constraint or undue influence, and that I am of sound mind and of legal age.

_____   _____
Signature of Testator   Printed Name of Testator

Page ___ of ___ pages   Testator's initials _____

We, the undersigned, being first sworn on oath and under penalty of perjury, state that:

On _____ , in the presence of all of us, the above-named Testator published and signed this Last Will and Testament, and then at Testator's request, and in Testator's presence, and in each other's presence, we all signed below as witnesses, and we declare that, to the best of our knowledge, the Testator signed this instrument freely, under no constraint or undue influence, and is of sound mind and legal age.

_____   _____
Signature of Witness   Signature of Witness

_____   _____
Printed Name of Witness   Printed Name of Witness

_____   _____
Address of Witness   Address of Witness

_____
Signature of Witness

_____
Printed Name of Witness

_____
Address of Witness

Notary Acknowledgment
State of _____
County of _____

On _____ , _____ the testator, and
_____ , _____ , and
_____ , the witnesses, personally came before me and, being duly sworn, did state that they are the persons described in the above document and that they signed the above document in my presence as a free and voluntary act for the purposes stated.

_____
Signature of Notary Public
Notary Public, In and for the County of _____
State of _____
My commission expires: _____   Notary Seal

Instructions for Will for Married Person with No Children

This will is appropriate for use by a married person with no children or grandchildren. Each spouse must prepare his or her own will. Do not attempt to prepare a joint will for both you and your spouse together.

This will contains the following standard clauses:

- Title Clause
- Identification Clause
- Marital Status Clause
- Specific Gifts Clause
- Residuary Clause
- Survivorship Clause
- Executor Clause
- Organ Donation Clause
- Funeral Arrangements Clause
- Signature and Witness Clause

Fill in each of the appropriate blanks in this will using the information that you included in your Property and Beneficiary Questionnaires. Cross out any information that is not appropriate to your situation. The necessary information to be filled-in is noted below and should be written into the place where the corresponding number appears in the following will form.

①　Full name of testator
②　Full name of testator (and any other names that you are known by)
③　Full address of testator

④　Spouse's full name (insert information on previous marriage, if necessary [see earlier instructions])

⑤　Complete description of specific gift (repeat for each specific gift)
⑥　Full name of beneficiary (repeat for each specific gift)
⑦　Relationship of beneficiary to testator (repeat for each specific gift)
⑧　Full name of alternate beneficiary (repeat for each specific gift)
⑨　Relationship of alternate beneficiary to testator (repeat for each specific gift)

⑩　Full name of residual beneficiary
⑪　Relationship of residual beneficiary to testator
⑫　Full name of alternate residual beneficiary
⑬　Relationship of alternate residual beneficiary to testator

⑭ Full name of executor
⑮ Relationship of executor to testator
⑯ Full address of executor
⑰ Full name of alternate executor
⑱ Relationship of alternate executor to testator
⑲ Full address of alternate executor

⑳ Name of funeral home
㉑ Address of funeral home
㉒ Name of cemetery
㉓ Address of cemetery

Number of total pages of will (fill in when will is typed or printed)
Date of signing of will (DO NOT FILL IN YET)
Signature of testator (DO NOT FILL IN YET)
Printed name of testator
Date of witnessing of will (DO NOT FILL IN YET)
Signature of witness (repeat for each witness) [DO NOT FILL IN YET]
Printed name of witness (repeat for each witness) [DO NOT FILL IN YET]
Address of witness (repeat for each witness) [DO NOT FILL IN YET]

㉔ Notary Acknowledgment (to be filled in by Notary Public)

Will for Married Person with No Children

Last Will and Testament of ①

I, ② ,
whose address is ③ ,
declare that this is my Last Will and Testament and I revoke all previous wills.

I am married to ④ .

I have no children or grandchildren living.

I make the following specific gifts:

I give ⑤ ,
to ⑥ ,
my ⑦ ,
or if not surviving, then to ⑧ ,
my ⑨ .

I give ⑤ ,
to ⑥ ,
my ⑦ ,
or if not surviving, then to ⑧ ,
my ⑨

I give ⑤ ,
to ⑥ ,
my ⑦ ,
or if not surviving, then to ⑧ ,
my ⑨

I give ⑤ ,
to ⑥ ,
my ⑦ ,
or if not surviving, then to ⑧ ,
my ⑨

Page ___ of ___ pages   Testator's initials _____

I give ⑤ ,
to ⑥ ,
my ⑦ ,
or if not surviving, then to ⑧ ,
my ⑨

I give ⑤ ,
to ⑥ ,
my ⑦ ,
or if not surviving, then to ⑧ ,
my ⑨

I give ⑤ ,
to ⑥ ,
my ⑦ ,
or if not surviving, then to ⑧ ,
my ⑨

I give ⑤ ,
to ⑥ ,
my ⑦ ,
or if not surviving, then to ⑧ ,
my ⑨

I give ⑤ ,
to ⑥ ,
my ⑦ ,
or if not surviving, then to ⑧ ,
my ⑨

I give all the rest of my property, whether real or personal, wherever located,
to ⑩ ,
my ⑪ ,
or if not surviving, to ⑫ ,
my ⑬ .

All beneficiaries named in this will must survive me by thirty (30) days to receive any gift under this will. If any beneficiary and I should die simultaneously, I shall be conclusively presumed to have survived that beneficiary for purposes of this will.

Page ____ of ____ pages   Testator's initials _____

I appoint ⑭ ,
my ⑮ ,
of ⑯ ,
as Executor, to serve without bond. If not surviving or otherwise unable to serve,
I appoint ⑰ ,
my ⑱ ,
of ⑲ ,
as Alternate Executor, also to serve without bond. In addition to any powers, authority, and discretion granted by law, I grant such Executor or Alternate Executor any and all powers to perform any acts, in his/her sole discretion and without court approval, for the management and distribution of my estate, including independent administration of my estate.

I also declare that, pursuant to the Uniform Anatomical Gift Act, I donate any of my body parts and/or organs to any medical institution willing to accept and use them, and I direct my executor to carry out such donation.

Funeral arrangements have been made with the ⑳ ,
of ㉑ ,
for burial at ㉒ ,
located in ㉓ ,
and I direct my Executor to carry out such arrangements.

I publish and sign this Last Will and Testament, consisting of _____ typewritten pages, on _____ , and declare that I do so freely, for the purposes expressed, under no constraint or undue influence, and that I am of sound mind and of legal age.

_____   _____
Signature of Testator   Printed Name of Testator

Page ___ of ___ pages   Testator's initials _____

We, the undersigned, being first sworn on oath and under penalty of perjury, state that:

On _____ , in the presence of all of us, the above-named Testator published and signed this Last Will and Testament, and then at Testator's request, and in Testator's presence, and in each other's presence, we all signed below as witnesses, and we declare that, to the best of our knowledge, the Testator signed this instrument freely, under no constraint or undue influence, and is of sound mind and legal age.

_____   _____
Signature of Witness   Signature of Witness

_____   _____
Printed Name of Witness   Printed Name of Witness

_____   _____
Address of Witness   Address of Witness

_____
Signature of Witness

_____
Printed Name of Witness

_____
Address of Witness

㉔ Notary Acknowledgment
State of _____
County of _____

On _____ , _____ the testator, and
_____ , _____ , and
_____ , the witnesses, personally came before me and, being duly sworn, did state that they are the persons described in the above document and that they signed the above document in my presence as a free and voluntary act for the purposes stated.

_____
Signature of Notary Public

Notary Public, In and for the County of _____
State of _____
My commission expires: _____   Notary Seal

Instructions for Will for Single Person with No Children

This will is appropriate for use by a single person with no children or grandchildren. This will contains the following standard clauses:

- Title Clause
- Identification Clause
- Marital Status Clause
- Specific Gifts Clause
- Residuary Clause
- Survivorship Clause
- Executor Clause
- Organ Donation Clause
- Funeral Arrangements Clause
- Signature and Witness Clause

Fill in each of the appropriate blanks in this will using the information that you included in your Property and Beneficiary Questionnaires. Cross out any information that is not appropriate to your situation. The necessary information to be filled-in is noted below and should be written into the place where the corresponding number appears in the following will form.

①   Full name of testator
②   Full name of testator (and any other names that you are known by)
③   Full address of testator

     (Insert information on previous marriage, if necessary [see earlier instructions])

④   Complete description of specific gift (repeat for each specific gift)
⑤   Full name of beneficiary (repeat for each specific gift)
⑥   Relationship of beneficiary to testator (repeat for each specific gift)
⑦   Full name of alternate beneficiary (repeat for each specific gift)
⑧   Relationship of alternate beneficiary to testator (repeat for each specific gift)

⑨   Full name of residual beneficiary
⑩   Relationship of residual beneficiary to testator
⑪   Full name of alternate residual beneficiary
⑫   Relationship of alternate residual beneficiary to testator

⑬   Full name of executor
⑭   Relationship of executor to testator
⑮   Full address of executor

⑯   Full name of alternate executor
⑰   Relationship of alternate executor to testator
⑱   Full address of alternate executor

⑲   Name of funeral home
⑳   Address of funeral home
㉑   Name of cemetery
㉒   Address of cemetery

     Number of total pages of will (fill in when will is typed or printed)
     Date of signing of will (DO NOT FILL IN YET)
     Signature of testator (DO NOT FILL IN YET)
     Printed name of testator
     Date of witnessing of will (DO NOT FILL IN YET)
     Signature of witness (repeat for each witness) [DO NOT FILL IN YET]
     Printed name of witness (repeat for each witness) [DO NOT FILL IN YET]
     Address of witness (repeat for each witness) [DO NOT FILL IN YET]

㉓   Notary Acknowledgment (to be filled in by Notary Public)

Will for Single Person with No Children

Last Will and Testament of ①

I, ② ,
whose address is ③ ,
declare that this is my Last Will and Testament and I revoke all previous wills.

I am not currently married.

I have no children or grandchildren living.

I make the following specific gifts:

I give ④ ,
to ⑤ ,
my ⑥ ,
or if not surviving, then to ⑦ ,
my ⑧ .

I give ④ ,
to ⑤ ,
my ⑥ ,
or if not surviving, then to ⑦ ,
my ⑧ .

I give ④ ,
to ⑤ ,
my ⑥ ,
or if not surviving, then to ⑦ ,
my ⑧ .

I give ④ ,
to ⑤ ,
my ⑥ ,
or if not surviving, then to ⑦ ,
my ⑧ .

Page ___ of ___ pages   Testator's initials _____

I give ④ ,
to ⑤ ,
my ⑥ ,
or if not surviving, then to ⑦ ,
my ⑧ .

I give ④ ,
to ⑤ ,
my ⑥ ,
or if not surviving, then to ⑦ ,
my ⑧ .

I give ④ ,
to ⑤ ,
my ⑥ ,
or if not surviving, then to ⑦ ,
my ⑧ .

I give ④ ,
to ⑤ ,
my ⑥ ,
or if not surviving, then to ⑦ ,
my ⑧ .

I give ④ ,
to ⑤ ,
my ⑥ ,
or if not surviving, then to ⑦ ,
my ⑧ .

I give ④ ,
to ⑤ ,
my ⑥ ,
or if not surviving, then to ⑦ ,
my ⑧ .

Page ___ of ___ pages

Testator's initials _____

I give all the rest of my property, whether real or personal, wherever located,
to ⑨ ,
my ⑩ ,
or if not surviving, to ⑪ ,
my ⑫ .

All beneficiaries named in this will must survive me by thirty (30) days to receive any gift under this will. If any beneficiary and I should die simultaneously, I shall be conclusively presumed to have survived that beneficiary for purposes of this will.

I appoint ⑬ ,
my ⑭ ,
of ⑮ ,
as Executor, to serve without bond. If not surviving or otherwise unable to serve,
I appoint ⑯ ,
my ⑰ ,
of ⑱ ,
as Alternate Executor, also to serve without bond. In addition to any powers, authority, and discretion granted by law, I grant such Executor or Alternate Executor any and all powers to perform any acts, in his/her sole discretion and without court approval, for the management and distribution of my estate, including independent administration of my estate.

I also declare that, pursuant to the Uniform Anatomical Gift Act, I donate any of my body parts and/or organs to any medical institution willing to accept and use them, and I direct my executor to carry out such donation.

Funeral arrangements have been made with the ⑲ ,
of ⑳ ,
for burial at ㉑ ,
located in ㉒ ,
and I direct my Executor to carry out such arrangements.

I publish and sign this Last Will and Testament, consisting of _____ typewritten pages,
on _____ , and declare that I do so freely, for the purposes expressed, under no constraint or undue influence, and that I am of sound mind and of legal age.

_____
Signature of Testator

_____
Printed Name of Testator

Page ___ of ___ pages

Testator's initials _____

We, the undersigned, being first sworn on oath and under penalty of perjury, state that:

On _____ , in the presence of all of us, the above-named Testator published and signed this Last Will and Testament, and then at Testator's request, and in Testator's presence, and in each other's presence, we all signed below as witnesses, and we declare that, to the best of our knowledge, the Testator signed this instrument freely, under no constraint or undue influence, and is of sound mind and legal age.

_____   _____
Signature of Witness   Signature of Witness

_____   _____
Printed Name of Witness   Printed Name of Witness

_____   _____
Address of Witness   Address of Witness

_____
Signature of Witness

_____
Printed Name of Witness

_____
Address of Witness

㉓ Notary Acknowledgment
State of _____
County of _____

On _____ , _____ the testator, and
_____ , _____ , and
_____ , the witnesses, personally came before me and, being duly sworn, did state that they are the persons described in the above document and that they signed the above document in my presence as a free and voluntary act for the purposes stated.

_____
Signature of Notary Public
Notary Public, In and for the County of _____
State of _____
My commission expires: _____   Notary Seal

Chapter 7

Preparing and Signing a Will

This chapter will explain how to prepare your will and have it readied for your signature. Using your Property and Beneficiary Questionnaires as guides, you should already have selected and filled in the necessary information on the appropriate will worksheet from Chapter 6.

Below are instructions for preparing the final version of your will. As you go about preparing your will, take your time and be very careful to proofread the original will before you sign it, to be certain that it states your desires exactly.

Instructions for Preparing Your Will

1. You should have before you a completed and filled-in photocopy or printed-out worksheet of the will that you have chosen. Then, carefully reread the entire worksheet version of your will to be certain that it is exactly as you wish.

2. After making any necessary changes, type or print-out the entire will on good quality 8-½" x 11" paper. (Note: if you are using the Forms-on-CD that accompanies this book, follow the instructions that are included in the Introduction of this book).

> **☼Toolkit Tip!**
>
> Before you type the final version of your will, reread the entire worksheet version of your will to be certain that it is exactly as you wish.

Definition:

Execution:
The formal signing of your will (or other legal document).

3.   After you have completed typing or printing out your will, fill in the total number of pages in the Signature paragraph. At the bottom of each page, also fill in the page number and the total number of pages. Do not yet sign your will, fill in the date, or initial the spaces on each page.

4.   Again, very carefully proofread your entire will. Be certain that there are no errors. If there are any errors, retype or reprint the particular page containing the error. *Do not* attempt to correct any errors with type-correcting fluid or tape, or with erasures of any kind. *Do not* cross-out or add anything to the typewritten words using a pen or pencil. Doing so will generally invalidate the will.

5.   When you have a perfect original of your will, with no corrections and no additions, staple all of the pages together in the upper left-hand corner. You are now ready to prepare for the *execution* (signing) of your will.

Warning!

Do not sign your will until you have all three of the necessary witnesses and Notary Public present.

Do not sign your will until you have read this chapter and have all of the necessary witnesses and Notary Public present. The legal requirements listed in this chapter regarding the proper signing of your will are extremely important and must not be deviated from in any manner in order for your will to be legally valid. These requirements are not at all difficult to follow, but they must be followed precisely. These formal requirements are what transform your will from a mere piece of paper outlining your wishes to a legal document that grants the power to dispose of your property under court order after your death.

The reasons for the formality of these requirements are twofold: first, by requiring a ceremonial-type signing of the document, it is hoped that the testator is made fully aware of the importance of what he or she is doing; and second, by requiring a formal signing witnessed by other adults, it is hoped that any instances of forgery, fraud, and coercion will be avoided, or at least minimized. Again, these legal formalities must be observed strictly. *Do not* deviate from these instructions in any way. The formal execution or signing of your will makes it legally valid and failure to properly sign your will renders it invalid.

Instructions for Signing Your Will

To properly execute your will, follow these few simple steps:

1. Select three (3) witnesses who will be available to assist you in witnessing your will. These persons may be any adults who are not mentioned in the will either as a beneficiary, executor, trustee, or guardian. The witnesses can be friends, neighbors, co-workers, or even strangers. However, it is prudent to choose persons who have been stable members of your community, since they may be called upon to testify in court someday.

2. Arrange for all of your witnesses to meet you at the office or home of a local Notary Public. Many banks, real estate offices, and government offices have notary services and most will be glad to assist you. (The Notary Public may *not* be one of the required three (3) witnesses.)

3. In front of all of the witnesses and the Notary Public, the following should take place in the order shown:

    (a)   You should state: "This is my Last Will and Testament, which I am about to sign. I ask that each of you witness my signature." There is no requirement that the witnesses know any of the terms of your will or that they read any of your will. All that is necessary is that they hear you state that it is your will, that you request them to be witnesses, that you observe you sign your will, and that they also sign the will as witnesses in each other's presence.

    (b)   You will then sign your will in ink, using a pen, at the end of the will in the place indicated, exactly as your name is typewritten on your will. You should also sign your initials on the bottom of each page of your will at this time.

    (c)   After you have signed, pass your will to the first witness, who should sign in the place indicated and fill in his or her address.

> **☼ Toolkit Tip!**
>
> Many banks and real estate offices have notary services and most will be glad to assist you. Some states allow notaries to charge small fees for their services.

⚡ **Warning!**

You should *never* under any circumstances sign a duplicate of your will. If you need a copy of your will, make a photocopy and be sure to label it clearly as a "COPY".

(d)   After the first witness has signed, have the will passed to the second witness, who should also sign in the place indicated and fill in his or her address.

(e)   After the second witness has signed, have the will passed to the third and final witness, who also signs in the place indicated and fills in his or her address. Throughout this ceremony, you and all of the witnesses must remain together. It is easier if you are all seated around a table or desk.

(f)   For the final step, the Notary Public completes the notary acknowledgment section of the will and signs in the space indicated. When this step is completed, your will is a valid legal document and you can be assured that your wishes will be carried out upon the presentation of your will to a probate court upon your death.

Safeguarding Your Will

Please note that you should *never* under any circumstances sign a duplicate of your will. Once your will has been properly executed following the steps above, you may make photocopies of it. It is a good idea to label any of these photocopies as "COPIES."

Having completed your will according to the instructions above, it is now time to place your will in a safe place. Many people keep their important papers in a safe deposit box at a local bank. Although this is an acceptable place for storing a will, be advised that there are certain drawbacks. Your will should be in a place that is readily accessible at a moment's notice to your executor. Often there are certain unavoidable delays in gaining access to a safe deposit box in an emergency situation. If you are married, and your safe deposit box is jointly held, many of these delays can be avoided. However, even in this situation, some states prevent immediate access to the safe deposit box of a deceased married person. If you decide to keep the original will in your safe deposit box, it is a good idea to keep a copy of your will clearly marked "COPY" at home in a safe but easily-located place, with a note as to where the original will can be found.

If in the future you should decide to make any changes to your will, make certain that your executor is informed of the changes and that the changes are kept with the original will. For more information regarding changing your will, please refer to the next chapter.

An acceptable alternative to a safe deposit box is a home file box or desk that is used for home storage of your important papers. If possible, this storage place should be fireproof and under lock and key. Wherever you decide to store your will, you will need to inform your chosen executor of its location. The executor will need to obtain the original of your will shortly after your demise to determine if there are any necessary duties that must be looked after without delay; for example, funeral plans or organ donations.

It is also a good practice to store any life insurance policies and a copy of your birth certificate in the same location as your original will. Additionally, it is also prudent to store a copy of your Property Questionnaire, Beneficiary Questionnaire, and Successor Trustee/Executor Information List with your will in order to provide your executor with an inventory and location list of your assets and a list of information regarding your heirs and beneficiaries. Any title documents or deeds relating to property that will be transferred under your will may also be stored with your will for the convenience of your executor. One final precaution: If you wish, allow the executor whom you have named to keep a copy of your will. Be careful, however, to be certain that you immediately inform him or her of any new will that you prepare, of any *codicils* (formal changes to your will) you make to your will, or of any decision to *revoke* (cancel) your will. Preparing a codicil to change your will is explained in the next chapter.

> ☼ **Toolkit Tip!**
>
> You should provide your chosen executor with a copy (not the original) of your will, your Executor Information List and the location of the original of your will.

Chapter 8

Changing a Will

In this chapter, instructions will be given on when and how to change your will and how to *revoke* (cancel) your will. It is most important to follow these instructions carefully should you desire to make *any* changes to your will. Failure to follow these instructions and an attempt to change your will by such methods as crossing out a name or penciling in an addition could have the disastrous effect of voiding portions of, or even perhaps, your entire will. Again, these instructions are not difficult to follow, but are very important to insure that your will remains legally valid.

If you desire to totally revoke your will, there are two acceptable methods:

- Signing a new will that expressly states that you revoke all prior wills. All wills prepared using this book contain such a provision.

- Completely destroying, burning, or mutilating the original of your will while it is in your possession, if you actually intend that there be a revocation of your will.

Regarding any potential changes that you may wish to make in your will at a later date, you should periodically review the provisions of your will, keeping in mind the following items as they relate to your present situation:

> **⚙ Toolkit Tip!**
>
> Whenever your personal life changes in any significant way (divorce, birth of child, marriage, etc.), you should be sure to review your existing will to be certain that it is still correct for your new circumstances.

- Have there been any substantial changes in your personal wealth?
- Have there been any changes in your ownership of any property mentioned in your will?
- Have any of the beneficiaries named in your will died or fallen into your disfavor?
- Are any of the persons whom you named as executor, guardian, or trustee in your will no longer willing or able to serve?
- Have you changed the state of your residence?
- Have you been married since the date of your will?
- Have you been divorced since the date of your will?
- Have you had any children since the date of your will?
- Have you adopted any children since the date of your will?
- Do you simply wish to make any corrections, deletions, or additions to any provisions in your will?

> **⊘ Definition:**
>
> **Codicil:**
> A formal written change to an existing will that has been signed and witnessed in the correct manner.

If any of these matters apply, you will need to change your will accordingly. Although it is possible to completely rewrite your will to take account of any of these changes, an easier method is to prepare and formally execute a *codicil*, or a written change to a will. Please bear in mind that all of the formalities surrounding the signing of your original will must again be followed in order for any such changes contained in a codicil to your will to be valid.

Never attempt to change any portions of your will by any other method. For example, *do not* attempt to add provisions in the margin of your will, either by typing or writing them in. *Do not* attempt to cross-out any portions of your will. These are not acceptable methods for the alteration of a will and could subject your will to a court battle to determine its subsequent validity.

Instructions for Changing Your Will

Following are standard clauses for changing provisions of your will and a general form for a codicil. Insert such changes as are necessary where indicated on the form. Prepare the codicil the same way as you prepared your original will using the following simple list of instructions:

Warning!

Never attempt to change your will by writing or typing new provisions or by crossing out items. You ***must*** either prepare an entirely new will or prepare and sign a codicil.

1. Make a photocopy or print out a copy of the codicil form. Using the photocopy as a worksheet, fill in the appropriate information for each chosen clause. For the main clause indicating the changes to your will, use one or more of the following phrases. If you wish to change a particular sentence in your will, you should first revoke the original sentence and then add the new sentence. If you merely wish to add new material to the will or revoke a portion of the will, use one of the phrases below:

   I revoke the following sentence of my will:

   and/or,

   I add the following sentence to my will:

2. Carefully reread your entire codicil to be certain that it is exactly as you wish.

3. After making any necessary changes, type or print out the entire codicil on good quality 8 ½" x 11" paper.

4. After you have completed typing or printing out your codicil, fill in the total number of pages in the Signature paragraph. *Do not* yet sign your codicil or fill in the date in any of the spaces indicated.

5. Again, proofread your entire codicil very carefully. Be certain that there are no errors. If there are any errors, retype that particular page. *Do not* attempt to correct any errors with type-correcting fluid or tape, or with erasures of any kind. *Do not* cross-out any words and *do not* add anything to the typewritten words using a pen or pencil.

6. When you have a perfect original of your codicil, with no corrections and no additions, staple all of the pages together in the upper left-hand corner. You are now ready to prepare for the *execution* (signing) of your codicil. For signing your codicil, please follow the same instructions that are provided in Chapter 7 for signing your will, substituting the statement:

This is my Codicil to my Last Will and Testament that I am about to sign.

As you fill in the information for each clause, keep in mind the following instructions:

Title Clause: The title clause is mandatory for all codicils and must be included. Fill in the name blank with your full legal name. If you have been known by more than one name, use your principal name. Be sure to use the exact same name as you used in the will that you are changing.

Warning!

Be sure to keep the original of your codicil with the original of your will.

Identification Clause: The identification clause is mandatory and must be included in all codicils. In the first blank, include any other names that you are known by. Do this by adding the phrase: "also known as" after your principal full name. For example:

John James Smith, also known as Jimmy John Smith.

In the spaces provided for your residence, use the location of your principal residence; that is, the place where you currently live permanently. Please note the exact date when you signed your current will.

Addition to Will Clause: Use of this clause is optional. Use if you wish to add additional provisions to your will. In the space provided, simply fill in whatever provisions you desired to be added. For example:

I add the following sentence to the [name of clause] clause of my will:

Revocation of Paragraph of Will Clause: This clause is optional. Use in those situations where you desire to delete a clause from your original will. Simply indicate which clause it is that you wish to revoke in the space indicated:

I revoke the following clause of my will:

I change the [name of clause] clause of my will to read as follows: [here include the new wording].

Correction of Will Clause: Use is optional. Use this clause for those situations where you wish to retain a particular clause in your will, but desire to change a portion of it (for example, substitution of the name of a different beneficiary). Where indicated in this clause, type the correct information that you wish to have become part of your will:

I change the [name of clause] clause of my will to read as follows:

Signature, Witness and Notary Clause: This clause is mandatory. You will fill in the number of pages and the appropriate dates where indicated after you have properly typed or printed out your codicil.. The use of the notary acknowledgment, although not a strict legal necessity, is strongly recommended. This allows the codicil to become "self-proving" and the witnesses need not be called upon to testify in court at a later date (after your death) that they, indeed, signed the codicil as witnesses. Although a few states have not enacted legislation to allow for the use of this type of sworn and acknowledged testimony to be used in court, the current trend is to allow for their use in probate courts. This saves time, money, and trouble in having your codicil admitted to probate when necessary.

Instructions for Completing a Codicil

You will sign your codicil in exactly the same manner as you sign your original will. The actual signing of the codicil by both you and your witnesses is explained in Chapter 7. Do *not* sign your codicil until you carefully follow the instructions contained in that chapter.

Fill in each of the appropriate blanks. Cross out any information that is not appropriate to your situation. The needed information to be filled in is noted below and should be written into the following codicil form in the place where the corresponding number appears.

①   Full name of testator
②   Full name of testator (and any other names that you are known by)
③   Full address of testator
④   Date of original will
⑤   Insert description of changes to original will
⑥   Date of signing of codicil (DO NOT FILL IN YET)

    Number of total pages of codicil (fill in when codicil is typed or printed)
    Date of signing of codicil (DO NOT FILL IN YET)
    Signature of testator (DO NOT FILL IN YET)
    Printed name of testator
    Date of witnessing of codicil (DO NOT FILL IN YET)
    Signature of witness (repeat for each witness) [DO NOT FILL IN YET]
    Printed name of witness (repeat for each witness) [DO NOT FILL IN YET]
    Address of witness (repeat for each witness) [DO NOT FILL IN YET]

⑦   Notary Acknowledgment (to be filled in by Notary Public)

Codicil

Codicil to the Last Will and Testament of

①_____

I, ②_____, whose address is ③_____,

declare that this is a codicil to my Last Will and Testament dated ④_____.

I make the following changes to my Last Will and Testament: ⑤

Page _____ of _____ pages   Testator's initials _____

On this date, _____, I republish my Last Will and Testament as modified by this Codicil, consisting of _____typewritten pages, and I declare that I do so freely, for the purposes expressed, under no constraint or undue influence, and that I am of sound mind and legal age.

_____

Signature of Testator

_____

Printed name of Testator

We, the undersigned, being first sworn on oath and under penalty of perjury, state that:

On _____ , in the presence of all of us, the above-named Testator published and signed this Codicil to his or her Last Will and Testament, and then at Testator's request, and in Testator's presence, and in each other's presence, we all signed below as witnesses, and we declare that, to the best of our knowledge, the Testator signed this instrument freely, under no constraint or undue influence, and is of sound mind and legal age.

_____   _____
Signature of Witness   Signature of Witness

_____   _____
Printed Name of Witness   Printed Name of Witness

_____   _____
Address of Witness   Address of Witness

_____
Signature of Witness

_____
Printed Name of Witness

_____
Address of Witness

Page _____ of _____ pages   Testator's initials _____

⑦ Notary Acknowledgment

State of _____
County of _____

On _____ , _____ the testator, and
_____ , _____ , and
_____ , the witnesses, personally came before me and,
being duly sworn, did state that they are the persons described in the above document and that
they signed the above document in my presence as a free and voluntary act for the purposes
stated.

_____
Signature of Notary Public

Notary Public, In and for the County of _____
State of _____

My commission expires: _____   Notary Seal

Chapter 9

Preparing a Living Trust

A living trust or *revocable trust* is a legal document that is used to pass on your assets to your beneficiaries upon your death. Thus, it accomplishes much the same results as a will. Like a will, it is revocable at any time during your life. Also, like a will, it allows you to retain control over your assets during your life and affords no direct tax advantages. A trust consists of assets of a *grantor* (the person who creates the trust) which are managed and distributed by a *trustee* to benefit one or more *beneficiaries* (those persons or organizations who will receive property under the trust). A living trust provides for all three of these designations to be held by the same person. You are the grantor, trustee, and beneficiary of your living trust while you are still alive. Upon your death, your chosen *successor trustee* succeeds you in the management of the trust and the distribution of your trust assets to your chosen beneficiaries.

A living trust is a legal document that allows for the transfer of property to the persons or organizations named in the living trust upon the death of the maker of the living trust. A living trust is only effective for the on-death distribution of property that has been previously transferred to the living trust. A living trust can be changed, modified, or revoked at any time by the grantor prior to death. A living trust may also be called a *revocable trust*, because during your lifetime you may *revoke*, or cancel the trust at any time. Upon your death, however, your living trust becomes irrevocable and its terms can no longer be altered in any way.

� Toolkit Tip!

A living trust generally provides that, initially, one person sets up the trust (the grantor), and is also both the initial beneficiary and the one who initially administers the trust (the trustee).

An increasingly popular estate planning tool, living or revocable trusts can be effectively used to avoid *probate*. As explained in Chapter 5, probate is an official series of court proceedings which begin with either proving a will is valid or determining that no will existed and then continuing with the distribution of the deceased person's property. To avoid probate, a living trust generally provides that all or most of a person's property be transferred to trust ownership. The owner of the property generally retains full control and management of the trust as trustee. In the trust document, beneficiaries are chosen, much the same as in a will. The terms of the trust can actually parallel the terms of a will. The difference is that, upon the death of the creator (grantor) of the trust, all of the property that has been transferred to trust ownership passes immediately and automatically to the beneficiaries without any court intervention or supervision and without an official probate proceeding.

The owner of the property (who is the creator or the trust) retains full control over the property until death and the creator of the trust can terminate this type of trust at any time prior to death. After the trust itself is prepared, all of the property that a person wishes placed in the living trust (stocks, bonds, bank accounts, real estate deeds, car titles, etc.) is actually transferred to the living trust.

It is equally important to understand that for a living trust to be valid, it must generally be prepared, signed, and notarized carefully. Although a living trust is perfectly valid if it Is written in plain English and does not use technical legal language, it must be prepared, signed, and notarized in the manner outlined in this book. These procedures are not at all difficult and consist generally of carefully typing your living trust in the manner outlined later, and signing it in the manner specified.

In some cases (for example, those involving extremely complicated business or personal financial holdings or the desire to create a complex trust arrangement) it is clearly advisable to consult an attorney for the preparation of your living trust. However, in most circumstances and for most people, the terms of a living trust that can provide for the necessary protection are relatively routine and may safely be prepared without the added expense of consulting a lawyer.

Advantages of a Living Trust
Avoiding the Expense and Delay of Probate

There are many reasons why it is desirable to have a living trust. One of the most important is that through the proper use of a living trust most or all of the expense and delay of probate is avoided. During a typical probate proceeding, an *executor* (a person appointed in a will) or a court-appointed administrator is authorized to collect, appraise, and distribute the assets of the deceased. Normally, the proper use of a living trust entirely eliminates or dramatically lessens the expenses of probate, since the disposition of all of your property has been planned in advance by you. Thus, the distribution takes place automatically upon your death, and the distribution is handled by the successor trustee that you name in your living trust.

Many people desire to avoid having their property be subject to probate proceedings. Although in some situations the probate process has been abused, there are valid reasons for allowing your property to be handled through probate after your death. It provides a process by which the improper distribution of your assets is guarded against by the probate court. Having your property distributed through a probate process also puts a definite limit on the length of time that a creditor can file a claim against your estate.

The drawbacks of probate are that it can substantially delay the distribution of your property while the probate process continues. The probate of an estate can take, generally, from four to 12 months, and sometimes much longer. Additionally, probate costs can be very significant. Court costs, appraisal fees, lawyer's fees, and accounting bills can all cut deeply into the amount of property and funds that will eventually be distributed to your beneficiaries. However, for small estates (generally, under $100,000.00) most states have simplified probate procedures that can be handled without lawyers and can substantially reduce these costs. (Check the Appendix for the rules regarding simplified probate in your state). The probate process itself is complex and will, in many cases, require the use of an attorney. The proper use of a living trust can allow all or most of your property to pass directly to

> **☼ Toolkit Tip!**
> Any property that is designated to pass to others using a living trust does not generally need to go through the probate process.

your chosen beneficiaries immediately upon your death, thus bypassing the probate process entirely. For many, this reason alone justifies the use of a living trust.

Avoiding Having the State Decide Who Will Receive Your Property

There are, however, numerous other valuable attributes of a living trust. Perhaps the next most important reason to have a living trust is to insure that it is you who decides how your estate is distributed on your death and to be assured that those loved ones whom you wish to share in your bounty actually receive your gifts.

What happens to your property and possessions if you do not have a valid and legal method by which to have your property distributed to your chosen *beneficiaries* (those persons or organizations to whom you decide to leave property) upon your death? If there is no valid living trust or will to use for direction, a probate judge must give a person's property to either the spouse, children, or the closest blood relatives of the deceased person. This result is required, even in situations when it is perfectly clear that the deceased person did not, under any circumstances, want those relatives to inherit the property.

Without such a valid living trust or will before him or her, a judge must rely on a legislative scheme which has been devised to make for an orderly distribution of property in all cases where there is no valid living trust or will. This scheme is present as law, in one form or another, in all 50 states and is generally referred to as *intestate distribution*.

The terms of state intestate distribution plans are very complex in most states. In general, a person's spouse is first in line to receive the property when there is no living trust or will at death. Most states provide that the spouse and children will either share the entire estate or the surviving spouse will take it all in the hopes that the spouse will share it with the children. Generally, the spouse will receive one-half and the children will receive one-half. In many states, if a person dies without a valid living trust or will and is survived by a spouse but not by any children, the spouse will inherit the entire estate and the surviving parents, brother, sisters, and any other blood relatives to the deceased will be entitled to nothing. Check on the listing in the Appendix for your own state's intestate distribution plan for specific details.

Each state has a complicated and often different method for deciding which particular family members will take property when there is no living trust or will. However, the results are often far from the desires of how the person actually wished to have the property distributed. Obviously, under this type of state distribution of your property, the individual circumstances of your family are not taken into consideration at all nor are any intentions that you may have had, regardless of how strongly you may have expressed them during your lifetime. The only way to avoid having the state decide who is to receive your property is to have prepared a legally valid living trust or will. If you die without a valid living trust or will, the state essentially writes one for you on its own terms.

Appointing a Trustee to Administer Your Property

Another very important reason for having a living trust is the ability to appoint a *successor trustee* of your own choice. A successor trustee is your personal representative for seeing that your wishes, as contained in your living trust, are carried out after your death and that your taxes and debts are paid. A successor trustee also collects and inventories all of your property and is in charge of seeing that it is distributed according to your wishes as expressed in your living trust.

> **⊘ Definition:**
>
> **Successor Trustee:**
> The person chosen to be trustee of a living trust after the initial trustee (generally, you) dies or is unable to handle their own affairs.

Typically, a spouse, sibling, or other close family member or trusted friend is chosen to act as successor trustee. However, it may be any responsible adult whom you would feel confident having this duty. It may even be a local bank or trust company. In that case of course, there will often be a substantial fee charged to your estate for the completion of these generally routine duties by the corporate successor trustee. If you choose an individual, he or she should be a resident of your home state. The living trust in this book enables you to appoint your successor trustee and an alternate successor trustee so that, in the event your first choice cannot perform, it is still your personal choice as to who will administer your living trust.

If you do not have a living trust or you do not choose a successor trustee in your living trust, a judge will appoint someone to administer the distribution of your property. Often it will be a local attorney, court official, or bank officer who may not know you or your beneficiaries at all. Your estate will then be distributed by a stranger who will charge your estate a hefty fee for the collection and distribution of your assets.

By appointing your own successor trustee, you are also able to waive the posting of a bond by your successor trustee. A *bond* is a type of insurance policy that a trustee would normally have to purchase to insure that he or she carries out his or her duties properly. The cost of the bond would come out of your *trust estate* (all of the trust's assets). You also provide that your successor trustee will not receive any compensation for serving as trustee. This will allow more of your assets to reach your beneficiaries, rather than paying for the expenses of administration of your estate.

Appointing a Trustee to Administer Property for a Minor Child

For those with minor children, the appointment of a trustee for any assets to be provided to the children is another very important matter which may be accomplished through the use of a living trust. You may set up a children's trust within your living trust and have your successor trustee administer your children's property until a time when you feel that your children will be able to handle their own affairs. Instructions to provide for this alternative are simply stated in a living trust, but are more difficult to accomplish without one. If such instruction is not provided for in a living trust and a minor child is left money or property by way of the state intestate succession laws, the courts will generally decide who should administer the property. Such court-supervised guardianship of the property or money will automatically end at the child's reaching the legal age of majority in the state (usually 18 years of age). At this age, without a living trust to direct otherwise, the child will receive full control over the property and/or money. This may not be the most prudent result, as many 18-year-olds are not capable of managing property or large sums of money. With a living trust, it is easy to arrange for the property or money to be held in trust and used to benefit the child until a later age, perhaps 21, 25, or even 30 years of age or older. Please note that you can *not* use a living trust to name a guardian for any minor children. You must use a will to accomplish this result.

Other Advantages of a Living Trust

There are a number of other significant advantages to using a living trust to distribute your property upon your death:

⚡ **Warning!**

Whenever your personal situation changes (marriage, divorce, or the purchase of major property, etc.), you should review the terms of your living trust to make certain that it still applies to your new situation.

- If you own real estate in a state other than that of your legal residence, the use of a living trust will generally allow that real estate to be passed to your beneficiary without an out-of-state probate proceeding.

- If you become incapacitated, a living trust allows your chosen successor trustee to manage your property. Without a living trust, a "conservator" or "guardian" would need to be authorized by a court to handle such matters. The legal proceeding to accomplish this is often long and expensive. (Note: you can also use a durable power of attorney to accomplish this result. Please see Chapter 13 regarding durable powers of attorney).

- With a living trust, the details of your estate plan remain confidential. Only your chosen successor trustee will need to know the actual specifics of your intentions. And even your successor trustee need only know the details of your estate plan after your death. A living trust only needs to be recorded with the county recorder in the event that real estate is transferred with such a trust.

- While you are alive, there are no required trust recordkeeping requirements, other than keeping track of the actual trust documents themselves. You need not have a trust bank account, file a trust federal or state income tax return,

✦Toolkit Tip!

You can change (either amend or revoke) your living trust at any time by simply preparing an amendment form.

or maintain any separate trust records. Of course, it is a good idea to keep careful track of the assets that you will place in the living trust.

• Another advantage is that it is much more difficult to challenge a living trust in court than it is to challenge a will.

• You can amend or revoke your living trust at any time, without any formal proceedings or actions. Simply use the forms provided later in this book to accomplish these actions.

• Finally, no lawyer is necessary to handle the distribution of your assets upon your death. If you follow the instructions in this book carefully, your chosen successor trustee should have no difficulty in distributing your assets to your chosen beneficiaries. This can save not only time, but considerable money as well.

Disadvantages of a Living Trust

There are a few disadvantages to using a living trust to distribute your property upon your death:

• Perhaps the most important disadvantage of using a living trust is the need to actually transfer to the trust all of the property intended to be put in trust. This requirement and the need to keep accurate trust records make the actual mechanics of a living trust more complicated than simply preparing a will. Setting up a living trust entails some paperwork. You must carefully prepare a trust document and the property and beneficiary schedules that will accompany it. You must also make certain that you have the selected property clearly transferred to the trust. If the property has a title or ownership document (such as a car or a piece of real estate), you must change the ownership documents to reflect that the ownership is being transferred to the trust. If the property has no ownership document, then simply listing the chosen property on the Trust Schedule of Assets will effectively transfer the property to the trust.

- In a very few situations and jurisdictions, there may be some limited transfer taxes, such as real estate transfer taxes or vehicle title transfer fees. In the vast majority of states, transfers of real estate to ownership by a living trust are exempt from any transfer taxes. Even if imposed, such transfer taxes are generally very minimal. Transfer of property to a living trust may also possibly trigger a reassessment of your property Please check specifically with your jurisdiction if this is an issue.

- There may be a few banks or finance companies that will balk at refinancing a property that has the title held by a trust. Most companies should be satisfied if you provide them with your trust document and all of the transfer documents (such as the new deed or title).

- A possible disadvantage to using a living trust is that it has no effect on your tax situation. It does not lessen any potential income, estate, or inheritance taxes.

- If you don't have much property, there really is no need to use a living trust to avoid probate, as your estate may likely qualify for simplified probate procedures.

- Finally, unlike a probate proceeding, there is no cutoff date for the filing of creditor's claims against the estate of a person who dies with a living trust. For the vast majority of people, this is not a problem as most estates do not have large unpaid liabilities. However, if you feel that your estate may be subject to large claims, you may wish to use a will, rather than a living trust, to distribute your property upon death.

> **⚡ Warning!**
>
> The use of a living trust does not effect your income tax situation. Its use is not for tax planning, but rather as a device to avoid probate.

Why You Still Need a Will

Although it can be short and simple, a living trust is an important document which can accomplish many tasks. The proper use of a living trust can eliminate much confusion for those left behind. Since it provides a clear and legal record of your wishes, it can avoid feuding and squabbles among your family members. Perhaps most importantly, it can make your last wishes come

⚡ Warning!

Even if you have prepared a living trust, you should always also have a will in case there is any property that was not included under the terms of your living trust or any other estate planning tools.

true. The main advantage to using a living trust instead of a will is that it allows your assets to be passed to your beneficiaries automatically upon your death, without any delay, probate, court intervention, or lawyer's fees. To many people, this very important advantage outweighs any disadvantages.

Even if you have used a living trust and the various other estate planning tools outlined in this book to attempt to have your estate avoid probate, a will is still highly recommended. There may be assets that you have neglected, forgotten about, or that will not be uncovered until your death. Even if you decide to use a living trust to pass your assets to your beneficiaries, you will also need to prepare a will. This is because regardless of your best efforts, generally, you will not be able to name each and every item of property that you own. Without a will as a backup, any property not named in the living trust will pass to your closest relatives, or if there are none, the property may be forfeited to the state. If you have a will as a backup to a living trust, you will retain the ability to be certain that all of your property will pass to those who you personally choose to receive it. In addition, a will is necessary to name a personal guardian for any minor children that you may have. Finally, if you wish to disinherit a child (or a spouse in a community property state), you must use a will to accomplish this. Chapter 6 provides basic wills for you to create to supplement your living trust.

Additional Types of Trusts

Please note that there are many, many other types of trusts that are available for estate planning purposes. A brief explanation of some of these type of trusts is below. As this book is an effort at simplifying the estate planning process, none of these more complex trust arrangements are covered in this book. If you feel that your situation may benefit from the use of one or more of these more complex trusts, please consult an attorney.

Support Trust: Authorizes the trustee to spend the principal and/or income of a trust for the health care, education, and general support of a beneficiary. The children's trust included in one of the living trusts in this chapter is one type of 'support trust".

Discretionary Trust: Authorizes the trustee to spend the principal and/or income of a trust in different amounts to various beneficiaries of a trust, in the sole discretion of the trustee.

Charitable Lead Trust: An irrevocable trust set up to support a charitable purpose for a set period of time, after which the trust assets revert to the grantor or beneficiaries.

Charitable Remainder Trust: An irrevocable trust with a beneficiary who receives the income for a certain period of time and then has a charity named as the final beneficiary.

Spendthrift Trust: Set up to provide for a person whom the grantor does not feel has the ability to manage their own affairs or for a person who may need protection from creditors.

Insurance Trust: This type of trust is used to purchase life insurance to benefit the beneficiaries or to pay any expected estate taxes.

Medicaid Trust: Set up to help one qualify for Medicaid benefits.

AB Trust: This type of trust is for estate tax avoidance purposes and provides that after the death of a first spouse, the surviving spouse is the beneficiary of the trust (but not the owner of the trust assets). This trust, thus, bypasses the surviving spouse and can save on estate taxes if the spouses combined assets are over $2 million (in 2008, but rising to $3.5 million in 2009).

QTIP Trust: For estate tax avoidance purposes, this trust provides that a surviving spouse becomes the beneficiary of the trust for his or her life. On the death of the surviving spouse, the remaining trust property passes to the beneficiaries named by the first spouse to die.

QDOT Trust: Also for estate tax avoidance. Provides a method that allows estate assets to be left to a non-U.S. citizen spouse and receive the estate tax marital deduction (which is normally limited for non-citizen spouses).

☆ Toolkit Tip!

There are many types of trusts (other than living trusts) that may be useful in your particular situation. If so, you should consult an attorney skilled in preparing complex trusts.

Creating a Living Trust

To create a living trust, you will first need to decide what property you wish to place in trust. To do this, you may use the property questionnaire that is provided in Chapter 3: Assets that are subject to being sold or discarded regularly should not be put in the trust. Next, you will need to decide who is to receive your assets upon your death. Again, you may use the beneficiary questionnaire that is included in Chapter 4. Finally, you will need to decide if you wish to retain all control over the trust. To achieve this end, you will name yourself as trustee.

> **⋄ Toolkit Tip!**
>
> You must actually transfer ownership to the trust of any property that you wish to have governed by the terms of your living trust.

Once you have created your living trust, you will need to actually transfer the ownership of all of the assets selected to the trust. This transfer may include obtaining a new title to your car, new bank accounts, and a new deed to any real estate. The new ownership will be in the name of the trust itself, with the name of the trustee specified; for example, *The Jane Smith Revocable Living Trust; Jane Smith, Trustee* might be the name on the deed or title. *Note*: In order to transfer property into your trust, you may need to use an Assignment to Living Trust form for personal property (see below) or a Quitclaim Deed for real estate (see Chapter 17: *Preparing a Quitclaim Deed*).

Living Trust: This is the main legal document that establishes your trust. Two versions of this main trust document are included: one for use by an individual with no minor children and one for use by an individual with minor children who wishes to set up a children's trust to handle any gifts to the minor children until they are of an age to be able to handle their own affairs.

Schedule of Assets of Living Trust: On this form, you will include a listing of all of the property that you wish to transfer into the trust. (For more information on property, please refer to Chapter 3: *Property and Taxation Information*.) This document should be attached to the living trust when completed. This form needs to be notarized.

Schedule of Beneficiaries of Living Trust: On this form, you will include a list of all of your chosen beneficiaries, alternate beneficiaries, and the trust property that you wish them to receive. You will also choose a residual beneficiary. (For more information on beneficiary choices, refer to Chapter 4). This form must be notarized.

Assignment to Living Trust: This form is used to transfer personal property to the trust. On this form, you will provide a full description of the property transferred. This form should also be notarized.

Registration of Living Trust: This form is used in those states (10 as of the date of printing this book) that require that a trust be registered with a county clerk. Please check the Appendix listing for "Additional Trust Requirement" to see if your state requires this registration.

> **·Ö·Toolkit Tip!**
> Check the Appendix to see if your state requires the registration of living trusts.

New York Notice of Assignment of Property to a Living Trust: This form is required in the state of New York for any assignments of property to a living trust.

Affidavit of Assumption of Duties by Successor Trustee: This form is useful if a successor trustee encounters any difficulty in having his or her authority to act under a living trust verified by a bank or other financial institution.

Note Regarding Individual State Requirements

A number of states have special requirements regarding the use of living trusts, generally involving the registration of the living trust in the county where the grantor is a resident or in which the trust itself will hold title to any real estate. A Registration of Living Trust is supplied for those states. In addition, New York state requires a Notice of Assignment of Property to a Living Trust form and this form and instructions are also included. Some states also require notification of beneficiaries when the grantor dies and the trust thus become irrevocable. Please check your state's requirements in the Appendix under the listing "Additional Trust Requirements".

Preparing Your Living Trust Declaration

Carefully read through all of the clauses in the appropriate blank living trust. Make a photocopy or print out a copy of the living trust form to use as a worksheet. If you wish, you may use this book itself as a worksheet (unless it is a library book!). The first set of instructions given apply to both trust declaration forms that are supplied with this book. Following these general instructions are the specific instructions for each of the two trust forms.

If you are at all unsure of the correct use of these forms, please consult a competent attorney. As you fill in the information for each clause, keep in mind the following instructions:

Title Clause: The title is mandatory for all living trusts. Fill in the name blank with your full legal name (such as the "Andrea Ann Doria Living Trust"). If you have been known under more than one name, use only your principal name.

Identification and Date Clause: The identification clause is mandatory and must be included in all living trusts. In the first blank, include any other names which you are known by. Do this by adding the phrase: "also known as" after your principal full name. For example:

"John James Smith, also known as Jimmy John Smith."

In the spaces provided for your residence, use the location of your principal residence; that is, where you currently live permanently. Fill in the date when you wish the living trust to take effect.

Name of Trust Clause: Fill in your own name prior to the title of the trust (for example: "The John Smith Living Trust").

Marital and Parental Status Clause: Depending upon your current marital and parental status you will choose one of the following clauses. If you have children, list the appropriate information for each child. This clause should be included in your living trust after the phrase "My marital status is that…:

⚡Toolkit Tip!

Before you create a living trust, be certain that you really need one. Often living trusts are used when other simpler probate avoidance techniques would work just as well (such as 'payable-on-death' accounts or joint tenancies).

- **"I am single and have no children."**

- **"I am currently married to [name of spouse] and we have no children."**

- **"I was previously married to [name of spouse] and that marriage ended on [date] by [death, divorce, or annulment] and we had no children."**

- **"I am single and have [number] child[ren] currently living. Their names and dates of birth are:"**

- **"I am currently married to [name of spouse] and we have [number] child[ren] currently living. Their names and dates of birth are:"**

- **"I was previously married to [name of spouse] and that marriage ended on [date] by [death, divorce, or annulment] and we have [number] child[ren] currently living. Their names and dates of birth are:"**

Trusteeship Clause: Under this clause, you declare that you will act as the trustee of the trust and any subtrusts which may be created by the trust (such as a children's trust).

Property Transfer Section: No additional information need be filled-in in this section. This section of your trust provides that you are transferring ownership of all of the property listed on your Schedule of Assets of Living Trust to the trust itself. You are also reserving the right to make any changes to your Schedule of Assets at any time, as long as they are in writing, notarized, and attached to the trust. You are also agreeing to prepare any additional paperwork that may be necessary to complete any such transfers of ownership, such as completing a deed or title transfer if necessary.

> **Toolkit Tip!**
>
> To transfer real estate to a living trust, you may use a quitclaim deed (explained in Chapter 17).

Grantor's Rights Section: No additional information need be filled-in for this section. Under this section, you retain full lifetime control of all of the trust's assets that you have transferred in the above section (and by other transfer documents, if necessary). Regarding your home, you specifically state that you retain the right of possession for your entire life and that any transfer to the trust does not interfere with any rights to homestead exemptions that you may have under state law.

⍟ Toolkit Tip!

Make sure that you read Chapter 5 before you make your selection of your successor or alternate successor trustees.

Successor Trustee Section: This section is included in every living trust in this book. With this clause, you will make your choice of successor trustee and alternate successor trustee, the persons who will administer and distribute your trust assets upon your death or who will take over the management of your trust upon your incapacitation or death. The various duties of your successor trustee are explained in Chapter 5. You also provide that any such incapacitation be certified by a physician before the successor trustee may assume management of your trust. The chosen alternate successor trustee will assume the powers of the trustee only if the successor trustee that you have chosen is not surviving or is otherwise unable to serve. A spouse, sibling, or other trusted party is usually chosen to act as successor trustee. The person chosen should be a resident of the state in which you currently reside. You also provide that he or she not be required to post a bond in order to be appointed to serve as successor trustee and that he or she will not be compensated for their service as trustee. Finally, you note that any reference to "trustee" in your document also refers to the successor or alternate successor trustee. Be sure to clearly identify the successor trustee and alternate successor trustee by full name and address.

Trustee's Powers Section: In this section, no additional information needs to be filled-in. You grant any trustee broad powers to manage your trust assets. The powers are granted without court supervision and without oversight by anyone else. The powers granted are the same power and authority as an individual person has over their own property.

Additional Trustee Powers Section: No additional information need be filled-in in this section. This section provides a detailed enumeration of the powers that are granted to the trustee. Although in the previous section you granted any powers granted by law, many businesses and financial institutions require that a trustee's actual power to perform a specific act be spelled-out in a trust document. As you can see, the powers granted to the trustee are very extensive and approximate the power that an individual would have over his or her property.

Incapacitation Section: No additional information needs to be filled-in for this section. This section goes into effect in the event that a grantor becomes incapacitated during his or her lifetime. This incapacitation must be certified by a physician, as noted in the successor trustee section above. In this event, the successor trustee is bound to manage the trust solely for the benefit of the grantor and in accordance with the grantor's accustomed manner of living. Thus, any beneficiaries of the trust cannot demand that the successor trustee stop spending trust assets to care for an incapacitated grantor and save the trust assets for them. Please note that the power and authority that a successor trustee has over the assets of a living trust when the original trustee is incapacitated is similar to the power and authority that an attorney-in-fact appointed under a durable power of attorney has over a person's assets when that person becomes incapacitated. If you are also intending on appointing an attorney-in-fact under a durable power of attorney in your estate plan, you should appoint the same person as successor trustee of your trust and as attorney-in-fact under your durable power of attorney. If you do not wish to appoint the same person for both roles, you will need to consult an attorney to be certain that the powers and authority that you provide to each separate person do not overlap and create a situation in which a court will have to intervene to determine which person has authority over which of your property.

> ## ⚡ Warning!
>
> If you will use both a living trust and a durable power of attorney for financial matters, you should appoint the same person as both successor trustee for the trust and attorney-in-fact for the power of attorney.

Children's Trust Fund Section: This clause is only present in the living trust in which a parent with children wishes to set up a children's trust fund (within the main living trust) for any gifts to be made to their minor children. The form in this book that contains this children's trust immediately follows these instructions. The second following trust is designed for individuals either without children or those who have children but do not wish to restrict their children's access to the gifts under the trust (generally parents with children above the age of 21).

Under this children's trust, you also may delay the time when they will actually have unrestricted control over your gift. It is not recommended, however, to attempt to delay receipt of control beyond the age of 35.

⚡ Warning!

You should not restrict access to a child's property beyond the age of 35 unless there are physical, mental, or psychological limitations that would prevent the child from handling their own affairs as an adult.

In this section, you will fill in two ages. First, you will select an age that a child must be under for the children's trust section to take effect. You may desire the gifts under the main trust to be held in the children's trust for any child under the age of, say, 30 years of age. Then you will also select an age when the children's trust will terminate and the then-adult will receive the property with no restrictions, for example, 35 years of age. The ages that you select may be any reasonable age.

The terms of the trust provide that the trustee may distribute any or all of the income or principal to the children as he or she deems necessary to provide for their health, support, and education. The trust will terminate when either the specific age is reached, all of the money is spent prior to that age, or the child dies prematurely. Upon termination, any remaining trust funds will be distributed to the child (beneficiary), if surviving. If the child is not surviving at the age when the trust is to terminate, the trust funds will be distributed to the heirs of the beneficiary (if there are any). If there are none, then the trust funds remaining will revert back to the residue of your trust (as noted on your Schedule of Beneficiaries of Living Trust) and be distributed accordingly. Additionally, since the trustee of the children's trust should be the same person who is successor trustee, you have already granted the trustee broad powers to manage the trust and also provided that he or she not be required to post a bond nor allowed compensation for services rendered.

Termination of Trust Section: This section provides that the trust shall become irrevocable upon the death of the grantor. Upon that event, the successor trustee will then be empowered to pay all of the valid debts, last expenses, and taxes of the grantor and then distribute the trust assets as specified on the Schedule of Beneficiaries of Living Trust. It is also noted in any of the trusts which contain a children's trust that any such distributions to beneficiaries are subject to the terms of the children's trust. This section also provides that the Schedule of Beneficiaries may be amended at any time (before it becomes irrevocable) by a written, notarized amendment which is attached to the trust.

Survivorship Section: This clause is included in every living trust. This clause provides for two possibilities. First, it provides for a required period of survival for any beneficiary to receive a gift under your living trust. The practical effect of this is to be certain that your property passes under your living trust and not that of a beneficiary who dies shortly after receiving your gift. The second portion of this clause provides for a determination of how your property should pass in the eventuality that both you and a beneficiary (most likely your spouse) should die in a manner that makes it impossible to determine who died first.

Without this clause in your living trust it would be possible that property would momentarily pass to a beneficiary under your living trust. When that person dies (possibly immediately if a result of a common accident or disaster) your property could wind up being left to the person whom your beneficiary designated, rather than to your alternate beneficiary. If you and your spouse are both preparing individual living trusts, it is a good idea to be certain that each of your living trusts contains identical survivorship clauses. If you are each other's primary beneficiary, it is also wise to attempt to coordinate who your alternate beneficiaries may be in the event of a simultaneous death.

Amendments and Revocations Section: This form of trust reserves the right to allow you to cancel (revoke) or amend this trust or any of the schedules at any time. However, any changes (amendments) must be in writing, notarized, and attached to the original trust document to be valid.

Governing Law Section: You will fill in the number of pages, including all schedules, and the state of your legal residence where indicated after you have properly typed or had your living trust typed. The laws of the state of your principal residence will govern any questions regarding the operation of the trust or the actions of any trustee.

Signature Section: The signature lines of your living trust will be completed in front of a notary public as explained next in the instructions on completing your living trust for signature.

> **-ϒ-Toolkit Tip!**
>
> Remember that you may alter or revoke your living trust at any time prior to your death, at which time the trust becomes irrevocable.

Completing Your Living Trust Forms

1. On the photocopy worksheet version of your living trust and schedules, cross out all of the instructions, circled numbers, and any other extraneous material which is not to become a part of your Living Trust. Carefully re-read the entire worksheet version of your living trust to be certain that it is exactly as you wish.

2. After making any necessary changes, type or print-out the entire living trust and the appropriate schedules on good quality letter-sized (8½" x 11") paper.

⚡ Warning!

You should never make corrections to your living trust by crossing out or writing in additional terms. All corrections must be in a written document that is signed and notarized and attached to the original trust.

3. After you have completed typing or printing out your living trust and schedules, fill in the total number of pages in the line above the signature section. Again, very carefully proofread your entire living trust. Be certain that there are no errors. If there are any errors, retype that particular page. Do not attempt to correct any errors with white-out type correcting fluid or tape or with erasures of any kind. Do not cross out or add anything to the typewritten words using a pen or pencil. The signature and notary acknowledgement spaces should be blank.

4. When you have a perfect original of your living trust and schedules, with no corrections and no additions, staple all of the pages together in the top left-hand corner.

5. Take the original of your living trust and schedules before a Notary Public. Many banks, real estate offices, and government offices have notary services and most will be glad to assist you. In front of the Notary Public, you should sign your living trust and schedules in the places indicated. (Note: unlike a will, the signing of a living trust need not be witnessed by anyone other than a notary public).

6. The final step is for the Notary Public to complete the Notary Acknowledgments, sign in the space indicated, and stamp with his or her Notary Seal. When this step is completed, your living trust is a valid legal document and you may be assured that your wishes will be carried out upon your death.

Safeguarding Your Living Trust

Having completed your living trust according to the foregoing instructions, it is now time to place your living trust in a safe place. Many people keep their important papers in a safe deposit box at a local bank. Although this is an acceptable place for storing a living trust, be advised that there are certain drawbacks. Your living trust should be in a place which is readily accessible to your successor trustee at a moment's notice. Often there are certain unavoidable delays in gaining access to a safe deposit box in an emergency situation. If you are married and your safe deposit box is jointly held, many of these delays can be avoided. However, even in this situation, some states prevent immediate access to the safe deposit box of a deceased married person. If you decide to keep the original in your safe deposit box, it is a good idea to keep a clearly-marked copy of your living trust at home in a safe but easily-located place, with a note as to where the original may be found.

> ⚡ **Warning!**
>
> If you make any photo-copies of your original living trust, you should clearly label any of these as "COPIES".

Wherever you decide to store your living trust, you will need to inform your chosen successor trustee of its location. The successor trustee will need to obtain the original of your living trust shortly after your demise to determine if there are any necessary duties which must be looked after without delay, for example: funeral plans or organ donations.

It is also a good practice to store any life insurance policies and a copy of your birth certificate in the same location. Additionally, it is also prudent to store a copy of your property questionnaire, beneficiary questionnaire, and the successor trustee information list with your living trust in order to provide your successor trustee with an inventory and location list of your assets and a list of information regarding your beneficiaries. Any title documents or deeds relating to property which is to be transferred under your living trust may also be stored with your living trust for the convenience of your successor trustee. A final precaution, if you desire, is to allow the successor trustee whom you have named to keep a copy of your living trust. Be careful, however, to be certain that you immediately inform him or her of any amendments to your living trust which you prepare or of any decision to revoke your living trust.

Instructions for Living Trust with a Children's Trust Included

This living trust is appropriate for use by an individual married person or a single person with one or more minor children, who desires to place the property and assets which may be left to the children in a trust fund. In most cases, a married person may desire to choose the other spouse as both successor trustee and trustee for any of their children's trusts, although this is not a legal requirement.

Fill in each of the appropriate blanks in this living trust, a Schedule of Assets of Living Trust, and a Schedule of Beneficiaries of Living Trust using the information which you included in your Property and Beneficiary Questionnaires. Cross out any information that is not appropriate to your situation. You will then complete the preparation of all your forms following the instructions later in this chapter.

To complete this form, you will need the following information:

①   The name of the living trust (generally, your full name is the name of the trust, such as the "Gwendolyn Smith Living Trust")

②   Your complete name
        The date on which you wish the living trust to take effect
        The name of the living trust
        Your complete name and
        Your marital status and the names of any children

③   No information needed

④   No information needed

⑤   The names and addresses of your chosen Successor Trustee and Alternate Successor Trustee

⑥   No information needed

⑦   No information needed

⑧   No information needed

⑨   The age of your child(ren) under which you wish the Children's Trust to take effect, and
        The age of each child when the Children's Trust will terminate

⑩   No information needed

⑪   No information needed

⑫   No information needed

⑬   The number of pages of the living trust, including schedules, and
        The state of your legal residence

⑭   Your signature and printed name (do not sign unless in front of a notary public)

⑮   The notary acknowledgment section (to be completed by notary public)

Living Trust with a Children's Trust Included

① ## Living Trust of _____

② Declaration of Trust

I, _____ , the grantor of this trust, declare and make this Living Trust on _____ (date).

This trust will be known as the _____ Living Trust.

I, _____ , will be trustee of this trust and any subtrusts created under this trust.

My marital status is that _____ .

③ Property Transfer

I transfer ownership to this trust of all of the assets which are listed on the attached Schedule of Assets of Living Trust, which is specifically made a part of this trust. I reserve the right to add or delete any of these assets at any time. In addition, I will prepare a separate Deed, Assignment, or any other documents necessary to carry out such transfers. Any additions or deletions to the Schedule of Assets of Living Trust must be written, notarized, and attached to this document to be valid.

④ Grantor's Rights

Until I die, I retain all rights to all income, profits, and control of the trust property. If my principal residence is transferred to this trust, I retain the right to possess and occupy it for my life, rent-free and without charge. I will remain liable for all taxes, insurance, maintenance, related costs, and expenses. The rights that I retain are intended to give me a beneficial interest in my principal residence such that I do not lose any eligibility that I may have for a state homestead exemption for which I am otherwise qualified.

⑤ Successor Trustee

Upon my death or if it is certified by a licensed physician that I am physically or mentally unable to manage this trust and my financial affairs, then I appoint _____

_____ (name), of _____
_____ (address), as Successor Trustee, to serve without bond and without compensation. If this successor trustee is not surviving or otherwise unable to serve, I ap-point _____ (name), of _____
_____ (address), as Alternate Successor Trustee, also to serve without bond and without compensation. The successor trustee or alternate successor trustee shall not be liable for any actions taken in good faith. References to "trustee" in this document shall include any successor or alternate successor trustees.

⑥ Trustee's Powers

In addition to any powers, authority, and discretion granted by law, I grant the trustee any and all powers to perform any acts, in his or her sole discretion and without court approval, for the management and distribution of this trust and any subtrusts created by this trust. I intend the trustee to have the same power and authority to manage and distribute the trust assets as an individual owner has over his or her own wholly-owned property.

⑦ Additional Trustee Powers

The trustee's powers include, but are not limited to: the power to sell trust property, borrow money, and encumber that property, specifically including trust real estate, by mortgage, deed of trust, or other method; the power to manage trust real estate as if the trustee were the absolute owner of it, including the power to lease or grant options to lease the property, make repairs or alterations, and insure against loss; the power to sell or grant options for the sale or exchange of any trust property, including stocks, bonds, and any other form of security; the power to invest trust property in property of any kind, including but not limited to bonds, notes, mortgages, and stocks; the power to receive additional property from any source and add to any trust created by this trust; the power to employ and pay reasonable fees to accountants, lawyers, or investment consultants for information or advice relating to the trust; the power to deposit and hold trust funds in both interest-bearing and non-interest-bearing accounts; the power to deposit funds in bank or other accounts uninsured by FDIC coverage; the power to enter into electronic fund transfer or safe deposit arrangements with financial institutions; the power to continue any business of the grantor; the power to institute or defend legal actions concerning the trust or grantor's affairs; and the power to execute any document necessary to administer any children's trust created in this trust.

⑧ Incapacitation

Should the successor trustee or alternate successor trustee assume management of this trust during the lifetime of the grantor, the successor trustee or alternate successor trustee shall manage the trust solely for the proper health care, support, maintenance, comfort, and/or welfare of the grantor, in accordance with the grantor's accustomed manner of living.

⑨ Children's Trust Fund

A   If any of my children who are named as beneficiaries on the attached Schedule of Beneficiaries of Living Trust are under _____ years old on my death, I direct that any property that I give them under this trust be held in an individual children's trust for each child under the following terms, until each shall reach the age of _____ years old.

B   In the trustee's sole discretion, the trustee may distribute any or all of the principal, income, or both as deemed necessary for the beneficiary's health, support, welfare, and education. Any income not distributed shall be added to the trust principal. Any such trust shall terminate when the beneficiary reaches the required age, dies prior to reaching the required age, or all trust funds have been distributed. Upon termination, any remaining undistributed principal and income shall pass to the beneficiary; or if not surviving, to the beneficiary's heirs; or if none, to the residue of the main trust created by this document.

⑩ Termination of Trust

Upon my death, this trust shall become irrevocable. The successor trustee shall then pay my valid debts, last expenses, and estate taxes from the assets of this trust. The successor trustee shall then distribute the remaining trust assets in the manner shown on the attached Schedule of Beneficiaries of Living Trust which is specifically made a part of this trust, subject to the provisions of any children's trust which is created by this document. I reserve the right to add and/or delete any beneficiaries at any time. Any additions or deletions to the Schedule of Beneficiaries of Living Trust must be written, notarized, and attached to this document to be valid.

⑪ Survivorship

All beneficiaries named in the Schedule of Beneficiaries of Living Trust must survive me by thirty (30) days to receive any gift under this living trust. If any beneficiary and I should die simultaneously, I shall be conclusively presumed to have survived that beneficiary for purposes of this living trust.

⑫ Amendments and Revocations

I reserve the right to amend any or all of this trust at any time. The amendments must be written, notarized, and attached to this document to be valid. I also reserve the right to revoke this trust at any time. A revocation of this trust must be written, notarized, and attached to this document to be valid.

⑬ Governing Law

This trust, containing _____ pages, was created on the date noted above and will be governed under the laws of the State of _____ .

⑭ Signature

_____

Signature of Grantor

_____

Printed Name of Grantor

⑮ Notary Acknowledgment

State of _____
County of _____

On _____ , _____ came before me personally and, under oath, stated that he or she is the person described in the above document and he or she signed the above document in my presence. I declare under penalty of perjury that the person whose name is subscribed to this instrument appears to be of sound mind and under no duress, fraud, or undue influence.

_____

Notary Public
In and for the County of _____
State of _____
My commission expires _____   Notary Seal

Instructions for Living Trust without a Children's Trust

This living trust is appropriate for use by a single person or an individual married person with or without children. If the person has children, this form is to be used only if the person desires that any assets to be transferred to the children at the grantor's death not be held in a children's trust, but rather be transferred directly to the children upon the death of the grantor. This will normally be used only when any children are already above the legal age of minority.

Fill in each of the appropriate blanks in this living trust, a Schedule of Assets of Living Trust, and a Schedule of Beneficiaries of Living Trust using the information which you included in your Property and Beneficiary Questionnaires. Cross out any information that is not appropriate to your situation. You will then complete the preparation of all your forms following the instructions later in this chapter.

To complete this form, you will need the following information:

①   The name of the living trust (generally, your full name is the name of the trust, such as the "Gwendolyn Smith Living Trust")

②   Your complete name
       The date on which you wish the living trust to take effect
       The name of the living trust
       Your complete name, and
       Your marital status and the names of any children

③   No information needed

④   No information needed

⑤   The names and addresses of your chosen Successor Trustee and Alternate Successor Trustee

⑥   No information needed

⑦   No information needed

⑧   No information needed

⑨   No information needed

⑩   No information needed

⑪   No information needed

⑫   The number of pages of the living trust, including schedules, and
       The state of your legal residence

⑬   Your signature and printed name (do not sign unless in front of a notary public)

⑭   The notary acknowledgment section (to be completed by notary public)

Living Trust without a Children's Trust

① Living Trust of _____

② Declaration of Trust

I, _____ , the grantor of this trust, declare and make this Living Trust on _____ (date).

This trust will be known as the _____ Living Trust.

I, _____ , will be trustee of this trust and any subtrusts created under this trust.

My marital status is that _____ .

③ Property Transfer

I transfer ownership to this trust of all of the assets which are listed on the attached Schedule of Assets of Living Trust, which is specifically made a part of this trust. I reserve the right to add or delete any of these assets at any time. In addition, I will prepare a separate Deed, Assignment, or any other documents necessary to carry out such transfers. Any additions or deletions to the Schedule of Assets of Living Trust must be written, notarized, and attached to this document to be valid.

④ Grantor's Rights

Until I die, I retain all rights to all income, profits, and control of the trust property. If my principal residence is transferred to this trust, I retain the right to possess and occupy it for my life, rent-free and without charge. I will remain liable for all taxes, insurance, maintenance, related costs, and expenses. The rights that I retain are intended to give me a beneficial interest in my principal residence such that I do not lose any eligibility that I may have for a state homestead exemption for which I am otherwise qualified.

⑤ Successor Trustee

Upon my death or if it is certified by a licensed physician that I am physically or mentally unable to manage this trust and my financial affairs, then I appoint _____ (name)

of_____ (ad-
dress), as Successor Trustee, to serve without bond and without compensation. If this
successor trustee is not surviving or otherwise unable to serve, I appoint _____
_____ (name), of _____
_____ (address), as Alternate Successor Trustee, also to serve without bond
and without compensation. The successor trustee or alternate successor trustee shall
not be liable for any actions taken in good faith. References to "trustee" in this document
shall include any successor or alternate successor trustees.

⑥ Trustee's Powers

In addition to any powers, authority, and discretion granted by law, I grant the trustee any
and all powers to perform any acts, in his or her sole discretion and without court approval,
for the management and distribution of this trust and any subtrusts created by this trust. I
intend the trustee to have the same power and authority to manage and distribute the trust
assets as an individual owner has over his or her own wholly-owned property.

⑦ Additional Trustee Powers

The trustee's powers include, but are not limited to: the power to sell trust property, borrow
money, and encumber that property, specifically including trust real estate, by mortgage,
deed of trust, or other method; the power to manage trust real estate as if the trustee were
the absolute owner of it, including the power to lease or grant options to lease the property,
make repairs or alterations, and insure against loss; the power to sell or grant options for
the sale or exchange of any trust property, including stocks, bonds, and any other form of
security; the power to invest trust property in property of any kind, including but not limited
to bonds, notes, mortgages, and stocks; the power to receive additional property from any
source and add to any trust created by this trust; the power to employ and pay reasonable
fees to accountants, lawyers, or investment consultants for information or advice relating to
the trust; the power to deposit and hold trust funds in both interest-bearing and non-interest-
bearing accounts; the power to deposit funds in bank or other accounts uninsured by FDIC
coverage; the power to enter into electronic fund transfer or safe deposit arrangements
with financial institutions; the power to continue any business of the grantor; the power to
institute or defend legal actions concerning the trust or grantor's affairs; and the power to
execute any document necessary to administer any children's trust created in this trust.

⑧ Incapacitation

Should the successor trustee or alternate successor trustee assume management of this
trust during the lifetime of the grantor, the successor trustee or alternate successor trustee

shall manage the trust solely for the proper health care, support, maintenance, comfort, and/or welfare of the grantor, in accordance with the grantor's accustomed manner of living.

⑨ Termination of Trust

Upon my death, this trust shall become irrevocable. The successor trustee shall then pay my valid debts, last expenses, and estate taxes from the assets of this trust. The successor trustee shall then distribute the remaining trust assets in the manner shown on the attached Schedule of Beneficiaries of Living Trust which is specifically made a part of this trust, subject to the provisions of any children's trust which is created by this document. I reserve the right to add and/or delete any beneficiaries at any time. Any additions or deletions to the Schedule of Beneficiaries of Living Trust must be written, notarized, and attached to this document to be valid.

⑩ Survivorship

All beneficiaries named in the Schedule of Beneficiaries of Living Trust must survive me by thirty (30) days to receive any gift under this living trust. If any beneficiary and I should die simultaneously, I shall be conclusively presumed to have survived that beneficiary for purposes of this living trust.

⑪ Amendments and Revocations

I reserve the right to amend any or all of this trust at any time. The amendments must be written, notarized, and attached to this document to be valid. I also reserve the right to revoke this trust at any time. A revocation of this trust must be written, notarized, and attached to this document to be valid.

⑫ Governing Law

This trust, containing _____ pages, was created on the date noted above and will be governed under the laws of the State of _____ .

⑬ Signature

_____
Signature of Grantor

_____
Printed Name of Grantor

⑭ Notary Acknowledgment

State of _____
County of _____

On _____ , _____ came before me personally
and, under oath, stated that he or she is the person described in the above document and he
or she signed the above document in my presence. I declare under penalty of perjury that the
person whose name is subscribed to this instrument appears to be of sound mind and under
no duress, fraud, or undue influence.

_____
Notary Public
In and for the County of _____
State of _____
My commission expires _____   Notary Seal

Completing Your Schedule of Assets of Living Trust Form

On this form, you will include a listing of all of the property that you wish to transfer into the trust. This document should be attached to the living trust when completed. It is relatively simple to complete. Simply fill in the title information (name and date of trust) and then carefully list the property that you have chosen to include in the trust.

Please refer to the Property Questionnaire in Chapter 3 that you completed to be certain that you include all of the property that you desire to be held in trust.

Always describe the property in as detailed and clear a manner as possible. In your description of the property, you should be as specific and precise as possible. For land, it is suggested that you use the description exactly as shown on the deed to the property. For personal property, be certain that your description clearly differentiates your gift from any other property.

Very Important Note: If the particular asset that you list on this Schedule has any type of ownership document, such as a title, deed, stock certificate, or similar document, you must also transfer the ownership of the asset to the trust by completing a new deed, title, or other transfer paperwork. Simply listing the asset on this form does not transfer it to the trust if an ownership document is required. For those items of personal property for which no such ownership document exists (such as a stereo system, appliances, antiques, etc.), the listing on the Schedule of Assets of Living Trust will effectively transfer the ownership to the Trust.

This Schedule of Assets will become a part of the living trust. It should be stapled to the original of the trust document. Any time that any changes are made to the assets that are to be included in the living trust, this schedule must be changed and an Amendment to living trust form should be filled out as explained in Chapter 10.

> ## ⚡ Warning!
>
> If any asset that you list on your Schedule of Assets also has any type of ownership documents, you must also transfer the actual ownership of the asset by completing the appropriate paperwork for such transfer.

Instructions for Schedule of Assets of Living Trust

This form should be used to list the assets of a single person or an individual spouse who is setting up an individual living trust. Please remember that any assets that have ownership documents must be transferred to the ownership of the trust using the appropriate method of documentary transfer (such as a deed or title).

Please refer to your Property Questionnaire to determine which property you desire to transfer to your living trust. The listing of property on this Schedule will effectively transfer the ownership of the property to the trust, unless an additional transfer of ownership document is necessary. Even if such additional paperwork is necessary, you should list the property on this Schedule of Assets. Please refer to the property instructions in Chapters 3 for details of how to list the property.

To complete this form, you will need the following information:

①   Date of assignment
      Full name of grantor
      Name of living trust, and
      Date original living trust was created
②   Full description of property to be transferred to the trust
③   Your signature and printed name (do not sign unless in front of a notary public)
④   The notary acknowledgment section (to be completed by notary public)

Schedule of Assets of Living Trust

①   This Schedule of Assets of Living Trust is made on _____ (date),
by _____ , the grantor, to the _____
_____ Living Trust dated _____ .

②   All grantor's right, title, and interest in the following property shall be the property of the trust:

③

_____
Signature of Grantor

_____
Printed Name of Grantor

④   Notary Acknowledgment

State of _____
County of _____

On _____ , _____ came before me personally
and, under oath, stated that he or she is the person described in the above document and he
or she signed the above document in my presence. I declare under penalty of perjury that the
person whose name is subscribed to this instrument appears to be of sound mind and under
no duress, fraud, or undue influence.

_____
Notary Public
In and for the County of _____
State of _____
My commission expires _____   Notary Seal

Completing Your Schedule of Beneficiaries of Living Trust Form

Using this form, you will direct how your property will be distributed by your Successor Trustee upon your death. You will select your beneficiaries, alternate beneficiaries, and the property that each of them will receive. Please refer to both your Schedule of Assets and back to your beneficiary questionnaire that you completed in Chapter 4 to prepare this form. The information that you compiled for that questionnaire will be your guide for preparing your living trust, both in terms of being certain that you have disposed of all of your Trust assets, and in terms of being certain that you have left gifts to all those persons or organizations that you wished to. Using the clauses in this section, you will be able to prepare a living trust in which you may:

☿ Toolkit Tip!

Make sure that you have your property questionnaire and your beneficiary questionnaire with you as you complete your Schedule of Beneficiaries form.

• Make specific gifts of cash, real estate, or personal property to anyone
• Make specific gifts of certain shares of your trust assets
• Make a gift of the rest (residue) of your assets to anyone

Specific Gifts Clause: Use this type of clause to provide specific gifts to your beneficiaries. If chosen, add this clause or clauses after the phrase "Upon the death of the grantor of the trust and the payment of all debts, taxes, and liabilities of the grantor, the Successor Trustee shall then distribute the remaining assets of the trust as follows:

To my [relationship], [name of beneficiary], or if not surviving, to my [relationship], [name of alternate beneficiary], the following trust assets shall be distributed:"

For making specific gifts, use as many of the "To my…" paragraphs as is necessary to complete your chosen gifts. In these paragraphs, you may make any type of gift that you wish, either a cash gift, a gift of a specific piece of personal property or real estate, or a specific share of your total trust estate. If you wish to give some of your trust estate in the form of portions of the total, it is recommended to use fractional portions. For example, if you wish to leave your trust estate in equal shares to two persons, name both parties after "To my…" and state "one-half of my total trust estate to each party."

Although none of the living trusts in this book contain a specific clause which states that you give one person your entire trust estate, you may make such a gift using this clause by simply stating after "The following trust assets shall be distributed:…"

"My entire trust estate"

⚡ Warning!

Any asset that you list on your Schedule of Beneficiaries must also have been listed on your Schedule of Assets form. You must also, if necessary, have completed the appropriate paperwork for the transfer of ownership to the trust.

Be sure that you do not attempt to give any other gifts. However, you should still include the residuary clause in your living trust, which is explained on the following pages.

You may only give away property that the trust itself owns. Be certain that any property included in any of the gift clauses is also included on your Schedule of Assets and has been effectively transferred to the Trust. In your description of the property, you should be as specific and precise as possible. For land, it is suggested that you use the description exactly as shown on the deed to the property. For personal property, be certain that your description clearly differentiates your gift from any other property. Use serial numbers, colors, or any other descriptive words to clearly indicate the exact nature of the gift. For cash gifts, specifically indicate the amount of the gift. For gifts of securities, state the amount of shares and the name of the company. You may add simple conditions to the gifts that you make, if you desire. Complex conditions, however, are not possible in this clause, and immoral or illegal conditions are not acceptable.

Be sure to clearly identify the beneficiary and alternate beneficiary by full name. You can also name joint beneficiaries, such as several children, if you choose. The space provided for an identification of the relationship of the beneficiary can be simply a descriptive phrase like "my wife," "my brother-in-law," or "my best friend." It does not mean that the beneficiary must be related to you personally.

The choice of alternate beneficiary is for the purpose of allowing you to designate someone to receive the gift if your first choice to receive the gift dies before you do (or, in the case of an organization chosen as primary beneficiary, is no longer in business). In this or any of the other gift clauses, your choice for alternate beneficiary may be one or more persons or an organization. It is recommended to always specifically name your beneficiary(s), rather than using a description only, such as "my children." In addition, you may delete the alternate beneficiary choice and substitute the words "*the residue*" instead. The result of this change will be that if your primary beneficiary dies before you do, your gift will pass under your residuary clause, which is discussed below. If additional gifts are desired, simply photocopy an additional page.

Residuary Clause: Although not a technical legal requirement, a residuary clause is included in every living trust in this book. With it, you will choose the person, persons, or organization to receive anything not covered by other clauses of your living trust. Even if you feel that you have given away everything that your trust owns under other clauses of your living trust, this can be a very important clause.

☆Toolkit Tip!

Recall that it is always recommended to prepare a will, even if you will be using a living trust in your estate plan.

If, for any reason, any other gifts under your living trust are not able to completed, this clause goes into effect. For example, if a beneficiary refuses to accept your gift or the chosen beneficiary has died and no alternate was selected or both the beneficiary and alternate has died, the gift is put back into your trust estate and will pass under the residuary clause. If there is no residuary clause included, any property not disposed of could potentially be forfeited to the state.

In addition, you may use this clause to give all of your estate (except your specific gifts) to one or more persons. For example: you make specific gifts of $1,000.00 to a sister and a car to a friend. By then naming your spouse as the residuary clause beneficiary, you will have gifted everything in your trust estate to your spouse—except the $1,000.00 and the car. You could then name your children, in equal shares, as the alternate residuary beneficiaries. In this manner, if your spouse were to die first, your children would then equally share your entire trust estate—except the $1,000.00 and the car.

Be sure to clearly identify the beneficiary by full name. The space provided for an identification of the relationship of the beneficiary can be simply a descriptive phrase like "my wife," or "my brother-in-law," or "my best friend." It does not mean that the beneficiary must be related to you personally.

After you have completed your Schedule of Beneficiaries of Living Trust form, you should revisit your living trust and the Asset and Beneficiary Schedules whenever there is any significant change in your life or circumstances. If you are married, divorced, have or adopt any children, or sell, transfer, or otherwise become dispossessed of any of the assets mentioned in your living trust schedules, you should make certain to make the appropriate changes in the trust itself, any schedules that are impacted, and any ownership documents relating to property that make have been affected.

Instructions for Schedule of Beneficiaries of Living Trust

This form should be used to list the beneficiaries of a single person or an individual spouse who is setting up an individual Living Trust.

Please refer to your Beneficiary Questionnaire to determine which property you desire to leave to which beneficiaries of your Living Trust. Please refer to the property and beneficiary instructions in Chapters 3 and 4 for details of how to list the property and beneficiaries.

To complete this form, you will need the following information:

① Date of assignment
   Full name of grantor
   Name of Living Trust, and
   Date original Living Trust was created

② For each item of property, complete the following:
   Name of beneficiary
   Relationship of beneficiary
   Name of alternate beneficiary (if main beneficiary has died first)
   Relationship of alternate beneficiary, and
   Full description of property to be transferred.

③ For your residuary clause, complete the following:
   Name of residuary beneficiary
   Relationship of residuary beneficiary
   Name of alternate residuary beneficiary (if main beneficiary has died first), and relationship of alternate residuary beneficiary

④ No information needed

⑤ Your signature and printed name (do not sign unless in front of a notary public)

⑥ The notary acknowledgment section (to be completed by notary public)

Schedule of Beneficiaries of Living Trust

① This Schedule of Beneficiaries is made on _____ (date), by
_____ , the grantor, to the _____
_____ Living Trust dated _____ .

② Upon the death of the grantor of the trust and the payment of all debts, taxes, and liabilities of the grantor, the Successor Trustee shall distribute the remaining assets of the Trust as follows:

To _____ (name), my _____
(relationship), or if not surviving, to _____ (name), my __
_____ (relationship), the following trust assets shall be distributed:

To _____ (name), my _____
(relationship), or if not surviving, to _____ (name), my __
_____ (relationship), the following trust assets shall be distributed:

To _____ (name), my _____
(relationship), or if not surviving, to _____ (name), my __
_____ (relationship), the following trust assets shall be distributed:

To _____ (name), my _____
(relationship), or if not surviving, to _____ (name), my __
_____ (relationship), the following trust assets shall be distributed:

To _____ (name), my _____
(relationship), or if not surviving, to _____ (name), my __
_____ (relationship), the following trust assets shall be distributed:

③ All the rest and residue of the trust assets shall be distributed to _____ _____ (name), my _____ (relationship), or if not surviving, to _____ (name), my _____ (relationship).

④ If any Beneficiary named on this Schedule of Beneficiaries is subject to the terms of any children's trust in the main trust document to which this Schedule pertains, then any property distributed to such Beneficiary shall be subject to the terms of any such children's trust.

⑤

_____
Signature of Grantor

_____
Printed Name of Grantor

⑥ Notary Acknowledgment

State of _____
County of _____

On _____ , _____ came before me personally and, under oath, stated that he or she is the person described in the above document and he or she signed the above document in my presence. I declare under penalty of perjury that the person whose name is subscribed to this instrument appears to be of sound mind and under no duress, fraud, or undue influence.

_____
Notary Public In and for the County of _____ ,

State of _____

My commission expires _____   Notary Seal

Instructions for Assignment to Living Trust

This form may be used if an assignment of ownership of personal property to a living trust is necessary.

An assignment of property is used for the transfer of personal property to the trust. Recall that you must complete transfer paperwork if the property in question is real estate, patents, copyrights, trademarks, motor vehicles, boats, stocks, bonds, or some other form of property that has ownership documents (such as a deed or title). For property with no ownership documentation, generally, the listing of property to be held by the trust on the Schedule of Trust Assets effectively transfers ownership of property to the trust. Thus, an assignment of property is not normally a legal necessity. However, some businesses or financial institutions may require this particular document to verify that the property has been technically "assigned" to the trust. In addition, this form is also necessary for assigning patents, copyrights, or trademarks to the trust. If such occasions arise, you may use this document.

To complete this form, you will need the following information:

①　Date of assignment
　　Full name of grantor
　　Name of Living Trust, and
　　Date original Living Trust was created
②　Full description of property to be assigned to the trust
③　No information needed
④　No information needed
⑤　Your signature and printed name (do not sign unless in front of a notary public)
⑥　The notary acknowledgment section (to be completed by notary public)

Assignment to Living Trust

① This Assignment to Living Trust is made on _____ (date) , between _____ , the grantor, and the _____ _____ Living Trust dated _____ .

② The grantor transfers and conveys possession, ownership, and all right, title, and interest in the following property to the Living Trust:

③ The grantor warrants that he or she owns this property and that he or she has the full authority to transfer and convey the property to the Living Trust. Grantor also warrants that the property is transferred free and clear of all liens, indebtedness, or liabilities.

④ Signed and delivered to the Living Trust on the above date.

⑤ _____

Signature of Grantor

_____

Printed Name of Grantor

⑥ Notary Acknowledgment

State of _____
County of _____

On _____ , _____ came before me personally and, under oath, stated that he or she is the person described in the above document and he or she signed the above document in my presence. I declare under penalty of perjury that the person whose name is subscribed to this instrument appears to be of sound mind and under no duress, fraud, or undue influence.

_____

Notary Public
In and for the County of _____-
State of _____
My commission expires _____   Notary Seal

Instructions for Registration of Living Trust

Residents of a number of states are required to register the main details regarding the existence of a Living Trust with their local courts when a trustee takes authority under the terms of the trust. Please check the Appendix listing for your state to determine if such registration is required in your state. Note also that even though such registration may technically be required for your state, there are generally no penalties or consequences for failing to do so.

①   Full name of trustee
      Name of Living Trust
      Date original Living Trust was created, and
      Full name of grantor of trust
②   No information needed.
③   Your signature and printed name (do not sign unless in front of a notary public)
④   The Notary Acknowledgment section (to be completed by notary public)

Registration of Living Trust

① I, _____, am Trustee of the _____ _____ Living Trust, which was created on the date of _____ , by the grantor, _____ .

② I hereby acknowledge that I accept the office of Trustee of the Trust, and am now acting as Trustee of the Trust.

③

_____
Signature of Trustee

_____
Printed Name of Trustee

④ Notary Acknowledgment

State of _____
County of _____

On _____ , _____ came before me personally and, under oath, stated that he or she is the person described in the above document and he or she signed the above document in my presence. I declare under penalty of perjury that the person whose name is subscribed to this instrument appears to be of sound mind and under no duress, fraud, or undue influence.

_____
Notary Public
In and for the County of _____
State of _____
My commission expires _____   Notary Seal

Instructions for New York Notice of Assignment of Property to Living Trust

This form may be used by residents of New York to provide notice that real or personal property has been assigned to the trust. You should attach a copy of your completed and notarized Schedule of Assets of Living Trust to this form.

To complete this form, you will need the following information:

①   Full name of grantor
       Name of Living Trust, and
       Date original Living Trust was created

②   Your signature and printed name (do not sign unless in front of a notary public)

③   The notary acknowledgment section (to be completed by notary public)

New York Notice of Assignment of Property to Living Trust

① I, _____ , as grantor, hereby provide Notice that all of the property listed on the attached **Schedule of Assets of Living Trust** has been transferred to the _____ Living Trust on the date of _____ .

②

_____
Signature of Grantor

_____
Printed Name of Grantor

③ Notary Acknowledgment

State of _____
County of _____

On _____ , _____ came before me personally and, under oath, stated that he or she is the **person** described in the above document and he or she signed the above document in my presence. I declare under penalty of perjury that the person whose name is subscribed to this instrument appears to be of sound mind and under no duress, fraud, or undue influence.

_____
Notary Public
In and for the County of _____
State of _____
My commission expires _____   Notary Seal

Instructions for Affidavit of Assumption of Duties by Successor Trustee

This document may be used if your successor trustee is having any difficulty with a business or financial institution accepting his or her authority to act on behalf of the trust, after the death of the original trustee. Some may insist on written verification that states that the successor trustee actually has the power to act on behalf of the trust. If this is the case, this form should satisfy those institutions or businesses. The successor trustee will need to attach a certified copy of the grantor's death certificate to this form.

①   Date of Affidavit, and
       Full name of successor trustee
②   Date of creation of living trust
       Full name of grantor
       Name of living trust, and
       Full name of successor trustee
③   Date of death of grantor, and
       Name of grantor
④   No information needed
⑤   Your signature and printed name (do not sign unless in front of a notary public)
⑥   The notary acknowledgment section (to be completed by notary public)

Affidavit of Assumption of Duties by Successor Trustee

① On this date, _____ , I, _____ ,
being of legal age and being duly sworn, declare the following:

② On the date of _____ , the grantor, _____
_____ , created the _____
Living Trust. The Living Trust provides that upon the death of the grantor, I, _____
_____ , become Trustee of the Trust.

③ On the date of _____ , the grantor, _____
_____ , died, as established in the certified copy of the Certificate of
Death, which is attached to this Affidavit.

④ I hereby accept the office of Trustee of the Trust, and am now acting as Trustee of the
Trust.

⑤ _____
Signature of Trustee

_____
Printed Name of Trustee

⑥ Notary Acknowledgment

State of _____
County of _____

On _____ , _____ came before me personally
and, under oath, stated that he or she is the person described in the above document and he
or she signed the above document in my presence. I declare under penalty of perjury that the
person whose name is subscribed to this instrument appears to be of sound mind and under
no duress, fraud, or undue influence.

_____
Notary Public
In and for the County of _____
State of _____
My commission expires _____   Notary Seal

215

Chapter 10

Changing a Living Trust

In this chapter, instructions will be given on when and how to change your living trust and how to revoke your living trust. It is most important to follow these instructions carefully should you desire to make any changes to your living trust. Failure to follow these instructions and an attempt to change your living trust by such methods as crossing out a name or penciling in an addition could have the disastrous effect of voiding portions of, or perhaps even your entire, living trust. Again, these instructions are not difficult to follow, but are very important to insure that your living trust remains legally valid.

Amending a Living Trust

Regarding any potential changes which you may wish to make in your living trust at a later date, you should periodically review the provisions of your living trust, keeping in mind the following items as they relate to your present situation:

- Have there been any substantial changes in your personal wealth?
- Have there been any changes in your ownership of any property mentioned in your living trust or schedules?
- Have any of the beneficiaries named in your living trust died or fallen into your disfavor?
- Are any of the persons whom you named as successor or

☼ **Toolkit Tip!**

You should review the terms of your living trust whenever there is a substantial change in your life or circumstances, such as marriage, divorce, child birth or adoption, or a change in the ownership of any of the trust assets.

alternative successor trustee in your living trust no longer willing or able to serve?

- Have you changed the state of your residence?
- Have you been married since the date of your living trust?
- Have you been divorced since the date of your living trust?
- Have you had any children since the date of your living trust?
- Have you adopted any children since the date of your living trust?
- Do you simply wish to make any corrections, deletions, or additions to any provisions in your living trust or schedules?

If any of these matters apply, you will need to change your living trust accordingly. Although it is possible to completely rewrite your living trust to take account of any of these changes, an easier method is to prepare and sign a written Amendment to a Living Trust. Please bear in mind that all of the formalities surrounding the signing of your original living trust must again be followed for any such changes to your living trust to be valid.

> ⚡ **Warning!**
> Do *not* attempt to change your living trust by making corrections on the form itself. You must use an Amendment of Living Trust form.

Never attempt to change any portions of your living trust by any other method. For example, do not attempt to add provisions in the margin of your living trust, either by typing or writing them in. Do not attempt to cross out any portions of your living trust. These methods are not acceptable methods for the alteration of a living trust, and could subject your living trust to a court battle to determine its subsequent validity.

Following these instructions, you will find an Amendment to Living Trust form. Complete this forms using the information requested as shown on the instructions page.

When you have completed the form and typed or printed it out, sign the form in the presence of a Notary Public and make certain that you store the original Amendment with the original of your living trust. You should also make certain that a copy of any amendment is provided to anyone who has a copy of your original living trust, such as your successor trustee. Make sure that you label the copy clearly as a "copy".

If you delete property from your Schedule of Assets of Living

⚡Toolkit Tip!

Make sure that any changes that you make to property ownership with an Amendment to Living Trust are also made on any ownership documents for the property involved.

Trust, you must be certain to officially transfer ownership of the property back to yourself using the appropriate ownership documentation as detailed in the previous chapter. And, of course, if you add property to your Schedule of Assets of Living Trusts, which requires additional ownership transfer documentation, you must complete these documents as soon as possible.

After the Amendment to Living Trust form, you will find a Revocation of Living Trust form. To complete this form, simply fill in the information as shown on the instruction page.

Instructions for Amendment to Living Trust

This form is for use by anyone who has created an individual living trust, whether or not he or she is married or has children. You may use this form for changes to the original Trust, Schedules of Assets, or Beneficiaries. For changes to the trust or schedules, you may use the following language in section of the form labeled ②:

- "The following wording is added to the Trust (or Schedule of Assets or Schedule of Beneficiaries) [here insert the added material]"
  OR
- "The following wording is deleted from the Trust (or Schedule of Assets or Schedule of Beneficiaries) [here insert the deleted material]"

To complete this form, you will need the following information:

①   Date of amendment
        Full name of grantor
        Name of living trust, and
        Date original living trust was created
②   Additions or deletions to trust, asset, or beneficiary schedules
③   No information needed
④   Your signature and printed name (do not sign unless in front of a notary public)
⑤   The notary acknowledgment section (to be completed by notary public)

Amendment to Living Trust

① This Amendment to Living Trust is made on _____ (date), by
_____ , the grantor, to the _____
_____ Living Trust dated _____ .

② The grantor modifies the original Trust as follows:

③ All other terms and conditions of the original Living Trust remain in effect without modification. This Amendment, including the original Living Trust, is the entire Living Trust as of this date. The grantor has signed this Amendment on the date specified at the beginning of this Amendment.

④

_____
Signature of Grantor

_____
Printed Name of Grantor

⑤ Notary Acknowledgment

State of _____
County of _____

On _____ , _____ came before me personally and, under oath, stated that he or she is the person described in the above document and he or she signed the above document in my presence. I declare under penalty of perjury that the person whose name is subscribed to this instrument appears to be of sound mind and under no duress, fraud, or undue influence.

_____
Notary Public
In and for the County of _____
State of _____
My commission expires _____   Notary Seal

Instructions for Revoking Your Living Trust

At some point in the future, you may desire to cancel or revoke your living trust entirely. Until you die, you have the right to revoke your living trust at any time.

When you have completed the form and retyped or printed it out, sign the form in the presence of a notary public and make certain that you store the original where you had stored the original of your living trust. You should also make certain that a copy of any revocation is provided to anyone who has a copy of your original living trust, such as your successor trustee. You should also then destroy the original and all copies of your living trust or cross out each page of the forms and mark "REVOKED" across them in bold print.

If you entirely revoke your living trust, you must be certain to officially transfer ownership of any trust assets back to yourself using the appropriate ownership documentation as explained in the previous chapter.

To complete this form, you will need the following information:

①   Date of revocation
       Full name of grantor
       Name of living trust, and
       Date original living trust was created
②   Your signature and printed name (do not sign unless in front of a notary public)
③   The Notary Acknowledgment section (to be completed by notary public)

Revocation of Living Trust

① On this date _____ , I, _____ ,
the grantor, fully and completely revoke the _____
Living Trust dated _____ . All property that is held in trust shall
be returned to the me, the grantor, as my sole property.

②

_____
Signature of Grantor

_____
Printed Name of Grantor

③ Notary Acknowledgment

State of _____
County of _____

On _____ , _____ came before me personally
and, under oath, stated that he or she is the person described in the above document and he
or she signed the above document in my presence. I declare under penalty of perjury that the
person whose name is subscribed to this instrument appears to be of sound mind and under
no duress, fraud, or undue influence.

_____
Notary Public
In and for the County of _____
State of _____
My commission expires _____   Notary Seal

Chapter 11

Preparing a Living Will

In this chapter, you will be given instructions on how to prepare a *living will,* a document that states your desires regarding end-of-life medical care. A living will is a relatively new legal document that has been made necessary due to recent technological advances in the field of medicine. These advances can allow for the continued existence of a person on advanced life support systems long after any normal semblance of "life," as many people consider it, has ceased.

The inherent problem that is raised by this type of extraordinary medical life support is that the person whose life is being artificially continued by such means may not wish to be kept alive beyond what they may consider to be the proper time for their life to end. However, since a person in such condition has no method of communicating their wishes to the medical or legal authorities in charge, a living will was developed that allows one to make these important decisions in advance of the situation.

The purpose of a living will is to provide doctors and other health care workers with clear directions regarding how you would like your medical care handled toward the end of your life. A living will makes it possible for you to specify, in advance, exactly what your preferences are regarding the use of life-sustaining medical procedures if you are ever in a terminal medical condition or in a vegetative state, and are unable to

> ⊘ **Definition:**
>
> **Terminal Condition:** An incurable medical condition that will cause imminent death and where the use of life support systems will only prolong the moment of death.

Definition:

Vegetative State:

A medical condition of complete and irreversible loss of brain function; a permanent coma.

Warning!

VERY IMPORTANT: You should read the provisions of your proposed living will very carefully, as they authorize actions that will *end your life*. If you do not fully understand the terms of your living will, you should consult an attorney.

give such directions yourself. *Terminal* is generally defined as an incurable condition that will cause imminent death such that the use of life-sustaining procedures only serve to prolong the moment of death. Likewise, a *vegetative state* is generally defined as a complete and irreversible loss of cognitive brain function and consciousness. Thus, a living will comes into effect only when there is no medical hope for a recovery from a particular injury or illness which will prove fatal or leave one in a permanent and irreversible coma.

As more and more advances are made in the medical field in terms of the ability to prevent "clinical" death, the difficult situations envisioned by a living will are destined to occur more often. The legal acceptance of a living will is currently at the forefront of law. Living wills are accepted in all states, but they must adhere to certain legal conditions. A few states do not currently have specific legislation providing express statutory recognition of living wills, but courts in those states have ruled that living wills are legally valid. Although a living will does not address all possible contingencies regarding terminally-ill patients, it does provide a written declaration for the individual to make known her or his decisions on life-prolonging procedures. A living will declares your wishes not to be kept alive by artificial or mechanical means if you are suffering from a terminal condition and your death would be imminent without the use of such artificial means. It provides a legally-binding written set of instructions regarding your wishes about this important matter.

In most states, in order to qualify for the use of a living will, you must meet the following criteria:

• You must be at least 19 years of age
• You must be of "sound mind"
• You must be able to comprehend the nature of your action in signing such a document

A living will becomes valid when it has been properly signed and witnessed. However, it is very important to remember that as long as you are capable of making decisions and giving directions regarding your medical care, your stated wishes must be followed–*not* those directions that are contained in your living will. Your living will only comes into force when you are in a terminal or vegetative condition, with no likelihood of recovery, and are unable to provide directions yourself. Until that time, *you*—and not your living will—will provide the directions for your health care. Generally, a licensed physician is required to determine when your condition has become terminal or vegetative with no likelihood of recovering.

There are 3 separate methods for preparing a living will in this book. First, this chapter contains a general, standardized living will (this standard living will is also contained on the CD). Next, the Forms-on-CD that accompanied this book also contains state-specific living will forms that have been taken directly from the most recent legislation regarding living wills in each state. A few states do not currently have specific legislation providing express statutory recognition of living wills. For those states, a living will has been prepared by legal professionals to comply with the basic requirements that courts in that state or other states have found important. In such states, be assured that courts, health care professionals, and physicians will be guided by this expression of your desires concerning life support as expressed in the living will prepared using this book and CD.

Finally, a living will is also part of the state-specific advance health care directives that are explained in Chapter 14 and these forms are also contained on the enclosed CD. You may use either the general living will form or the state-specific statutory form for your state explained in this chapter, or you may choose to use the living will in the advance health care directive for your state. Please compare your state's specific living will form in the advance health care directives with the standardized form in this chapter and on the CD and select the appropriate form that you feel best expresses your wishes regarding health care if you are in a terminal or vegetative condition.

Typical Living Will Provisions

Nearly all states have passed legislation setting up a statutorily-accepted living will form. Those states that have not expressed a preference for a specific type of living will have, nevertheless,

> ### ☼ Toolkit Tip!
>
> This book provides 3 methods for completing a living will: 1) a standardized living will, 2) a state-specific living will (on the CD), and 3) a living will that is part of a state-specific advance health care directive (also on the CD).

⛭ Toolkit Tip!

You should usually prepare a living will and a health care power of attorney. Note that the advance health care directives explained in Chapter 14 contain both of these important forms.

accepted living wills that adhere to general legal requirements. There are many different types of living wills, from very brief statements such as the following from the State of Illinois:

> "If at any time I should have an incurable and irreversible injury, disease, or illness judged to be a terminal condition by my attending physician who has personally examined me and has determined that my death is imminent except for death-delaying procedures, I direct that such procedures which would only prolong the dying process be withheld or withdrawn, and that I be permitted to die naturally with only the administration of medication, sustenance, or the performance of any medical procedure deemed necessary by my attending physician to provide me with comfort care."

to lengthy and elaborate multi-page forms with detailed and very specific instructions. All of the various state forms try to assure that a person's own wishes are followed regarding health care decisions. Many states have drafted their legislation with the intention that people prepare both a living will and a health care power of attorney (or similar form) which appoints a person of your choosing to act on your behalf in making health care decisions when you are unable to make such decisions for yourself. It is advisable that you prepare both of these advance health care forms in order to cover most, if not all, eventualities that may arise regarding your health care in difficult situations. Health care powers of attorney are explained in Chapter 12.

In general, the purpose of your living will is to convey your wishes regarding life-prolonging treatment and artificially provided nutrition and hydration if you no longer have the capacity to make your own decisions, and have either a terminal condition, or become permanently unconscious. You should very carefully think about your own personal desires should either of these conditions arise. Please also note that the basic living will included in this book also contains a release of medical information under the federal HIPAA guidelines for privacy of medical information.

You should also read through this statement concerning the importance of the decisions that you make in a living will (This notice is also part of the living will itself):

Notice to the Adult Signing this Document:

This is an important legal document. This document directs the medical treatment you are to receive in the event you are unable to participate in your own medical decisions and you are in a terminal condition. This document may state what kind of treatment you want or do not want to receive. This document can control whether you live or die. Prepare this document carefully. If you use this form, read it completely.

You may want to seek professional help to make sure the form does what you intend and is completed without mistakes. This document will remain valid and in effect until and unless you revoke it. Review this document periodically to make sure it continues to reflect your wishes. You may amend or revoke this document at any time by notifying your physician and other health-care providers. You should give copies of this document to your physician and your family. This form is entirely optional. If you choose to use this form, please note that the form provides signature lines for you, the three witnesses whom you have selected and a notary public.

> **ϒ Toolkit Tip!**
>
> If you decide to use a state-specific living will (found on the CD), please use the instructions outlined on the following pages and also in the Introduction for completing these forms.

Finally, the Federal Patient Self-Determination Act encourages all people to make their own decisions about the type of medical care they wish to receive. This act also requires all health care agencies (hospitals, long-term care facilities, and home health agencies) receiving Medicare and Medicaid reimbursement to recognize a living will and/or health care power of attorney as advance directives that indicate the patient's wishes. Under this Act, all health care agencies must ask you if you have advance directives and must give you materials with information about your rights under state law. The living will in this chapter and/or the state-specific living wills on the CD must be recognized by all health care agencies.

Instructions for Preparing and Signing a Living Will

If you desire that your life not be prolonged artificially when there is no reasonable chance for recovery and death is imminent, please follow the instructions below for completion of your living will. The entire following form is should be used if you choose to use this form. It has been adapted to be valid in all states. Courts, health care professionals, members of your family, and physicians will be guided by this expression of your desires concerning life support. Please consult the Appendix for further information regarding recognition of living wills in your state.

1. Make a photo-copy or printout a copy of the entire living will form from this chapter or the state-specific living will form from the Forms-on-CD. Using the photo-copy as a worksheet, please fill in the correct information in the appropriate blanks as noted below:

    ① Name of person making living will
    ② Name of person making living will
    ③ State whose laws will govern the living will
    ④ Any additional directions, terms or conditions that you wish to add
    ⑤ Number of pages of entire living will (fill in after printing out final copy)
    ⑥ Date of signing of living will (fill in upon signing)
    ⑦ Your signature and printed name (do not sign unless in front of a notary public)
    ⑧ Date, signatures and printed names of witnesses to signing of living will
    ⑨ The notary acknowledgment section (to be completed by notary public)

2. On clean, white, 8 1/2 x 11" paper, type or printout the entire living will exactly as shown with your information added. Carefully re-read this original living will to be certain that it exactly expresses your desires on this very important matter. When you have a clean, clear original version, staple all of the pages together in the upper left-hand corner. Do not yet sign this document or fill in the date.

3. You should now assemble two or three witnesses and a Notary Public to witness your signature. Note that the standardized living will provides for three witnesses so that it will be legally valid in all states. Most of the state-specific living wills provide for only two witnesses, although some will require three. As noted on the document itself, these witnesses should have no connection with you from a health care or beneficiary standpoint (exception: see note following). Specifically, the witnesses must:

    • Be at least 19 years of age
    • Not be related to you in any manner: by blood, marriage, or adoption
    • Not be your attending physician, or a patient or employee of your attending physician; or a patient, physician, or employee of the health care facility in which you may be a patient. However, please see below.

- Not be entitled to any portion of your estate on your death under any laws of intestate succession, nor under your will or any codicil
- Have no claim against any portion of your estate on your death
- Not be directly financially responsible for your medical care
- Not have signed the living will for you, even at your direction
- Not be paid a fee for acting as a witness

Note: a few states have laws in effect regarding witnesses when the declarant is a patient in a nursing home, boarding facility, hospital, or skilled or intermediate health care facility. In those situation, it is advisable to have a patient ombudsman, patient advocate, or the director of the health care facility to act as the third witness to the signing of a living will. Please check the Appendix for your state's requirements.

4. In front of all of the witnesses and in front of the Notary Public, the following should take place in the order shown:

- You will then sign your living will at the end, exactly as your name is typewritten on your living will, where indicated, in ink using a pen.

- After you have signed, pass your living will to the first witness, who should sign where indicated and fill in his or her address.

- After the first witness has signed, have the living will passed to the second witness, who should also sign where indicated.

- If you are using a living will that requires a third witness, then after the second witness has signed, have the living will passed to the third and final witness, who also signs where indicated and fills in his or her address. Throughout this ceremony, you and all of the witnesses must remain together.

The final step is for the notary public to sign in the space indicated. When this step is completed, your living will is a valid legal document. Have several copies made and, if appropriate, deliver a copy to your attending physician to have placed in your medical records file. You may also desire to give a copy to the person you have chosen as the executor of your will (or successor trustee of your living trust), a copy to your clergy, and a copy to your spouse or other trusted relative.

Living Will Declaration and Directive to Physicians of

① _____

Notice to Adult Signing This Document: This is an important legal document. This document directs the medical treatment you are to receive in the event you are unable to participate in your own medical decisions and you are in a terminal condition. This document may state what kind of treatment you want or do not want to receive. This document can control whether you live or die. Prepare this document carefully. If you use this form, read it completely. You may want to seek professional help to make sure the form does what you intend and is completed without mistakes. This document will remain valid and in effect until and unless you revoke it. Review this document periodically to make sure it continues to reflect your wishes. You may amend or revoke this document at any time by notifying your physician and other health-care providers. You should give copies of this document to your physician and your family. This form is entirely optional. If you choose to use this form, please note that the form provides signature lines for you, the three witnesses whom you have selected and a notary public.

② I, _____ , being of sound mind, willfully and voluntarily make known my desire that my life not be artificially prolonged under the circumstances set forth below, and, ③ pursuant to any and all applicable laws in the State of _____ , I declare that:

If at any time I should have an incurable injury, disease, or illness which has been certified as a terminal condition by my attending physician and one additional physician, both of whom have personally examined me, and such physicians have determined that there can be no recovery from such condition and my death is imminent, and where the application of life prolonging procedures would serve only to artificially prolong the dying process, then:

I direct that such procedures be withheld or withdrawn, and that I be permitted to die naturally with only the administration of medication, the administration of nutrition and/or hydration, or the performance of any medical procedure deemed necessary to provide me with comfort, care, or to alleviate pain.

If at any time I should have been diagnosed as being in a persistent vegetative state which has been certified as incurable by my attending physician and one additional physician, both of whom have personally examined me, and such physicians have determined that there can be no recovery from such condition, and where the application of life prolonging procedures would serve only to artificially prolong the dying process, then:

I direct that such procedures be withheld or withdrawn, and that I be permitted to die naturally with only the administration of medication, the administration of nutrition and/or hydration, or the performance of any medical procedure deemed necessary to provide me with comfort, care, or to alleviate pain.

In the absence of my ability to give directions regarding my treatment in the above situations, including directions regarding the use of such life prolonging procedures, then:

It is my intention that this declaration shall be honored by my family, my physician, and any court of law, as the final expression of my legal right to refuse medical and surgical treatment. I declare that I fully accept the consequences for such refusal.

④ If I have any additional directions, I will state them here:

If I have also signed a Health Care Power of Attorney, Appointment of Health Care Agent, or Health Care Proxy, I direct the person who I have appointed with such instrument to follow the directions that I have made in this document. I intend for my agent to be treated as I would be with respect to my rights regarding the use and disclosure of my individually identifiable health information or other medical records. This release authority applies to any information governed by the Health Insurance Portability and Accountability Act of 1996 (aka HIPAA), 42 USC 1320d and 45 CFR 160-164.

If I am diagnosed as pregnant, this document shall have no force and effect during my pregnancy.

I understand the full importance of this declaration, and I am emotionally and mentally competent to make this declaration and Living Will. I also understand that I may revoke this document at any time.

⑤ I publish and sign this Living Will and Directive to Physicians, consisting of _____ ⑥ typewritten pages, on _____, 20_____ , and declare that I do so freely, for the purposes expressed, under no constraint or undue influence, and that I am of sound mind and of legal age.

⑦ _____
Declarant's Signature

_____
Printed Name of Declarant

⑧ On _____, 20_____, in the presence of all of us, the above-named Declarant published and signed this Living Will and Directive to Physicians, and then at the Declarant's request, and in the Declarant's presence, and in each other's presence, we all signed below as witnesses, and we each declare, under penalty of perjury, that, to the best of our knowledge:

1. The Declarant is personally known to me and, to the best of my knowledge, the Declarant signed this instrument freely, under no constraint or undue influence, and is of sound mind and memory and legal age, and fully aware of the possible consequences of this action.

2. I am at least 19 years of age and I am not related to the Declarant in any manner: by blood, marriage, or adoption.

3. I am not the Declarant's attending physician, or a patient or employee of the Declarant's attending physician; or a patient, physician, or employee of the health care facility in which the Declarant is a patient, unless such person is required or allowed to witness the execution of this document by the laws of the state in which this document is executed.

4. I am not entitled to any portion of the Declarant's estate on the Declarant's death under the laws of intestate succession of any state or country, nor under the Last Will and Testament of the Declarant or any Codicil to such Last Will and Testament.

5. I have no claim against any portion of the Declarant's estate on the Declarant's death.

6. I am not directly financially responsible for the Declarant's medical care.

7. I did not sign the Declarant's signature for the Declarant or on the direction of the Declarant, nor have I been paid any fee for acting as a witness to the execution of this document.

⑨

_____
Signature of Witness #1

_____
Printed name of Witness #1

_____
Address of Witness #1

_____

Signature of Witness #2

_____

Signature of Witness #3

_____

Printed name of Witness #2

_____

Printed name of Witness #3

_____

Address of Witness #2

_____

Address of Witness #3

Notary Acknowledgement

⑪ County of _____
State of _____

On _____ , 20_____, before me personally appeared _____ ,
the Declarant, and _____, the first witness, _____ , the
second witness, _____ , the third witness, and, being first sworn on oath
and under penalty of perjury, state that, in the presence of all the witnesses, the Declarant
published and signed the above Living Will Declaration and Directive to Physicians, and then,
at Declarant's request, and in the presence of the Declarant and of each other, each of the
witnesses signed as witnesses, and stated that, to the best of their knowledge, the Declarant
signed said Living Will Declaration and Directive to Physicians freely, under no constraint
or undue influence, and is of sound mind and memory and legal age and fully aware of the
potential consequences of this action. The witnesses further state that this affidavit is made at
the direction of and in the presence of the Declarant.

_____

Signature of Notary Public

_____

Printed name of Notary Public

Notary Public,
In and for the County of _____
State of _____
My commission expires: _____   Notary Seal

Instructions for Revoking a Living Will

All states which have recognized living wills have provided methods for the easy revocation of them. Since they provide authority for medical personnel to withhold life-support technology which will likely result in death to the patient, great care must be taken to insure that a change of mind by the patient is heeded.

If revocation of your living will is an important issue, please consult your state's law directly. The name of your particular state's law relating to living wills is provided in the Appendix of this book.

For the revocation of a living will, any one of the following methods of revocation is generally acceptable:

• Physical destruction of the living will, such as tearing, burning, or mutilating the document.

• A written revocation of the living will by you or by a person acting at your direction. A form for this is provided at the end of this chapter. You may use two witnesses on this form, although most states do not require the use of witnesses for the written revocation of a living will to be valid.

• An oral revocation in the presence of a witness who signs and dates a writing confirming a revocation. This oral declaration may take any manner. Most states allow for a person to revoke such a document by any indication (even non-verbal) of the intent to revoke a living will, regardless of their physical or mental condition.

To use the Revocation of Living Will form provided on the next page, simply fill in the following information:

① Name of person revoking living will
② Date of original living will
③ Date of signing revocation of living will
④ Signature and printed name of person revoking living will
⑤ Signatures and printed names of two witnesses to signing of revocation

Revocation of Living Will

① I, _____ , am the Declarant and maker of a Living Will and Directive to
② Physicians, dated _____ , 20_____ .

By this written revocation, I hereby entirely revoke such Living Will and Directive to Physicians and intend that it no longer have any force or effect whatsoever.

③ Dated _____ , 20_____ .

④ _____
Declarant's Signature

_____
Printed Name of Declarant

⑤ _____
Signature of Witness

_____
Printed name of Witness

_____
Address of Witness

_____
Signature of Witness

_____
Printed name of Witness

_____
Address of Witness

Chapter 12

Preparing a Health Care Power of Attorney

·Ϙ·Toolkit Tip!

A health care power of attorney is the only type of power of attorney that can be used to authorize someone to make health care decisions for you if you are unable to communicate.

A power of attorney is a document that is used to allow one person to give authority to another person to act on their behalf. The person signing the power of attorney grants legal authority to another to "stand in their shoes" and act legally for them. The person who receives the power of attorney is called an *attorney-in-fact*. This title and the power of attorney form does not mean that the person receiving the power has to be a lawyer. Power of attorney forms are useful documents for many occasions. They can be used to authorize someone else to sign certain documents if you can not be present when the signatures are necessary. Traditionally, financial and property matters were the type of actions handled with powers of attorney.

Increasingly people are using a specific type of power of attorney to authorize other persons to make health care decisions on their behalf in the event of a disability which makes the person unable to communicate their wishes to doctors or other health care providers. This broad type of power of attorney is called a *health care power of attorney*. It is different from *durable power of attorney for financial affairs*, which gives another person the authority handle a person's financial affairs, but is intended to remain in effect even if a person becomes disabled or incompetent. A *durable power of attorney for financial affairs* does not confer authority on another person to make health care decisions on someone else's behalf. Only a *durable health care power of attorney* can do that.

When You Should Use a Health Care Power of Attorney

Health care powers of attorney are useful documents that go beyond the provisions of a living will. They provide for health care options that living wills do not cover, and are important additions to the use of a living will. Basically, a health care power of attorney allows you to appoint someone to act for you in making health care decisions when you are unable to make them for yourself. A living will does not provide for this. Also, a health care power of attorney generally applies to all medical decisions (unless you specifically limit the power). Most living wills only apply to certain decisions regarding life support at the end of your life and are most useful in "terminal illness" or "permanent unconsciousness" situations. Note that a health care power of attorney is also a 'durable' type power of attorney, the term durable meaning that the power of attorney is not effected by your incapacitation and will remain in effect. Health care powers of attorney will be referred to as durable for the rest of this discussion.

Additionally, a durable health care power of attorney can provide your chosen agent with a valuable flexibility in making decisions regarding medical choices that may arise. Often, during the course of medical treatment, unforeseen situations may occur that require immediate decision-making. If you are unable to communicate your desires regarding such choices, the appointment of a *health care representative* for you (appointed with a durable health care power of attorney) will allow such decisions to be made on your behalf by a trusted person.

Finally, a durable health care power of attorney can provide specific detailed instructions regarding what you would like done by your attending physician in specific circumstances. Generally, living wills are limited to options for the withholding of life support. In order to be certain that you have made provisions for most potential health care situations, it is recommended you prepare both a living will and a durable health care power of attorney. Not everyone, however, has a trusted person available to serve as their health care representative. In these situations, the use of a living will alone will be necessary. It is, of course, possible

⊘ Definition:

Durable:
When used to describe a power of attorney, this means that the document is still effective if the maker is incapacitated. A standard (non-durable) power of attorney becomes invalid if the maker is incapacitated.

to add additional instructions to any living will to clearly and specifically indicate your desires.

Your health care representative can be a relative or close friend. It should be someone who knows you very well and whom you trust completely. Your representative should be someone who is not afraid to ask questions of health care providers and is able to make difficult decisions. Your representative may need to be assertive on your behalf. You should discuss your choice with your representative and make certain that he or she understands the responsibilities involved.

All states have enacted legislation regarding this type of form and recognize the validity of this type of legal document. In some states, they are called Appointment of Health Care Agent; in others, they are referred to as a Health Care Proxy. The form included in this book is officially titled Durable Health Care Power of Attorney and Appointment of Health Care Agent and Proxy, and is designed to be legally valid in all states. Information regarding each state's provisions are included in the Appendix.

The durable health care power of attorney included in this chapter is intended to be used to confer a very powerful authority to another person. In some cases, this may actually mean that you are giving that other person the power of life or death over you. This is not a power that should be conferred lightly. Very serious thought should be given to both who you appoint as your health care attorney-in-fact (the person you authorize to act on your behalf) and to any specific directions that you may want to give to that person regarding health care decisions. You may, of course, revoke your durable health care power of attorney at any time prior to your incapacitation (and even during any incapacitation if you are able to make your desire to revoke the power known). Remember, however, that should you become disabled or incapacitated and unable to communicate your wishes to anyone, you may be unable to communicate your desire to revoke your durable health care power of attorney.

Please note that this form also provides a release for your health care representative to receive your medical records under the federal HIPAA regulations relating to the privacy of health care records. Also, at the beginning of the form is a notice that clearly explains the importance of caution in the use of this form and is applicable to all states. Please read it carefully before you sign your durable health care power of attorney.

There are two methods for preparing a durable health care power of attorney with this book. This chapter contains a general, standardized durable health care power of attorney. The enclosed CD contains state-specific health care powers of attorney as part of the state-specific advance health care directives that have been taken directly from the most recent legislation regarding health care powers of attorney in each state. (Note: these are explained in Chapter 14). A few states do not currently have specific legislation providing express statutory recognition of health care powers of attorney. For those states, the durable health care power of attorney in this chapter has been prepared by legal professionals to comply with the basic requirements that courts in that state or other states have found important. In such states, be assured that courts, health care professionals, and physicians will be guided by this expression of your desires concerning life support as expressed in the durable health care power of attorney prepared using this book. You may use either the general durable health care power of attorney form or the state-specific advance health care directive form for your state. Please compare your state's form (in your state's advance health care directive on the CD) with the standardized form in this chapter and select the appropriate form that you feel best expresses your wishes regarding the appointment of a health care agent to make your health care decisions for you if you are unable to make those decisions for yourself.

The Federal Patient Self-Determination Act encourages all people to make their own decisions about the type of medical care they wish to receive. This act also requires all health care agencies (hospitals, long-term care facilities, and home health agencies) receiving Medicare and Medicaid reimbursement to recognize a living will and/or health care power of attorney as advance directives. Under this Act, all health care agencies must ask you if you have advance directives and must give you materials with information about your rights under state law. The

⚡ Warning!

Be very careful as to who you appoint as your health care representative. They will have the authority to make life and death decisions if you are unable to make them yourself.

durable health care power of attorney included in this chapter and/or the state-specific health care power of attorney included in the state-specific advance health care directives on the CD must be recognized by all health care agencies.

Revoking Your Durable Health Care Power of Attorney

All states have provided methods for the easy revocation of durable health care powers of attorney. Since such forms provide authority to medical personnel to withhold life-support technology that will likely result in death to the patient, great care must be taken to insure that a change of mind by the patient is heeded. For the revocation of a durable power of attorney for health care, any one of the following methods of revocation is generally acceptable:

- Physical destruction of the durable power of attorney for health care, such as tearing, burning, or mutilating the document.

- A written revocation of the durable power of attorney for health care by you or by a person acting at your direction. A form for this is provided later in this chapter and on the CD.

- An oral revocation in the presence of a witness who signs and dates an affidavit confirming a revocation. This oral declaration may take in any manner (verbal or non-verbal). Most states allow for a person to revoke such a document by any indication (even non-verbal) of the intent to revoke a durable power of attorney for health care, regardless of his or her physical or mental condition. A form for this (Witness Affidavit of Oral Revocation of Durable Health Care Power of Attorney) is included later in this chapter and on the CD.

☼ Toolkit Tip!

If you use the revocation forms in this chapter or if you physically destroy your health care power of attorney, make sure that you provide a copy (or notice) of this revocation to anyone or any health care facility that has a copy or original of the durable power of attorney for health care that you are revoking.

Instructions for Durable Health Care Power of Attorney and Appointment of Health Care Agent and Proxy

This form should be used for preparing a durable health care power of attorney that appoints another person whom you chose to have the authority to make health care decisions for you in the event that you become incapacitated.

To complete this form, you will need the following information:

①   Name and address of person granting power of attorney

②   Name and address of person appointed as the "health care representative" (same as the "attorney-in-fact for health care decisions")

③   State whose laws will govern the powers granted

④   Signature of person granting power of attorney.

    IMPORTANT NOTE: You should only sign this section if you have carefully read and agree with the statement that grants your health care representative the authority to order the withholding of nutrition, hydration, and any other medical care when you are diagnosed as being in a persistent vegetative state.

⑤   Any additional terms or conditions that you wish to add

⑥   Date of signing of durable health care power of attorney

⑦   Your signature and printed name (do not sign unless in front of a notary public and witnesses)

⑧   Signature and printed name of witnesses (signed in front of a notary)

⑨   The notary acknowledgment section (to be completed by notary public)

⑩   Signature and printed name of person appointed as health care representative (This signature need not be witnessed or notarized)

Please note that there are additional requirements for residents of the states of California, Delaware, Georgia, and Vermont. An additional statement is required to be signed by a patient advocate, ombudsman (in California, Delaware and Vermont) or facility director (in Georgia or Vermont), if the principal is a patient in a skilled nursing facility. If you are a resident of these states and are a resident of a skilled nursing facility, you should use the additional statement and witness signature information shown on page 247. Note that this additional page is also contained in the durable health care power of attorney forms that are included on the enclosed CD.

Durable Health Care Power of Attorney and Appointment of Health Care Agent and Proxy

NOTICE TO ADULT SIGNING THIS DOCUMENT: This is an important legal document. Before executing this document, you should know these facts: This document gives the person you designate (the attorney-in-fact) the power to make MOST health care decisions for you if you lose the capacity to make informed health care decisions for yourself. This power is effective only when your attending physician determines that you have lost the capacity to make informed health care decisions for yourself. Regardless of this document, as long as you have the capacity to make informed health care decisions for yourself, you retain the right to make all medical and other health care decisions for yourself. You may include specific limitations in this document on the authority of the attorney-in-fact to make health care decisions for you. Subject to any specific limitations you include in this document, if your attending physician determines that you have lost the capacity to make an informed decision on a health care matter, the attorney-in-fact GENERALLY will be authorized by this document to make health care decisions for you to the same extent as you could make those decisions yourself, if you had the capacity to do so. The authority of the attorney-in-fact to make health care decisions for you GENERALLY will include the authority to give informed consent, to refuse to give informed consent, or to withdraw informed consent to any care, treatment, service, or procedure to maintain, diagnose, or treat a physical or mental condition. Additionally, when exercising authority to make health care decisions for you, the attorney-in-fact will have to act consistently with your desires or, if your desires are unknown, to act in your best interest. You may express your desires to the attorney-in-fact by including them in this document or by making them known to the attorney-in-fact in another manner. When acting pursuant to this document, the attorney-in-fact GENERALLY will have the same rights that you have to receive information about proposed health care, to review health care records, and to consent to the disclosure of health care records. You can limit that right in this document if you so choose. GENERALLY, you may designate any competent adult as the attorney-in-fact under this document. You have the right to revoke the designation of the attorney-in-fact and the right to revoke this entire document at any time and in any manner. Any such revocation generally will be effective when you express your intention to make the revocation. However, if you made your attending physician aware of this document, any such revocation will be effective only when you communicate it to your attending physician, or when a witness to the revocation or other health care personnel to whom the revocation is communicated by such a witness communicates it to your attending physician. If you execute this document and create a valid Health Care Power of Attorney with it, this will revoke any prior, valid power of attorney for health care that you created, unless you indicate otherwise in this document. This document is not valid as a Health Care Power of

Attorney unless it is acknowledged before a notary public or is signed by at least two adult witnesses who are present when you sign or acknowledge your signature. No person who is related to you by blood, marriage, or adoption may be a witness. The attorney-in-fact, your attending physician, and the administrator of any nursing home in which you are receiving care also are ineligible to be witnesses. If there is anything in this document that you do not understand, you should ask a lawyer to explain it to you.

① I, _____ (printed name) , residing at _____, appoint the following person as my attorney-in-fact for health care decisions, my health care agent, and confer upon this person my health care proxy. This person shall hereafter referred to as my "health care representative":
② _____ (printed name) , residing at _____.

③ I grant my health care representative the maximum power under law to perform any acts on my behalf regarding health care matters that I could do personally under the laws of the State of _____, including specifically the power to make any health decisions on my behalf, upon the terms and conditions set forth below. My health care representative accepts this appointment and agrees to act in my best interest as he or she considers advisable. This health care power of attorney and appointment of health care agent and proxy may be revoked by me at any time and is automatically revoked on my death. However, this power of attorney shall not be affected by my present or future disability or incapacity.

This health care power of attorney and appointment of health care agent and proxy has the following terms and conditions:

If I have signed a Living Will or Directive to Physicians, and it is still in effect, I direct that my health care representative abide by the directions that I have set out in that document. If at any time I should have an incurable injury, disease, or illness which has been certified as a terminal condition by my attending physician and one additional physician, both of whom have personally examined me, and such physicians have determined that there can be no recovery from such condition and my death is imminent, and where the application of life prolonging procedures would serve only to artificially prolong the dying process, then:

I direct my health care representative to assure that such procedures be withheld or withdrawn, and that I be permitted to die naturally with only the administration of medication, the administration of nutrition and/or hydration, or the performance of any medical procedure deemed necessary to provide me with comfort, care, or to alleviate pain. If at any time I should have been diagnosed as being in a persistent vegetative state which has been certified as incurable by my attending physician and one additional physician, both of whom have personally examined me, and such physicians have determined that there can be no recovery from such condition, and where the application of life prolonging procedures would serve only to artificially prolong the dying process, then: I direct that my health care representative assure that such procedures be withheld or withdrawn, and that I be permitted to die naturally with only the administration of medication, the administration of nutrition and/or hydration, or the performance of any medical procedure deemed necessary to provide me with comfort, care, or to alleviate pain.

④ **THE FOLLOWING INSTRUCTIONS (IN BOLDFACE TYPE) ONLY APPLY IF I HAVE SIGNED MY NAME IN THIS SPACE:** _____

However, if at any time I should have been diagnosed as being in a persistent vegetative state which has been certified as incurable by my attending physician and one additional physician, both of whom have personally examined me, and such physicians have determined that there can be no recovery from such condition, I also direct that my health care representative have sole authority to order the withholding of any aid, including the administration of nutrition, hydration, and any other medical procedure deemed necessary to provide me with comfort, care, or to alleviate pain.

If I am able to communicate in any manner, including even blinking my eyes, I direct that my health care representative try and discuss with me the specifics of any proposed health care decision.

⑤ If I have any further terms or conditions, I state them here:

I have discussed my health care wishes with the person whom I have herein appointed as my health care representative, I am fully satisfied that the person who I have herein appointed as my health care representative will know my wishes with respect to my health care and I have full faith and confidence in their good judgement.

I further direct that my health care representative shall have full authority to do the following, should I lack the capacity to make such a decision myself, provided however, that this listing shall in no way limit the full authority that I give my health care representative to make health care decisions on my behalf:
a. to give informed consent to any health care procedure;
b. to sign any documents necessary to carry out or withhold any health care procedures on my behalf, including any waivers or releases of liabilities required by any health care provider;
c. to give or withhold consent for any health care or treatment;
d. to revoke or change any consent previously given or implied by law for any health care treatment;

e. to arrange for or authorize my placement or removal from any health care facility or institution;

f. to require that any procedures be discontinued, including the withholding of any medical treatment and/or aid, including the administration of nutrition, hydration, and any other medical procedure deemed necessary to provide me with comfort, care, or to alleviate pain, subject to the conditions earlier provided in this document;

g. to authorize the administration of pain-relieving drugs, even if they may shorten my life.

I desire that my wishes with respect to all health care matters be carried out through the authority that I have herein provided to my health care representative, despite any contrary wishes, beliefs, or opinions of any members of my family, relatives, or friends. I have read the Notice that precedes this document. I understand the full importance of this appointment, and I am emotionally and mentally competent to make this appointment of health care representative. I intend for my health care representative to be treated as I would be with respect to my rights regarding the use and disclosure of my individually identifiable health information or other medical records. This release authority applies to any information governed by the Health Insurance Portability and Accountability Act of 1996 (aka HIPAA), 42 USC 1320d and 45 CFR 160-164.

I declare to the undersigned authority that I sign and execute this instrument as my health care power of attorney and that I sign it willingly, or willingly direct another to sign for me, that I execute it as my free and voluntary act for the purposes expressed in this document and that I am nineteen years of age or older, of sound mind and under no constraint or undue influence ,and that I have read and understand the contents of the notice at the beginning of this document, and .that I understand the purpose and effect of this document.

⑥ Dated _____ , 20_____

⑦ _____
Signature of person granting health care power of attorney and appointing health care representative

_____
Printed name of person granting health care power of attorney and appointing health care representative

⑧ Witness Attestation

I, _____(printed name), the first witness, and I, _____(printed name), the second witness, sign my name to the foregoing power of attorney being first duly sworn and do declare to the undersigned authority that the principal signs and executes this instrument as his/her power of attorney and that he/she signs it willingly, or willingly directs another to sign for him/her, and that I, in the presence and hearing of the principal, sign this power of attorney as witness to the principal's signing and that to the best of my knowledge the principal is nineteen years of age or older, of sound mind and under no constraint or undue influence. I am nineteen years of age or older. I am not appointed as the health care representative or attorney-in-fact by this document. I am not related to the principal by blood, adoption or marriage, nor am I entitled to any portion of the principal's estate under the laws of intestate succession or under any will or codicil of the principal. I also do not provide health care services to the principal, nor an employee of any health care facility in which the principal is a patient and am not financially responsible for the principal's health care.

_____   _____
Signature of First Witness   Address of First Witness

_____   _____
Signature of Second Witness   Address of Second Witness

⑨ Notary Acknowledgment
State of _____   County of _____

Subscribed, sworn to and acknowledged before me on this date _____ , 20_ _____ by _____, the principal, who came before me personally, and under oath, stated that he or she is the person described in the above document and he or she signed the above document in my presence, or willingly directed another to sign for him or her. I declare under penalty of perjury that the person whose name is subscribed to this instrument appears to be of sound mind and under no duress, fraud, or undue influence. This document was also subscribed and sworn to before me on this date by _____, the first witness, and _____,the second witness .

_____
Notary Signature
Notary Public, In and for the County of _____   State of _____
My commission expires: _____   Notary Seal

Acceptance of Appointment as Health Care Attorney-in-Fact and Health Care Representative

I have read the attached durable health care power of attorney and am the person identified as the attorney-in-fact and health care representative for the principal. I hereby acknowledge that I accept my appointment as health care attorney-in-fact and health care representative and that when I act as agent I shall exercise the powers in the best interests of the principal.

⑩_____

Signature of person granted health care power of attorney and appointed health care representative

_____

Printed name of person granted health care power of attorney and appointed as health care representative

In California, Delaware, Georgia, and Vermont, the following statement is required to be signed by a patient advocate, ombudsman (in California, Delaware and Vermont) or facility director (in Georgia or Vermont, if the principal is a patient in a skilled nursing facility:

Statement of Patient Advocate or Ombudsman: I declare under penalty of perjury under the laws of the State of _____ that I am a patient advocate or ombudsman (or medical facility director) and am serving as a witness required by the laws of this state and that the principal appeared to be of sound mind and under no duress, fraud, or undue influence.

Dated _____

_____   _____
Signature of Patient Advocate or Ombudsman   Printed name and title of witness

Instructions for Revocation of a Durable Health Care Power of Attorney

On the following page, there is included a revocation of health care power of attorney. You have the right at any time to revoke your health care power of attorney. Remember, however, that should you become disabled or incapacitated and unable to communicate your wishes to anyone, you may be unable to communicate your desire to revoke your health care power of attorney. In any event, if you choose to revoke your health care power of attorney, a copy of this revocation should be provided to the person to whom the power was originally given. Copies should also be given to any party that may have had dealings with the attorney-in-fact before the revocation and to any party with whom the attorney-in-fact may be expected to attempt to deal with after the revocation, for example, your family physician.

Also note that you may also revoke a health care power of attorney by an oral revocation that takes place in the presence of a witness who then signs and date a written statement that confirms the revocation. Your oral declaration may take any manner, even a non-verbal indication (such as nodding your head or blinking your eyes) that signifies your intent to revoke the health care power of attorney. Such revocation can take place regardless of your physical or mental condition, as long as you are able to communicate, in some recognizable manner, your clear intent to revoke the power that was granted. For an oral revocation, use the Witness Affidavit of Oral Revocation of Durable Health Care Power of Attorney.

If you are able to, this form should be filled out and signed by the person revoking the health care power of attorney. It should also be notarized.

1. Name and address of person granting original health care power of attorney
2. Date of original durable health care power of attorney (that is now being revoked)
3. Name and address of person originally appointed as the "health care representative"
4. Date of signing of Revocation of Durable Health Care Power of Attorney
5. Your signature and printed name

Revocation of Durable Health Care Power of Attorney

① I, _____ (printed name),
of (address) _____

② do revoke the Durable Health Care Power of Attorney dated _____ , 20_____ ,
③ which was granted to _____ (printed name),
of (address) _____ , to act
as my attorney-in-fact for health care decisions and I revoke any appointment of the above
person as my health care agent, health care representative, or health care proxy.

④ Dated _____ , 20_____

⑤ _____
Signature of person revoking power of attorney

_____
Printed name of person revoking power of attorney

Instructions for Witness Affidavit of Oral Revocation of Durable Health Care Power of Attorney

If it is necessary to use the Witness Affidavit of Oral Revocation of Durable Health Care Power Of Attorney form, the witness should actually observe your indication of an intention to revoke your durable health care power of attorney. This may take the form of any verbal or non-verbal direction, as long as your intent to revoke is clearly and unmistakably evident to the witness. This form does not need to be notarized to be effective. Make sure that you provide a copy of this revocation to anyone or any health care facility that has a copy or original of the durable health care power of attorney that you are revoking.

To complete this document, fill in the following information:

① Name and address of person who originally signed health care power of attorney (principal)
② Date of original health care power of attorney
③ State in which health care power of attorney was originally signed
④ Printed name of witness to act of revocation
⑤ Date of act of revocation
⑥ Witness signature
⑦ Date of witness signature
⑧ Printed name of witness

Witness Affidavit of Oral Revocation of Durable Health Care Power of Attorney

The following person ① _____ , referred to as the Principal, was the maker and signatory of a Durable Health Care Power of Attorney which was dated ② _____ , and which was executed by him or her for use in the State of ③ _____ .

By this written affidavit, I, ④ _____ , the witness, hereby affirm that on the date of ⑤ _____ , I personally witnessed the above-named declarant make known to me, through verbal and/or non-verbal methods, his or her clear and unmistakable intent to entirely revoke such Durable Health Care Power of Attorney, or any other appointment or designation of a person to make any health care decisions on his or her behalf. It is my belief that the above-named principal fully intended that all of the above-mentioned documents no longer have any force or effect whatsoever.

Witness Acknowledgment

The declarant is personally known to me and I believe him or her to be of sound mind and under no duress, fraud, or undue influence.

Witness Signature ⑥ _____ Date ⑦ _____

Printed Name of Witness ⑧ _____

Chapter 13

Preparing a Durable Unlimited Power of Attorney for Financial Affairs

A durable power of attorney is a specific type of power of attorney that gives another person the authority to sign legal papers, transact business, buy or sell property, etc., and is only effective in one of two scenarios: (1) it may be written so that it *remains* in effect *even* if a person becomes disabled or incompetent, or (2) one that *only* goes into effect *if and when* a person becomes disabled or incompetent. A *durable unlimited power of attorney* provides that your agent will have total authority to act on your behalf *only* for all financial and/or business matters. A durable power of attorney does not confer authority on another person to make health care decisions on someone else's behalf. Only a durable *health care* power of attorney can do that. There are two durable power of attorney forms contained in this book: one is written for the first scenario above (remains in effect if a person becomes incapacitated) and the other is written for the second scenario (it will only go into effect when and if a person becomes incapacitated). In addition, there are also state-specific durable powers of attorney for certain states contained on the enclosed CD. (These are explained further on pages 254-255).

(These are explained further on pages 254-255).

🔆 Toolkit Tip!

There are two types of durable financial powers of attorney: 1) one that goes into effect immediately and remains in effect upon the makers incapacitation, and 2) one that *only* goes into effect upon the maker's incapacitation.

When You Should Use a Durable Unlimited Power of Attorney for Financial Affairs

A *durable unlimited power of attorney for financial affairs* allows you to appoint an agent (who is then referred to as an 'attorney-in-fact') to handle your financial affairs during a period that you are unable to handle them yourself. With this form, you are giving another person the right to manage your financial and business matters on your behalf. They are given the power to act as you could, if you were able. If there is someone available who can be trusted implicitly to act on your behalf, the appointment of such a person can eliminate many problems that may arise if you are unable to handle your own affairs.

The appointment of an agent for your financial affairs allows for the paying of bills, writing of checks, etc. while you are unable to do so yourself. With the forms in this book, you are granting the appointed agent very broad powers to handle your affairs. You will give your agent the maximum power under law to perform any and all acts relating to any and all of your financial and/or business affairs. Your attorney-in-fact (agent) is granted full power to act on your behalf in the same manner as if you were personally present.

The person you appoint (remember: attorney-in-fact) will have the authority to handle real estate transactions; goods and services transactions; stock, bond, share and commodity transactions; banking transactions; business operating transactions; insurance transactions; estate transactions; legal claims and litigation; personal relationships and affairs; benefits from military service; records, reports and statements; retirement benefit transactions; making gifts to a spouse, children, parents and other descendants (if any); and tax matters.

You should appoint someone whom you trust completely. This is not a power that should be conferred lightly. Very serious thought should be given to both who you appoint as your attorney-in-fact (the person you authorize to act on your behalf) and to any spe-

> ⊘ **Definition:**
>
> **Attorney-in-Fact:**
> The designation given to the person that you appoint in your financial power of attorney. This does *not* mean that the person has to be an attorney.

⚡ Warning!

If you decide to use the power of attorney that goes into effect immediately, remember that as soon as you sign this form, your appointed attorney-in-fact will have total control over your finances.

cific directions that you may want to give to that person regarding financial decisions. You do not have to appoint anyone to handle your financial affairs, but it is often very useful to do so.

By accepting their appointment, your agent agrees to act in your best interest as he or she considers advisable. A durable unlimited power of attorney for financial matters may be revoked by you at any time and is automatically revoked on your death.

If you wish to limit the powers that you give to your agent, you may wish to use a *limited power of attorney* instead of a durable unlimited power of attorney. However, because of its limited scope, this type of power of attorney is not as practical in situations when a *durable* power of attorney is generally used. Some of the state-specific forms allow this, but if you are in a state that does not provide a state-specific form and if you wish to limit the powers that you grant in your durable power of attorney, you will need to consult an attorney.

The first durable unlimited power of attorney for financial affairs that is provided immediately appoints your chosen attorney-in-fact and provides that such appointment will remain in effect *even if* you become incapacitated. The second durable unlimited power of attorney for financial affairs that is provided will become effective *only* upon your incapacitation, as certified by your primary physician or, if your primary physician is not available, by any other attending physician. Neither power of attorney grants any power or authority to your designated attorney-in-fact regarding health care decisions. Only the *durable health care power of attorney* can confer those powers (explained in Chapter 12). You may, of course, choose to select the very same person to act as both your health care representative and your agent for financial affairs.

At the beginning of each of the documents are notices regarding the use of a durable power of attorney. They clearly explain the importance of caution in the use of this form and are applicable to all states. Please read each carefully to decide which of these forms are appropriate for your situation. Please note that the forms in the book provide a release for your attorney-in-fact to receive your medical records under the federal HIPAA regulations relating to the privacy of health care records. This does not confer any authority for your attorney-in-fact to make health care decisions on your behalf. The HIPAA release is for the purpose of allowing your attorney-in-fact to have access to your medical files for the purpose of paying or examining medical bills and charges.

State-Specific Power of Attorney Forms

Although, the forms provided in this book are legally-valid in all states, some states provide their own particular form for a durable power of attorney. You may choose to use a state-specific form if they are provided for your state or you may use the forms in this chapter. A 'state-specific statutory form' is a form that has been taken directly from the laws of your particular state. The legal effects of the language in such a document have been approved by the legislature of the state. This provides an advantage in that the legal language in such a 'statutory' form is generally familiar to most financial institutions in the particular state and they know that such language has been approved. This does not mean, however, that other 'non-statutory' forms are not legally valid in the state as well. All states specifically provide, in their legislation regarding powers of attorney, that power of attorney forms other than those contained in the statute itself are legally valid. All of the forms in this book meet such required legal standards. The following states have developed state-specific statutory forms for durable powers of attorney and they are included on the enclosed CD:

> *Alaska, Arkansas, California, Colorado, Connecticut, District of Columbia, Georgia, Illinois, Montana, Nebraska, New Hampshire, New Mexico, New York, North Carolina, Oklahoma, Pennsylvania, Rhode Island, Texas*

In all other states, the legislatures have not developed specific forms for durable powers of attorney. In such situations, you may use the individual durable unlimited power of attorney forms provided in this chapter which have been prepared following any guidelines or requirements set out by the particular state's legislature. These forms are also provided on the enclosed CD in both PDF and text formats.

✓ Toolkit Tip!

If you live in the states noted below, you may wish to compare the state-specific form for your state (provided on the CD) with the forms in this chapter and select the one that best fits your particular circumstances. Note that the forms in this chapter are also provided on the CD.

Instructions for Durable Unlimited Power of Attorney for Financial Affairs - Effective Immediately

(1) Goes into effect immediately and remains in effect even upon your incapacitation

This form should be used only in situations where you desire to authorize another person to act for you in *all* transactions immediately and you wish the power to remain in effect in the event that you become incapacitated and unable to handle your own affairs. The grant of power under this document is unlimited (except for health care decisions). This form gives the person whom you designate as your "attorney-in-fact" broad powers to handle your property during your lifetime, which may include powers to mortgage, sell, or otherwise dispose of any real or personal property without advance notice to you or approval by you. This document does not authorize anyone to make medical or other health care decisions. You must execute a health care power of attorney to accomplish this. This form does provide a HIPPA medical records privacy release that will allow the person that you appoint to access any hospital or medical bills or records on you behalf. This form also provides that you will also name a successor attorney-in-fact who will have the same powers as the original person appointed, but who will only have the powers if the original person appointed is unable to perform the necessary tasks required by the power of attorney. The authority granted by this power of attorney may be revoked by you at any time and is automatically revoked if you die. If there is anything about this form that you do not understand, you should ask a lawyer to explain it to you. To complete this form, fill in the following:

1. Name and address of person granting power (principal)
2. Name and address of person granted power (attorney-in-fact)
3. Name and address of successor to person originally granted power (successor attorney-in-fact) (optional-if not used, write N/A in this space)
4. Printed name of principal, date of signature, and signature of principal (signed in front of notary public)
5. Witnesses printed names and signatures (signed in front of notary public)
6. Notary acknowledgement should be completed by the notary public
7. Printed name and signature of attorney-in-fact and successor attorney-in-fact (need not be witnessed or notarized)
8. Printed name and signature of attorney-in-fact and successor attorney-in-fact (optional-if not used, write N/A in this space) (need not be witnessed or notarized)

Durable Unlimited Power of Attorney For Financial Affairs (Effective Immediately)

NOTICE TO ADULT SIGNING THIS DOCUMENT: This is an important document. Before signing this document, you should know these important facts. By signing this document, you are not giving up any powers or rights to control your finances and property yourself. In addition to your own powers and rights, you are giving another person, your attorney-in-fact, broad powers to handle your finances and property, which may include powers to encumber, sell or otherwise dispose of any real or personal property without advance notice to you or approval by you. THE POWERS GRANTED UNDER THIS DOCUMENT ARE EFFECTIVE IMMEDIATELY AND WILL REMAIN IN EFFECT IF YOU BECOME DISABLED OR INCAPACITATED. This document does not authorize anyone to make medical or other health care decisions for you. If you own complex or special assets such as a business, or if there is anything about this form that you do not understand, you should ask a lawyer to explain this form to you before you sign it. If you wish to change your durable unlimited power of attorney, you must complete a new document and revoke this one. You have the right to revoke the designation of the attorney-in-fact and the right to revoke this entire document at any time and in any manner. You may revoke this document at any time by destroying it, by directing another person to destroy it in your presence or by signing a written and dated statement expressing your intent to revoke this document. If you revoke this document, you should notify your attorney-in-fact and any other person to whom you have given a copy of the form. You also should notify all parties having custody of your assets. These parties have no responsibility to you unless you actually notify them of the revocation. If your attorney-in-fact is your spouse and your marriage is annulled, or you are divorced after signing this document, this document may become invalid. Since some third parties or some transactions may not permit use of this document, it is advisable to check in advance, if possible, for any special requirements that may be imposed. You should sign this form only if the attorney-in- fact you name is reliable, trustworthy and competent to manage your affairs. Generally, you may designate any competent adult as the attorney-in-fact under this document.

① I, _____ (printed name),
of (address) _____,
as principal, ② do appoint _____ (printed name),
of (address) _____, as
my attorney-in- fact to act in my name, place and stead in any way which I myself could do, if I were personally present, with respect to all of the following matters to the extent that I am permitted by law to act through an agent: I grant my attorney-in-fact the maximum power under

law to perform any act on my behalf that I could do personally, including but not limited to, all acts relating to any and all of my financial transactions and/or business affairs including all banking and financial institution transactions, all real estate or personal property transactions, all insurance or annuity transactions, all claims and litigation, and any and all business transactions. **This power of attorney shall become effective immediately and shall remain in full effect upon my disability or incapacitation.** This power of attorney grants no power or authority regarding healthcare decisions to my designated attorney-in-fact.

③

If the attorney-in-fact named above is unable or unwilling to serve, then I appoint
_____(printed name),
of _____ (address),
to be my successor attorney-in-fact for all purposes hereunder.

My attorney-in-fact is granted full and unlimited power to act on my behalf in the same manner as if I were personally present. My attorney-in-fact accepts this appointment and agrees to act in my best interest as he or she considers advisable. To induce any third party to rely upon this power of attorney, I agree that any third party receiving a signed copy or facsimile of this power of attorney may rely upon such copy, and that revocation or termination of this power of attorney shall be ineffective as to such third party until actual notice or knowledge of such revocation or termination shall have been received by such third party. I, for myself and for my heirs, executors, legal representatives and assigns, agree to indemnify and hold harmless any such third party from any and all claims that may arise against such third party by reason of such third party having relied on the provisions of this power of attorney. This power of attorney may be revoked by me at any time and is automatically revoked upon my death. My attorney-in-fact shall not be compensated for his or her services nor shall my attorney-in-fact be liable to me, my estate, heirs, successors, or assigns for acting or refraining from acting under this document, except for willful misconduct or gross negligence. Revocation of this document is not effective unless a third party has actual knowledge of such revocation. I intend for my attorney-in-fact under this Power of Attorney to be treated as I would be with respect to my rights regarding the use and disclosure of my individually identifiable health information or other medical records. This release authority applies to any information governed by the Health Insurance Portability and Accountability Act of 1996 (aka HIPAA), 42 USC 1320d and 45 CFR 160-164.

④

Signature and Declaration of Principal

I, _____(printed name), the principal, sign my name to this power of attorney this _____day of _____and, being first duly sworn, do declare to the undersigned authority that I sign and execute this instrument as my power of attorney and that I sign it willingly, or willingly direct another to sign for me, that I execute it as my free and voluntary act for the purposes expressed in the power of attorney and that I am eighteen years of age or older, of sound mind and under no constraint or undue influence, and that I have read and understand the contents of the notice at the beginning of this document.

_____
Signature of Principal

⑤ **Witness Attestation**

I, _____ (printed name), the first witness, and
I, _____ (printed name), the second witness, sign my name to the foregoing power of attorney being first duly sworn and do declare to the undersigned authority that the principal signs and executes this instrument as his/her power of attorney and that he/she signs it willingly, or willingly directs another to sign for him/her, and that I, in the presence and hearing of the principal, sign this power of attorney as witness to the principal's signing and that to the best of my knowledge the principal is eighteen years of age or older, of sound mind and under no constraint or undue influence.

_____
Signature of First Witness

_____
Signature of Second Witness

⑥ **Notary Acknowledgment**

The State of _____
County of _____
Subscribed, sworn to and acknowledged before me by _____, the principal, and subscribed and sworn to before me by _____, the first witness, and _____, the second witness on this date _____.

_____
Notary Public Signature

Notary Public, In and for the County of _____ State of _____
My commission expires: _____   Notary Seal

⑦ Acknowledgment and Acceptance of Appointment as Attorney-in-Fact

I, _____, (printed name) have read the attached power of attorney and am the person identified as the attorney-in-fact for the principal. I hereby acknowledge that I accept my appointment as attorney-in-fact and that when I act as agent I shall exercise the powers for the benefit of the principal; I shall keep the assets of the principal separate from my assets; I shall exercise reasonable caution and prudence; and I shall keep a full and accurate record of all actions, receipts and disbursements on behalf of the principal.

_____   _____

Signature of Attorney-in-Fact   Date

⑧ Acknowledgment and Acceptance of Appointment as Successor Attorney-in-Fact

I, _____, (printed name) have read the attached power of attorney and am the person identified as the successor attorney-in-fact for the principal. I hereby acknowledge that I accept my appointment as successor attorney-in-fact and that, in the absence of a specific provision to the contrary in the power of attorney, when I act as agent I shall exercise the powers for the benefit of the principal; I shall keep the assets of the principal separate from my assets; I shall exercise reasonable caution and prudence; and I shall keep a full and accurate record of all actions, receipts and disbursements on behalf of the principal.

_____   _____

Signature of Successor Attorney-in-Fact   Date

Instructions for Durable Unlimited Power of Attorney for Financial Affairs - Effective on Incapacitation

(2) Goes into effect only upon your incapacitation as certified by your primary physician, or another physician, if your primary physician is not available.

This form should be used only in situations where you desire to authorize another person to act for you in all transactions but you desire that the powers granted will not take effect until you become incapacitated and unable to handle your own affairs. This documents also provides that your incapacitation must be certified by your primary physician, or another attending physician if your primary physician is not available. The grant of power under this document is unlimited (except for health care decisions). This form gives the person whom you designate as your "attorney-in-fact" broad powers to handle your property during your incapacitation, which may include powers to mortgage, sell, or otherwise dispose of any real or personal property without advance notice to you or approval by you. This document does not authorize anyone to make medical or other health care decisions. You must execute a durable health care power of attorney to accomplish this. This form does provide a HIPPA medical records privacy release that will allow the person that you appoint to access any hospital or medical bills or records on you behalf. This form also provides that you will also name a successor attorney-in-fact who will have the same powers as the original person appointed, but who will only have the powers if the original person appointed is unable to perform the necessary tasks required by the power of attorney. The authority granted by this power of attorney may be revoked by you at any time and is automatically revoked if you die. If there is anything about this form that you do not understand, you should ask a lawyer to explain it to you. Please note that this form provides a release for your attorney-in-fact to receive your medical records under the federal HIPAA regulations relating to the privacy of health care records.

To complete this form, fill in the following:

1. Name and address of person granting power (principal)
2. Name and address of person granted power (attorney-in-fact)
3. Name and address of successor to person originally granted power (successor attorney-in-fact) (optional-if not used, write N/A in this space)
4. Printed name of principal, date of signature, and signature of principal (signed in front of notary public)
5. Witnesses printed names and signatures (signed in front of notary public)
6. Notary acknowledgement should be completed by the notary public
7. Printed name and signature of attorney-in-fact and successor attorney-in-fact (need not be witnessed or notarized)
8. Printed name and signature of attorney-in-fact and successor attorney-in-fact (optional-if not used, write N/A in this space) (need not be witnessed or notarized)

261

Durable Unlimited Power of Attorney For Financial Affairs (Effective Only Upon Incapacitation)

NOTICE TO ADULT SIGNING THIS DOCUMENT: This is an important document. Before signing this document, you should know these important facts. By signing this document, you are not giving up any powers or rights to control your finances and property yourself. In addition to your own powers and rights, you are giving another person, your attorney-in-fact, broad powers to handle your finances and property, which may include powers to encumber, sell or otherwise dispose of any real or personal property without advance notice to you or approval by you. THE POWERS GRANTED UNDER THIS DOCUMENT WILL ONLY GO INTO EFFECT IF YOU BECOME DISABLED OR INCAPACITATED, AS CERTIFIED BY YOUR PRIMARY PHYSICIAN, OR BY ANOTHER ATTENDING PHYSICIAN, IF YOUR PRIMARY PHYSICIAN IS NOT AVAILABLE. This document does not authorize anyone to make medical or other health care decisions for you. If you own complex or special assets such as a business, or if there is anything about this form that you do not understand, you should ask a lawyer to explain this form to you before you sign it. If you wish to change your durable unlimited power of attorney, you must complete a new document and revoke this one. You have the right to revoke the designation of the attorney-in-fact and the right to revoke this entire document at any time and in any manner. You may revoke this document at any time by destroying it, by directing another person to destroy it in your presence or by signing a written and dated statement expressing your intent to revoke this document. If you revoke this document, you should notify your attorney-in-fact and any other person to whom you have given a copy of the form. You also should notify all parties having custody of your assets. These parties have no responsibility to you unless you actually notify them of the revocation. If your attorney-in-fact is your spouse and your marriage is annulled, or you are divorced after signing this document, this document may become invalid. Since some third parties or some transactions may not permit use of this document, it is advisable to check in advance, if possible, for any special requirements that may be imposed. You should sign this form only if the attorney-in-fact you name is reliable, trustworthy and competent to manage your affairs. Generally, you may designate any competent adult as the attorney-in-fact under this document.

① I, _____(printed name), of (address) _____, as principal,
② do appoint _____(printed name), of (address) _____, as my attorney-in-fact to act in my name, place and stead in any way which I myself could do, if I were personally present, with respect to all of the following matters to the extent that I am permitted by law to act through an agent: I grant my attorney-in-fact the maximum power under

law to perform any act on my behalf that I could do personally, including but not limited to, all acts relating to any and all of my financial transactions and/or business affairs including all banking and financial institution transactions, all real estate or personal property transactions, all insurance or annuity transactions, all claims and litigation, and any and all business transactions. **This power of attorney shall only become effective upon my disability or incapacitation, as certified by my primary physician, or if my primary physician is not available, by any other attending physician.** This power of attorney grants no power or authority regarding healthcare decisions to my designated attorney-in-fact.

③

If the attorney-in-fact named above is unable or unwilling to serve, then I appoint

_____(printed name),

of _____ (address),

to be my successor attorney-in-fact for all purposes hereunder.

My attorney-in-fact is granted full and unlimited power to act on my behalf in the same manner as if I were personally present. My attorney-in-fact accepts this appointment and agrees to act in my best interest as he or she considers advisable. To induce any third party to rely upon this power of attorney, I agree that any third party receiving a signed copy or facsimile of this power of attorney may rely upon such copy, and that revocation or termination of this power of attorney shall be ineffective as to such third party until actual notice or knowledge of such revocation or termination shall have been received by such third party. I, for myself and for my heirs, executors, legal representatives and assigns, agree to indemnify and hold harmless any such third party from any and all claims that may arise against such third party by reason of such third party having relied on the provisions of this power of attorney. This power of attorney may be revoked by me at any time and is automatically revoked upon my death. My attorney-in-fact shall not be compensated for his or her services nor shall my attorney-in-fact be liable to me, my estate, heirs, successors, or assigns for acting or refraining from acting under this document, except for willful misconduct or gross negligence. Revocation of this document is not effective unless a third party has actual knowledge of such revocation.

I intend for my attorney-in-fact under this Power of Attorney to be treated as I would be with respect to my rights regarding the use and disclosure of my individually identifiable health information or other medical records. This release authority applies to any information governed by the Health Insurance Portability and Accountability Act of 1996 (aka HIPAA), 42 USC 1320d and 45 CFR 160-164.

④ **Signature and Declaration of Principal**

I, _____ (printed name), the principal, sign my name to this power of attorney this _____day of _____and, being first duly sworn, do declare to the undersigned authority that I sign and execute this instrument as my power of attorney and that I sign it willingly, or willingly direct another to sign for me, that

I execute it as my free and voluntary act for the purposes expressed in the power of attorney and that I am eighteen years of age or older, of sound mind and under no constraint or undue influence ,and that I have read and understand the contents of the notice at the beginning of this document.

_____

Signature of Principal

⑤ Witness Attestation

I, _____ (printed name), the first witness, and
I, _____ (printed name), the second witness,
sign my name to the foregoing power of attorney being first duly sworn and do declare to the undersigned authority that the principal signs and executes this instrument as his/her power of attorney and that he/she signs it willingly, or willingly directs another to sign for him/her, and that I, in the presence and hearing of the principal, sign this power of attorney as witness to the principal's signing and that to the best of my knowledge the principal is eighteen years of age or older, of sound mind and under no constraint or undue influence.

_____   _____

Signature of First Witness   Signature of Second Witness

⑥ Notary Acknowledgment

The State of _____
County of _____
Subscribed, sworn to and acknowledged before me by _____,the
principal, and subscribed and sworn to before me by _____, the
first witness, and _____,the second witness on this date _____.

_____

Notary Public Signature
Notary Public, In and for the County of _____State of _____
My commission expires: _____ Notary Seal

⑦ **Acknowledgment and Acceptance of Appointment as Attorney-in-Fact**

I, _____ (printed name) have read the attached power of attorney and am the person identified as the attorney-in-fact for the principal. I hereby acknowledge that I accept my appointment as attorney-in-fact and that when I act as agent I shall exercise the powers for the benefit of the principal; I shall keep the assets of the principal separate from my assets; I shall exercise reasonable caution and prudence; and I shall keep a full and accurate record of all actions, receipts and disbursements on behalf of the principal.

_____   _____

Signature of Attorney-in-Fact   Date

⑧ **Acknowledgment and Acceptance of Appointment as Successor Attorney-in-Fact**

I, _____ (printed name) have read the attached power of attorney and am the person identified as the successor attorney-in-fact for the principal. I hereby acknowledge that I accept my appointment as successor attorney-in-fact and that, in the absence of a specific provision to the contrary in the power of attorney, when I act as agent I shall exercise the powers for the benefit of the principal; I shall keep the assets of the principal separate from my assets; I shall exercise reasonable caution and prudence; and I shall keep a full and accurate record of all actions, receipts and disbursements on behalf of the principal.

_____   _____

Signature of Successor Attorney-in-Fact   Date

Instructions for Revocation of Power of Attorney

This document may be used with either of the previous power of attorney forms. The revocation is used to terminate the original authority that was granted to the other person in the first place. Some limited powers of attorney specify that the powers that are granted will end on a specific date. If that is the case, you will not need a revocation unless you wish the powers to end sooner than the date specified. If the grant of power was for a limited purpose and that purpose is complete but no date for the power to end was specified, this revocation should be used as soon after the transaction as possible. In any event, if you choose to revoke a power of attorney, a copy of this revocation should be provided to the person to whom the power was given. Copies should also be given to any party that may have had dealings with the attorney-in-fact before the revocation and to any party with whom the attorney-in-fact may be expected to attempt to deal with after the revocation. If you feel that it is important to verify the revocation of your power of attorney, you should have any third party that you supply with a copy of the revocation sign another copy for you to keep. If that is not possible, you should mail a copy of the revocation to that person or institution by first class mail, with a return receipt requested that requires a signature to verify delivery.

Although this revocation may be used to revoke a health care power of attorney, please also note that there is a specific form for revocation of a health care power of attorney and that there are other acceptable methods to revoke a health care power of attorney. These are noted in Chapter 12.

To complete this document, fill in the following information:

① Printed name and address of person who originally granted power (principal)
② Date of original power of attorney
③ Printed name and address of person granted power (attorney-in-fact)
④ Date of revocation of power of attorney
⑤ Signature of person revoking power of attorney (principal) (signed in front of notary)
⑥ Notary to complete the notary acknowledgement

Revocation of Power of Attorney

① I, _____ (printed name) ,
address: _____

② do revoke the power of attorney dated _____ , 20 _____ ,
③ which was granted to _____ (printed name),
address:_____ ,

to act as my attorney-in-fact.

④ This Revocation is dated _____ , 20 _____

⑤ _____
Signature of Person Revoking Power of Attorney

⑥ **Notary Acknowledgement**

State of _____
County of _____

On _____ , 20 _____ , _____ personally
came before me and, being duly sworn, did state that he or she is the person described in the
above document and that he or she signed the above document in my presence.

_____
Signature of Notary Public

Notary Public, In and for the County of _____
State of _____

My commission expires: _____   Notary Seal

Chapter 14

Preparing an Advance Health Care Directive

What is an Advance Health Care Directive?

An advance health care directive is a legal document that may be used in any state and that allows you to provide written directions relating to your future health care should you become incapacitated and unable to speak for yourself. Advance health care directives give you a direct voice in medical decisions in situations when you cannot make those decisions yourself. Your advance health care directive will not be used as long as you are able to express your own decisions. You can always accept or refuse medical treatment and you always have the legal right to revoke your advance health care directive at any time. Instructions regarding revocations are discussed later in these instructions. The Federal Patient Self-Determination Act encourages all people to make their own decisions about the type of medical care they wish to receive. This act also requires all health care agencies (hospitals, long-term care facilities, and home health agencies) receiving Medicare and Medicaid reimbursement to recognize a living will and health care power of attorney as advance directives. Under this Act, all health care agencies must ask you if you have advance directives and must give you materials with information about your rights under state law.

Advance health care directives are not only for senior citizens. Serious life-threatening accidents or disease can strike anyone and leave them unable to communicate their desires. In fact,

> **⚬ Toolkit Tip!**
>
> An advance health care directive contains a living will and a health care power of attorney. Thus, it can take the place of these two important estate planning documents.

the rise of the use of advance health care directives can be attributed in part, to legal cases involving medical care to young people, particularly Karen Ann Quinlan and Nancy Cruzan, and most recently, Terry Schiavo. Anyone over the age of 18 (19 in Alabama) who is mentally competent should complete an advance health care directive. Be aware, however, that advance health care directives are intended for non-emergency medical treatment. Most often, there is no time for health care providers to consult and analyze the provisions of an advance health care directive in an emergency situation.

The advance health care directives that are contained on the CD that is enclosed with this book all contain four separate sections, each dealing with different aspects of potential situations that may arise during a possible period of incapacitation:

- Living will
- Selection of health care agent (generally, by health care power of attorney)
- Designation of primary physician
- Organ donation

In addition, this book also provides (in Chapter 13) a fifth legal form that may be useful in many health care situations if you are unable to handle your own financial affairs: a durable unlimited power of attorney for financial affairs. A brief explanation of each of the forms included in an advance health care directive follows:

Living Will: A *living will* is a document that can be used to state your desire that extraordinary life support means not be used to artificially prolong your life in the event that you are stricken with a terminal disease or injury. Its use has been recognized in all states in recent years. The purpose of a living will is to provide doctors and other health care workers with clear directions regarding how you would like your medical care handled toward the end of your life. A living will makes it possible for you to specify, in advance, exactly what your preferences are regarding the use of life-sustaining medical procedures if you are ever in a terminal medical condition or in a vegetative state, and are unable to give such directions yourself. For instructions and forms for preparing a living will that is not part of an advance health care directive, please see Chapter 11.

> ⚡ **Warning!**
>
> VERY IMPORTANT: You should read the provisions of your proposed living will very carefully, as they authorize actions that will *end your life.* If you do not fully understand the terms of your living will, you should consult an attorney.

Health Care Power of Attorney: This relatively new legal document has been developed to allow a person to appoint another person to make health care decisions on one's behalf, in the event that he or she becomes incapacitated or incompetent. Generally, a *health care power of attorney* will only take effect upon a person becoming unable to manage his or her own affairs, and only after this incapacitation has been certified by an attending physician. The person appointed will then have the authority to view your medical records, consult with your doctors and make any required decisions regarding your health care. This document may be carefully tailored to fit your needs and concerns and can be used in conjunction with a living will. It can be a valuable tool for dealing with difficult healthcare situations. For instructions and forms for preparing an individual durable health care power of attorney that is not part of an advance health care directive, please refer to Chapter 12.

Designation of Primary Physician: Through the use of this document, you will be able to designate your choice for your primary physician in the event you are unable to communicate your wishes after an accident or during an illness. Although your family may know your personal doctor, it may still be a good idea to put this choice in writing so that there is no question regarding who your choice for a doctor may be. For instructions and a form to designate your choice for your primary physician that is not part of an advance health care directive, please refer to Chapter 15.

Organ Donation: You may also wish that your vital organs or, indeed, your entire body be used after your death for various medical purposes. Every year, many lives are saved and much medical research is enhanced by organ donations. All states allow for you to personally declare your desires regarding the use of your body and/or organs after death. For instructions and a form to designate your choice regarding organ donations that is not part of an advance health care directive, please refer to Chapter 16. Also please note that you must be certain that any organ donation decisions must be coordinated with any such donation decisions that you may have made in any other manner, such as on your driver's license or with your state motor vehicles department.

☀ Toolkit Tip!

You can either prepare a complete advance health care directive as one form, or you may choose to prepare each (or only certain) of the four component forms as separate documents.

The combination of these four forms provides a comprehensive method by which you may provide, in advance, for a situation in which you may be unable to communicate your desires to your family, your friends, and your health care providers. It is an opportunity to carefully plan how you would like various medical situations to be handled should they arise.

Using this book and the enclosed CD, there are two methods that you may use. You may choose to complete an entire comprehensive advance health care directive or you may simply wish to prepare separate individual forms. Either method is acceptable. If you intend to prepare a living will and a health care power of attorney, however, you are encouraged to use the state-specific advance health care directive for your state, which contains a state-specific living will and a state-specific health care power of attorney form as part of that document. This will allow the provisions in your living will and the provisions in your health care power of attorney (both as part of your complete advance health care directive) to complement each other. It is important that these two documents be coordinated so that the actions that your health care agent may be asked to take on your behalf (when you are unable to communicate) are in line with your stated desires as shown in your living will. Keeping these two documents together as part of a comprehensive advance health care directive makes such coordination much more likely.

> **Toolkit Tip!**
>
> Your advance health care directive will *not* be used as long as you are still able to make known your decisions about your health care.

The individual forms that comprise an advance health care directive are provided on the enclosed CD (under the listing for their particular chapter) and are explained in more detail in their respective chapters. The individual forms have been prepared to meet the minimum legal requirements in all states and are legally-valid in all states. The forms explained in this chapter are comprehensive state-specific advance health care directives and are provided on the enclosed CD. Please also note that you may elect to only adopt certain of the individual sections of the comprehensive advance health care directives, such as, for example, adopting the living will and health care power of attorney sections, but not adopting the designation of primary physician or the organ donation section. Please review your own state's advance health care directive form. Finally, please note that if you wish to make any changes to an individual form, you must use the text format version of the form that is provided on the CD.

When You Should Use an Advance Health Care Directive

A *'state-specific advance health care directive'* is a form that has been taken directly from the laws of your particular state. The legal effects of the language in such a document have been approved by the legislature of the state. This provides an advantage in that the legal language in such a 'statutory' form is generally familiar to health care providers in the particular state and they know that such language has been approved. This does not mean, however, that other 'non-statutory' forms are not legally valid in the state as well. Anyone may use a 'non-statutory' legal form with language that they find appropriate to their own situation, as long as the document meets certain minimum legal standards for a particular state.

You need not necessarily adopt all four sections of the document for your own use. You may select and complete any or all of the four separate sections of the form. For example, if you choose not to select a health care agent, you may use the other three parts of the form and not complete that section. Instructions for filling in the forms are contained later in this chapter. Many people find using a single comprehensive document easier than completing each separate form as an individual document. This method also provides a simple compact package that contains your entire advance health care directive with forms using legal language that most health care providers in your state are familiar with. In a few states, the legislatures have not developed specific language for one or more of the forms. These few instances are noted under the state's heading in the appendix of this book. In addition, in such situations, an appropriate and legally-valid form has been added to the directives for those states. Any such forms have been prepared following any guidelines set out by the state's legislature.

Important Note: The state-specific advance health care directive forms *do not* contain a durable unlimited power of attorney for financial affairs. As this form is not directly related to health care decision issues, it is provided only as a separate individual form located in Chapter 6. Should you desire to use this type of document to authorize someone to handle your financial affairs in the event of your disability or incapacitation, you should use one of the forms provided in Chapter 6.

Witness and Notary Requirements

All states have provided protections to ensure the validity of an advance health care directive. They have also provided legal protections against persons using undue influence to force or coerce someone into signing an advance health care directive. There are various requirements regarding who may be a witness to your signing of your advance health care directive. In general, these protections are for the purpose of ensuring that the witnesses have no actual or indirect stake in your death. These witnesses should have no connection with you from a health care or beneficiary standpoint. In most states, the witnesses must:

> ⌀ **Definition:**
>
> **Declarant:**
> The formal name for the person who signs an advance health care directive; ie. the person that 'declares' the decisions made in the document.

- Not be under 18 years of age (19 in Alabama)
- Not be related to you in any manner either by blood, marriage, or adoption
- Not be your attending physician
- Not be a patient or employee of your attending physician
- Not be a patient, physician, or employee of the health care facility in which you may be a patient
- Not be entitled to any portion of your estate upon your death under any laws of intestate succession, nor under your will or any codicil
- Not have a claim against any portion of your estate upon your death
- Not be directly financially responsible for your medical care
- Not have signed the advance health care directive for you, even at your direction
- Not be paid a fee for acting as a witness

In addition, please note that several states and the District of Columbia (Washington D.C.) have laws in effect regarding witnesses when the *declarant* (the person signing the advance health care directive) is a patient in a nursing home, boarding facility, hospital, or skilled or intermediate health care facility. In those situations, it is advisable to have a patient ombudsman, patient advocate, or the director of the health care facility act as the third witness to the signing of an advance health care directive.

These restrictions on who may be a witness to your signing of an advance health care directive require, in most cases, that the witnesses either be 1) friends who will receive nothing from you under your will, or 2) strangers. Please review the requirements for your own state in the witness statements on your particular state's form.

> **⚬ Toolkit Tip!**
>
> Even if you choose to use an advance health care directive, you can choose not to adopt a particular part of the form (such as the organ donation section).

In addition, all of the advance health care directive forms included on this book's CD are designed to be notarized. This is a requirement in most states for most forms and has been made mandatory on all of the forms in this book. The purpose of notarization in this instance is to add another level of protection against coercion or undue pressure being exerted to force anyone to sign any of these legal forms against their wishes. Sadly, such undue pressure has been applied in some cases to force senior citizens to sign legal documents against their own wishes. The requirement that one sign a document in front of a notary and in front of two additional witnesses can significantly lessen the opportunity for such abuse.

Instructions for Preparing Your Advance Health Care Directive

1. Select the appropriate form from the CD. Carefully read through each section of your Advance Health Care Directive. You may wish to make a copy of the form that you choose. This will allow you to use the copy as a draft copy.

2. Note that you will need to initial your choices in the first section of the form as to which sections of the entire advance health care directive you wish to be effective. The choices are:

- Living will
- Selection of health care agent
- Designation of primary physician
- Organ donation

Please note that you may choose to exclude any of the above portions of your form and the remaining portions will be valid. If you wish to exclude one or more portions, DO NOT place your initials in the space before the section that you wish to exclude. Be careful so that you are certain you are expressing your desires exactly as you wish on these very important matters. If you do not wish to use a particular main section of the entire form, cross out that section of the form clearly and do not initial that section in either the first paragraph of the Directive or in the paragraph directly before your signature near the end of the Directive. If you do not wish to use a particular paragraph within one of the four main sections of the form, cross out that paragraph also.

> **☼ Toolkit Tip!**
>
> If your additional instructions or limitations do not fit in the space provided on the form, you will need to use an "Additional Information for Advance Health Care Directive" form.

Make the appropriate choices in each section where indicated by initialing the designated place or filling in the appropriate information. Depending on which form that you use, you may have many choices to initial or you may have no choices to initial. Please carefully read through the paragraphs and clauses that require choices to be certain that you understand the choices that you will be making. If you wish to add additional instructions or limitations in an area of the form, you should do so within the Adobe Acrobat Reader® program. If you need to add additional pages, please use the form titled "Additional Information for Advance Health Care Directive" which is also provided on the CD. If you need and use additional pages, be certain that you initial and date each added page and that you clearly label each additional page regarding which paragraph or section of the form to which it pertains.

3. In the form or section on organ donations, you may choose to either donate all of your organs or limit your donation to certain specific organs. Likewise, you may provide that the organs be used for any purpose or you may limit their use to certain purposes.

4. Print out (or type) a final copy of your advance health care directive. You will now need to complete the signature and witness/notary sections of your forms. When you have a completed original with no erasures or corrections, staple all of the pages together in the upper left-hand corner. Do not sign this document, initial your choices or fill in the date yet. You should now assemble your witnesses and a notary public to witness your signature. Be certain that your witnesses meet your specific state requirements. In addition, please note that several states and the District of Columbia have laws in effect regarding witnesses when the declarant is a patient in a nursing home, boarding facility, hospital, or skilled or intermediate health care facility. In those situations, it is advisable to have a patient ombudsman, patient advocate, or the director of the health care facility to act as the third witness to the signing of an advance health care directive. In order that your advance health care directive be accepted by all legal and medical authorities with as little difficulty as possible, it is highly recommended that you have your signing of this important document witnessed by both your appropriate witnesses and a notary public.

> ### ·̣φ̣·Toolkit Tip!
> At the formal signing of your directive, you will initial your choices as to which sections of the form you wish to adopt.

5. In front of all of the witnesses and the notary public, the following should take place in the order shown:

(a) There is no requirement that the witnesses know any of the terms of your advance health care directive or other legal forms, or that they read any of your advance health care directive or legal forms. All that is necessary is that they observe you sign your advance health care directive and that they also sign the advance health care directive as witnesses in each other's presence.

(b) You will sign your legal form at the end where indicated, exactly as your name is shown on the form, in ink using a pen. At this time, you should also again initial your choices as to which sections you have chosen (directly before your signature space). You will also need to fill in the date on the first page of the directive or form, date and initial each additional information page (if you have used any), and fill in your address after your signature. Once you have signed and completed all of the necessary information, pass your advance health care directive or other legal form to the first witness, who should sign and date the acknowledgment where indicated and also print his or her name.

(c) After the first witness has signed, have the advance health care directive or other legal form passed to the second witness, who should also sign and date the acknowledgment where indicated and print his or her name.

(d) Throughout this ceremony, you and all of the witnesses must remain together. The final step is for the notary public to sign in the space where indicated and complete the notarization block on the form.

(e) If you have chosen individuals to act as your health care agent (durable power of attorney for health care), you should have them sign the form at the end where shown acknowledging that they accept their appointment.

6. When this step is completed, your advance health care directive or individual legal form that you have signed is a valid legal document. Have several photo-copies made and, if appropriate, deliver a copy to your attending physician to have placed in your medical records file. You should also provide a copy to any person who was selected as either your health care agent or your agent for financial affairs. You may also desire to give a copy to the person you have chosen as the executor of your will (or successor trustee of your living trust), your clergy, and your spouse or other trusted relative.

> **⚡ Toolkit Tip!**
>
> Remember that you may revoke or change your advance health care directive at any time.

If you need to add additional pages to your advance health care directive, please use the form titled "Additional Information for Advance Health Care Directive" at the end of this chapter. If you need and use additional pages, be certain that you initial and date each added page and that you clearly label each additional page regarding which paragraph or section of the form to which it pertains. You should also note in the form itself that you are using additional pages by printing or writing "See attached additional page which is incorporated by reference" in the section of the form where you wish to insert additional instructions or information.

Revoking Your Advance Health Care Directive

All states have provided methods for the easy revocation of advance health care directives and the forms that they contain. Since such forms provide authority to medical personnel to withhold life-support technology that will likely result in death to the patient, great care must be taken to insure that a change of mind by the patient is heeded. Any one of the following methods of revocation is generally acceptable:

- Physical destruction of the advance health care directive, such as tearing, burning, or mutilating the document.

- A written revocation of the advance health care directive by you or by a person acting at your direction. A form for this is provided later in this chapter and on the CD.

- An oral revocation in the presence of a witness who signs and dates an affidavit confirming a revocation. This oral declaration may take place in any manner (verbal or non-verbal). Most states allow for a person to revoke such a document by any indication (even non-verbal) of the intent to revoke an advance health care directive, regardless of his or her physical or mental condition. A form for this effect is included later in this chapter and on the CD, titled "Witness Affidavit of Oral Revocation of Advance Health Care Directive."

If your revoke your advance health care directive, make sure that you provide a copy (or notice) of this revocation to anyone or any health care facility that has a copy or original of the advance health care directive that you are revoking.

Instructions for Revocation of Advance Health Care Directive

To complete this document, fill in the following information:

① Name of person who originally signed the advance health care directive (principal or declarant)
② Date of original advance health care directive
③ State in which original advance health care directive was signed
④ Signature of person revoking advance health care directive
⑤ Date of revocation of advance health care directive

Revocation of Advance Health Care Directive

① I, _____ , am the maker and signatory of an Advance Health Care Directive which was dated ② _____ , and which was executed by me for use in the State of ③_____ .

By this written revocation, I hereby entirely revoke such Advance Health Care Directive, any Living Will, any Durable Power of Attorney for Health Care, any Organ Donation, or any other appointment or designation of a person to make any health care decisions on my behalf. I intend that all of the above mentioned documents have no force or effect whatsoever.

BY SIGNING HERE I INDICATE THAT I UNDERSTAND THE PURPOSE AND EFFECT OF THIS DOCUMENT.

④ Signature _____

⑤ Date _____

Instructions for Witness Affidavit of Oral Revocation of Advance Health Care Directive

If it is necessary to use the Witness Affidavit of Oral Revocation of Advance Health Care Directive form, the witness should actually observe your indication of an intention to revoke your Advance Health Care Directive. This may take the form of any verbal or non-verbal direction, as long as your intent to revoke is clearly and unmistakably evident to the witness. This form does not need to be notarized to be effective. Make sure that you provide a copy of this revocation to anyone or any health care facility that has a copy or original of the Advance Health Care Directive that you are revoking.

To complete this document, fill in the following information:

① Name of person who originally signed the advance health care directive (principal or declarant)
② Date of original advance health care directive
③ State in which original advance health care directive was signed
④ Printed name of witness
⑤ Date of act of revocation
⑥ Signature of witness to the oral or non-verbal revoking of advance health care directive
⑦ Date of witness signature
⑧ Printed name of witness

Witness Affidavit of Oral Revocation of Advance Health Care Directive

The following person, ① _____ , herein referred to as the declarant, was the maker and signatory of an Advance Health Care Directive which was dated ② _____ , and which was executed by him or her for use in the State of ③ _____ .

By this written affidavit, I, ④ _____ , the witness, hereby affirm that on the date of ⑤ _____ , I personally witnessed the above-named declarant make known to me, through verbal and/or non-verbal methods, their clear and unmistakable intent to entirely revoke such Advance Health Care Directive, any Living Will, any Durable Power of Attorney for Health Care, any Organ Donation, or any other appointment or designation of a person to make any health care decisions on his or her behalf. It is my belief that the above-named declarant fully intended that all of the above-mentioned documents no longer have any force or effect whatsoever.

Witness Acknowledgment

The declarant is personally known to me and I believe him or her to be of sound mind and under no duress, fraud, or undue influence.

Witness Signature ⑥ _____ Date ⑦ _____

Printed Name of Witness ⑧ _____

Instructions for Additional Information for Advance Health Care Directive

If you need to add additional pages to your advance health care directive document, please use the form titled "Additional Information for Advance Health Care Directive" which is provided on the following page and on the CD. If you need to use additional pages, be certain that you initial and date each added page and that you clearly label each additional page regarding which paragraph or section of the form to which it pertains. You should also note in the form itself that you are using additional pages by printing or writing "See attached additional information page, which is incorporated by reference" in the section of the form where you wish to insert additional instructions or information. Note that this form should be attached to the original advance health care directive document prior to the signing and notarization of the original document.

To complete this document, fill in the following information:

1. Date of original advance health care directive
2. Name and address of person who originally signed advance health care directive (declarant)
3. Detailed statement of any additional information or instructions in advance health care directive (Be certain that you note the paragraph or section of the original advance health care directive where the additional information or instructions will apply).
4. Initials of declarant and date of advance health care directive

Additional Information for Advance Health Care Directive

The following information is incorporated by reference and is to be considered as a part of the Advance Health Care Directive, dated ① _____,
which was signed by the following declarant ② _____,

Declarant must initial and date at bottom of form and insert additional information here: ③

④ Initials of Declarant _____   Date _____

Chapter 15

Preparing a Designation of Primary Physician

This form allows you to make known your personal choice of the doctor whom you would like to care for you should you be unable to make known your choice. Generally, people desire that their personal family physician be designated as their primary physician since this person is most aware of their personal wishes and desires concerning health care issues. This form may also be useful in conjunction with other estate planning forms that may call for a certification by a primary physician of a person's disability or incapacitation, such as with a durable power of attorney or health care power of attorney. The use of this form is optional. You should keep a copy of this document attached to any such form that may require action by your primary physician. In addition, you should request that a copy of this document be placed into your main medical files. This form need not be acknowledged by a notary public.

> **☼ Toolkit Tip!**
>
> This form is also part of the state-specific advance health care directives explained in Chapter 14. Use the form in this chapter if you choose to prepare this form as a separate document.

Instructions for Designation of Primary Physician

To complete this form, fill in the following information:

① Your name and address
② Name and address of doctor selected as your primary physician
③ Date of signing of Designation of Primary Physician
④ Your signature and printed name

Designation of Primary Physician

① I, _____, address:

do hereby designate the following doctor as my primary physician for all medical issues:

② _____, address:

③ Date _____

④ _____
Signature of person designating primary physician

_____
Printed name of person designating primary physician

Chapter 16

Preparing an Organ Donation Form

The use of this form allows you to make a donation of your organs for medical use after your death. Using this form, you may make choices about whether and how you may wish any of your organs to be donated for medical, scientific, or educational uses after your death. All states have versions of a state law usually referred to as an "Anatomical Gift Act," which provides that individuals may make personal choices about whether and how to provide for the gift of their organs after death. Because of the many lives that can be saved though the use of transplanted donated organs, many states actually actively encourage such donations. This form allows for a selection of which of your organs or body parts you wish to donate and a selection of how those items that you have chosen to donate may be used (such as for any purpose, for research, therapy, transplantation, medical education, or other limitations on their use).

Please read through this carefully and make your appropriate decisions. You may choose to select the donation of your whole body or only of specific parts. You may also choose to allow your donation to be used for any medical or scientific purpose or you may limit the uses of your donation in any way. Naturally, the use of this form is entirely optional. If you do complete this form, it is a good idea to leave a copy of this form with your will and/or living trust and, additionally, to have a copy placed in your main medical file of your primary family physician. As the viability of organs for donation is very time-sensitive, it may also be a good

☀️ Toolkit Tip!

Make certain that any organ donation that you make using this form is identical to any organ donation decision that you may have made previously (for example, on your driver's license.

idea to inform your closest relatives of your decision regarding the use of your organs after your death. This form is designed to be notarized.

Please note that this form specifically states that such donation be made regardless of the objections of any family member. This clause is included because there have been many successful efforts by surviving family members to prevent organ donations after the death of a person who has signed a valid organ donation form. This clause makes known your desire that such donations are your strong personal desire, regardless of the objections of any family members.

Also note that you should be certain that the choices that you make using this document should be identical to any choices that you may have made in any other document, including in your will or on a driver's license organ donation designation.

> **⚡Toolkit Tip!**
>
> An organ donation form is also part of the advance health care directive in this book. You should complete either one, but not both, of these forms to make your organ donation decision.

Instructions for Organ Donation Form

To complete this form, fill in the following information:

①   Your name and address
②   Initial your selection of either any organs/parts or which specific organs or parts
③   Initial your selection of either any purposes or which specific purposes limitations on the use of your organs or parts
④   Date of signing of organ donation form
⑤   Your signature and printed name (Sign in front of notary public)
⑥   The notary acknowledgement section is completed by a notary public

Organ Donation Form

①   I, _____, address:

being of sound mind, do hereby donate the following organs for the noted medical purposes, and I specifically intend that such donations take place regardless of any objections of any of my family member:

② In the event of my death, I have placed my *initials* next to the following part(s) of my body that I wish donated for the purposes that I have *initialed* below:

[   ] any organs or parts **OR**

[   ] eyes   [   ] bone and connective tissue   [   ] skin

[   ] heart   [   ] kidney(s)   [   ] liver

[   ] lung(s)   [   ] pancreas   [   ] other _____

③ for the purposes of:

[   ] any purpose authorized by law **OR**

[   ] transplantation   [   ] research   [   ] therapy

[   ] medical education   [   ] other limitations

④ Dated _____

⑤ _____
        Signature of person donating organs

_____
        Printed name of person donating organs

⑥ **Notary Acknowledgement**

State of _____

County of _____

On _____ , 20_____ , _____ came before me personally and, under oath, stated that he/she is the person described in the above document and he/she signed the above document in my presence.

_____

Notary Public

In and for the County of _____   State of _____

My commission expires: _____   Notary Seal

Chapter 17

Preparing a Quitclaim Deed

This form is used to transfer property from the owner (called the 'grantor' on the deed) to another person or persons (called the 'grantee' on the deed) without any warranties that he or she actually owns the property involved. By using a quitclaim deed, the owner is not, in any way, guaranteeing that she or he actually owns any interest in the property. The owner is simply agreeing to transfer whatever interest in the property he our she may actually own. As with all transfers of real estate, transfers for estate planning purposes must be in writing. This type of quitclaim deed is intended to be used in estate planning situations in two general situation: first, when an individual wishes to transfer real estate into a living trust, and second, in situations when individuals or couples wish to transfer property between co-owners.

When using a quitclaim deed to transfer property into a living trust, the person setting up the living trust who would also be the owner of the real estate that will be placed in the living trust. That person's name (as shown on the current deed to the property) will be the grantor on the new quitclaim deed. The grantee on the new deed would be the trust itself, such as the "Andrea Ann Doria Living Trust, dated June 4, 2006, Andrea Ann Doria, Trustee".

If you are using a quitclaim deed to transfer property from one form of co-ownership to another, such as from ownership as

> ⊘ **Definition:**
>
> **Quitclaim:**
> To release any claim that you might have to the ownership of a parcel of real estate to the grantee.

tenants-in-common to ownership as joint tenants with rights of survivorship, you are advised to check with a title company, real estate professional, or attorney in the county where the property is located to determine the exact wording that is necessary in your jurisdiction. There are many variations from state to state regarding the terminology used to effectively transfer property into a joint tenancy or a tenancy-by-the-entireties (a type of co-tenancy between a wife and husband). An example of such a transaction would be that the grantors would be "Jane and John Smith, as tenants in common" and the grantees would be "Jane and John Smith, as joint tenants with right of survivorship." Again, be sure that you use the correct terminology for your state and locale. For this deed form to be recorded, it must be properly witnessed and notarized.

For estate planning purposes, it may often be useful to add another person to the ownership of real estate. In order to do so, the current owner(s) of the property would be listed as the grantor on a quitclaim deed and the new owner(s) would be listed as the grantees. For example, Bill and Mary Smith own a home and would like to add their daughter, Jane, to the ownership of the property. Bill and Mary Smith would be the grantors on a quitclaim deed to accomplish this and Bill Smith, Mary Smith and Jane Smith would be the grantees on the quitclaim deed. Again, you should be certain as to the type of terminology that you wish to use on your quitclaim deed. In the above example, if no other designation is used, Bill, Mary, and Jane Smith would own the property as tenants-in-common, meaning that they would each own a one-third interest in the property. If the Smith's would like to have their property pass to their daughter without going through probate they would need to designate the ownership of the property to be shared as "joint tenants with right of survivorship". You should review the rules pertaining to property that are outlined in Chapter 3 and check the information relating to property ownership in your state that is listed in the Appendix. Note: If you will be preparing this deed with more than one grantor or grantee, you will need to use the text version of this form. Make certain that you provide a three inch margin at the top of each page and a one inch margin on both the sides and bottom of each page. These margin requirements are necessary for the proper recording of the deed in your local recorder's or county clerk's office.

Instructions for Quitclaim Deed

To prepare this deed, simply fill in the following information:

1. Name of person requesting recording of deed (generally, you)
2. Name and address of person who prepared the deed
3. Name and address of person to whom the recorded deed should be mailed by the recorder's office (not necessary if you bring the deed to the recorder's office personally)
4. Property Tax Parcel number or Tax account number (generally found on latest tax bill)
5. Date of signing deed
6. Name of grantor (the one transferring the property)
7. Address of grantor
8. Name of grantee (the one receiving the property)
9. Address of grantee
10. Street address of property itself
11. Legal description of property (should be taken from current deed)
12. Current year for property taxes (taxes will be prorated between grantor and grantee for the portion of the tax year that each party owned the property)
13. Date of signing of deed by grantor
14. Signature of grantor (signed in the front of notary public)
15. Printed Name of grantor
16. Signatures and printed names of two witnesses (signed in front of notary public)
17. Notary Acknowledgement to be completed by notary public

Recording requested by: ① _____ corder

Quitclaim Deed

Space above reserved for Re-

Document prepared by:

When recorded, mail to:

Name ② _____

Name ③ _____

Address _____

Address _____

Property Tax Parcel/Account Number: ④ _____

This Quitclaim Deed is made on ⑤ _____ , 20 _____ , between
⑥ _____, grantor, address: ⑦ _____
_____

and ⑧_____ , grantee, address: ⑨ _____
_____
_____ .

For valuable consideration, the grantor hereby quitclaims and transfers all right, title, and interest held by the Grantor in the following described real estate to the grantee, and his or her heirs or assigns, to have and hold forever, located at ⑩ _____ , City of _____ , State of _____ , and described as follows: ⑪

Subject to all easements, rights of way, protective covenants, and mineral reservations of record, if any. Taxes for the Tax year of ⑫ _____ shall be prorated between the Grantor and Grantee as of the date of recording this deed.

Dated:⑬ _____ , 20 _____

⑭_____

Signature of Grantor

⑮_____

Printed Name of Grantor

⑯_____
Signature of Witness 1

⑯_____
Printed Name of Witness 1

⑯_____
Signature of Witness 2

⑯_____
Printed Name of Witness 2

⑰ **Notary Acknowledgement**

State of _____
County of _____
On _____ , 20 _____ , _____ personally
came before me, is personally known to me or has proved his or her identity to me on the basis
of satisfactory evidence, and, being duly sworn, did state that he or she is the person described
in the above document and that he or she signed the above document in my presence.

_____
Signature of Notary Public
Notary Public, In and for the County of _____
State of _____
My commission expires: _____   Notary Seal

Appendix: State Estate Planning Laws

This Appendix contains a summary of the laws relating to estate planning issues for all states and the District of Columbia (Washington D.C.). It has been compiled directly from the most recently-available statutes and has been abridged for clarity and succinctness. It is recommended that you review the listing that pertains to your home state and any state in which you own real estate before you complete your estate plan. As you review your state's particular laws, keep in mind that your estate plan documents are going to be interpreted under the laws of the state where you resided at the time of your death. Your personal property will be also distributed according to the laws of the state in which you were a resident at the time of your death. Your real estate, however, will be distributed under the laws of the state in which it is located, regardless of where you were a resident.

Every effort has been made to ensure that the information contained in this Appendix is as complete and up-to-date as possible. However, state laws are subject to constant change. While most laws relating to estates are relatively stable, it is advisable to check your particular state statutes to be certain there have been no major modifications since this book was prepared, especially for those legal points that are particularly important in your situation. To simplify this process as much as possible, the exact name of the statute and the chapter or section number of where the information can be found is noted after each section of information. Any of these official statute books should be available at any public library or on the internet. A librarian will be glad to assist you in locating the correct book and in finding the appropriate pages.

The correct terminology for each state is used in these listings. However, some states use certain language interchangeably. In those states, the most commonly-used language is stated. Although it has been simplified to some extent, you will find that the language in the Appendix is somewhat more complicated than the language used in the rest of this book. This is due to the fact that much of the language in the Appendix has been taken directly from the laws and statutes of each state, and most legislators are lawyers. We apologize for this. We feel, however, that, as a reference, the technical details of the laws should be provided. Use the Glossary located at the end of this book to translate this language. Please note that you may view this Appendix (and increase the size of the type) on your computer by using the PDF format version that is included on the Forms-on-CD. The state-by-state listings following in this Appendix contain the following information for each state:

State Website: This listing provides the internet website address of the location of the state's statutes. The addresses were current at the time of this book's publication; however, like most websites, the page addresses are subject to change. If an expired state webpage is not automatically redirected to a new site, laws can be searched at http://www.findlaw.com

State Law Description: This is the title where most of the relevant state laws on wills, living wills and probate are contained.

Uniform Acts Adopted: This listing notes the various Uniform Trust Acts relating to trusts that have been enacted and lists their citations (*i.e.*, Uniform Trustees' Powers Act, Uniform Gifts to Minors Act, etc.).

Court with Probate Jurisdiction: This listing provides the name of the particular court in each state that has exclusive jurisdiction over probate and will-related legal matters.

Minimum Age for Disposing of Property by Will: This listing details the minimum age for having a legally-valid will. For most states, this age is 18, but there are a few states that have differing laws.

Required Number of Witnesses for Wills: For most states, the *minimum* number of required witnesses is two. Be advised, however, that it is recommended to use at least three witnesses for your will. Some states will disqualify a witness that is a beneficiary and, if this happens, two additional witnesses are required for the will to be valid.

Can Witnesses Be Beneficiaries?: Under this listing is information regarding whether witnesses to the signing of the will can be beneficiaries under the will. Again, be advised that to be safe, your witnesses should *not* be beneficiaries.

Are There Provisions for Self-Proving Wills?: This listing details whether there are specific state law provisions for self-proving wills. All wills (except Louisiana) provided in this book are designed to be self-proving when completed as indicated.

Are Holographic Wills Permitted?: Under this listing, the name of any relevant state law regarding living wills is shown.

How Does Divorce Affect the Will?: The effect of divorce on the will under state law is shown in this listing. State law varies widely on this point and in some states a divorce may automatically revoke your entire will. It is highly recommended that you review and update your will if you are ever divorced.

How Does Marriage Affect the Will?: This listing provides the state law on the effect of marriage on the will. Again, state law provides various provisions and marriage may have the drastic effect of entirely revoking your will. It is, therefore, recommended that you review and update your will if you are ever married.

Who Must Be Mentioned in the Will?: Under this listing is shown which parties must be specifically mentioned in the will. Certain parties must be mentioned in your will or they may be entitled to an intestate share of your estate regardless of your will. Most states provide this protection for children born after a will is made and for new spouses from a marriage that takes place after a will is prepared. However, it is recommended that you review and change your will if you adopt or have any new children, are married, or if any of your named beneficiaries die.

Spouse's Right to Property Regardless of Will: This listing provides the results of a spouse's right of election against the will. In all states, the surviving spouse has a right to a certain share of the deceased spouse's estate regardless of any provisions in the will of the deceased spouse that may give the surviving spouse less than this "statutory" or "community" property share.

Laws of Intestate Succession (Distribution If No Will): Under this listing the complex state provisions regarding intestate distribution of estates are outlined. This provides an overview of how your property would be distributed in the event that you die without a valid will. The laws in this area are extremely complex and differ widely from state to state. The outline of laws shown in this listing is intended to provide a simplified example of the particular state distribution scheme. If specific details of your state's distribution plan are needed, please consult the state statute directly.

A few definitions may be useful in deciphering the information listed in this section. The terms "per capita" and "per stirpes" are often used in these state plans. *Per capita* refers to a distribution to each member of a group equally. *Per stirpes* means distribution to a lower-level group based on "representation" in the upper level. For example, a parent has two children, each of whom have two grandchildren for a total of six descendents. However, one of the children died before the parent, leaving only five descendents. When the parent dies, a per capita distribution would divide the estate into five equal shares, with each descendent taking one-fifth. In a per stirpes distribution, the estate is divided into two equal halves; one for each original child's share. The living child takes one-half and the grandchildren who are children of the deceased child each take one-fourth. In effect, they share by "representation" their deceased parent's share of the estate. The grandchildren who are children of the living child would take nothing under a per stirpes distribution.

Another definition which may be useful is a "life estate." A *life estate* in real estate is provided to the surviving spouse in some states upon a spouse's death. A life estate means that the surviving spouse has the full use and enjoyment of any real estate for his or her entire life. However, upon his or her death, the property will pass automatically to the person who has the remaining share of the estate. Most often, this will be a child of the original, or first, deceased. The spouse who is given a life estate cannot leave such a property interest to anyone else.

Property Ownership: Whether the state follows the community property or common-law system of ownership of marital property is shown in this listing.

State Gift, Inheritance, or Estate Taxes: This listing shows the tax situation in each state as it relates to estates and wills. There are three basic taxes that apply: gift taxes, inheritance taxes, and estate taxes. Each individual state may impose any of these taxes and each tax rate may vary, depending on the state.

Simplified Probate Procedures: Under this listing are shown the various state exceptions to standard probate procedures. All states (except Georgia and Louisiana)) have some method by which small estates are exempted from formal probate procedures. They generally take two forms: a method of probate using affidavits, and/or an exemption from standard probate procedures for estates that fall below a certain dollar value.

Living Will Form: Under this listing, the exact location of a state's official Simplified Probate Procedures: Living Will Form is provided.

Other Directives: The existence and location of additional official state directives relating to advance health care and powers of attorney are indicated in this listing. Examples of such forms are Durable Power of Attorney for Health Care, Durable Power of Attorney for Financial Affairs, Anatomical Gift Act forms (organ donation forms), Designation of Primary Physician, and other related forms.

Living Will Effective: This listing indicates the requirements of state law regarding when a living will becomes effective. Most states require that two physicians must diagnose and document that a patient either has a terminal illness with no hope of recovery or is in a permanent state of unconsciousness, or some similar diagnosis.

Living Will Witness Requirements: Under this listing are noted the specific state requirements for witnesses to the signing of a living will and any related advance health care directives. In general, most states require that there are two witnesses, and that the witnesses be over eighteen, not related by blood or marriage to the declarant, not entitled to any part of the declarant's estate, and not financially responsible for the declarant's health care costs. Note that a few states require that, if the declarant is a patient in a nursing home or hospital, one of the witnesses be a patient advocate or patient ombudsman. In some states, the patient advocate or ombudsman is required to be a third witness, in addition to the other two required witnesses.

Trustee Residency Requirements: Here is noted if a trustee must be a resident of the state in which the trust is formed and any qualifications.

Minimum Age for Grantor or Trustee: This listing specifies the minimum age that a person must be to be either a grantor or trustee of a trust. There is no minimum age to be a beneficiary of a trust in any state.

Trust-Writing Requirements: Which trust provisions must be in writing are noted in this listing. All states require trusts relating to real estate to be in writing. Some states require that all trust provisions be in writing.

Trust Pour-Over to Will: The requirements for a trust that is used to add property to an existing will are noted in this section.

Additional Trust Requirements: Here are listed any additional state-specific requirements for trusts, such as registration of a trust, etc.

Alabama

State Website: www.legislature.state.al.us/CodeofAlabama/1975/coatoc.htm

State Law Reference: Code of Alabama.

Uniform Acts Adopted: Uniform Testamentary Additions to Trusts Act: (Section 43-8-140). Uniform Trustee Powers Act: (Section 19-3-322) Uniform Gift to Minors Act: (Sections 35-5A-1+).

Court with Probate Jurisdiction: Probate Court. (Section 12-13-1).

Minimum Age for Disposing of Property by Will: 18. (Section 43-8-130).

Required Number of Witnesses for Signing of Will: Two. (Section 43-8-131).

Can Witnesses Be Beneficiaries?: Yes. (Section 43-8-134).

Are There Provisions for Self-Proving Wills?: Yes. (Section 43-8-132).

Are Holographic Wills Permitted?: No provision.

How Does Divorce Affect the Will?: Revokes the will as to the divorced spouse unless expressly provided otherwise. (Sections 43-8-137 and 43-8-252).

How Does Marriage Affect the Will?: Revokes the will as to the spouse if he or she is not otherwise provided for. Spouse may still be entitled to his or her statutory share under the state intestate laws. (Section 43-8-90).

Who Must Be Mentioned in the Will?: Children, born or adopted; surviving spouse. (Sections 43-8-90 and 43-8-91).

Spouse's Right to Property Regardless of Will: The surviving spouse is entitled to either: (a) all of the deceased spouse's estate, reduced by the value of the surviving spouse's "augmented" estate; or (b) 1/3 of the "augmented" estate of the deceased spouse. In general, the "augmented" estate includes both the property that passes under the will and any other property that passes by other "non-will" transfers, such as under the terms of a living trust or a joint tenancy arrangement. (Section 43-8-70).

Laws of Intestate Succession (Distribution If No Will): *Spouse and children of spouse surviving:* $50,000.00 and 1/2 of balance to spouse and 1/2 of balance to children.

Spouse and children not of spouse surviving: 1/2 to spouse and 1/2 to children.

Spouse, but no children or parent(s) surviving: All to spouse.

Spouse and parent(s), but no children surviving: $100,000.00 and 1/2 of balance to spouse and 1/2 of balance to parent(s).

Children, but no spouse surviving: All to children equally or to their children per stirpes.

Parent(s), but no spouse or children surviving: All to parents equally or to the surviving parent.

No spouse, children, or parent(s) surviving: All to brothers and sisters per stirpes; or if none, to grandparents or their children per stirpes; or if none, to deceased spouse's next-of-kin. (Sections 43-8-41 and 43-8-42).

Property Ownership: Common-law state. Tenancy-in-common is presumed if real estate is held jointly unless title creates joint tenancy with right of survivorship or similar words. No tenancy-by-the-entirety is recognized. Joint bank account deposits are payable to any survivor. (Section 35-4-7).

State Gift, Inheritance, or Estate Taxes: No gift tax; no inheritance tax; imposes state estate tax based on federal estate tax. (Sections 40-15-1 to 40-15-19).

Simplified Probate Procedures: No affidavit procedure. Simplified probate for estates up to $3,000 of personal property. (Section 43-2-690+).

Simplified Probate Procedures: No affidavit procedure. Simplified probate allowed for estates up to $3,000 in personal property. (Section 43-2-692).

Living Will Form: Living Will (Section 22-8A-4).

Other Directives: Anatomical Gift Act (Section 22-19-40).

Living Will Effective: Two (2) physicians, one being the attending physician, must diagnose and document in the medical records that you either have a terminal illness or injury or are in a permanent state of unconsciousness. (Section 22-8A-4).

Living Will Witness Requirements: Living will must be signed in the presence of two (2) or more witnesses at least nineteen (19) years of age. Witnesses cannot be related by blood, adoption, or marriage, entitled to any part of your estate, or be directly financially responsible for your health care. (Section 22-8A-4).

Advance Health Care Directive: Referred to as a Living Will. (Section 22-8A-4).

Health Care Power of Attorney: State specific form is part of Advance Health Care Directive. See Chapter 10 for instructions for form on CD. (Section 22-8A-4).

Durable Power of Attorney: No state-specific form. See Chapter 6 for form. (Section 26-1-2).

Trustee Residency Requirements: No provision.

Minimum Age for Grantor or Trustee: Nineteen (19). (Section 26-1-1).

Trust-Writing Requirements: A trust holding real estate must be in writing. A trust holding personal or other property can be written or oral. (Section 8-9-2).

Trustee Bond Requirements: Trustee must provide bond of double the amount of the supposed value of the trust, unless waived by the trust itself. (Section 19-3-233).

Trustee Pour-Over to Will: The trust must be identified in the will. The terms of the trust must be in a document other than the will and signed before or at the same time as the will. (Section 43-8-140).

Additional Trust Requirements: None.

Alaska

State Website: www.legis.state.ak.us/folhome.htm

State Law Reference: Alaska Statutes.

Uniform Acts Adopted: Uniform Probate Code: (Sections 13.06.005+). Uniform Testamentary Additions to Trusts Act: (Section 13.12.511). Uniform Transfer to Minors Act: (Sections 13.46.010+). Uniform Powers of Trustees Act: (Section 13.36.109).

Court with Probate Jurisdiction: Superior Court.

Minimum Age for Disposing of Property by Will: 18. (Section 13.12.501).

Required Number of Witnesses for Signing of Will: Two. (Section 13.12.502).

Can Witnesses Be Beneficiaries?: Yes. (Section 13.12.505).

Are There Provisions for Self-Proving Wills?: Yes. (Section 13.12.504).

Are Holographic Wills Permitted?: Yes. (Section 13.12.502).

How Does Divorce Affect the Will?: Revokes the will as to the divorced spouse unless expressly provided otherwise. (Section 13.12.802).

How Does Marriage Affect the Will?: Revokes the will as to the spouse if he or she is not otherwise provided for. Spouse may still be entitled to his or her statutory share under the state intestate laws. (Section 13.12.301).

Who Must Be Mentioned in the Will?: Children, born or adopted; surviving spouse. (Sections 13.12.202 and 13.12.302).

Spouse's Right to Property Regardless of Will: The surviving spouse is entitled to 1/3 of the "augmented" estate of the deceased spouse. In general, the "augmented" estate includes both the property that passes under the will and any other property that passes by other "non-will" transfers, such as under the terms of a living trust or a joint tenancy arrangement. (Sections 13.12.202 and 13.12.203).

Laws of Intestate Succession (Distribution If No Will): *Spouse and children of spouse surviving:* All to spouse.
Spouse and children not of spouse surviving: 1/2 to spouse and 1/2 to children or grandchildren per stirpes.
Spouse, but no children or parent(s) surviving: All to spouse.
Spouse and parent(s), but no children surviving: $200,000.00 and 3/4 of balance to spouse and 1/4 of balance to parent(s).
Children, but no spouse surviving: All to children equally or to their children per stirpes.
Parent(s), but no spouse or children surviving: All to parents equally or to the surviving parent.
No spouse, children, or parent(s) surviving: All to brothers and sisters per stirpes; or if none, 1/2 to paternal grandparents and their children per stirpes and 1/2 to maternal grandparents and their children per stirpes. (Sections 13.12.102 and 13.12.103).

Property Ownership: Common-law state. However, spouses may, by written agreement, declare that any or all of their property is community property with a right of survivorship. No joint tenancy in real property (except for spouses). Persons with undivided interests in real estate are tenants-in-common. Spouses who acquire real estate hold it as tenants-by-the-entirety unless stated otherwise. Joint bank account deposits are payable to any survivor. (Sections 34.15.110 and 34.77.030).

State Gift, Inheritance, or Estate Taxes: No gift tax; no inheritance tax; imposes state estate tax based on federal estate tax. (Sections 43.31.011 to 43.31.430).

Simplified Probate Procedures: Affidavit allowed for estates with personal property up to $15,000.00. Simplified probate allowed for estates up to value of homestead, exempt property allowance, family allowances, last illness and burial expenses. (Sections 13.16.680, 13.16.690, and 13.16.695).

Living Will Form: Declaration Relating to Use of Life-Sustaining Procedures serves as Living Will (Section 13.52.300).

Other Directives: Anatomical Gift Act (Section 13.52.170 through 13.52.280).

Living Will Effective: Two (2) physicians determine that you are in a terminal condition and your death will result without using life-sustaining procedures. Your physician must then record your diagnosis and the contents of your Declaration in your medical records. (Section 13.52.300).

Living Will Witness Requirements: Sign your Declaration, or direct another to sign it, in the presence of two (2) adult witnesses or a notary public. Witnesses cannot be related by blood or marriage. (Section 13.52.300).

Advance Health Care Directive: (Section 13.52.300).

Durable Power of Attorney for Health Care: State specific form is part of Advance Health Care Directive. See Chapter 10 for instructions for form on CD. (Section 13.52.300)

Durable Power of Attorney: State specific form. See Chapter 9. (Sections 13.26.332 and 13.26.353).

Trustee Residency Requirements: If out-of-state trustee is appointed, trust must be registered. (Section 13.36.025).

Minimum Age for Grantor or Trustee: Eighteen (18). (Section 25.20.010).

Trust-Writing Requirements: All trusts must be in writing. (Sections 9.25.010 & 34.40.070).

Trustee Bond Requirements: None, unless required by trust, requested by beneficiary, or ordered by court. (Section 13.36.085).

Trustee Pour-Over to Will: The trust must be identified in the will. The terms of the trust must be in a document other than the will and signed before or at the same time as the will. (Section 13.12.511).

Additional Trust Requirements: Residents should register a "Registration of Living Trust" form with the local court in their county of residence. This requirement is mandatory, although there are no penalties or consequences for failure to register. Please see proper form in Chapter 9.

Arizona

State Website: www.azleg.state.az.us/

State Law Reference: Arizona Revised Statutes Annotated.

Uniform Acts Adopted: Uniform Probate Code: (Sections 14-1102+). Uniform Trustees' Powers Act: (Sections 14-7232 & 14-7233). Uniform Transfer to Minors Act: (Sections 14-7651+). Uniform Testamentary Additions to Trusts Act: (Section 14-2511).

Court with Probate Jurisdiction: Superior Court.

Minimum Age for Disposing of Property by Will: 18. (Section 14-2501).

Required Number of Witnesses for Signing of Will: Two. (Section 14-2502).

Can Witnesses Be Beneficiaries?: Yes. (Section 14-2505).

Are There Provisions for Self-Proving Wills?: Yes. (Section 14-2504).

Are Holographic Wills Permitted?: Yes. (Section 14-2503).

How Does Divorce Affect the Will?: Revokes the will as to the divorced spouse unless expressly provided otherwise. (Section 14-2802).

How Does Marriage Affect the Will?: Revokes the will as to the spouse if he or she is not otherwise provided for. Spouse may still be entitled to his or her statutory share under the state intestate laws. (Section 14-2301).

Who Must Be Mentioned in the Will?: Children, born or adopted; surviving spouse. (Sections 14-2301 and 14-2302).

Spouse's Right to Property Regardless of Will: Community property right to 1/2 of the deceased spouse's "community" property. In addition, the surviving spouse is entitled to a one-time allowance of $18,000.00. (Section 14-2402).

Laws of Intestate Succession (Distribution If No Will): *Spouse and children of spouse surviving:* All of decedent's separate property and 1/2 of decedent's community property to spouse and 1/2 of decedent's community property to children.

Spouse and children not of spouse surviving: 1/2 of decedent's separate property to spouse and 1/2 of decedent's separate property and all of decedent's community property to children.

Spouse, but no children or parent(s) surviving: All to spouse.

Spouse and parent(s), but no children surviving: All to spouse.

Children, but no spouse surviving: All to children equally or to their children per stirpes.

Parent(s), but no spouse or children surviving: All to parents equally or to the surviving parent.

No spouse, children, or parent(s) surviving: All to brothers and sisters per stirpes; or if none, to the next-of-kin. (Sections 14-2102 and 14-2103).

Property Ownership: Community property state. Property acquired during marriage outside state before moving into state is quasi-community property. Joint tenancy with right of survivorship between spouses if stated. Tenancy-by-the-entirety is not recognized. Joint bank account deposits are payable to any survivor unless clear evidence exists that deposit is payable only to specified survivor. Allows beneficiary deeds to transfer property on death. (Section 25-211 and Section 33-431).

State Gift, Inheritance, or Estate Taxes: No gift tax; no inheritance tax; no state estate tax. (Sections 42-4051 and 42-4052)

Simplified Probate Procedures: Affidavit and simplified probate allowed for estates up to $50,000.00 (Sections 14-3971.B. 14-3971.E, and 14-3973)

Living Will Form: Living Will (Sections 36-3261 and 36-3262).

Other Directives: Anatomical Gift Act (Sections 36-841 through 36-850).

Living Will Effective: For the living will to become operative, a physician must certify that your condition is terminal, irreversible, or incurable. (Section 36-3251)

Living Will Witness Requirements: Sign in the presence of one (1) or more witnesses or a notary public. Witnesses cannot be related by blood, adoption, or marriage, entitled to any part of your estate, or be directly financially responsible for your health care. (Section 36-3261 and 36-3221).

Advance Health Care Directive: Referred to as a Living Will. (Sections 36-3261 and 36-3261).

Health Care Power of Attorney: State specific form is part of Advance Health Care Directive. See Chapter 10 for instructions for form on CD. (Sections 36-3221 through 36-3224)

Durable Power of Attorney: State specific form. See Chapter 9. (Section 14-5501).

Trustee Residency Requirements: None.

Minimum Age for Grantor or Trustee: Eighteen (18). (Section 8-101).

Trust-Writing Requirements: A trust holding real estate must be in writing. A trust holding personal property can be written or oral. (Section 44-101).

Trustee Bond Requirements: None, unless required by trust, requested by beneficiary, or required by court order. (Section 14-7304).

Trustee Pour-Over to Will: The trust must be identified in the will. The terms of the trust must be in a document other than the will and signed before or at the same time as the will. (Section 14-2511).

Additional Trust Requirements: None.

Arkansas

State Website: http://www.arkleg.state.ar.us/

State Law Reference: Arkansas Code.

Uniform Acts Adopted: Uniform Testamentary Additions to Trusts Act: (Sections 28-27-101+). Uniform Trustees' Powers Act: (Sections 28-69-033 & 28-69-304). Uniform Gifts to Minors Act: (Sections 9-26-201+).

Court with Probate Jurisdiction: Probate Court. (Section 28-1-104).

Minimum Age for Disposing of Property by Will: 18. (Section 28-25-101).

Required Number of Witnesses for Signing of Will: Two. (Section 28-25-102).

Can Witnesses Be Beneficiaries?: Yes, but still must have 2 other disinterested witnesses. (Section 28-25-102).

Are There Provisions for Self-Proving Wills?: Yes. (Section 28-25-106).

Are Holographic Wills Permitted?: Yes. (Section 28-25-104).

How Does Divorce Affect the Will?: Revokes the will as to the divorced spouse. (Section 28-25-109).

How Does Marriage Affect the Will?: Does not revoke the will. (Section 28-25-109).

Who Must Be Mentioned in the Will?: Children, born or adopted; surviving spouse. (Sections 28-39-401 and 28-39-407).

Spouse's Right to Property Regardless of Will: Intestate share: 1/3 of personal property and 1/3 of real estate for life. (Section 28-39-401).

Laws of Intestate Succession (Distribution If No Will): *Spouse and children of spouse surviving:* Real estate: 1/3 life estate to spouse and 2/3 to children equally or their children per stirpes. Personal property: 1/3 to spouse and 2/3 to children equally or their children per stirpes.

Spouse and children not of spouse surviving: Real estate: 1/3 life estate to spouse and 2/3 to children equally or their children per stirpes. Personal property: 1/3 to spouse and 2/3 to children equally or their children per stirpes.

Spouse, but no children or parent(s) surviving: All to spouse if married over 3 years. If married less than 3 years, 1/2 to spouse and 1/2 to brothers and sisters equally or their children per stripes; or if no siblings or siblings' children, all to ancestors (up to great-grandparents); or if none, all to spouse.

Spouse and parent(s), but no children surviving: All to spouse if married over 3 years. If married less than 3 years, 1/2 to spouse and 1/2 to parent(s).

Children, but no spouse surviving: All to children equally or to their children per capita.

Parent(s), but no spouse or children surviving: All to parents equally or to the surviving parent.

No spouse, children, or parent(s) surviving: All to brothers and sisters per stripes; or if none, to grandparents and their children per stirpes. (Sections 28-9-204, 28-9-205, and 28-9-206).

Property Ownership: Common-law state. Property acquired in a community property state is community property. Tenancy-in-common and joint tenancy are recognized. Tenancy-by-the-entirety is recognized when conveyance is to husband and wife. Joint bank account deposits are payable to any survivor. Allows beneficiary deeds to transfer property on death. (Sections 18-12-106 and 18-12-603, and 23-47-204).

State Gift, Inheritance, or Estate Taxes: No gift tax; no inheritance tax; no state estate tax. (Sections 26-59-101 to 26-59-122)

Simplified Probate Procedures: No affidavit procedure. Simplified probate for estates up to $100,000.00 plus some limited amounts for surviving spouse or children. (Section 28-41-101).

Living Will Form: Declaration serves as Living Will (Section 20-17-202).

Other Directives: Anatomical Gift Act (Section 20-17-1201+).

Living Will Effective: Declaration applies when two (2) physicians diagnose you to have an incurable or irreversible condition that will cause death in a relatively short time. (20-17-203).

Living Will Witness Requirements: Sign in the presence of two (2) witnesses. No other restrictions apply. (Section 20-17-202).

Advance Health Care Directive: Referred to as a Declaration. (Section 20-17-202).

Durable Power of Attorney for Health Care: No state specific form. See Chapter 7 for form. Also may use Advance Health Care Directive. See Chapter 10 for instructions for form on CD. (Section 20-13-104).

Durable Power of Attorney: State specific form. See Chapter 9. (Section 28-68-402).

Trustee Residency Requirements: Out-of-state trustee must qualify to do business in Arkansas. (Section 4-31-202).

Minimum Age for Grantor or Trustee: Eighteen (18). (Section 9-25-101).

Trust-Writing Requirements: A trust holding real estate must be in writing. (Section 4-59-103).

Trustee Bond Requirements: Yes, unless not required by trust. (Section 28-4-201).

Trustee Pour-Over to Will: The trust must be identified in the will. The terms of the trust must be in a document other than the will and signed before or at the same time as the will. (Section 28-27-101).

Additional Trust Requirements: None.

California

State Website: www.leginfo.ca.gov/

State Law Reference: California Law.

Uniform Acts Adopted: Uniform Testamentary Additions to Trusts Act: (Probate Code, Section 6300). Uniform Trustees' Powers Act: (Probate Code, Sections 16200+). Uniform Transfers to Minors Act: (Probate Code, Sections 3900+).

Court with Probate Jurisdiction: Superior Court.

Minimum Age for Disposing of Property by Will: 18. (Probate Code, Section 6100).

Required Number of Witnesses for Signing of Will: Two. (Probate Code, Section 6110).

Can Witnesses Be Beneficiaries?: Yes. (Probate Code, Section 6112).

Are There Provisions for Self-Proving Wills?: Yes. (Probate Code, Section 8221).

Are Holographic Wills Permitted?: Yes. (Probate Code, Section 6111).

How Does Divorce Affect the Will?: Revokes the will as to the divorced spouse unless expressly provided otherwise. (Probate Code, Section 6122).

How Does Marriage Affect the Will?: Revokes the will as to the surviving spouse. However, spouse may still be entitled to statutory share. (Probate Code, Section 21610).

Who Must Be Mentioned in the Will?: Children, born or adopted; grandchildren of deceased child; surviving spouse. (Probate Code, Sections 21610 and 21620).

Spouse's Right to Property Regardless of Will: Community property right to 1/2 of the deceased spouse's "community" property. (Probate Code, Section 100).

Laws of Intestate Succession (Distribution If No Will): *Spouse and children of spouse surviving:* All of decedent's community property to spouse. If 1 child, 1/2 of decedent's separate property to spouse and 1/2 to child per stirpes. If more than 1 child, 1/3 of decedent's separate property to spouse and 2/3 to children per stirpes.

Spouse and children not of spouse surviving: 1/2 of community property, 1/3 life estate in separate real property, and 1/3 separate personal property to spouse; balance to children or grandchildren per stirpes.

Spouse, but no children or parent(s) surviving: All of decedent's community property to spouse. 1/2 of decedent's separate property to spouse and 1/2 of decedent's separate property to brothers and sisters equally or to their children per stirpes; or if none, all to spouse.

Spouse and parent(s), but no children surviving: All of decedent's community property to spouse. 1/2 of decedent's separate property to spouse and 1/2 of decedent's separate property to parents or surviving parent.

Children, but no spouse surviving: All to children equally or to their children per stirpes.

Parent(s), but no spouse or children surviving: All to parents equally or to the surviving parent.

No spouse, children, or parent(s) surviving: All to brothers and sisters per stirpes; or if none, to the next-of-kin. (Probate Code, Sections 6401 and 6402).

Property Ownership: Community property state. Property in names of spouses as joint tenants is not community property unless stated. Joint tenancy with right of survivorship must be stated. Tenancy-by-the-entirety is not recognized. Joint bank account deposits are payable to survivor if account had rights of survivorship stated. Allows transfer-on-death vehicle titles. (Family Code, Sections 750, 760, and 770 and Civil Code, Section 683).

State Gift, Inheritance, or Estate Taxes: No gift tax; no inheritance tax; imposes state estate tax based on federal estate tax. (Revenue and Taxation Code, Sections 13301 and 13302).

Simplified Probate Procedures: Affidavit allowed for estates up to $100,000.00. Simplified probate allowed for estates up to $100,000.00 (unlimited amount for surviving spouse's community property). (Probate Code, Section 13050,

13100+, 13200+, and 13500+).

Living Will Form: California Advanced Health Care Directive serves as Living Will (Probate Code, Section 4701)

Other Directives: Anatomical Gift Act (Health and Safety Code, Sections 7150 +).

Living Will Effective: This Directive becomes effective in the event that you have an incurable and irreversible condition that will result in death within a relatively short time, become unconscious and, to a reasonable degree of medical certainty, will not regain consciousness, or the likely risks and burdens of treatment would outweigh the expected benefits. (Probate Code, Section 4701).

Living Will Witness Requirements: Sign in the presence of two (2) adult witnesses. A witness cannot be the person you appointed as your agent, your health care provider or an employee of your health care provider, or the operator or employee of a residential care facility for the elderly. Witnesses cannot be related to you by blood, marriage, or adoption, or be entitled to any part of your estate. A third witness, who must be a patient advocate or ombudsman, is required if the patient is in a skilled nursing facility (Probate Code, Section 4701).

Advance Health Care Directive: (Probate Code, Section 4701).

Power of Attorney for Health Care: State specific form is part of Advance Health Care Directive. See Chapter 10 for instructions for form on CD. (Probate Code, Sections 4701, 4673, 4674, and 4675).

Durable Power of Attorney: State specific form. See Chapter 9. (Probate Code, Sections 4120 +).

Trustee Residency Requirements: Out-of-state trustee's actions are severely restricted, please refer directly to the statute. (Probate Code, Sections 17003 & 17005).

Minimum Age for Grantor or Trustee: Eighteen (18). (Family Code, Section 6500-02).

Trust-Writing Requirements: A trust holding real estate must be in writing. Trusts holding personal property need clear and convincing evidence if not in writing. (Probate Code, Sections 15206 & 15207).

Trustee Bond Requirements: None, unless required by the trust or court order. (Probate Code, Section 15602).

Trustee Pour-Over to Will: The trust must be identified in the will. The terms of the trust must be in a document other than the will and signed before or at the same time as the will. (Probate Code, Section 6300).

Additional Trust Requirements: When a living trust becomes irrevocable in California (upon the death of the grantor or surviving grantor), the trustee must notify all beneficiaries of the trust in writing. There are specific requirements for the notice which are contained in California Probate Code, Section 16061.5+.

Colorado

State Website: www.leg.state.co.us/

State Law Reference: Colorado Revised Statutes.

Uniform Acts Adopted: Uniform Probate Code: (Sections 15-10-101+ and 15-11-101+). Uniform Testamentary Additions to Trusts Act: (Section 15-11-511). Uniform Trustees' Powers Act: (Section 15-1-804). Uniform Gifts to Minors Act: (Sections 11-50-101+).

Court with Probate Jurisdiction: District Court (Probate Court in Denver). (Section 13-9-103).

Minimum Age for Disposing of Property by Will: 18. (Section 15-11-501).

Required Number of Witnesses for Signing of Will: Two. (Section 15-11-502(1)(c)).

Can Witnesses Be Beneficiaries?: Yes. (Section 15-11-505).

Are There Provisions for Self-Proving Wills?: Yes. (Section 15-11-504).

Are Holographic Wills Permitted?: Yes. (Section 15-11-502(2)).

How Does Divorce Affect the Will?: Revokes the will as to the divorced spouse. (Section 15-11-804).

How Does Marriage Affect the Will?: Revokes the will as to the spouse if he or she is not otherwise provided for. Spouse may still be entitled to his or her statutory share under the state intestate laws. (Section 15-11-301).

Who Must Be Mentioned in the Will?: Children, born or adopted; surviving spouse. (Sections 15-11-301 and 15-11-302).

Spouse's Right to Property Regardless of Will: The surviving spouse is entitled to 1/2 of the "augmented" estate of the deceased spouse. However, the amount is also dependent on the length of the marriage in years. In general, the "augmented" estate includes both the property that passes under the will and any other property that passes by other "non-will" transfers, such as under the terms of a living trust or a joint tenancy arrangement. (Section 15-11-201).

Laws of Intestate Succession (Distribution If No Will): *Spouse and children of spouse surviving:* Spouse receives entire estate. (Section 15-11-102(1)(b)).

Spouse and children not of spouse surviving: $150,000.00 and 1/2 to spouse and 1/2 to children and grandchildren per stirpes. (Section 15-11-102(3)).

Spouse, but no children or parent(s) surviving: $200,000.00 and 3/4 of remainder to spouse, 1/4 to parent(s). (Section 15-11-102(1)(A)).

Spouse and parent(s), but no children surviving: All to spouse. (Section 15-11-102(2)).

Children, but no spouse surviving: All to children equally or to their children per capita at each generation. (Section 15-11-103(1)).

Parent(s), but no spouse or children surviving: All to parents equally or to the surviving parent. (Section 15-11-103(2)).

No spouse, children, or parent(s) surviving: All to brothers and sisters per capita at each generation; or if none, to grandparents and their children per capita at each generation; or if none, to nearest lineal ancestors and their children. (Section 15-11-102).

Property Ownership: Common-law state. Tenancy-in-common is presumed unless otherwise stated. Joint tenancy is recognized. Tenancy-by-the-entirety is not recognized. Allows beneficiary deeds to transfer property on death. (Section 38-11-101).

State Gift, Inheritance, or Estate Taxes: No gift tax; no inheritance tax; no state estate tax. (Sections 39-23.5+).

Simplified Probate Procedures: Affidavit allowed for estates up to $50,000.00. Simplified probate allowed for up to value of exempt property allowance, family allowances, last illness and burial expenses. (Sections 15-12-1201 and 15-12-1203).

Living Will Form: Colorado Declaration as to Medical or Surgical Treatment serves as Living Will (Section 15-18-103).

Other Directives: Anatomical Gift Act (Section 12-34-101).

Living Will Effective: Two (2) physicians must determine that you are in a terminal condition and your death will result without using life-sustaining procedures. Your physician must then record your diagnosis and the contents of your Declaration in your medical records. (Sections 15-18-103 and 15-18-104).

Living Will Witness Requirements: Sign in the presence of two (2) adult witnesses. A witness cannot be a person who has claim against your estate upon your death, stands to inherit from your estate, or a physician, an employee of your attending physician or treating health care facility, or a patient of your treating health care facility. (Sections 15-18-105 and 15-18-106).

Advance Health Care Directive: Referred to as a Declaration as to Medical or Surgical Treatment. (Section 15-18-104).

Durable Power of Attorney for Health Care: State specific form is part of Advance Health Care Directive. See Chapter 10 for instructions for form on CD. (Section 15-14-506).

Durable Power of Attorney: State specific form. See Chapter 9. (Sections 15-1-1301+, 15-14-501+, and 15-14-601+).

Trustee Residency Requirements: Trust managed by out-of-state trustee must be registered. (Section 15-16-105).

Minimum Age for Grantor or Trustee: Eighteen (18). (Section 13-22-101).

Trust-Writing Requirements: A trust holding real estate must be in writing. (Section 38-10-118).

Trustee Bond Requirements: None unless required by trust or beneficiary. (Section 15-16-304).

Trustee Pour-Over to Will: The trust must be identified in the will. The terms of the trust must be in a document other than the will and signed before or at the same time as the will. (Section 15-15-101).

Additional Trust Requirements: Upon the Grantor's death, the Successor Trustee must notify all beneficiaries of the existence of the trust. Residents should register a "Registration of Living Trust" form with the local court in their county of residence. This requirement is mandatory, although there are no penalties or consequences for failure to register. Please see proper form in Chapter 9.

Connecticut

State Website: www.cga.ct.gov/

State Law Reference: Connecticut General Statutes Annotated.

Uniform Acts Adopted: Uniform Testamentary Additions to Trusts Act: (Section 45a-260). Uniform Gifts to Minors Act: (Sections 45a-557+). Uniform Trustees' Powers Act: (Sections 45a-234+).

Court with Probate Jurisdiction: Probate Court.

Minimum Age for Disposing of Property by Will: 18. (Section 45a-250).

Required Number of Witnesses for Signing of Will: Two. (Section 45a-251).

Can Witnesses Be Beneficiaries?: Yes, but must still have 2 other disinterested witnesses. (Section 45a-258).

Are There Provisions for Self-Proving Wills?: Yes.

Are Holographic Wills Permitted?: No provision.

How Does Divorce Affect the Will?: Revokes the will completely. (Section 45a-257c).

How Does Marriage Affect the Will?: Revokes the will completely unless spouse was not a beneficiary under the will. (Section 45a-257a).

Who Must Be Mentioned in the Will?: Children, born or adopted; surviving spouse. (Section 45a-257).

Spouse's Right to Property Regardless of Will: The surviving spouse is entitled to 1/3 of the deceased spouse's real estate and personal property for the rest of his or her life. (Section 45a-436).

Laws of Intestate Succession (Distribution If No Will): *Spouse and children of spouse surviving:* $100,000.00 and 1/2 of balance to spouse and 1/2 of balance to children or grandchildren per stirpes. (Section 45a-437(3)).

Spouse and children not of spouse surviving: 1/2 to spouse and 1/2 to children or grandchildren per stirpes. (Sections 45a-437(4) and 45a-438).

Spouse, but no children or parent(s) surviving: All to spouse. (Section 45a-437(1)).

Spouse and parent(s), but no children surviving: $100,000.00 and 3/4 of balance to spouse and 1/4 of balance to parents or surviving parent. (Section 45a-437(2)).

Children, but no spouse surviving: All to children equally or to their children per stirpes. (Section 45a-438).

Parent(s), but no spouse or children surviving: All to parents equally or to the surviving parent. (Section 45a-439(a)(1)).

No spouse, children, or parent(s) surviving: All to brothers and sisters per stirpes; or if none, to next-of-kin. (Section 45a-439(2)-(3)).

Property Ownership: Common-law state. Tenancy-in-common is presumed unless words "joint tenants" follow names. Joint tenancy automatically includes right of survivorship. Tenancy-by-the-entirety is recognized. Allows transfer-on-death vehicle titles. (Section 47-14a).

State Gift, Inheritance, or Estate Taxes: No gift tax; no inheritance tax; imposes state estate tax. (Sections 12-391 to 12-398).

Simplified Probate Procedures: No affidavit procedure. Simplified probate allowed for estates up to $20,000.00 in personal property. (Section 45a-273).

Living Will Form: Connecticut Health Care Instructions serves as Living Will (Section 19a-575).

Other Directives: Anatomical Gift Act (Section 19a-279+).

Living Will Effective: When you have an incurable or irreversible medical condition which, without the use of life support, will result in death in a relatively short period of time, or you are in a permanent coma or a persistent vegetative state. (Section 19a-575).

Living Will Witness Requirements: Sign in the presence of two (2) adult witnesses. Your appointed agent cannot be a witness. If you reside in a resident facility operated or licensed by the department of mental health or department of mental retardation, additional Living Will Witness Requirements must be met and you should consult an attorney. (Sections 19a-575 and 19a-576).

Advance Health Care Directive: Referred to as Connecticut Health Care Instructions. (Section 19a-575).

Health Care Power of Attorney: Connecticut Health Care Instructions also contain Appointment of Health Care Agent and Appointment of Attorney-In-Fact for Health Care Decisions. State specific form is part of Advance Health Care Directive. See Chapter 10 for instructions for form on CD. (Section 19a-575).

Durable Power of Attorney: State specific form. See Chapter 9. (Section 45a-562).

Trustee Residency Requirements: If out-of-state trustee is appointed, then a resident agent must also be appointed. (Section 45a-477).

Minimum Age for Grantor or Trustee: Eighteen (18). (Sections 1-1(d) and 1-56(r)).

Trust-Writing Requirements: A trust holding real estate must be in writing. (Section 52-550).

Trustee Bond Requirements: Yes, unless not required by trust. (Section 45a-473).

Trustee Pour-Over to Will: The trust must be identified in the will. The terms of the trust must be in a document other than the will and signed before or at the same time as the will. (Section 45a-260).

Additional Trust Requirements: None.

Delaware

State Website: www.delcode.delaware.gov/index.shtml
State Law Reference: Delaware Code Annotated.
Uniform Acts Adopted: Uniform Gifts to Minors Act: (Sections 12-4501+).
Court with Probate Jurisdiction: Chancery Court.
Minimum Age for Disposing of Property by Will: 18. (Section 12-201).
Required Number of Witnesses for Signing of Will: Two. (Section 12-202).
Can Witnesses Be Beneficiaries?: Yes. (Section 12-203).
Are There Provisions for Self-Proving Wills?: Yes. (Section 12-1305).

Are Holographic Wills Permitted?: No. (Section 12-202).

Are Living Wills Recognized?: Yes. (Sections 16-2501 to 16-2518).

How Does Marriage Affect the Will?: Revokes the will as to the spouse if he or she is not otherwise provided for. The surviving spouse may still claim his or her statutory share of the decedent's estate. (Section 12-323).

Who Must Be Mentioned in the Will?: Children, born or adopted; surviving spouse. (Sections 12-301 to 12-321).

Spouse's Right to Property Regardless of Will: The surviving spouse is entitled to 1/3 of the deceased spouse's estate or $20,000.00, whichever is less. (Section 12-901(a)).

Laws of Intestate Succession (Distribution If No Will): *Spouse and children of spouse surviving:* Real estate: life estate to spouse and all the rest to children or grandchildren per stirpes. Personal property: $50,000.00 and 1/2 of balance to spouse and 1/2 of balance to children or grandchildren per stirpes. (Section 12-502(3)).

Spouse and children not of spouse surviving: Real estate: life estate to spouse and all the rest to children or grandchildren per stirpes. Personal property: 1/2 to spouse and 1/2 to children or grandchildren per stirpes. (Section 12-502(4)).

Spouse, but no children or parent(s) surviving: All to spouse. (Section 12-502(1)).

Spouse and parent(s), but no children surviving: Real estate: life estate to spouse; remainder to parents or surviving parent. Personal property: $50,000.00 and 1/2 of balance to spouse and 1/2 of balance to parents or surviving parent. (Section 12-502).

Children, but no spouse surviving: All to children equally or to their children per stirpes. (Section 12-503(1)).

Parent(s), but no spouse or children surviving: All to parents equally or to the surviving parent. (Section 12-503(2)).

No spouse, children, or parent(s) surviving: All to brothers or sisters or their children per stirpes; or if none, to the next-of-kin per stirpes. (Section 12-503(3)(4)).

Property Ownership: Common-law state. Tenancy-in-common is presumed. If joint owners are married, tenancy-by-the-entirety is created. Joint tenancy created only if stated. Joint bank account deposits are payable to any survivor. (Sections 25-309, 25-311, and 25-701).

State Gift, Inheritance, or Estate Taxes: No inheritance tax; no state estate tax. (Sections 30-1501+)

Simplified Probate Procedures: Affidavit allowed for estates up to $30,000.00 in personal property. However, beneficiaries can only be relatives of decedent, trustee, or funeral director. No simplified probate procedure. (Section 12-2306).

Living Will Form: Instructions for Health Care serves as Living Will (Section 16-2503).

Other Directives: Anatomical Gift Act (Sections 16-2710 - 16-2719).

Living Will Effective: Two (2) physicians determine in writing that you have a terminal condition and/or are in a permanent state of unconsciousness. (Section 16-2505).

Living Will Witness Requirements: Sign in the presence of two (2) adult witnesses. A witness cannot be a person who has claim against your estate upon your death, stands to inherit from your estate, be directly financially responsible for your health care, or be an owner, operator, or employee of a residential long-term health care institution in which you reside. If declarant is a patient in a nursing home, one of the witnesses must be a patient advocate or ombudsman. (Sections 16-2503 and 16-2505).

Advance Health Care Directive: Referred to as Instructions for Health Care. Delaware Advance Directive contains Power of Attorney for Health Care and Instructions for Health Care. (Section 16-2503).

Health Care Power of Attorney: State specific form is part of Advance Health Care Directive. See Chapter 10 for instructions for form on CD. (Section 16-2503).

Durable Power of Attorney: No state-specific form. See Chapter 6 for form. (Section 12-4901+).

Trustee Residency Requirements: None.

Minimum Age for Grantor or Trustee: Eighteen (18). (Section 1-701).

Trust-Writing Requirements: A trust holding real estate must be in writing. (Section 6-2714).

Trustee Bond Requirements: No provision.

Trustee Pour-Over to Will: The trust must be identified in the will. The terms of the trust must be in a document other than the will and signed before or at the same time as the will. (Section 12-211).

Additional Trust Requirements: None.

District of Columbia (Washington D.C.)

State Website: http://government.westlaw.com/linkedslice/default.asp?SP=DCC-1000

State Law Reference: District of Columbia Code Annotated.

Uniform Acts Adopted: Uniform Testamentary Additions to Trusts Act: (Section 18-306). Uniform Transfers to Minors Act: (Sections 21-301+). Uniform Fiduciaries Act: (Sections 21-1701+).

Court with Probate Jurisdiction: Superior Court. (Section 16-3101).

Minimum Age for Disposing of Property by Will: 18. (Section 18-102).

Required Number of Witnesses for Signing of Will: Two. (Section 18-103).

Can Witnesses Be Beneficiaries?: No, if they are eligible to take any portion of the estate under District intestacy law. (Section 18-104).

Are There Provisions for Self-Proving Wills?: No provision.

Are Holographic Wills Permitted?: No provision.

How Does Divorce Affect the Will?: Does not revoke the will. (Section 18-109).

How Does Marriage Affect the Will?: Does not revoke the will. (Section 18-109).

Who Must Be Mentioned in the Will?: Surviving spouse. (Sections 19-113).

Spouse's Right to Property Regardless of Will: The surviving spouse is entitled to 1/3 of the deceased spouse's estate. (Sections 19-113 and 19-302).

Laws of Intestate Succession (Distribution If No Will): *Spouse and children of spouse and decedent surviving:* Real estate: 2/3 to spouse 1/3 to children.

Spouse and both children of spouse and children of spouse but not of decedent surviving: 1/2 to spouse, and 1/2 to children of spouse and decedent.

Spouse and any children of decedent who are not children of surviving spouse: 1/2 to spouse, and 1/2 to decedent's children.

Spouse, but no children, grandchildren, or parent(s) surviving: all to spouse.

Spouse and parent(s), but no children surviving: 3/4 to spouse, and 1/4 to parent(s).

Children but no spouse surviving: all to the children equally or to their children per stirpes.

Parent(s), but no spouse or children surviving: all to parent(s) equally, or to surviving parent.

No spouse, children, or parent(s) surviving: all to brothers and sisters or their children per stirpes, or if none, to collaterals; or if none, to grandparent(s). (Sections 301-302 and 305-312)

Property Ownership: Common-law state. Tenancy-in-common is presumed unless joint tenancy is stated. Joint ownership by husband and wife is presumed to be tenancy-by-the-entirety. Joint bank account deposits are payable to any survivor. (Section 42-516).

State Gift, Inheritance, or Estate Taxes: No gift tax; no inheritance tax; imposes limited state estate tax. (Sections 47-3701 to 47-3723).

Simplified Probate Procedures: Affidavit allowed if estate is only up to two automobiles, after all debts are paid.

Simplified probate allowed for estates up to $40,000.00. (Section 20-351+).

Living Will Form: District of Columbia Declaration serves as Living Will (Section 7-622).

Other Directives: Anatomical Gift Act (Section 7-1521.04).

Living Will Effective: Two (2) physicians determine that you are in a terminal condition and your death will result without using life-sustaining procedures. Your physician must then record your diagnosis and the contents of your Declaration in your medical records. (Sections 7-621 and 7-622).

Living Will Witness Requirements: Sign in the presence of two (2) adult witnesses. A witness cannot be your appointed attorney-in-fact, health care provider, or an employee of your health care provider. Witnesses also cannot be related by blood, marriage, or adoption, stand to inherit from your estate, or be financially responsible for your health care. (Section 7-622).

Advance Health Care Directive: Referred to as a Declaration. (Section 7-622).

Health Care Power of Attorney: State specific form is part of Advance Health Care Directive. See Chapter 10 for instructions for form on CD. (Section 21-2207).

Durable Power of Attorney: State Specific form. See Chapter 9. (Section 21-2081).

Trustee Residency Requirements: No provision.

Minimum Age for Grantor or Trustee: Eighteen (18). (Section 30-401).

Trust-Writing Requirements: A trust holding real estate must be in writing. (Section 28-3503).

Trustee Bond Requirements: Yes, if appointed by court or can be waived by the trust itself. (Section 16-601).

Trustee Pour-Over to Will: The trust must be identified in the will. The terms of the trust must be in a document other than the will and signed before or at the same time as the will. (Section 18-306).

Additional Trust Requirements: None.

Florida

State Website: http://www.flsenate.gov/statutes/index.cfm

State Law Reference: Florida Statutes Annotated.

Uniform Acts Adopted: Uniform Trustees' Powers Act: (Sections 737.401+). Uniform Testamentary Additions to Trusts Act: (Section 732.513). Uniform Transfers to Minors Act: (Section 710).

Court with Probate Jurisdiction: Circuit Court.

Minimum Age for Disposing of Property by Will: 18. (Section 732.501).

Required Number of Witnesses for Signing of Will: Two. (Section 732.502(1)(b)).

Can Witnesses Be Beneficiaries?: Yes. (Section 732.504).

Are There Provisions for Self-Proving Wills?: Yes. (Section 732.503).

Are Holographic Wills Permitted?: No. (Section 732.502).

How Does Divorce Affect the Will?: Revokes the will as to the divorced spouse. (Section 732.507(2)).

How Does Marriage Affect the Will?: Revokes the will as to the spouse if he or she is not otherwise provided for. Spouse will still be entitled to his or her statutory share under the state intestate laws regardless of prior will. (Section 732.301).

Who Must Be Mentioned in the Will?: Children, born or adopted; surviving spouse. (Sections 732.301 and 732.302).

Spouse's Right to Property Regardless of Will: The surviving spouse is entitled to 30 percent of the deceased spouse's estate. [Note: the head of a household is prohibited from leaving a family home in his or her will to anyone other than a child or a spouse, if either are alive.]. (Section 732.2065 and Florida Constitution Article 10, Section 4).

Laws of Intestate Succession (Distribution If No Will): *Spouse and children of spouse surviving:* $60,000.00 and 1/2 of balance to spouse and 1/2 of balance to children and grandchildren per stirpes. (Sections 732.102) and 732.103). *Spouse and children not of spouse surviving:* 1/2 to spouse and 1/2 to children and grandchildren per stirpes. (Section 732.102).
Spouse, but no children or parent(s) surviving: All to spouse. (Section 732.102).
Spouse and parent(s), but no children surviving: All to spouse. (Section 732.102).
Children, but no spouse surviving: All to children equally or to their children per stirpes. (Section 732.103).
Parent(s), but no spouse or children surviving: All to parents equally or to the surviving parent. (Section 732.103).
No spouse, children, or parent(s) surviving: All to brothers and sisters or their children per stirpes; or if none, 1/2 to maternal next-of-kin and 1/2 to paternal next-of-kin beginning with grandparents. (Section 732.103).

Property Ownership: Common-law state. Personal property or real estate owned by husband and wife is presumed to be a tenancy-by-the-entirety with survivorship. Joint tenancy includes survivorship only if stated. Joint bank account deposits are payable to any survivor. (Sections 689.11 and 689.15).

State Gift, Inheritance, or Estate Taxes: No gift tax; no inheritance tax; imposes limited state estate tax. (Sections 198.01 to 198.44).

Simplified Probate Procedures: Affidavit allowed for very small estates of only personal property. Simplified probate allowed for estate up to $75,000.00 that is not subject to creditor's claims. (Sections 735.201+, and 735.301).

Living Will Form: Living Will (Section 765-303).

Other Directives: Anatomical Gift Act (Sections 765.510 - 765.546).

Living Will Effective: Two (2) physicians determine in writing that you have a terminal condition, and/or are in a permanent state of unconsciousness and can no longer make your own health care decisions. (Section 765.306).

Living Will Witness Requirements: Sign in the presence of two (2) adult witnesses. At least one (1) of your witnesses must not be related to you by marriage or blood. (Section 765.302).

Advance Health Care Directive: Referred to as a Living Will. (Section 765.303).

Health Care Power of Attorney: State specific form is part of Advance Health Care Directive. See Chapter 10 for instructions for form on CD. (Section 765.203).

Durable Power of Attorney: No state specific form. See Chapter 6 for form. (Section 709.08).

Trustee Residency Requirements: If requested by beneficiary or directed by trust, an out-of-state trustee must register the trust. (Section 737.105).

Minimum Age for Grantor or Trustee: Eighteen (18). (Section 744.102).

Trust-Writing Requirements: A trust holding real estate must be in writing. (Section 689.05).

Trustee Bond Requirements: None, unless required by trust, requested by beneficiary, or ordered by court. (Section 737.304).

Trustee Pour-Over to Will: The trust must be identified in the will. The terms of the trust must be in a document other than the will and signed before or at the same time as the will. (Section 732.513).

Additional Trust Requirements: Upon the Grantor's death, the Successor Trustee must notify all beneficiaries of the existence of the trust. Additionally, residents should register a "Registration of Living Trust" form with the local court in their county of residence. This requirement is mandatory, although there are no penalties or consequences for failure to register. Please see proper form in Chapter 9.

Georgia

State Website: www.legis.state.ga.us

State Law Reference: Code of Georgia Annotated.

Uniform Acts Adopted: Uniform Testamentary Additions to Trusts Act: (Section 53-12-71). Uniform Trustees' Powers Act: (Section 53-12-55). Uniform Gifts to Minors Act: (Sections 44-5-110+). Georgia Transfer to Minors Act. (Sections 45-5-110+).

Court with Probate Jurisdiction: Probate Court. (Section 15-9-30).

Minimum Age for Disposing of Property by Will: 14. (Section 53-4-10).

Required Number of Witnesses for Signing of Will: Two. (Section 53-4-20).

Can Witnesses Be Beneficiaries?: Yes, but any gift to a witness who is a beneficiary is void unless there are also 2 other disinterested witnesses. (Section 53-4-23).

Are There Provisions for Self-Proving Wills?: Yes. (Section 53-4-24).

Are Holographic Wills Permitted?: No provision.

How Does Divorce Affect the Will?: Revokes the will completely unless expressly provided otherwise. (Section 53-4-49).

How Does Marriage Affect the Will?: Revokes the will completely unless expressly provided otherwise. (Section 53-4-48).

Who Must Be Mentioned in the Will?: Statute contains detailed provisions regarding this matter. Please refer directly to statute text or consult an attorney if this is a critical factor. (Section 53-4-48).

Spouse's Right to Property Regardless of Will: The surviving spouse is entitled to 1 year's support from the deceased spouse's estate. (Section 53-3-1).

Laws of Intestate Succession (Distribution If No Will): *Spouse and children of spouse surviving:* Children or grandchildren and spouse all take equal shares with at least 1/4 to spouse. (Section 53-2-1).

Spouse and children not of spouse surviving: Children or grandchildren and spouse all take equal shares with at least 1/4 to spouse. (Section 53-2-1).

Spouse, but no children or parent(s) surviving: All to spouse. (Section 53-2-1).

Spouse and parent(s), but no children surviving: All to spouse. (Section 53-2-1).

Children, but no spouse surviving: All to children equally or to their children per stirpes. (Section 53-2-1).

Parent(s), but no spouse or children surviving: All to parents, brothers, and sisters equally or to their children per stirpes. (Section 53-2-1).

No spouse, children, or parent(s) surviving: All to brothers and sisters or their children per stirpes; or if none, to paternal and maternal next-of-kin. (Section 53-2-1).

Property Ownership: Common-law state. Tenancy-in-common is presumed unless "joint tenants" or similar language is stated specifically. Joint tenancy can only be created in document of transfer (such as a deed). Tenancy-by-the-entirety is not recognized. Joint bank account deposits are payable to any survivor unless clear evidence exists that deposit is payable only to specified survivor. (Section 44-6-120).

State Gift, Inheritance, or Estate Taxes: No gift tax; no inheritance tax; imposes limited state estate tax. (Sections 48-12-1 to 48-12-6).

Simplified Probate Procedures: No affidavit or simplified probate procedure allowed.

Living Will Form: Georgia Living Will (Section 31-32-3).

Other Directives: Anatomical Gift Act (Section 44-5-140).

Living Will Effective: Two (2) physicians determine in writing that you have a terminal condition, and/or are in a permanent state of unconsciousness. (Sections 31-32-2 and 31-32-8).

Living Will Witness Requirements: Sign in the presence of two (2) adult witnesses. A witness cannot be a person who has claim against your estate upon your death, stands to inherit from your estate, be directly financially responsible for your health care, or be an owner, operator, or employee of a health care institution in which you are a patient. Witnesses also cannot be related by blood or marriage. (Section 31-32-5).

Advance Health Care Directive: Referred to as Georgia Advance Directive for Health Care. (Section 31-32-4).

Health Care Power of Attorney: State specific form is part of Advance Health Care Directive. See Chapter 10 for instructions for form on CD. (Section 31-32-4).

Durable Financial Power of Attorney: State specific form. See Chapter 9. (Sections 10-6-140 through 10-6-142).

Trustee Residency Requirements: None. (Section 53-12-24).

Minimum Age for Grantor or Trustee: Eighteen (18). (Section 53-12-22).

Trust-Writing Requirements: A trust holding real estate must be in writing. (Section 13-5-30).

Trustee Bond Requirements: Court may require a successor trustee to post bond; otherwise, no bond unless required by trust or requested by beneficiary. (Section 53-12-174).

Trustee Pour-Over to Will: The trust must be identified in the will. The terms of the trust must be in a document other than the will and signed before or at the same time as the will. (Section 53-12-71).

Additional Trust Requirements: None.

Hawaii

State Website: http://www.capitol.hawaii.gov/

State Law Reference: Hawaii Revised Statutes.

Uniform Acts Adopted: Uniform Probate Code: (Sections 560:1-101+). Uniform Trustees' Powers Act: (Sections 554A-3 & 560:7-401). Uniform Testamentary Additions to Trusts Act: (Section 560:2-511). Uniform Gifts to Minors Act: (Sections 553A-1+).

Court with Probate Jurisdiction: Circuit Court. (Section 603-21.6).

Minimum Age for Disposing of Property by Will: 18. (Section 560:2-501).

Required Number of Witnesses for Signing of Will: Two. (Section 560:2-502(3)).

Can Witnesses Be Beneficiaries?: Yes. (Section 560:2-505(b)).

Are There Provisions for Self-Proving Wills?: Yes. (Section 560:2-504).

Are Holographic Wills Permitted?: Yes. (Sections 560:2-502(b) and 560:2-503).

How Does Divorce Affect the Will?: Revokes the will as to the divorced spouse unless expressly provided otherwise. (Section 560:2-802).

How Does Marriage Affect the Will?: Revokes the will as to the spouse if he or she is not otherwise provided for. Spouse may still be entitled to his or her statutory share under the state intestate laws. (Section 560:2-301).

Who Must Be Mentioned in the Will?: Children, born or adopted; surviving spouse. (Sections 560:2-301 and 560:2-302).

Spouse's Right to Property Regardless of Will: The surviving spouse is entitled to 1/2 of the community property on the death of the other spouse. The surviving spouse's right to additional property regardless of provisions in the will depends on the length of the marriage. Please refer to the statute for details. (Section 510:10 and 560:2-202).

Laws of Intestate Succession (Distribution If No Will): *Spouse and children of spouse surviving:* All to spouse.

(Section 560:2-102(1)(A)).

Spouse and children not of spouse surviving: $150,000.00 and 1/2 of remaining estate to spouse and 1/2 to children equally or to the grandchildren. (Section 560:2-102(3)).

Spouse, but no children or parent(s) surviving: All to spouse. (Section 560:2-102(1)(A)).

Spouse and parent(s), but no children surviving: $200,000.00 and 3/4 of remaining estate to spouse and 1/4 to parents equally or surviving parent. (Section 560:2-102(2)).

Children, but no spouse surviving: All to children equally or to their children per stirpes. (Section 560:2-103(1)).

Parent(s), but no spouse or children surviving: All to parents equally or to the surviving parent. (Section 560:2-103(a)).

No spouse, children, or parent(s) surviving: All to brothers and sisters or their children per stirpes; or if none, to grandparents; or if none, to uncles and aunts equally. (Section 560:2-103(3)(4)).

Property Ownership: Common-law state. Tenancy-in-common is presumed unless joint tenancy or tenancy-by-the-entirety is stated. Joint bank account deposits are payable to any survivor unless clear evidence exists that deposit is payable only to a specified survivor. [Note: a community property system was in effect in Hawaii from 1945 to 1949. Community property established during this time period is governed under Section 510] (Sections 509-1, 509-2, and 510-22+).

State Gift, Inheritance, or Estate Taxes: No gift tax; no inheritance tax; imposes state estate tax based on federal estate tax. (Section 236D-3).

Simplified Probate Procedures: Affidavit allowed for estates up to $100,00.00 of personal property. No simplified probate procedures. (Sections 560:3-1201+ and 560:3-1203+).

Living Will Form: Instruction for Health Care serves as Living Will (Section 327E-3).

Other Directives: Anatomical Gift Act (Section 327-1).

Living Will Effective: In the event that you have an incurable and irreversible condition that will result in death within a relatively short time, become unconscious and, to a reasonable degree of medical certainty, will not regain consciousness, or the likely risks and burdens of treatment would outweigh the expected benefits. (Section 327E-3).

Living Will Witness Requirements: Sign in the presence of two (2) adult witnesses. At least one (1) of your witnesses cannot be related to you by marriage or blood or entitled to any part of your estate. A witness cannot be the person you appoint as your agent, health care provider, or an employee of your health care provider. (Section 327E-3).

Advance Health Care Directive: Referred to as Instructions for Health Care. (Section 327E-3).

Health Care Power of Attorney: State specific form is part of Advance Health Care Directive. See Chapter 10 for instructions for form on CD. (Section 327E-3).

Durable Power of Attorney: No state specific form. See Chapter 6 for form. (Sections 551D-1 through 551D-7).

Trustee Residency Requirements: If out-of-state trustee is appointed to a living trust, the trust must be registered. (Section 560:7-101).

Minimum Age for Grantor or Trustee: Eighteen (18). (Section 577-1).

Trust-Writing Requirements: A trust holding real estate must be in writing. (Section 656-1).

Trustee Bond Requirements: None, unless required by trust, requested by beneficiary, or ordered by court. (Section 560:7-304).

Trustee Pour-Over to Will: The trust must be identified in the will. The terms of the trust must be in a document other than the will and signed before or at the same time as the will. (Section 560:2-511).

Additional Trust Requirements: Residents should register a "Registration of Living Trust" form with the local court in their county of residence. This requirement is mandatory, although there are no penalties or consequences for failure to register. Please see proper form in Chapter 9.

Idaho

State Website: http://www3.state.id.us/

State Law Reference: Idaho Code.

Uniform Acts Adopted: Uniform Probate Code: (Sections 15-1-101+). Uniform Trustees' Power Act. (Sections 15-7-401 & 15-7-402). Uniform Testamentary Additions to Trusts Act: (Section 15-2-511). Uniform Gifts to Minors Act: (Sections 68-801+).

Court with Probate Jurisdiction: District Court. (Section 1-103).

Minimum Age for Disposing of Property by Will: 18, or emancipated from parents. (Section 15-2-501).

Required Number of Witnesses for Signing of Will: Two. (Section 15-2-502).

Can Witnesses Be Beneficiaries?: Yes. (Section 15-2-505).

Are There Provisions for Self-Proving Wills?: Yes. (Section 15-2-504).

Are Holographic Wills Permitted?: Yes. (Section 15-2-503).

How Does Divorce Affect the Will?: Revokes the will as to the divorced spouse unless expressly provided otherwise. (Section 15-2-802).

How Does Marriage Affect the Will?: Revokes the will as to the spouse if he or she is not otherwise provided for. Spouse may still be entitled to his or her statutory share under the state intestate laws. (Section 15-2-301).

Who Must Be Mentioned in the Will?: Children, born or adopted; surviving spouse. (Sections 15-2-301 and 15-2-302).

Spouse's Right to Property Regardless of Will: Community property right to 1/2 of the deceased spouse's "community" property. (Section 15-2-301).

Laws of Intestate Succession (Distribution If No Will): *Spouse and children of spouse surviving:* All of decedent's community property to spouse; $50,000.00 and 1/2 of balance of decedent's separate property to spouse and 1/2 of balance to children or grandchildren per stirpes. (Sections 15-2-102(1)(3) and 15-2-103(a)).

Spouse and children not of spouse surviving: All of decedent's community property to spouse; 1/2 of decedent's separate property to spouse and 1/2 to children or grandchildren per stirpes. (Section 15-2-102(a)).

Spouse, but no children or parent(s) surviving: All to spouse. (Section 15-2-102(a)(1)).

Spouse and parent(s), but no children surviving: All of decedent's community property to spouse; $50,000.00 and 1/2 of balance of decedent's separate property to spouse and 1/2 of balance to parents or surviving parent. (Section 15-2-102(a)(2)).

Children, but no spouse surviving: All to children or to their children per stirpes. (Section 15-2-103(a)).

Parent(s), but no spouse or children surviving: All to parents equally or to the surviving parent. (Section 15-2-103(b)).

No spouse, children, or parent(s) surviving: All to brothers and sisters or their children, if surviving. If not, then 1/2 to living maternal grandparents or their children and 1/2 to paternal grandparents or their children. (Section 15-2-103(d)).

Property Ownership: Community property state. Tenancy-in-common is presumed unless joint tenancy is stated or property is acquired as partnership or as community property. Tenancy-by-the-entirety is not recognized. Joint bank account deposits are payable to any survivor unless clear evidence exists that deposit is payable only to specified survivor. (Sections 32-903 and 32-906, and Section 55-508).

State Gift, Inheritance, or Estate Taxes: No gift tax; no inheritance tax; no state estate tax. (Sections 14-401 to 14-413).

Simplified Probate Procedures: Affidavit allowed for estates up to $100,000 of personal property. Simplified probate allowed for estates up to value of homestead, exempt property allowance, family allowances, last illness and burial expenses. (Sections 15-3-1201+ and 15-3-1203+).

Living Will Form: Idaho Living Will (Section 39-4510).

Other Directives: Anatomical Gift Act (Section 39-3401).

Living Will Effective: Two (2) physicians determine that you are in a terminal condition, your death will result without using life-sustaining procedures, or you are in a persistent vegetative state. (Section 39-4510).

Living Will Witness Requirements: Although Idaho does not have any witness requirements, we suggest that you sign in the presence of two adult witnesses or a notary public, and we suggest that witnesses should not be your appointed attorney-in-fact, your health care provider, or a person related to you by blood, marriage or adoption.

Advance Health Care Directive: Referred to as Idaho Living Will. (Section 39-4510).

Health Care Power of Attorney: State specific form is part of Advance Health Care Directive. See Chapter 10 for instructions for form on CD. (Section 39-4510).

Durable Power of Attorney: No state specific form. See Chapter 6 for form. (Section 15-5-501+).

Trustee Residency Requirements: Out-of-state trustee must qualify to do business in Idaho. A trustee, whether a resident or not, must register the trust. (Section 15-7-105).

Minimum Age for Grantor or Trustee: Eighteen (18). (Section 32-101).

Trust-Writing Requirements: A trust holding real estate must be in writing. (Section 9-503).

Trustee Bond Requirements: None, unless required by trust, requested by beneficiary, or ordered by court. (Section 15-7-304).

Trustee Pour-Over to Will: The trust must be identified in the will. The terms of the trust must be in a document other than the will and signed before or at the same time as the will. (Section 15-2-511).

Additional Trust Requirements: Residents should register a "Registration of Living Trust" form with the local court in their county of residence. This requirement is mandatory, although there are no penalties or consequences for failure to register. Please see proper form in Chapter 9.

Illinois

State Website: http://www.ilga.gov/

State Law Reference: Illinois Compiled Statutes.

Uniform Acts Adopted: Uniform Testamentary Additions to Trusts Act: (755 ILCS 4-4). Uniform Gifts to Minors Act: (755 ILCS 5/11-1). Uniform Trustees' Powers Act: (755 ILCS 4-1+).

Court with Probate Jurisdiction: Circuit Court. (755 ILCS 5/1+)

Minimum Age for Disposing of Property by Will: 18. (755 ILCS 5/4-1).

Required Number of Witnesses for Signing of Will: Two. (755 ILCS 5/4-3).

Can Witnesses Be Beneficiaries?: Yes, but any gift to a beneficiary who was a witness will be void unless there were also 2 other disinterested witnesses. However, a witness-beneficiary may still receive his or her intestate share. (755 ILCS 5/4-3).

Are There Provisions for Self-Proving Wills?: Yes. (755 ILCS 5/4-6).

Are Holographic Wills Permitted?: No provision.

How Does Divorce Affect the Will?: Revokes will as to the divorced spouse. (755 ILCS -5/4-7).

How Does Marriage Affect the Will?: Does not revoke the will. (755 ILCS 5/4-7).

Who Must Be Mentioned in the Will?: Children, born or adopted; surviving spouse. (755 ILCS 5/4-10 and 755 ILCS 5/15-1).

Spouse's Right to Property Regardless of Will: Generally, the surviving spouse is entitled to 1/2 of the deceased

spouse's estate if there are no children and to only 1/3 if there are children. However, please refer directly to the statute as the provisions are detailed. (755 ILCS 5/2-8).

Laws of Intestate Succession (Distribution If No Will): *Spouse and children of spouse surviving:* 1/2 to spouse and 1/2 to children equally or to the grandchildren per stirpes.

Spouse and children not of spouse surviving: 1/2 to spouse and 1/2 to children equally or to the grandchildren per stirpes.

Spouse, but no children or parent(s) surviving: All to spouse.

Spouse and parent(s), but no children surviving: All to spouse.

Children, but no spouse surviving: All to children equally or to their children per stirpes.

Parent(s), but no spouse or children surviving: All to parents, brothers, sisters, or children of brothers and sisters per stirpes. If only 1 surviving parent, he or she takes a double share.

No spouse, children, or parent(s) surviving: 1/2 to maternal grandparents and 1/2 to paternal grandparents equally or to surviving grandparent; or if none, to their children per stirpes; or if none, 1/2 to maternal great-grandparents and 1/2 to paternal great-grandparents equally or to surviving great-grandparent; or if none, to their children per stirpes; or if none of the above, all to the next-of-kin. (755 ILCS 5/2-1).

Property Ownership: Common-law state. Tenancy-in-common is presumed. Joint tenancy with right of survivorship created only by statement that property is held in joint tenancy and not tenancy-in-common. Tenancy-by-the-entirety is recognized only for real estate. Joint bank account deposits are payable to any survivor. (205 ILCS 105/4 to 205 ILCS 105/8 and 765 ILCS 1005/1 to 765 ILCS 1005/4a).

State Gift, Inheritance, or Estate Taxes: No gift tax; no inheritance tax; state estate tax based on federal estate tax. (35 ILCS 405/1 to 35 ILCS 405/18).

Simplified Probate Procedures: Affidavit allowed for estates up to $100,000.00 in personal property. Simplified probate allowed for estates up to $100,000.00 if all heirs and beneficiaries consent in writing. (755 ILCS 5/25-1+).

Living Will Form: Illinois Declaration serves as Living Will (755 ILCS 35/3).

Other Directives: Anatomical Gift Act (755 ILCS 50).

Living Will Effective: If death would occur without the use of death-delaying procedures. Your physician must personally examine you and certify in writing that you are terminally ill. (755 ILCS 35/2).

Living Will Witness Requirements: Sign in the presence of two (2) adult witnesses. Witnesses cannot be entitled to any part of your estate or financially responsible for your medical care. (755 ILCS 35/3).

Advance Health Care Directive: Referred to as Illinois Declaration (755 ILCS 35/3)

Health Care Power of Attorney: State specific form is part of Advance Health Care Directive. See Chapter 10 for instructions for form on CD. **(755 ILCS 45/4-1+)_**)

Durable Power of Attorney: State specific form. See Chapter 9. (755 ILCS 45/2-1+).

Trustee Residency Requirements: None.

Minimum Age for Grantor or Trustee: Eighteen (18). (760 ILCS 5/11-1).

Trust-Writing Requirements: A trust holding real estate must be in writing. (740 ILCS 80/9).

Trustee Bond Requirements: None, unless required by trust.

Trustee Pour-Over to Will: The trust must be identified in the will. The terms of the trust must be in a document other than the will and signed before or at the same time as the will. (755 ILCS 4-4).

Additional Trust Requirements: None.

Indiana

State Website: http://www.in.gov/legislative/ic/code/

State Law Reference: Indiana Code Annotated.

Uniform Acts Adopted: Uniform Testamentary Additions to Trusts Act: (Section 29-1-6-1). Uniform Gifts to Minors Act: (Sections 30-2-8.5-1+). Uniform Trustees' Powers Act: (Section 30-4-3-3).

Court with Probate Jurisdiction: Circuit or Superior Court (Probate Court in St. Joseph and Vigo Counties).

Minimum Age for Disposing of Property by Will: 18, however, no minimum age if a member of Armed Forces or Merchant Marines. (Section 29-1-5-1).

Required Number of Witnesses for Signing of Will: Two. (Section 29-1-5-3).

Can Witnesses Be Beneficiaries?: Yes, but any gift to a beneficiary who was a witness will be void. However, if the witness-beneficiary is entitled to receive an intestate share of the estate, he or she may receive the lesser of the intestate share or the property gifted to him or her under the will. (Section 29-1-5-2).

Are There Provisions for Self-Proving Wills?: Yes. (Section 29-1-5-3).

Are Holographic Wills Permitted?: No provision.

How Does Divorce Affect the Will?: Revokes the will as to the divorced spouse. (Section 29-1-5-8).

How Does Marriage Affect the Will?: Does not revoke the will. (Section 29-1-5-8).

Who Must Be Mentioned in the Will?: Children, born or adopted; surviving spouse. (Sections 29-1-3-1 and 29-1-3-8).

Spouse's Right to Property Regardless of Will: The surviving spouse is entitled to 1/2 of the deceased spouse's estate. If there are surviving children of a prior spouse, a second or subsequent spouse is entitled to 1/3 of the deceased's personal property and 1/3 of the deceased's real estate for the rest of his or her life. (Section 29-1-3-1).

Laws of Intestate Succession (Distribution If No Will): *Spouse and children of spouse surviving:* 1/2 to spouse and 1/2 to children.

Spouse and children not of spouse surviving: Real estate: an amount equal to 1/4 of the fair market value of real estate to spouse and balance to children. Personal property: 1/2 to spouse and 1/2 to children.

Spouse, but no children or parent(s) surviving: All to spouse.

Spouse and parent(s), but no children surviving: 3/4 to spouse and 1/4 to parents or surviving parent.

Children, but no spouse surviving: All to children equally or their children per stirpes.

Parent(s), brothers, sisters, and children of brothers and sisters, but no spouse or children surviving: Surviving parents, brothers, sisters all share equally, but each surviving parent is entitled to at least 1/4 of estate.

No spouse, children, parent(s), or brothers or sisters surviving: All to brothers' and sisters' children per stirpes; or if none, to grandparents; or if none, to aunts and uncles per stirpes. (Section 29-1-2-1).

Property Ownership: Common-law state. Joint tenancy, tenancy-in-common, and tenancy-by-the-entirety are recognized. Tenancy-in-common is presumed unless joint tenancy stated. Joint ownership by husband and wife is presumed to be a tenancy-by-the-entirety (for real estate only). Joint bank account deposits are payable to any survivor. (Section 6-4.1-8-4 and 32-17-2-1, 32-17-3-1).

State Gift, Inheritance, or Estate Taxes: No gift tax; imposes an inheritance tax of up to 20 percent; imposes state estate tax. (Sections 6-4.1-5-1 and 6-4.1-11-2).

Simplified Probate Procedures: Affidavit allowed for estates up to $50,000.00 in personal property. Simplified probate allowed for estates up to $50,000.00. (Sections 29-1-8-1, and 29-1-8-3+).

Living Will Form: Indiana Living Will Declaration (Section 16-36-4-10).

Other Directives: Anatomical Gift Act (Section 29-2-16-1).

Living Will Effective: Your physician must certify in writing that you are in a terminal condition and your death would occur within a short period of time without the use of life-sustaining medical care. (Section 16-36-4-10).

Living Will Witness Requirements: Sign in the presence of two (2) adult witnesses. Witnesses cannot be entitled to any part of your estate, related to you by blood or marriage, financially responsible for your medical care, or be the person who signed the Declaration on your behalf. (Section 16-36-4-8).

Advance Health Care Directive: Referred to as Indiana Living Will Declaration. (Section 16-36-4-10).

Health Care Power of Attorney: State specific form is part of the Advance Health Care Directive. See Chapter 10 for instructions for form on CD. (Section 16-36-4-10).

Durable Power of Attorney: No state specific form. See Chapter 6 for form. (Section 29-3-5).

Trustee Residency Requirements: None.

Minimum Age for Grantor or Trustee: Eighteen (18). (Sections 30-4-2-10 & 30-4-2-11).

Trust-Writing Requirements: Yes.

Trustee Bond Requirements: None, unless required by trust. (Section 30-4-6-8).

Trustee Pour-Over to Will: The trust must be identified in the will. The terms of the trust must be in a document other than the will and signed before or at the same time as the will. (Section 29-1-6-1).

Additional Trust Requirements: None.

Iowa

State Website: http://www.legis.state.ia.us/

State Law Reference: Iowa Code Annotated.

Uniform Acts Adopted: Uniform Testamentary Additions to Trusts Act: (Sections 633-275+). Uniform Gifts to Minors Act: (Sections 565B.1+). Uniform Trustees' Powers Act: (Section 633.699).

Court with Probate Jurisdiction: District Court. (Section 633.10).

Minimum Age for Disposing of Property by Will: 18 ("full age"). (Section 633.264).

Required Number of Witnesses for Signing of Will: Two. (Section 633.279).

Can Witnesses Be Beneficiaries?: Yes, but any gift to a beneficiary who was a witness will be void unless there were also 2 other disinterested witnesses. However, a witness-beneficiary is still entitled to receive any intestate share. (Section 633.281).

Are There Provisions for Self-Proving Wills?: Yes. (Section 633.279).

Are Holographic Wills Permitted?: No provision.

Are Living Wills Recognized?: Yes, under the "Iowa Life Sustaining Procedures Act." (Sections 144A.1 to 144A.12).

How Does Divorce Affect the Will?: Revokes the will as to divorced spouse unless he or she remarries. (Section 633.271).

How Does Marriage Affect the Will?: Revokes the will as to the spouse if he or she is not otherwise provided for. Spouse may still be entitled to his or her statutory share under the state intestate laws. (Section 633.236).

Who Must Be Mentioned in the Will?: Children, born or adopted; surviving spouse. (Sections 633.236 and 633.267).

Spouse's Right to Property Regardless of Will: The surviving spouse is entitled to 1/3 of the deceased spouse's estate. (Section 633.238).

Laws of Intestate Succession (Distribution If No Will): *Spouse and children of spouse surviving:* All to spouse.

Spouse and children not of spouse surviving: $50,000.00 and 1/2 of balance to spouse and 1/2 of balance to children.
Spouse, but no children or parent(s) surviving: All to spouse.
Spouse and parent(s), but no children surviving: All to spouse.
Children, but no spouse surviving: All to children equally or to their children per stirpes.
Parent(s), but no spouse or children surviving: All to parents equally or to the surviving parent.
No spouse, children, or parent(s) surviving: All to brothers and sisters or their children per stirpes; or if none, to ancestors and their children per stirpes; or if none, to spouse or heirs of spouse. (Sections 633.211, 633.212, and 633.219).

Property Ownership: Common-law state. Tenancy-in-common is presumed unless joint tenancy stated. Tenancy-by-the-entirety not recognized. Joint bank account deposits are payable to any survivor. (Sections 534.302 and 557.15).

State Gift, Inheritance, or Estate Taxes: No gift tax; imposes an inheritance tax of up to 15 percent; no state estate tax. (Sections 450.10 and 451.2).

Simplified Probate Procedures: Affidavit allowed for estates up to $25,000.00 in personal property. Simplified probate allowed for estates up to $50,000.00 if left to spouse or child, up to $15,000.00 if left to parent or grandchild, and up to $10,000.00 if left to other relatives. (Sections 633.356 and 635.1).

Living Will Form: Iowa Declaration serves as Living Will (Section 144A.3).

Other Directives: Anatomical Gift Act (Section 142C).

Living Will Effective: Two (2) physicians must certify in writing that you are in a terminal condition and your death would occur within a short period of time without the use of life-sustaining medical care. (Section 144A.5).

Living Will Witness Requirements: Sign in the presence of two (2) witnesses eighteen (18) years or older or a notary public. A witness cannot be your health care provider or an employee of your health care provider. (Section 144A.3).

Advance Health Care Directive: Referred to as Iowa Declaration. (Section 144A.3)

Health Care Power of Attorney: State specific form is part of Advance Health Care Directive. See Chapter 10 for instructions for form on CD. (Section 144B.2).

Durable Power of Attorney: No state-specific form. See Chapter 6 for form. (Section 633B.1+).

Trustee Residency Requirements: None. (Section 633.64).

Minimum Age for Grantor or Trustee: Eighteen (18). (Section 599.1).

Trust-Writing Requirements: A trust holding real estate must be in writing. (Section 557.10).

Trustee Bond Requirements: Yes, unless not required by trust. (Section 633.169).

Trustee Pour-Over to Will: The trust must be identified in the will. The terms of the trust must be in a document other than the will and signed before or at the same time as the will. (Section 633.275).

Additional Trust Requirements: None.

Kansas

State Website: http://www.kslegislature.org/

State Law Reference: Kansas Statutes Annotated.

Uniform Acts Adopted: Uniform Trustees' Powers Act: (Sections 58-1202 & 58-1203). Uniform Testamentary Additions to Trusts Act: (Sections 59-3101). Uniform Gifts to Minors Act: (Sections 38-1701+).

Court with Probate Jurisdiction: District Court.

Minimum Age for Disposing of Property by Will: 18, unless the testator is married, then the minimum age is 16. (Section 38-101 and 59-601).

Required Number of Witnesses for Signing of Will: Two. (Section 59-606).

Can Witnesses Be Beneficiaries?: Yes, but a gift to a beneficiary who was a witness will be void unless there were also 2 other disinterested witnesses. If entitled to take under intestacy statutes, then witness takes lesser of intestate share or gift under the will. (Section 59-604).

Are There Provisions for Self-Proving Wills?: Yes. (Section 59-606).

Are Holographic Wills Permitted?: No provision.

How Does Divorce Affect the Will?: Revokes the will as to divorced spouse. (Section 59-610).

How Does Marriage Affect the Will?: Revokes the will if a child is later born to or adopted into the marriage. (Section 59-610).

Who Must Be Mentioned in the Will?: Surviving spouse. (Section 59-610).

Spouse's Right to Property Regardless of Will: The amount to which a surviving spouse is entitled to is dependent on the length of marriage. Please refer directly to the statute as the provisions are detailed. (Section 59-6a202).

Laws of Intestate Succession (Distribution If No Will): *Spouse and children of spouse surviving:* 1/2 to spouse and 1/2 to children or grandchildren per stirpes.

Spouse and children not of spouse surviving: 1/2 to spouse and 1/2 to children or grandchildren per stirpes.

Spouse, but no children or parent(s) surviving: All to spouse.

Spouse and parent(s), but no children surviving: All to spouse.

Children, but no spouse surviving: All to children equally or to their children per stirpes.

Parent(s), but no spouse or children surviving: All to parents equally or to the surviving parent.

No spouse, children, or parent(s) surviving: All to brothers and sisters per stirpes. (Sections 59-504 to 59-508).

Property Ownership: Common-law state. Tenancy-in-common is presumed unless joint tenancy is stated. Tenancy-by-the-entirety not recognized. Joint bank account deposits are payable to any survivor. Allows beneficiary deeds and transfer-on death vehicle titles to transfer property on death. (Section 17-2213 and Section 58-501).

State Gift, Inheritance, or Estate Taxes: No gift tax; no inheritance tax; imposes state estate tax until 2009. (Section 79-102 and Sections 79-15,201+).

Simplified Probate Procedures: Affidavit allowed for estates up to $20,000.00 in personal property. Simplified probate allowed for any estate if court and heirs agree. (Sections 59-1507b and 59-3202+).

Living Will Form: Kansas Declaration serves as Living Will (Section 65-28,103).

Other Directives: Anatomical Gift Act (Section 65-3209+).

Living Will Effective: Two (2) physicians must certify in writing that you are in a terminal condition and your death would occur within a short period of time without the use of life-sustaining medical care. (Section 65-28,103).

Living Will Witness Requirements: Sign in the presence of two (2) witnesses eighteen (18) years or older or a notary public. Witnesses cannot be entitled to any part of your estate, be financially responsible for your medical care, be related to you by blood or marriage, or be the person who signed the Declaration on your behalf. (Section 65-28,103).

Advance Health Care Directive: Referred to as Kansas Declaration. (Section (65-28,103).

Health Care Power of Attorney: State specific form is part of Advance Health Care Directive. See Chapter 10 for instructions for form on CD. (Section 58-629).

Durable Power of Attorney: No state specific form. See Chapter 6 for form. (Section 58-650+).

Trustee Residency Requirements: None, but if out-of-state trustee is appointed, a resident agent must also be appointed. (Section 59-1706).

Minimum Age for Grantor or Trustee: Eighteen (18). (Section 38-101).

Trust-Writing Requirements: A trust holding real estate must be in writing. (Section 33-106).

Trustee Bond Requirements: Yes, unless not required by trust. (Section 59-1101).

Trustee Pour-Over to Will: The trust must be identified in the will. The terms of the trust must be in a document other than the will and signed before or at the same time as the will. (Section 59-3101).

Additional Trust Requirements: Upon the Grantor's death, the Successor Trustee must notify all beneficiaries of the existence of the trust.

Kentucky

State Website: http://lrc.ky.gov/

State Law Reference: Kentucky Revised Statutes.

Uniform Acts Adopted: Uniform Trustees' Powers Act: (Sections 386.800+). Uniform Testamentary Additions to Trusts Act: (Section 394.076). Uniform Gifts to Minors Act: (Sections 385.012+).

Court with Probate Jurisdiction: District Court. (Section 24A.120).

Minimum Age for Disposing of Property by Will: 18. (Section 394.020).

Required Number of Witnesses for Signing of Will: Two. (Section 394.040).

Can Witnesses Be Beneficiaries?: Yes, but interested witness may not take more than intestate share, if any. (Section 394.210).

Are There Provisions for Self-Proving Wills?: Yes. (Section 394.225).

Are Holographic Wills Permitted?: Yes. (Section 394.040).

How Does Divorce Affect the Will?: Revokes the will as to the divorced spouse unless expressly provided otherwise. (Section 394.092).

How Does Marriage Affect the Will?: Does not revoke the will. (Section 394.090).

Who Must Be Mentioned in the Will?: Children, born or adopted; surviving spouse. (Section 394.382).

Spouse's Right to Property Regardless of Will: The surviving spouse is entitled to 1/3 of the real estate acquired during the marriage and 1/2 of the deceased spouse's real estate and personal property. (Section 392.020).

Laws of Intestate Succession (Distribution If No Will): *Spouse and children of spouse surviving:* Real estate: life estate of 1/3 of fee simple property acquired during marriage and 1/2 of other real estate to spouse; balance to children or grandchildren per stirpes. Personal property: 1/2 to spouse and 1/2 to children equally or to grandchildren per stirpes. Spouse or surviving children if no surviving spouse are entitled to up to $15,000.00 in personal property exempt from other distribution.

Spouse and children not of spouse surviving: Real estate: life estate of 1/3 of fee simple property acquired during marriage and 1/2 of other real estate to spouse; balance to children or grandchildren per stirpes. Personal property: 1/2 to spouse and 1/2 to children equally or to grandchildren per stirpes.

Spouse, but no children or parent(s) surviving: 1/2 to parents' children; or if none, all to spouse.

Spouse and parent(s), but no children surviving: 1/2 to spouse and 1/2 to parents or surviving parent.

Children, but no spouse surviving: All to children equally or to their children per stirpes.

Parent(s), but no spouse or children surviving: All to parents equally or surviving parent.

No spouse, children, or parent(s) surviving: All to brothers and sisters or their children per stirpes; or if none, 1/2 to maternal next-of-kin and 1/2 to paternal next-of-kin and their children per stirpes. (Sections 391.010 and 392.020).

Property Ownership: Common-law state. Tenancy-in-common is presumed between husband and wife unless joint tenancy stated. Tenancy-by-the-entirety is recognized only for real estate. Joint bank account deposits are payable to any survivor. (Sections 381.130 and Section 391.315).

State Gift, Inheritance, or Estate Taxes: No gift tax;no inheritance tax; no state estate tax. (Sections 140.070 and

140.130).

Simplified Probate Procedures: No affidavit procedure. Simplified probate allowed for estates where assets are less than debts or in other specialized circumstances. Please refer directly to statute. (Sections 391.030 and 395.455).

Living Will Form: Living Will Directive (Section 311.625).

Other Directives: Anatomical Gift Act (Sections 311.165 through 311.235).

Living Will Effective: When you become unable to make your own medical decisions. (Section 311.625).

Living Will Witness Requirements: Sign in the presence of two (2) witnesses eighteen (18) years or older or a notary public. Witnesses cannot be entitled to any part of your estate, financially responsible for your medical care, or related to you by blood or marriage. (Section 311.625).

Advance Health Care Directive: Referred to as Living Will Directive. (Section 311.625).

Health Care Power of Attorney: State specific form is part of Advance Health Care Directive. See Chapter 10 for instructions for form on CD. (Section 311.625).

Durable Power of Attorney: No state specific form. See Chapter 6 for form. (Section 386.093).

Trustee Residency Requirements: No provision.

Minimum Age for Grantor or Trustee: Eighteen (18). (Section 2.015).

Trust-Writing Requirements: A trust holding real estate must be in writing. (Section 371.010).

Trustee Bond Requirements: None, unless required by trust, requested by beneficiary, or ordered by court. (Section 386.720).

Trustee Pour-Over to Will: The trust must be identified in the will. The terms of the trust must be in a document other than the will and signed before or at the same time as the will. (Section 394.076).

Additional Trust Requirements: None.

Louisiana

State Website: http://www.legis.state.la.us/

State Law Reference: Louisiana Revised Statutes and Louisiana Civil Code Annotated.

Uniform Acts Adopted: Uniform Gifts to Minors Act: (Revised Statutes, Sections 9:751+).

Court with Probate Jurisdiction: District Court.

Minimum Age for Disposing of Property by Will: 16. (Civil Code, Section 1476).

Required Number of Witnesses for Signing of Will: Two Witnesses and One Notary. (Civil Code, Section 1577).

Can Witnesses Be Beneficiaries?: No. (Civil Code, Section 1582 and 1582.1).

Are There Provisions for Self-Proving Wills?: Yes. **(Note: Will forms in this book are not valid in Louisiana).**

Are Holographic Wills Permitted?: Yes. (Civil Code, Section 1575).

How Does Divorce Affect the Will?: Revokes the will. (Civil Code, Section 1608).

How Does Marriage Affect the Will?: Does not revoke the will. (Civil Code, Section 1691).

Who Must Be Mentioned in the Will?: Children, born or adopted; surviving spouse. However, children may be disinherited for a just cause. (Civil Code, Section 1619-1624).

Spouse's Right to Property Regardless of Will: The Louisiana Civil Code provisions regarding this matter are detailed and should be consulted directly. (Civil Code, Sections 890+).

Laws of Intestate Succession (Distribution If No Will): *Spouse and children of spouse surviving:* All community property to descendants per stirpes. However, the spouse has the right to use the property until remarried. All separate property to children equally or to grandchildren per stirpes.

Spouse and children not of spouse surviving: All community property to descendants per stirpes. However, the spouse has the right to use the property until remarried. All separate property to children equally or to grandchildren per stirpes.

Spouse, but no children or parent(s) surviving: All community property to spouse. All separate property to brothers and sisters or to their children per stirpes; or if none, to parent(s); or if none, all to spouse.

Spouse and parent(s), but no children surviving: All community property to spouse. All separate property to brothers and sisters or their children per stirpes; or if none, to parent(s); or if none, all to spouse.

Children, but no spouse surviving: All to children equally or to their children per stirpes.

Parent(s), but no spouse or children surviving: All to parents equally or to the surviving parent.

No spouse, children, or parent(s) surviving: To brothers and sisters equally or their children per stirpes; or if none, to next-of-kin. (Civil Code, Sections 880 to 991).

Property Ownership. Community property state. Joint ownership is presumed if 2 or more persons are listed as owners. No tenancy-by-the-entirety or tenancy-in-common. Joint bank account deposits are payable to any survivor. (Revised Statutes, Title 6, Section 1255 and Civil Code, Sections 2334 and 2335).

State Gift, Inheritance, or Estate Taxes: Imposes a state gift tax; imposes a minimal inheritance tax; imposes a state estate tax. (Revised Statutes, Title 47, Sections 2403 and 2432).

Simplified Probate Procedures: No affidavit or simplified probate procedures allowed.

Living Will Form: Louisiana Declaration serves as Living Will (Revised Statutes, Section 40:1299.58.3).

Other Directives: Anatomical Gift Act (Revised Statutes, Section 17:2354).

Living Will Effective: Two (2) physicians must certify in writing that you are in a terminal condition and your death would occur within a short period of time without the use of life-sustaining medical care. (Revised Statutes, Section 40:1299.58.2).

Living Will Witness Requirements: Sign in the presence of two (2) adult witnesses. Witnesses cannot be entitled to any part of your estate or related by blood or marriage. (Revised Statutes, Sections 40:1299.58.2 and 40:1299.58.3).

Advance Health Care Directive: Referred to as Louisiana Declaration. (Revised Statutes, Section 40:1299.58.3).

Health Care Power of Attorney: No state specific form. See Chapter 7 for form. Also may use Advance health Care Directive. See Chapter 10 for instructions for form on CD. (Revised Statutes, Section 40:1299.53).

Durable Financial Power of Attorney: No state specific form. See Chapter 6 for form. (Civil Code, Section 3026).

Trustee Residency Requirements: None.

Minimum Age for Grantor or Trustee: Eighteen (18). (Civil Code, Section 29).

Trust-Writing Requirements: A trust holding real estate must be in writing. (Civil Code, Section 2440).

Trustee Bond Requirements: Yes, unless not required by trust. (Revised Statutes, Section 9:2157).

Trustee Pour-Over to Will: The trust must be identified in the will. The terms of the trust must be in a document other than the will and signed before or at the same time as the will and with the same formalities as required for a will in Louisiana. (Revised Statutes, Sections 9:1733 & 9:1751).

Additional Trust Requirements: None.

Maine

State Website: http://janus.state.me.us/legis/statutes/

State Law Reference: Maine Revised Statutes Annotated.

Uniform Acts Adopted: Uniform Probate Code: (Sections 18A-1-101+). Uniform Testamentary Additions to Trusts Act: (Section 18A-2-511). Uniform Gifts to Minors Act: (Sections 33-1651+). Uniform Trustees' Powers Act: (Sections

18A-7-401+).

Court with Probate Jurisdiction: Probate Court. (Section 4-201-406).

Minimum Age for Disposing of Property by Will: 18. (Section 18A-2-501).

Required Number of Witnesses for Signing of Will: Two. (Section 18A-2-502).

Can Witnesses Be Beneficiaries?: Yes. (Section 18A-2-505).

Are There Provisions for Self-Proving Wills?: Yes. (Section 18A-2-504).

Are Holographic Wills Permitted?: Yes. (Section 18A-2-503).

How Does Divorce Affect the Will?: Revokes the will as to the divorced spouse unless expressly provided otherwise. (Section 18A-2-508).

How Does Marriage Affect the Will?: Revokes the will as to the spouse if he or she is not otherwise provided for. Spouse may still be entitled to his or her statutory share under the state intestate laws. (Section 18A-2-301).

Who Must Be Mentioned in the Will?: Children, born or adopted; grandchildren of deceased child; surviving spouse. (Sections 18A-2-301 and 18A-2-302).

Spouse's Right to Property Regardless of Will: The surviving spouse is entitled to 1/3 of the entire estate of the deceased spouse. (Section 18A-2-201).

Laws of Intestate Succession (Distribution If No Will): *Spouse and children of spouse surviving:* $50,000.00 and 1/2 of balance to spouse and 1/2 of balance to children or grandchildren per capita at each generation. (Note: Surviving registered domestic partners are entitled to the same intestate share as a surviving spouse.)

Spouse and children not of spouse surviving: 1/2 to spouse and 1/2 to children or grandchildren per capita at each generation.

Spouse, but no children or parent(s) surviving: All to spouse.

Spouse and parent(s), but no children surviving: $50,000.00 and 1/2 of balance to spouse and 1/2 of balance to parents or surviving parent.

Children, but no spouse surviving: All to children equally or to their children per capita at each generation.

Parent(s), but no spouse or children surviving: All to parents equally or to the surviving parent.

No spouse, children, or parent(s) surviving: All to children of parents per capita; or if none, then 1/2 to paternal grandparents or their children per capita and 1/2 to maternal grandparents or their children per capita. (Sections 2-102 and 2-103).

Property Ownership: Common-law state. Ownership by 2 or more is presumed to be a tenancy-in-common unless joint tenancy is stated. Tenancy-by-the-entirety not recognized. Joint bank account deposits are payable to any survivor. (Sections 33-7-159 and 33-7-160).

State Gift, Inheritance, or Estate Taxes: No gift tax; no inheritance tax; imposes state estate tax. (Section 18A-3-916).

Simplified Probate Procedures: Affidavit allowed for estates up to $20,000.00. Simplified probate allowed for estates up to value of homestead, exempt property allowance, family allowances, last illness and burial expenses. (Sections 18A-3-1201 and 18A-3-1203).

Living Will Form: Instructions for Health Care serves as Living Will (Section 18A-5-804).

Other Directives: Anatomical Gift Act (Section 22-2-2901+).

Living Will Effective: The Living Will becomes effective in the event that you have an incurable and irreversible condition that will result in death within a relatively short time, become unconscious and, to a reasonable degree of medical certainty, will not regain consciousness, or the likely risks and burdens of treatment would outweigh the expected benefits. (Section 18A-5-804).

Living Will Witness Requirements: Sign in the presence of two (2) adult witnesses. No other restrictions apply. (Section 18A-5-804).

Advance Health Care Directive: Referred to as Instructions for Health care. (Section 18A-5-801).

Health Care Power of Attorney: State specific form is part of Advance Health Care Directive. See Chapter 10 for instructions for form on CD. (Section 18A-5-506).

Durable Power of Attorney: No state specific form. See Chapter 6 for form. (Section 18A-5-508).

Trustee Residency Requirements: Out-of-state trustee must qualify to do business in Maine. (Section 18A-7-105).

Minimum Age for Grantor or Trustee: Eighteen (18). (Section 1-1-72).

Trust-Writing Requirements: A trust holding real estate must be in writing. (Section 33-851).

Trustee Bond Requirements: None, unless required by trust, requested by beneficiary, or ordered by court. (Section 18B).

Trustee Pour-Over to Will: The trust must be identified in the will. The terms of the trust must be in a document other than the will and signed before or at the same time as the will. (Section 18A-2-511).

Additional Trust Requirements: Upon the Grantor's death, the Successor Trustee must notify all beneficiaries of the existence of the trust. Residents should register a "Registration of Living Trust" form with the local court in their county of residence. This requirement is mandatory, although there are no penalties or consequences for failure to register. Please see proper form in Chapter 9.

Maryland

State Website: http://mlis.state.md.us/

State Law Reference: Maryland Code.

Uniform Acts Adopted: Uniform Gifts to Minors Act: (Estates and Trusts, Sections 13-301+). Uniform Trustees' Powers Act: (Estates and Trusts, Sections 15-101 & 15-102).

Court with Probate Jurisdiction: Orphan's Court (Circuit Court in Hartford and Montgomery Counties).

Minimum Age for Disposing of Property by Will: 18. (Estates and Trusts 4-101).

Required Number of Witnesses for Signing of Will: Two. (Estates and Trusts 4-102).

Can Witnesses Be Beneficiaries?: Yes. (Estates and Trusts 4-102).

Are There Provisions for Self-Proving Wills?: Yes. (Estates and Trusts 5-303).

Are Holographic Wills Permitted?: Yes, if made outside U.S. by a member of the Armed Forces. Expires 1 year after testator's discharge from service if he or she is alive and has testamentary capacity. (Estates and Trusts 4-103).

How Does Divorce Affect the Will?: Revokes the will as to the divorced spouse. (Estates and Trusts 4-105).

How Does Marriage Affect the Will?: Revokes the will if a child is later born to or adopted into the marriage and survives the maker of the will. (Estates and Trusts 4-105).

Who Must Be Mentioned in the Will?: Children, born or adopted; grandchildren of deceased child; surviving spouse. (Estates and Trusts 4-105).

Spouse's Right to Property Regardless of Will: Generally, the surviving spouse is entitled to 1/2 of the deceased spouse's estate if there are no children, and only 1/3 if there are children. However, please refer directly to the statute for details. (Estates and Trusts 3-102).

Laws of Intestate Succession (Distribution If No Will): *Spouse and children of spouse surviving:* If any surviving children are minors, 1/2 to spouse and 1/2 to children equally or grandchildren per stirpes; if no surviving children are minors, $15,000.00 and 1/2 of balance to spouse and 1/2 of balance to children equally or grandchildren per stirpes. *Spouse and children not of spouse surviving:* If any surviving children are minors, 1/2 to spouse and 1/2 to children equally or grandchildren per stirpes; if no surviving children are minors, $15,000.00 and 1/2 of balance to spouse and 1/2 of balance to children equally or grandchildren per stirpes.

Spouse, but no children or parent(s) surviving: All to spouse.

Spouse and parent(s), but no children surviving: $15,000.00 to spouse and then 1/2 of balance to spouse and 1/2 of balance to parents or surviving parent.

Children, but no spouse surviving: All to children or to their children per stirpes.

Parent(s), but no spouse or children surviving: All to parents equally or to the surviving parent.

No spouse, children, or parent(s) surviving: 1/2 to paternal grandparents and 1/2 to maternal grandparents and their next-of-kin. (Title 3, Sections 3-102 to 3-104).

Property Ownership: Common-law state. Tenancy-in-common is recognized. Joint tenancy must be stated. Joint ownership by spouses is presumed to be a tenancy-by-the-entirety unless stated otherwise. Joint bank accounts are payable to any survivor. (Financial Institutions 1-204 and Real Property 2-117 and 4-108).

State Gift, Inheritance, or Estate Taxes: No gift tax; imposes an inheritance tax of 10 percent; imposes state estate tax based on federal estate tax. (Tax General 7-204 and 7-304).

Simplified Probate Procedures: No affidavit procedure. Simplified probate allowed for estates up to $30,000.00 ($50,000.00 if spouse is sole beneficiary). (Estates and Trusts 5-601)

Living Will Form: Advance Medical Directive Health Care Instructions serve as Living Will (Health General, Section 5-603).

Other Directives: Anatomical Gift Act (Estates & Trusts, Section 4-501).

Living Will Effective: Two (2) physicians must agree in writing that you are incapable of making an informed health care decision, but you are not unconscious or unable to communicate by any other means. (Health General, Section 5-606).

Living Will Witness Requirements: Sign in the presence of two (2) adult witnesses. The person you assign as your agent cannot be a witness. At least one (1) of your witnesses must be a person who is not entitled to any portion of your estate or financial benefit by reason of your death. (Health General, Section 5-603).

Advance Health Care Directive: Referred to as Maryland Advance Directive: Planning for future Health Care Decisions. (Health General, Section 5-603).

Health Care Power of Attorney: State specific form is part of Advance Health Care Directive. See Chapter 10 for instructions for form on CD. (Health General, Section 5-603).

Durable Power of Attorney: No state specific form. See Chapter 6 for form. (Estates and Trusts, Section 13-601).

Trustee Residency Requirements: No provision.

Minimum Age for Grantor or Trustee: Eighteen (18). (Commercial Law, Section 1-103).

Trust-Writing Requirements: A trust holding real estate must be in writing. (Real Property, Section 5-105).

Trustee Bond Requirements: None.

Trustee Pour-Over to Will: The trust must be identified in the will. The terms of the trust must be in a document other than the will and signed before or at the same time as the will. (Estates and Trusts, Sections 4-411 & 4-412).

Additional Trust Requirements: None.

Massachusetts

State Website: http://www.mass.gov/legis/laws/mgl/

State Law Reference: Massachusetts General Laws.

Uniform Acts Adopted: Uniform Testamentary Additions to Trusts Act: (Chapter 203, Section 3B). Uniform Gifts to Minors Act: (Chapter 201A, Sections 1+). Uniform Trustees' Powers Act: (Chapter 184B, Section 2).

Court with Probate Jurisdiction: Probate and Family Court. (Chapter 215, Section 1+).

Minimum Age for Disposing of Property by Will: 18. (Chapter 191, Section 1).

Required Number of Witnesses for Signing of Will: Two. (Chapter 191, Section 1).

Can Witnesses Be Beneficiaries?: Yes, but any gift to a beneficiary who was a witness will be void unless there were also 2 other disinterested witnesses. (Chapter 191, Section 2).

Are There Provisions for Self-Proving Wills?: Yes. (Chapter 192, Section 2).

Are Holographic Wills Permitted?: No.

How Does Divorce Affect the Will?: Revokes the will as to the divorced spouse. (Chapter 191, Section 9).

How Does Marriage Affect the Will?: Revokes the will. (Chapter 191, Section 9).

Who Must Be Mentioned in the Will?: Children, born or adopted; grandchildren (if of deceased child); surviving spouse. (Chapter 191, Sections 15 and 20).

Spouse's Right to Property Regardless of Will: Generally, the surviving spouse is entitled to $25,000.00 and 1/2 of the deceased spouse's remaining estate if there are no children, and only 1/3 if there are children. However, please refer directly to the statute as the provisions are detailed. (Chapter 191, Section 15).

Laws of Intestate Succession (Distribution If No Will): *Spouse and children of spouse surviving:* 1/2 to spouse and 1/2 to children equally or grandchildren per stirpes.

Spouse and children not of spouse surviving: 1/2 to spouse and 1/2 to children equally or grandchildren per stirpes.

Spouse, but no children or parent(s) surviving: $200,000.00 and 1/2 of balance to spouse and 1/2 of balance to brothers and sisters equally or their children per stirpes; or if none, to next-of-kin; or if none, all to spouse.

Spouse and parent(s), but no children surviving: $200,000.00 and 1/2 of balance to spouse and 1/2 of balance to parents equally or the surviving parent.

Children, but no spouse surviving: All to children equally or to their children per stirpes.

Parent(s), but no spouse or children surviving: All to parents equally or to the surviving parent.

No spouse, children, or parent(s) surviving: All to brothers and sisters equally or their children per stirpes; or if none, to the next-of-kin. (Chapter 190, Section 1).

Property Ownership: Common-law state. Tenancy-in-common, joint tenancy, and tenancy-by-the-entirety are recognized. Joint ownership by husband and wife creates a tenancy-in-common, unless otherwise stated. (Chapter 184, Section 7).

State Gift, Inheritance, or Estate Taxes: No gift tax; no inheritance tax; imposes limited state estate tax. (Chapter 65C, Section 1).

Simplified Probate Procedures: No affidavit procedure. Simplified probate allowed for estates up to $15,000.00 in personal property if beneficiaries are immediate family. (Chapter 195, Sections 16 and 16A).

Living Will Form: No state statute governing the use of Living Wills. However, you have a constitutional right to state your wishes about medical care. A form is provided in this book.

Living Will Effective: In the event that you develop an irreversible condition that prevents you from making your own medical decisions.

Living Will Witness Requirements: Because Massachusetts does not have a statute governing the use of Living Wills, there are no specific requirements to make your Living Will legally binding. We suggest that you sign in the presence of two (2) witnesses eighteen (18) years or older or a notary public. A witness should not be your health care provider or an employee of your health care provider. Witnesses should not be entitled to any part of your estate, financially responsible for your medical care, or related to you by blood or marriage.

Advance Health Care Directive: No state statute. Form provided on CD.

Health Care power of Attorney: No state specific form. See Chapter 7 for form. Also may use Advance Health Care Directive. See Chapter 10 for instructions for form on CD. (Chapter 201D, Sections 1-17).

Durable Power of Attorney: No state specific form. See Chapter 6 for form.

Trustee Residency Requirements: If out-of-state trustee is appointed and trust holds Massachusetts land, trust must be registered. (Chapter 203, Section 10).

Minimum Age for Grantor or Trustee: Eighteen (18). (Chapter 231, Section 85P).

Trust-Writing Requirements: A trust holding real estate must be in writing. (Chapter 203, Section 1).

Trustee Bond Requirements: None, unless required by trust. (Chapter 205, Section 5).

Trustee Pour-Over to Will: The trust must be identified in the will. The terms of the trust must be in a document other than the will and signed be fore or at the same time as the will. (Chapter 203, Section 3B).

Additional Trust Requirements: None.

Michigan

State Website: http://www.michiganlegislature.org/

State Law Reference: Michigan Compiled Laws Annotated.

Uniform Acts Adopted: Uniform Probate Code: (Sections 701-713).

Court with Probate Jurisdiction: Probate Court. (Section 700.1302).

Minimum Age for Disposing of Property by Will: 18. (Section 700.1106(c)).

Required Number of Witnesses for Signing of Will: Two. (Section 700.2502).

Can Witnesses Be Beneficiaries?: Yes, but any gift to a beneficiary who was a witness will be void beyond the amount that the witness-beneficiary would have received as an intestate share unless there were also 2 other disinterested witnesses. (Section 700.2505).

Are There Provisions for Self-Proving Wills?: Yes. (Section 700.2504).

Are Holographic Wills Permitted?: Yes. (Section 700.2502).

How Does Divorce Affect the Will?: Revokes the will as to the divorced spouse. (Section 700.2801).

How Does Marriage Affect the Will?: Revokes the will as to the spouse if he or she is not otherwise provided for. Spouse may still be entitled to his or her statutory share under the state intestate laws. (Section 700.2301).

Who Must Be Mentioned in the Will?: Children, born or adopted; surviving spouse. (Sections 700.2301 and 700.2302).

Spouse's Right to Property Regardless of Will: Generally, the surviving spouse is entitled to 1/2 of the deceased spouse's estate if there are no children, and only 1/4 if there are children. However, please refer directly to the statute as the provisions are detailed. (Sections 700.2201 to 700.2206).

Laws of Intestate Succession (Distribution If No Will): *Spouse and children of spouse surviving:* $150,000.00 and 1/2 of balance to spouse and 1/2 of balance to children per stirpes. (Note: All amounts are adjusted for cost-of-living increases each year (Section 100.1210).

Spouse and children not of spouse surviving: First $100,000.00 to spouse and then 1/2 to spouse and 1/2 to children per stirpes.

Spouse, but no children or parent(s) surviving: All to spouse.

Spouse and parent(s), but no children surviving: $150,000.00 and 3/4 of balance to spouse and 1/4 of balance to parents or surviving parent.

Children, but no spouse surviving: All to children or to their children per stirpes.

Parent(s), but no spouse or children surviving: All to parents equally or to the surviving parent.

No spouse, children, or parent(s) surviving: All to brothers and sisters equally or to their children per stirpes; or if none, 1/2 to maternal grandparents or their children per stirpes and 1/2 to paternal grandparents or their children per stirpes. (Sections 700.2101 to 700.2114).

Property Ownership: Common-law state. Tenancy-in-common, joint tenancy and tenancy-by-the-entirety are recognized. Joint tenancy created only if stated. Joint tenancy by spouses and joint ownership of real estate by spouses is presumed to be a tenancy-by-the-entirety unless otherwise stated. Joint tenancy with right of survivorship must be in writing. Joint bank account deposits are payable to any survivor. (Sections 554.44, 554.45, and 557.101).

State Gift, Inheritance, or Estate Taxes: No gift tax or inheritance tax; imposes state estate tax based on federal estate tax. (Section 205.202(a)).

Simplified Probate Procedures: Affidavit allowed for estates up to $15,000.00 in personal property. Simplified probate allowed for estates up to $15,000.00 and for estates up to value of homestead, exempt property allowance, family allowances, last illness and burial expenses. (Sections 700.3982, 700.3983, and 700.3987).

Living Will Form: No state statute governing the use of Living Wills. However, you have a constitutional right to state your wishes about medical care. A form is provided in this book.

Living Will Effective: In the event that you develop an irreversible condition that prevents you from making your own medical decisions.

Living Will Witness Requirements: Because Michigan does not have a statute governing the use of Living Wills, there are no specific requirements to make your Living Will legally binding. We suggest that you sign in the presence of two (2) witnesses eighteen (18) years or older or a notary public. A witness should not be your health care provider or an employee of your health care provider. Witnesses should not be entitled to any part of your estate, be financially responsible for your medical care, or be related to you by blood or marriage.

Advance Health Care Directive: No state statute. Form provided on CD.

Health Care Power of Attorney: No state specific form. See Chapter 7 for form. Also may use Advance Health Care Directive. See Chapter 10 for instructions for form on CD. (Sections 700.5506+).

Durable Power of Attorney: No state specific form. See Chapter 6 for form. (Sections 700.5501+).

Trustee Residency Requirements: Out-of-state trustee must qualify to do business in Michigan. (Section 700.7105).

Minimum Age for Grantor or Trustee: Eighteen (18). (Section 722.522).

Trust-Writing Requirements: Yes. (Section 566.106).

Trustee Bond Requirements: None, unless required by trust, requested by beneficiary, or required by court. (Section 700.7304).

Trustee Pour-Over to Will: The trust must be identified in the will. The terms of the trust must be in a document other than the will and signed before or at the same time as the will. (Sections 555.461–555.464).

Additional Trust Requirements: Upon the Grantor's death, the Successor Trustee must notify all beneficiaries of the existence of the trust. Residents should register a "Registration of Living Trust" form with the local court in their county of residence. This requirement is mandatory, although there are no penalties or consequences for failure to register. Please see proper form in Chapter 9. (Section 700.7101).

Minnesota

State Website: http://www.revisor.leg.state.mn.us/stats/

State Law Reference: Minnesota Statutes Annotated.

Uniform Acts Adopted: Uniform Probate Code: (Sections 524.1-101+). Uniform Trustees' Powers Act: (Section 501B.81). Uniform Testamentary Additions to Trusts Act: (Section 501B.08). Uniform Gifts to Minors Act: (Sections 527.21+).

Court with Probate Jurisdiction: District Court. (Section 524.1-201).

Minimum Age for Disposing of Property by Will: 18. (Section 524.2-501).

Required Number of Witnesses for Signing of Will: Two. (Section 524.2-502).

Can Witnesses Be Beneficiaries?: Yes. (Section 524.2-505).

Are There Provisions for Self-Proving Wills?: Yes. (Section 524.2-504).

Are Holographic Wills Permitted?: No.

How Does Divorce Affect the Will?: Revokes the will as to the divorced spouse. (Section 524.2-804).

How Does Marriage Affect the Will?: Revokes the will as to the spouse if he or she is not otherwise provided for. Spouse may still be entitled to his or her statutory share under the state intestate laws. (Section 524.2-301).

Who Must Be Mentioned in the Will?: Children, born or adopted; grandchildren (if of deceased child); surviving spouse. (Sections 524.2-202 and 524.2-302).

Spouse's Right to Property Regardless of Will: The elective share amount is dependent on length of marriage. (Sections 524.2-201 and 524.2-202).

Laws of Intestate Succession (Distribution If No Will): *Spouse and children of spouse surviving:* All to spouse.

Spouse and children not of spouse surviving: $150,000.00 and 1/2 of balance of estate to spouse and 1/2 to children or grandchildren per stirpes.

Spouse, but no children or parent surviving: All to spouse.

Spouse and parent(s), but no children surviving: All to spouse.

Children, but no spouse surviving: All to children equally or to their children per stirpes.

Parent(s), but no spouse or children surviving: All to parents equally or to the surviving parent.

No spouse, children, or parent(s) surviving: All to brothers and sisters equally or their children per stirpes; or if none, to the next-of-kin. (Sections 524.2-102 and 524.2-103).

Property Ownership: Common-law state. Tenancy-in-common is presumed unless joint tenancy in writing. Tenancy-by-the-entirety not recognized. Joint bank account deposits are payable to any survivor unless clear evidence exists that deposit is payable only to specified survivor. (Sections 500.19 and 524.6-203).

State Gift, Inheritance, or Estate Taxes: No gift tax; no inheritance tax; imposes state estate tax based on federal estate tax. (Section 291.03).

Simplified Probate Procedures: Affidavit allowed for estates up to $20,000.00 in personal property. Simplified probate allowed if court determines value of estate is less than value of homestead, exempt property allowance, family allowances, last illness and burial expenses. (Sections 524.3-1201 and 524.3-1203).

Living Will Form: Health Care Living Will (Section 145B-04).

Other Directives: Anatomical Gift Act (Sections 525.9211+).

Living Will Effective: Living Will becomes effective in the event that you can no longer make your own medical decisions. (Sections 145B.02 and 145B.04).

Living Will Witness Requirements: Sign in the presence of two (2) witnesses eighteen (18) years or older or a notary public. A witness cannot be the person whom you appointed as your agent. At least one (1) witness cannot be your health care provider or an employee of your health care provider. (Section 145B.03).

Advance Health Care Directive: Referred to as Health Care Living Will. (Section 145B.04).

Health Care Power of Attorney: State specific form is part of Advance Health Care Directive. See Chapter 10 for instructions for form on CD. (Section 145B.04).

Durable Power of Attorney: No state specific form. See Chapter 6 for form. (Section 523.07).

Trustee Residency Requirements: No, unless in trust. (Section 524.3-913).

Minimum Age for Grantor or Trustee: Eighteen (18). (Section 645.451).

Trust-Writing Requirements: Yes. (Section 513.03).

Trustee Bond Requirements: No provision.

Trustee Pour-Over to Will: The trust must be identified in the will. The terms of the trust must be in a document other than the will and signed before or at the same time as the will. (Section 524.2-511).

Additional Trust Requirements: None.

Mississippi

State Website: http://www.mscode.com/

State Law Reference: Mississippi Code Annotated.

Uniform Acts Adopted: Uniform Trustees' Powers Act: (Sections 91-9-101+). Uniform Testamentary Additions to Trusts Act: (Section 91-5-11). Uniform Gifts to Minors Act: (Sections 91-20-1+).

Court with Probate Jurisdiction: Chancery Court. (Section 9-5-83).

Minimum Age for Disposing of Property by Will: 18. (Section 91-5-1).

Required Number of Witnesses for Signing of Will: Two. (Section 91-5-1).

Can Witnesses Be Beneficiaries?: No, however a witness-beneficiary is still entitled to receive a share of the estate not to exceed the amount he or she is entitled to as an intestate share. (Section 91-5-9).

Are There Provisions for Self-Proving Wills?: Yes. (Section 91-7-7).

Are Holographic Wills Permitted?: Yes. (Section 91-5-1).

How Does Divorce Affect the Will?: Does not revoke the will. (Section 91-5-27).

How Does Marriage Affect the Will?: Does not revoke the will. (Section 91-5-27).

Who Must Be Mentioned in the Will?: Children, born or adopted; surviving spouse. (Section 91-5-27).

Spouse's Right to Property Regardless of Will: Generally, the surviving spouse is entitled to 1/2 of the deceased spouse's estate if there are no children, and only 1/3 if there are children. However, please refer directly to the statute as the provisions are detailed. (Sections 91-5-25 and 91-5-27).

Laws of Intestate Succession (Distribution If No Will): *Spouse and children of spouse surviving:* Spouse and any surviving children or grandchildren each take equal shares.

Spouse and children not of spouse surviving: Spouse and any surviving children or grandchildren each take equal shares.

Spouse, but no children or parent(s) surviving: All to spouse.

Spouse and parent(s), but no children surviving: All to spouse.

Children, but no spouse surviving: All to children equally or to their children per stirpes.

Parent(s), but no spouse or children surviving: All to parents, brothers, and sisters equally, or to children of brothers and sisters per stirpes. If no brothers or sisters or children of brothers or sisters, all to parents equally or the surviving parent.

No spouse, children, or parent(s) surviving: All to brothers and sisters equally, or to their children per stirpes; or if none, to grandparents, uncles, and aunts equally, or to their children per stirpes; or if none, to the next-of-kin. (Sections 91-1-3, 91-1-7, and 91-1-11).

Property Ownership: Common-law state. Tenancy-in-common, joint tenancy and tenancy-by-the-entirety are recognized. Ownership by 2 or more persons is presumed to be tenancy-in-common unless joint tenancy is stated. Joint bank account deposits are payable to any survivor. (Section 89-1-7).

State Gift, Inheritance, or Estate Taxes: No gift tax; no inheritance tax; imposes limited state estate tax. Section 27-9-5).

Simplified Probate Procedures: Affidavit allowed for estates consisting only of bank account up to $12,500.00. No simplified probate procedure. (Section 81-14-383).

Living Will Form: Instructions for Health Care serves as Living Will (Section 41-41-209).

Other Directives: Anatomical Gift Act (Sections 41-39-31+).

Living Will Effective: In the event that you have an incurable and irreversible condition that will result in death within a relatively short time, become unconscious and, to a reasonable degree of medical certainty, will not regain consciousness, or the likely risks and burdens of treatment would outweigh the expected benefits. (Section 41-41-209).

Living Will Witness Requirements: Sign in the presence of two (2) witnesses eighteen (18) years or older or a notary public. A witness cannot be the person whom you appointed as your agent, health care provider, or an employee of your health care provider. At least one (1) witness cannot be related to you by blood or marriage or entitled to your estate upon your death. (Section 41-41-209).

Advance Health Care Directive: (Section 41-41-209).

Health Care Power of Attorney: State specific form is part of Advance Health Care Directive. See Chapter 10 for instructions for form on CD. (Section 41-41-209).

Durable Power of Attorney: No state specific form. See Chapter 6 for form. (Sections 87-3-105).

Trustee Residency Requirements: Out-of-state trustee must qualify to do business in Mississippi.

Minimum Age for Grantor or Trustee: Twenty-one (21). (Section 1-3-27).

Trust-Writing Requirements: Yes. (Section 91-9-1).

Trustee Bond Requirements: None, unless required by trust.

Trustee Pour-Over to Will: The trust must be identified in the will. The terms of the trust must be in a document other than the will and signed before or at the same time as the will. (Section 91-5-11).

Additional Trust Requirements: None.

Missouri

State Website: http://www.moga.state.mo.us/STATUTES/STATUTES.HTM#T

State Law Reference: Missouri Annotated Statutes.

Uniform Acts Adopted: Uniform Trustees' Powers Act: (Section 456.7-801+). Uniform Gifts to Minors Act: (Sections 404.005+).

Court with Probate Jurisdiction: Circuit Court. (Section 478.260).

Minimum Age for Disposing of Property by Will: 18. (Section 474.310).

Required Number of Witnesses for Signing of Will: Two. (Section 474.320).

Can Witnesses Be Beneficiaries?: Yes, but interested witness is limited to intestate share, if any, unless signed by 2 other disinterested witnesses. (Section 474.330).

Are There Provisions for Self-Proving Wills?: Yes. (Section 474.337).

Are Holographic Wills Permitted?: No provision.

How Does Divorce Affect the Will?: Revokes the will as to the divorced spouse. (Section 474.420).

How Does Marriage Affect the Will?: Spouse may still be entitled to his or her statutory share under the state intestate laws. (Section 474.420).

Who Must Be Mentioned in the Will?: Children, born or adopted; surviving spouse. (Sections 474.160 and 474.240).

Spouse's Right to Property Regardless of Will: Generally, the surviving spouse is entitled to 1/2 of the deceased spouse's estate if there are no children, and only 1/3 if there are children. However, please refer directly to the statute as the provisions are detailed. (Section 474.160).

Laws of Intestate Succession (Distribution If No Will): *Spouse and children of spouse surviving:* $20,000.00 and 1/2 of balance to spouse and 1/2 of balance to children or grandchildren per stirpes.

Spouse and children not of spouse surviving: 1/2 to spouse and 1/2 to children or grandchildren per stirpes.

Spouse, but no children or parent(s) surviving: All to spouse.

Spouse and parent(s), but no children surviving: All to spouse.

Children, but no spouse surviving: All to children equally or to their children per stirpes.

Parent(s), but no spouse or children surviving: All to parents, brothers, and sisters equally, or to their children per stirpes; or if none, all to parents or to the surviving parent.

No spouse, children, or parent(s) surviving: All to brothers and sisters equally or to their children per stirpes; or if none, to grandparents, uncles, and aunts and their children per stirpes; or if none, to the nearest lineal ancestor and their children. (Section 474.010).

Property Ownership: Common-law state. Tenancy-in-common, joint tenancy and tenancy-by-the-entirety are recognized. Ownership by 2 or more persons is presumed to be a tenancy-in-common unless joint tenancy is stated. Joint bank account deposits are payable to any survivor. Allows beneficiary deeds and transfer-on-death vehicle titles to transfer property on death. (Sections 442.025, 442.030, and 442.035).

State Gift, Inheritance, or Estate Taxes: No gift tax; no inheritance tax; no state estate tax. (Section 145.011).

Simplified Probate Procedures: No affidavit procedure. Simplified probate allowed for estates up to $40,000.00. (Section 473.097).

Living Will Form: Missouri Declaration serves as Living Will (Section 459.015).

Other Directives: Anatomical Gift Act (Sections 194.210+).

Living Will Effective: The Declaration becomes effective in the event that you have an incurable or irreversible medical condition which, without the use of life support, will result in death in a relative short period of time, or you are in a permanent coma or persistent vegetative state. (Section 459.025)

Living Will Witness Requirements: Sign in the presence of two (2) adult witnesses. If you have someone sign the Declaration on your behalf, that person cannot serve as a witness. (Section 459.015).

Advance Health Care Directive: Referred to as Missouri Declaration. (Section 459.015).

Health Care Power of Attorney: No state specific form. See Chapter 7 for form. Also may use Advance Health Care Directive. See Chapter 10 for instructions for form on CD. (Section 404.822).

Durable Power of Attorney: No state specific form. See Chapter 6 for form. (Section 404.705).

Trustee Residency Requirements: Out-of-state trustee must qualify to do business in Missouri.

Minimum Age for Grantor or Trustee: Eighteen (18). (Section 431.055).

Trust-Writing Requirements: A trust holding real estate must be in writing. (Section 432.010).

Trustee Bond Requirements: Yes, unless not required by trust, or court. (Section 456.7-702).

Trustee Pour-Over to Will: The trust must be identified in the will. The terms of the trust must be in a document other than the will and signed before or at the same time as the will. (Section 456.021).

Additional Trust Requirements: Residents should register a "Registration of Living Trust" form with the local court in their county of residence. This requirement is mandatory, although there are no penalties or consequences for failure to register. Please see proper form in Chapter 9.

Montana

State Website: http://data.opi.state.mt.us/bills/mca_toc/index.htm

State Law Reference: Montana Code Annotated.

Uniform Acts Adopted: Uniform Probate Code: (Sections 72-1-101+). Uniform Trustees' Powers Act: (Sections 72-34-301+). Uniform Testamentary Additions to Trusts Act: (Sections 72-2-531+). Uniform Gifts to Minors Act: (Sections 72-26-501+).

Court with Probate Jurisdiction: District Court. (Section 3-5-302).

Minimum Age for Disposing of Property by Will: 18. (Section 72-2-521).

Required Number of Witnesses for Signing of Will: Two. (Section 72-2-522).

Can Witnesses Be Beneficiaries?: Yes. (Section 72-2-525).

Are There Provisions for Self-Proving Wills?: Yes. (Section 72-2-524).

Are Holographic Wills Permitted?: Yes. (Section 72-2-522).

How Does Divorce Affect the Will?: Revokes the will as to the divorced spouse. (Sections 72-2-528 and 72-2-814).

How Does Marriage Affect the Will?: Revokes the will as to the spouse if he or she is not otherwise provided for. Spouse will still be entitled to his or her statutory share under the state intestate laws. (Section 72-2-331).

Who Must Be Mentioned in the Will?: Children, born or adopted; surviving spouse. (Sections 72-2-221 and 72-2-332).

Spouse's Right to Property Regardless of Will: The surviving spouse is entitled to an elective share of the deceased spouse's "augmented" estate that ranges from a "supplemental amount" for spouses married for less than 1 year, 3 percent of the "augmented" estate for spouses married from 1-2 years, and up to 50 percent for spouses married over 15 years. Please consult the statute directly for complete details. In general, the "augmented" estate includes both the property that passes under the will and any other property that passes by other "non-will" transfers, such as under the terms of a living trust or a joint tenancy arrangement. (Section 72-2-221).

Laws of Intestate Succession (Distribution If No Will): *Spouse and children of spouse surviving:* All to spouse.

Spouse and children not of spouse surviving: If 1 child surviving, 1/2 to spouse and 1/2 to child; if more than 1 child surviving, 1/3 to spouse and 2/3 to children equally.

Spouse, but no children or parent(s) surviving: All to spouse.

Spouse and parent(s), but no children surviving: All to spouse.

Children, but no spouse surviving: All to children equally or to their children per stirpes.

Parent(s), but no spouse or children surviving: All to parents equally or to the surviving parent.

No spouse, children, or parent(s) surviving: All to brothers and sisters equally or their children per stirpes; or if none, 1/2 to paternal grandparents or their children and 1/2 to maternal grandparents or their children per stirpes. (Sections 72-2-112 and 72-2-113).

Property Ownership: Common-law state. Tenancy-in-common and joint tenancy (called interests in common and joint interests) are recognized. No tenancy-by-the-entirety is recognized. Tenancy-in-common is presumed unless joint tenancy stated. Joint bank account deposits are payable to any survivor. (Section 40-2-105 and Section 70-1-310).

State Gift, Inheritance, or Estate Taxes: No gift tax or inheritance tax. no state estate tax. (Section 72-16-904).

Simplified Probate Procedures: Affidavit allowed for estates up to $50,000.00 in personal property. Simplified probate allowed for estates up to value of homestead, exempt property allowance, family allowances, last illness and burial expenses. (Sections 72-3-1101 and 72-3-1103)

Living Will Form: Montana Declaration serves as Living Will (Section 50-9-103).

Other Directives: Anatomical Gift Act (Section 72-17-101+).

Living Will Effective: Becomes effective when you have an incurable or irreversible medical condition which, without the use of life support, will result in death in a relatively short period of time, or you are in a permanent coma or persistent vegetative state. (Section 50-9-105).

Living Will Witness Requirements: Sign in the presence of two (2) adult witnesses. No other restrictions apply. Do not use your appointed health care agent as one of your witnesses. (Section 50-9-103).

Advance Health Care Directive: Referred to as Montana Declaration. (Section 50-9-103).

Health Care Power of Attorney: State specific form is part of Advance Health Care Directive. See Chapter 10 for instructions for form on CD. (Section 50-9-103).

Durable Power of Attorney: State specific form. See Chapter 9. (Section 72-5-501).

Trustee Residency Requirements: Out-of-state trustee must qualify to do business in Montana.

Minimum Age for Grantor or Trustee: Eighteen (18). (Section 41-1-101).

Trust-Writing Requirements: Yes. (Section 72-33-208).

Trustee Bond Requirements: None, unless required by trust or court. (Section 72-33-603).

Trustee Pour-Over to Will: The trust must be identified in the will. The terms of the trust must be in a document other than the will and signed before or at the same time as the will. (Section 72-2-531).

Additional Trust Requirements: None.

Nebraska

State Website: http://www.unicam.state.ne.us/web/public/home

State Law Reference: Revised Statutes of Nebraska.

Uniform Acts Adopted: Uniform Probate Code: (Section 30-2201). Uniform Testamentary Additions to Trusts Act: (Sections 30-3602). Uniform Trustees' Powers Act: (Sections 30-3880). Uniform Gifts to Minors Act: (Sections 43-2701+).

Court with Probate Jurisdiction: County Court. (Section 24-517).

Minimum Age for Disposing of Property by Will: 18, but no minimum age for married persons. (Section 30-2326).

Required Number of Witnesses for Signing of Will: Two. (Section 30-2327).

Can Witnesses Be Beneficiaries?: Yes, however interested witness may be limited to receiving intestate share. (Section 30-2330).

Are There Provisions for Self-Proving Wills?: Yes. (Section 30-2329).

Are Holographic Wills Permitted?: Yes. (Section 30-2328).

How Does Divorce Affect the Will?: Revokes the will as to the divorced spouse. (Section 30-2333).

How Does Marriage Affect the Will?: Spouse will still be entitled to his or her statutory share under the state intestate laws. (Section 30-2320).

Who Must Be Mentioned in the Will?: Children, born or adopted; surviving spouse. (Sections 30-2313 and 30-2321).

Spouse's Right to Property Regardless of Will: The surviving spouse is entitled to 1/2 of the "augmented" estate of the deceased spouse. In general, the "augmented" estate includes both the property that passes under the will and any other property that passes by other "non-will" transfers, such as under the terms of a living trust or a joint tenancy arrangement. (Section 30-2313).

Laws of Intestate Succession (Distribution If No Will): *Spouse and children of spouse surviving:* $50,000.00 and 1/2 of balance to spouse and 1/2 of balance to children.

Spouse and children not of spouse surviving: 1/2 to spouse and 1/2 to children.

Spouse, but no children or parent(s) surviving: All to spouse.

Spouse and parent(s), but no children surviving: $50,000.00 and 1/2 of balance to spouse and 1/2 of balance to parents or surviving parent.

Children, but no spouse surviving: All to children equally or to their children per stirpes.

Parent(s), but no spouse or children surviving: All to parents equally or to the surviving parent.

No spouse, children, or parent(s) surviving: All to brothers and sisters equally, or their children per stirpes; or if none, 1/2 to paternal grandparents or their children and 1/2 to maternal grandparents or their children per stirpes. (Sections 30-2302 and 30-2303).

State Property Ownership: Common-law state. Tenancy-in-common and joint tenancy are recognized. Tenancy-by-the-entirety is not recognized. Joint bank account deposits are payable to any survivor unless clear evidence exists that deposit is payable only to specified survivor. (Section 76-118).

State Gift, Inheritance, or Estate Taxes: No gift tax; imposes an inheritance tax of up to 16 percent; no state estate tax. (Sections 77-2001 to 77-2006 and 77-2101.01)

Simplified Probate Procedures: Affidavit allowed for estates up to $25,000.00. Simplified probate allowed for estates up to value of homestead, exempt property allowance, family allowances, last illness and burial expenses. (Sections 30-24,125 and 30-24,127)

Living Will Form: Nebraska Declaration serves as Living Will (Section 20-404).

Other Directives: Anatomical Gift Act (Section 71-4804).

Living Will Effective: Declaration becomes effective when your attending physician determines you to have an incurable or irreversible medical condition which, without the use of life support, will result in death in a relatively short period of time, or you are in a permanent coma or persistent vegetative state. (Section 20-405).

Living Will Witness Requirements: Sign in the presence of two (2) adult witnesses. Witnesses cannot be employees of your life or health insurance provider and at least one (1) witness must not be an administrator or employee of your treating health care provider. (Section 20-404).

Advance Health Care Directive: Referred to as Nebraska Declaration. (Section 20-404).

Health Care Power of Attorney: State specific form is part of Advance Health Care Directive. See Chapter 10 for instructions for form on CD. (Section 30-3408).

Durable Power of Attorney: State specific form. See Chapter 9. (Section 49-1522).

Trustee Residency Requirements: Out-of-state trustee must qualify to do business in Nebraska. (Section 30-3820).

Minimum Age for Grantor or Trustee: Eighteen (18). (Section 43-2101).

Trust-Writing Requirements: A trust holding real estate must be in writing. (Section 36-103).

Trustee Bond Requirements: None, unless required by trust, requested by beneficiary, or court order. (Section 30-3858).

Trustee Pour-Over to Will: The trust must be identified in the will. The terms of the trust must be in a document other than the will and signed before or at the same time as the will. (Section 30-3602).

Additional Trust Requirements: Upon the Grantor's death, the Successor Trustee must notify all beneficiaries of the existence of the trust. Residents should register a "Registration of Living Trust" form with the local court in their county of residence. This requirement is mandatory, although there are no penalties or consequences for failure to register. Please see proper form in Chapter 9.

Nevada

State Website: http://www.leg.state.nv.us/NRS/

State Law Reference: Nevada Revised Statutes Annotated.

Uniform Acts Adopted: Uniform Testamentary Additions to Trusts Act: (Sections 136.220+). Uniform Trustees' Powers Act: (Sections 163.260+). Uniform Gifts to Minors Act: (Sections 167.010+).

Court with Probate Jurisdiction: District Court. (Section 136.010).

Minimum Age for Disposing of Property by Will: 18. (Section 133.020).

Required Number of Witnesses for Signing of Will: Two. Electronic wills are also valid in Nevada. (Section 133.040 and 133.085).

Can Witnesses Be Beneficiaries?: No, unless there are 2 other competent witnesses. (Section 133.060).

Are There Provisions for Self-Proving Wills?: Yes. (Section 133.050).

Are Holographic Wills Permitted?: Yes. (Section 133.090).

How Does Divorce Affect the Will?: Revokes the will as to the divorced spouse, if will was signed prior to entry of divorce decree. (Section 133.115).

How Does Marriage Affect the Will?: Revokes the will as to the spouse if he or she is not otherwise provided for. Spouse may still be entitled to his or her statutory share under the state intestate laws. (Section 133.110).

Who Must Be Mentioned in the Will?: Statute contains detailed provisions regarding this. Please refer directly to statute or consult an attorney if this is a critical factor. (Sections 133.160 and 134.005).

Spouse's Right to Property Regardless of Will: Community property right to 1/2 of the deceased spouse's "community" property. (Section 123.250).

Laws of Intestate Succession (Distribution If No Will): *Spouse and children of spouse surviving:* All of decedent's community property to spouse. If only 1 child is surviving, 1/2 of decedent's separate property to spouse and 1/2 to child or grandchildren per stirpes; if more than 1 child is surviving, 1/3 of separate property to spouse and 2/3 to the children or grandchildren per stirpes.

Spouse and children not of spouse surviving: All of decedent's community property to spouse. If only 1 child is surviving, 1/2 of decedent's separate property to spouse and 1/2 to child or grandchildren per stirpes; if more than 1 child is surviving, 1/3 of separate property to spouse and 2/3 to the children or grandchildren per stirpes.

Spouse, but no children or parent(s) surviving: All of decedent's community property to spouse. 1/2 of decedent's separate property to spouse and 1/2 to brothers and sisters equally or their children per stirpes; or if none, all to spouse.

Spouse and parent(s), but no children surviving: All of decedent's community property to spouse. 1/2 of decedent's separate property to spouse and 1/2 to parents equally or surviving parent.

Children, but no spouse surviving: All to children or their children per stirpes.

Parent(s), but no spouse or children surviving: All to parents equally or to the surviving parent.

No spouse, children, or parent(s) surviving: All to brothers and sisters equally, or their children per stirpes; or if none, to the next-of-kin. There are additional distribution possibilities listed in the statute. (Sections 134.040 to 134.160).

Property Ownership: Community property state. Tenancy-in-common, joint tenancy, and community property with right of survivorship are recognized. Tenancy-by-the-entirety is not recognized. Joint bank account deposits are payable to any survivor. Allows beneficiary deeds to transfer property on death. (Sections 111.060 and 111.065).

State Gift, Inheritance, or Estate Taxes: No gift tax; no inheritance tax; Imposes a state estate tax based on federal estate tax. (Section 375A.100).

Simplified Probate Procedures: Affidavit allowed for estates up to $20,000 in personal property if left to family members and no real estate is owned in Nevada. Simplified probate allowed for estates up to $100,000.00 with court approval. (Sections 146.020, 146.070, and 146.080).

Living Will Form: Nevada Declaration serves as Living Will (Section 449-610).

Other Directives: Anatomical Gift Act (Sections 451.500+).

Living Will Effective: Declaration becomes effective when your doctor determines that your death would occur without the use of life-sustaining medical care. (Section 449.617).

Living Will Witness Requirements: Sign in the presence of two (2) adult witnesses. No other restrictions apply. (Section 449.610).

Advance Health Care Directive: Referred to as Nevada Declaration. (Section 449.610).

Health Care Power of Attorney: State specific form is part of Advance Health Care Directive. See Chapter 10 for instructions for form on CD. (Section 449.830).

Durable Power of Attorney: No state specific form. See Chapter 6 for form. (Section 111.460).

Trustee Residency Requirements: No provision.

Minimum Age for Grantor or Trustee: Eighteen (18). (Section 129.010).

Trust-Writing Requirements: A trust holding real estate must be in writing. (Section 111.235).

Trustee Bond Requirements: None, unless required by trust or ordered by court. (Section 153.120).

Trustee Pour-Over to Will: Trust must be identified in the will. Terms of the trust must be in a document other than the will and signed before or at the same time as the will. (Sections 163.220–163.250).

Additional Trust Requirements: None.

New Hampshire

State Website: http://gencourt.state.nh.us/rsa/html/indexes/default.asp

State Law Reference: New Hampshire Revised Statutes.

Uniform Acts Adopted: Uniform Trustees' Powers Act: (Sections 564-A:1+). Uniform Testamentary Additions to Trusts Act: (Sections 563-A:1+). Uniform Gifts to Minors Act: (Sections 463-A:1+).

Court with Probate Jurisdiction: Probate Court. (Section 547:3).

Minimum Age for Disposing of Property by Will: 18, but no minimum for married persons. (Section 551:1).

Required Number of Witnesses for Signing of Will: Two. (Section 551:2).

Can Witnesses Be Beneficiaries?: Yes, but any gift to a beneficiary who was a witness will be void unless there were also 2 other disinterested witnesses. (Section 551:3).

Are There Provisions for Self-Proving Wills?: Yes. (Section 551:2a).

Are Holographic Wills Permitted?: No provision.

How Does Divorce Affect the Will?: Revokes the will as to the former spouse. (Section 551:13).

How Does Marriage Affect the Will?: Spouse may elect to receive statutory share. (Section 560:10).

Who Must Be Mentioned in the Will?: Children, born or adopted; grandchildren; surviving spouse. (Sections 551:10 and 560:10).

Spouse's Right to Property Regardless of Will: Generally, the surviving spouse is entitled to 1/2 of the deceased

spouse's estate if there are no children, and only 1/3 if there are children. However, please refer directly to the statute as the provisions are detailed. (Section 560:10).

Laws of Intestate Succession (Distribution If No Will): *Spouse and children of spouse surviving:* $250,000.00 and 1/2 of balance to spouse and 1/2 of balance to children or grandchildren per stirpes. ($150,000.00 and 1/2 of the balance if surviving spouse also has children which are not decedents)

Spouse and children not of spouse surviving: 1/2 to spouse and 1/2 to children or grandchildren per stirpes.

Spouse, but no children or parent(s) surviving: All to spouse.

Spouse and parent(s), but no children surviving: $250,000.00 and 3/4 of balance to spouse and 1/4 of balance to parents or surviving parent.

Children, but no spouse surviving: All to children or to their children per stirpes.

Parent(s), but no spouse or children surviving: All to parents equally or to the surviving parent.

No spouse, children, or parent(s) surviving: All to brothers and sisters equally, or their children per stirpes; or if none, 1/2 to maternal grandparents or their children and 1/2 to paternal grandparents or their children per stirpes. (Section 561:1).

Property Ownership: Common-law state. Tenancy-in-common is presumed unless joint tenancy stated. Ownership by spouses creates joint tenancy. Tenancy-by-the-entirety is not recognized. Joint bank account deposits are payable to any survivor. (Sections 477:18 and 477:19).

State Gift, Inheritance, or Estate Taxes: No gift tax or inheritance tax. no state estate tax. (Section 87:01).

Simplified Probate Procedures: No affidavit procedure. Simplified probate allowed for estates left to a spouse or an only child. (Section 553:32)

Living Will Form: New Hampshire Declaration serves as Living Will (Section 137-J:20).

Other Directives: Anatomical Gift Act (Section 291-A).

Living Will Effective: Two (2) physicians must certify in writing that you are in a terminal condition and your death would occur within a short period of time without the use of life-sustaining medical care. (Section 137-J:20).

Living Will Witness Requirements: Sign in the presence of two (2) witnesses eighteen (18) years or older or a notary public. A witness cannot be a person who has a claim against your estate, stands to inherit from your estate, be your spouse, or be your doctor or a person acting under direction or control of your doctor. If you are a resident of a health care facility or a patient in a hospital, one of your witnesses may be your doctor or an employee of your doctor. (Section 137-J:14).

Advance Health Care Directive: Referred to as New Hampshire Declaration. (Section 137-J:19).

Health Care Power of Attorney: No state specific form. See Chapter 7 for form. Also may use Advance Health Care Directive. See Chapter 10 for instructions for form on CD. (Section 137-J:19).

Durable Power of Attorney: State specific form. See Chapter 9. (Section 506:6).

Trustee Residency Requirements: If out-of-state trustee is appointed, a resident agent must also be appointed.

Minimum Age for Grantor or Trustee: Eighteen (18). (Section 21-B:1).

Trust-Writing Requirements: A trust holding real estate must be in writing. (Section 477:17).

Trustee Bond Requirements: None, unless required by trust or ordered by court. (Section 564-B:7-702).

Trustee Pour-Over to Will: The trust must be identified in the will. The terms of the trust must be in a document other than the will and signed before or at the same time as the will. (Sections 563-A:1 and 563-A:4).

Additional Trust Requirements: None.

New Jersey

State Website: http://www.njleg.state.nj.us

State Law Reference: New Jersey Revised Statutes.

Uniform Acts Adopted: Uniform Probate Code: (Sections 3B:3-1+). Uniform Testamentary Additions to Trusts Act: (Sections 3B:4-1+). Uniform Trustees' Powers Act: (Section 3B:14-23). Uniform Gifts to Minors Act: (Sections 46:38A-1+).

Court with Probate Jurisdiction: Surrogate's Court.

Minimum Age for Disposing of Property by Will: 18. (Section 3B:3-1).

Required Number of Witnesses for Signing of Will: Two. (Section 3B:3-2).

Can Witnesses Be Beneficiaries?: Yes. (Section 3B:3-8).

Are There Provisions for Self-Proving Wills?: Yes. (Section 3B:3-4).

Are Holographic Wills Permitted?: Yes. (Section 3B:3-3).

How Does Divorce Affect the Will?: Revokes the will as to the divorced spouse. (Section 3B:3-14).

How Does Marriage Affect the Will?: Spouse shall still be entitled to his or her statutory share under the state intestate laws. (Section 3B:5-15).

Who Must Be Mentioned in the Will?: Children born or adopted; grandchildren; surviving spouse. (Sections 3B:5-15 and 3B:5-16).

Spouse's Right to Property Regardless of Will: The surviving spouse is entitled to 1/3 of the "augmented" estate of the deceased spouse. In general, the "augmented" estate includes both the property that passes under the will and any other property that passes by other "non-will" transfers, such as under the terms of a living trust or a joint tenancy. (Section 3B:8-1).

Laws of Intestate Succession (Distribution If No Will): *Spouse and children of spouse surviving:* 1/4 of estate (at least $50,000.00 but no more than 200,000.00) and 1/2 of balance to spouse and 1/2 of balance to children or grandchildren per stirpes.

Spouse and children not of spouse surviving: 1/2 to spouse and 1/2 to children or grandchildren per stirpes.

Spouse, but no children or parent(s) surviving: All to spouse.

Spouse and parent(s), but no children surviving: 1/4 of estate (at least $50,000.00 but no more than 200,000.00) and 1/2 of balance to spouse and 1/2 of balance to parents or surviving parent.

Children, but no spouse surviving: All to children or to their children per stirpes.

Parent(s), but no spouse or children surviving: All to parents equally or to the surviving parent.

No spouse, children, or parent(s) surviving: All to brothers and sisters equally, or their children per stirpes; or if none, 1/2 to maternal grandparents or their children and 1/2 to paternal grandparents or their children per stirpes. (Sections 3B:5-3 and 3B:5-4).

Property Ownership: Common-law state. Tenancy-in-common, joint tenancy and tenancy-by-the-entirety are recognized. Ownership by spouses is presumed to be a tenancy-by-the-entirety unless stated otherwise. Tenancy-in-common is presumed unless joint tenancy stated. Joint bank account deposits are payable to any survivor. (Sections 46:3-17, 46:3-17.1, and 46:3-17.2).

State Gift, Inheritance, or Estate Taxes: No gift tax; imposes an inheritance tax of up to 16 percent; imposes state estate tax. (Sections 54-34+ and 54:38-1)

Simplified Probate Procedures: Affidavit allowed for intestate estates up to $20,000.00 to spouse or $5,000.00 to other persons. No simplified probate allowed. (Sections 3B:10-3 and 3B:10-4).

Living Will Form: New Jersey Instruction Directive serves as Living Will (Section 26-2H-55).

Other Directives: Anatomical Gift Act (Section 26:6-57+).

Living Will Effective: Your doctor or treating health care institution must receive this document. Your attending physician and one (1) other physician must confirm that you are unable to make health care decisions. (Sections 26:2H-59 and 26:2H-60).

Living Will Witness Requirements: Sign in the presence of two (2) witnesses eighteen (18) years or older or a notary public. A witness cannot be the person whom you appointed as your agent. (Section 26:2H-56).

Advance Health Care Directive: Referred to as Advance Directive for Health Care. (Section 26:2H-58).

Health Care Power of Attorney: No state specific form. See Chapter 7 for form. Also may use Advance Health Care Directive. See Chapter 10 for instructions for form on CD. (Section 26:2H-56).

Durable Power of Attorney: No state specific form. See Chapter 6 for form. (Section 46:2B-8.1).

Trustee Residency Requirements: None.

Minimum Age for Grantor or Trustee: Eighteen (18). (Section 9:17B-4).

Trust-Writing Requirements: A trust holding real estate must be in writing. (Section 25:1-11).

Trustee Bond Requirements: Yes, if the trustee is not the appointed trustee, the trust requires it, or court orders it. (Section 3B:15-1).

Trustee Pour-Over to Will: The trust must be identified in the will. The terms of the trust must be in a document other than the will and signed before or at the same time as the will. (Sections 3B:4-1+).

Additional Trust Requirements: None.

New Mexico

State Website: http://www.legis.state.nm.us/

State Law Reference: New Mexico Statutes Annotated.

Uniform Acts Adopted: Uniform Probate Code: (Sections 45-1-101+). Uniform Trustees' Powers Act: (Section 46A-8-801+). Uniform Testamentary Additions to Trusts Act: (Sections 45-2-511+) Uniform Gifts to Minors Act: (Sections 46-7-11+).

Court with Probate Jurisdiction: Probate or District Court. (Section 34-7-1+).

Minimum Age for Disposing of Property by Will: 18. (Section 45-2-501).

Required Number of Witnesses for Signing of Will: Two. (Section 45-2-502).

Can Witnesses Be Beneficiaries?: Yes. (Section 45-2-505).

Are There Provisions for Self-Proving Wills?: Yes. (Section 45-2-504).

Are Holographic Wills Permitted?: No.

How Does Divorce Affect the Will?: Revokes the will as to the divorced spouse. (Section 45-2-802).

How Does Marriage Affect the Will?: Spouse will still be entitled to his or her statutory share under the state intestate laws. (Section 45-2-301).

Who Must Be Mentioned in the Will?: Children, born or adopted; surviving spouse. (Sections 45-2-301 and 45-2-302).

Spouse's Right to Property Regardless of Will: Community property right to 1/2 of the deceased spouse's "community" property. (Section 45-2-805).

Laws of Intestate Succession (Distribution If No Will): *Spouse and children of spouse surviving:* All of decedent's community property to spouse. 1/4 of decedent's separate property to spouse and 3/4 to children or grandchildren per stirpes.

Spouse and children not of spouse surviving: All of decedent's community property to spouse. 1/4 of decedent's separate property to spouse and 3/4 to children or grandchildren per stirpes. *Spouse, but no children or parent(s) surviving:* All to spouse.

Spouse and parent(s), but no children surviving: All to spouse.

Children, but no spouse surviving: All to children equally or to their children per stirpes.

Parent(s), but no spouse or children surviving: All to parents equally or to the surviving parent.

No spouse, children, or parent(s) surviving: All to brothers and sisters equally, or their children per stirpes; or if none, 1/2 to maternal grandparents or their children and 1/2 to paternal grandparents or their children per stirpes. (Sections 45-2-102 and 45-2-103).

Property Ownership: Community property state. Tenancy-in-common, joint tenancy, and community property are recognized. Spouses may hold real estate as joint tenants. Tenancy-by-the-entirety is not recognized. Joint bank account deposits are payable to any survivor unless clear evidence exists that deposit is payable only to specified survivor. Allows beneficiary deeds to transfer property on death. (Section 47-1-15).

State Gift, Inheritance, or Estate Taxes: No gift tax; no inheritance tax; imposes state estate tax based on federal estate tax. (Sections 7-7-3 and 7-7-4).

Simplified Probate Procedures: Affidavit allowed for estates up to $30,000.00 and estates of couples with community property principal residence of up to $100,000.00. Simplified probate allowed for estates up to value of homestead, exempt property allowance, family allowances, last illness and burial expenses. (Sections 45-3-1201, 45-3-1203, and 45-3-1205).

Living Will Form: Optional Advance Health Care Directive (Section 24-7A-4).

Other Directives: Anatomical Gift Act (Sections 24-6B-1+).

Living Will Effective: This document becomes effective in the event that you have an incurable and irreversible condition that will result in death within a relatively short time, become unconscious and, to a reasonable degree of medical certainty, will not regain consciousness, or the likely risks and burdens of treatment would outweigh the expected benefits. (Section 24-7A-4).

Living Will Witness Requirements: The law does not require that your advance directive be witnessed. To avoid future concerns, we recommend that you sign in the presence of two (2) witnesses eighteen (18) years or older or a notary public. A witness should not be the person whom you appointed as your agent. (Section 24-7A-4)

Advance Health Care Directive: (Section 24-7A-4).

Health Care Power of Attorney: State specific form is part of Advance Health Care Directive. See Chapter 10 for instructions for form on CD.

Durable Power of Attorney: State specific form. See Chapter 9. (Section 46B-1-104).

Trustee Residency Requirements: None.

Minimum Age for Grantor or Trustee: Eighteen (18). (Section 28-6-1).

Trust-Writing Requirements: A trust holding real estate must be in writing, requested by beneficiaries, or court order.

Trustee Bond Requirements: None, unless required by trust.

Trustee Pour-Over to Will: The trust must be identified in the will. The terms of the trust must be in a document other than the will and signed before or at the same time as the will. (Section 45-2-511+).

Additional Trust Requirements: Upon the Grantor's death, the Successor Trustee must notify all beneficiaries of the existence of the trust.

New York

State Website: http://assembly.state.ny.us/leg/

State Law Reference: New York Consolidated Laws.

Uniform Acts Adopted: Uniform Testamentary Additions to Trusts Act: (Estates, Powers and Trusts, Section 3-3.7). Uniform Trustees' Powers Act: (Estates, Powers and Trusts, Section 11-1.1). Uniform Gifts to Minors Act: (Estates, Powers and Trusts, Sections 7-6.1+).

Court with Probate Jurisdiction: Probate Court. (Surrogate's Court Procedure, Section 1409).

Minimum Age for Disposing of Property by Will: 18. (Estates, Powers and Trusts, Section 3-1.1).

Required Number of Witnesses for Signing of Will: Two. (Estates, Powers and Trusts, Section 3-2.1).

Can Witnesses Be Beneficiaries?: Yes, but any gift to a beneficiary who was a witness will be void unless there were also 2 other disinterested witnesses. (Estates, Powers and Trusts, Section 3-3.2).

Are There Provisions for Self-Proving Wills?: Yes. (Surrogate's Court Procedure, Section 1406).

Are Holographic Wills Permitted?: Yes, but restricted to members of the armed forces. (Estates, Powers and Trusts, Section 3-2.2).

How Does Divorce Affect the Will?: Revokes the will as to divorced spouse. (Estates, Powers and Trusts, Section 5-1.4).

How Does Marriage Affect the Will?: Does not revoke the will. Surviving spouse has right to take elective share of estate. (Estates, Powers and Trusts, Section 5-1.3).

Who Must Be Mentioned in the Will?: Children, born or adopted; surviving spouse. (Estates, Powers and Trusts, Sections 5-1.1-A and 5-3.2).

Spouse's Right to Property Regardless of Will: Generally, the surviving spouse is entitled to $50,000.00 or 1/3 of the deceased spouse's estate. However, please refer directly to the statute as the provisions are detailed. (Estates, Powers and Trusts, Section 5-1.1-A).

Laws of Intestate Succession (Distribution If No Will): *Spouse and children of spouse surviving:* $50,000.00 and 1/2 of balance to spouse and 1/2 of balance to children or grandchildren per stirpes.

Spouse and children not of spouse surviving: $50,000.00 and 1/2 of balance to spouse and 1/2 of balance to children or grandchildren per stirpes.

Spouse, but no children or parent(s) surviving: All to spouse.

Spouse and parent(s), but no children surviving: All to spouse.

Children, but no spouse surviving: All to children equally or to their children per stirpes.

Parent(s), but no spouse or children surviving: All to parents equally or to the surviving parent.

No spouse, children, or parent(s) surviving: All to brothers and sisters equally, or their children per stirpes; or if none, to grandparents equally or their children per capita; or if none, to the next-of-kin. (Estates, Powers and Trusts, Section 4-1.1).

Property Ownership: Common-law state. Tenancy-in-common, joint tenancy and tenancy-by-the-entirety are recognized, however, tenancy-by-the-entirety in personal property is not recognized. Joint ownership by spouses is presumed to be a tenancy-by-the-entirety unless specified otherwise. Tenancy-in-common is presumed unless joint tenancy is stated. Joint bank account deposits are payable to any survivor. (Real Property, Section 240b).

State Gift, Inheritance, or Estate Taxes: Imposes a gift tax; no inheritance tax; imposes a state estate tax of up to 21 percent. (Tax, Article 26, Sections 951+).

Simplified Probate Procedures: Affidavit may be used by executor under simplified probate procedures. Simplified probate allowed for estates up to $20,000.00 in personal property, excluding spousal and minor children's exempt property up to $56,000.00. (Surrogate's Court Procedure Section 1301).

Living Will Form: Order not to resuscitate acts as Living Will. (Public Health, Section 2960+).

Other Directives: Anatomical Gift Act (Public Health, Section 4300+).

Living Will Effective: The Living Will becomes effective when you become terminally ill, permanently unconscious, or minimally conscious due to brain damage and will never regain the ability to make decisions. (Public Health, Section 2965).

Living Will Witness Requirements: Order not to resuscitate acts as Living Will in New York. You must sign in the presence of two (2) adult witnesses who do not benefit from your estate. (Public Health, Section 2964).

Advance Health Care Directive: Referred to as Order Not To Resuscitate. (Public Health, Sections 2960+).

Health Care Power of Attorney: State specific form is part of Advance Health Care Directive. See Chapter 10 for instructions for form on CD. (Public Health, Sections 2980+).

Durable Power of Attorney: State specific form. See Chapter 9. (General Obligations, Sections 5-1501+).

Trustee Residency Requirements: None.

Minimum Age for Grantor or Trustee: Eighteen (18). (Estates, Powers and Trusts, Section 2.-1.10).

Trust-Writing Requirements: Yes. (Estates, Powers and Trusts, Section 13-2.1).

Trustee Bond Requirements: None, unless required by trust.

Trustee Pour-Over to Will: The trust must be identified in the will. The terms of the trust must be in a document other than the will and signed before or at the same time as the will. (Estates, Powers and Trusts, Section 3-3.7).

Additional Trust Requirements: Residents of New York will need to prepare a "Notice of Assignment Property to Living Trust." Please see proper form that is included on the Forms-on-CD.

North Carolina

State Website: http://www.ncga.state.nc.us/

State Law Reference: North Carolina General Statutes.

Uniform Acts Adopted: Uniform Testamentary Additions to Trusts Act: (Section 31-47). Uniform Trustees' Powers Act: (Sections 32-25+). Uniform Gifts to Minors Act: (Sections 33A-1+).

Court with Probate Jurisdiction: Superior Court.

Minimum Age for Disposing of Property by Will: 18. (Section 31-1).

Required Number of Witnesses for Signing of Will: Two. (Section 31-3.3).

Can Witnesses Be Beneficiaries?: Yes, but any gift to a beneficiary who was a witness will be void unless there were also 2 other disinterested witnesses. (Section 31-10).

Are There Provisions for Self-Proving Wills?: Yes. (Section 31-11.6).

Are Holographic Wills Permitted?: Yes. (Section 31-3.4).

How Does Divorce Affect the Will?: Revokes the will as to the divorced spouse. (Section 31-5.4).

How Does Marriage Affect the Will?: Does not revoke the will. (Section 31-5.3).

Who Must Be Mentioned in the Will?: Children, born or adopted; surviving spouse. (Section 29-30 and Section 31-5.5).

Spouse's Right to Property Regardless of Will: Generally, the surviving spouse has 2 choices if there is a will: (1) the surviving spouse is entitled to 1/2 of the deceased spouse's estate if there are 1 or no children of the spouses surviving, and only 1/3 of the estate if there are 2 or more children or grandchildren surviving; or (2) the surviving spouse may choose a life estate of 1/3 of all real estate that the decedent owned on his or her death. Please consult the statute directly as the terms are complex. (Section 29-30 and Section 30-3.1).

Laws of Intestate Succession (Distribution If No Will): *Spouse and children of spouse surviving:* If only 1 child surviving, $30,000.00 (from personal property, if any) and 1/2 of balance to spouse and 1/2 of balance to children or grandchildren per stirpes. If more than 1 child surviving, $30,000.00 (from personal property, if any) and 1/3 of balance to spouse and 2/3 of balance to children or grandchildren per stirpes.

Spouse and children not of spouse surviving: If only 1 child surviving, $30,000.00 (from personal property, if any) and 1/2 of balance to spouse and 1/2 of balance to children or grandchildren per stirpes. If more than 1 child surviving, $30,000.00 (from personal property, if any) and 1/3 of balance to spouse and 2/3 of balance to children or grandchildren per stirpes.

Spouse, but no children or parent(s) surviving: All to spouse.

Spouse and parent(s), but no children surviving: $50,000.00 (from personal property, if any) and 1/2 of balance to spouse and 1/2 of balance to parents or surviving parent.

Children, but no spouse surviving: All to children equally or to their children per stirpes.

Parent(s), but no spouse or children surviving: All to parents equally or to the surviving parent.

No spouse, children, or parent(s) surviving: All to brothers and sisters equally, or their children per stirpes; or if none, 1/2 to maternal grandparents or their children and 1/2 to paternal grandparents or their children per stirpes. (Sections 29-14 and 29-15).

Property Ownership: Common-law state. Tenancy-in-common, joint tenancy, and tenancy-by-the-entirety are recognized. However, a tenancy-by-the-entirety in personal property not recognized. Joint bank account deposits are payable to any survivor. (Sections 39-7+).

State Gift, Inheritance, or Estate Taxes: Imposes a gift tax; does not impose an inheritance tax; imposes a state estate tax based on federal estate tax. (Section 105-32.2).

Simplified Probate Procedures: Affidavit allowed for estates up to $10,000.00 in personal property ($20,000.00 if intestate and spouse is sole beneficiary). No other simplified probate allowed. (Sections 28A-25-1).

Living Will Form: Declaration of a Desire for a Natural Death serves as Living Will (Section 90-321).

Other Directives: Anatomical Gift Act (Section 130A-402+).

Living Will Effective: Two (2) physicians must certify in writing that you are in a terminal condition and your death would occur within a short period of time without the use of life-sustaining medical care. (Section 90-321).

Living Will Witness Requirements: Sign in the presence of two (2) adult witnesses and a notary public. A witness cannot be a person who has claim against your estate upon your death, stands to inherit from your estate, be directly financially responsible for your health care, or be an owner, operator, or employee of a health care institution in which you are a patient. Witnesses also cannot be related by blood or marriage. (Section 90-321).

Advance Health Care Directive: Referred to as Declaration of a Desire for a Natural Death. (Section 90-321).

Health Care Power of Attorney: State specific form is part of Advance Health Care Directive. See Chapter 10 for instructions for form on CD. (Sections 32A-15+)

Durable Power of Attorney: State specific form. See Chapter 9. (Section 32A-1+).

Trustee Residency Requirements: If out-of-state trustee is appointed, a resident agent must also be appointed.

Minimum Age for Grantor or Trustee: Eighteen (18). (Section 48A-2).

Trust-Writing Requirements: A trust holding real estate must be in writing. (Section 22-2).

Trustee Bond Requirements: Yes, if the trustee is not the appointed trustee. Otherwise, not unless required by trust or ordered by court.

Trustee Pour-Over to Will: The trust must be identified in the will. The terms of the trust must be in a document other than the will and signed before or at the same time as the will. (Section 31-47).

Additional Trust Requirements: None.

North Dakota

State Website: http://www.legis.nd.gov/information/statutes/cent-code.html

State Law Reference: North Dakota Century Code.

Uniform Acts Adopted: Uniform Probate Code: (Sections 30.1-01-01+). Uniform Testamentary Additions to Trusts Act: (Sections 30.1-08-11+). Uniform Trustees' Powers Act: (Sections 59-16-01+). Uniform Gifts to Minors Act: (Sections 47-24.1-01+).

Court with Probate Jurisdiction: District Court. (Section 30.1-02-02).

Minimum Age for Disposing of Property by Will: 18. (Section 30.1-08-01).

Required Number of Witnesses for Signing of Will: Two. (Section 30.1-08-02).

Can Witnesses Be Beneficiaries?: Yes. (Section 30.1-08-05).

Are There Provisions for Self-Proving Wills?: Yes. (Section 30.1-08-04).

Are Holographic Wills Permitted?: No.

How Does Divorce Affect the Will?: Revokes the will as to the divorced spouse. (Section 30.1-10-02).

How Does Marriage Affect the Will?: Spouse will still be entitled to his or her statutory share under the state intestate laws. (Section 30.1-06-01).

Who Must Be Mentioned in the Will?: Children, born or adopted; surviving spouse. (Sections 30.1-06-01 and 30.1-06-02).

Spouse's Right to Property Regardless of Will: The surviving spouse is entitled to 1/3 of the "augmented" estate of the deceased spouse. In general, the "augmented" estate includes both the property that passes under the will and any other property that passes by other "non-will" transfers, such as under the terms of a living trust or a joint tenancy arrangement. (Section 30.1-05-01).

Laws of Intestate Succession (Distribution If No Will): *Spouse and children of spouse surviving:* All to spouse.

Spouse and children not of spouse surviving: $150,000.00 and 1/2 of balance to spouse and 1/2 to children or grandchildren per stirpes.

Spouse, but no children or parent(s) surviving: All to spouse.

Spouse and parent(s), but no children surviving: $200,000.00 and 3/4 of balance to spouse and 1/4 of balance to parents or surviving parent.

Children, but no spouse surviving: All to children equally or to their children per stirpes.

Parent(s), but no spouse or children surviving: All to parents equally or to the surviving parent.

No spouse, children, or parent(s) surviving: All to brothers and sisters equally, or their children per stirpes; or if none, 1/2 to maternal next-of-kin and 1/2 to paternal next-of-kin. (Sections 30.1-04-02 and 30.1-04-03).

Property Ownership: Common-law state. Tenancy-in-common and joint tenancy are recognized. Tenancy-by-the-entirety is not recognized. Joint bank account deposits are payable to any survivor. (Section 47-02-06).

State Gift, Inheritance, or Estate Taxes: No gift tax; no inheritance tax; imposes state estate tax based on federal estate tax. (Sections 57-37.1-02 and 57-37.1-02).

Simplified Probate Procedures: Affidavit allowed for estates up to $50,000.00 in personal property. Simplified probate allowed for estates up to value of homestead, exempt property allowance, family allowances, last illness and burial expenses. (Sections 30.1-23-01+, and 30.1-23-03

Living Will Form: Declaration serves as Living Will (Section 23-06.5-17).

Other Directives: Anatomical Gift Act (Sections 23-06.6-01+).

Living Will Effective: Two (2) physicians must certify in writing that you are in a terminal condition and your death would occur within a short period of time without the use of life-sustaining medical care (Section 23-06.5-17).

Living Will Witness Requirements: Sign in the presence of two (2) adult witnesses and a notary public. A witness cannot be a person who has claim against your estate upon your death, stands to inherit from your estate, be directly financially responsible for your health care, or be your doctor. Witnesses also cannot be related by blood or marriage. If you are presently living in a nursing home or other long-term care facility, one (1) of your witnesses must be one (1) of the following: a member of the clergy, a lawyer licensed to practice in North Dakota, or a person designated by the Department of Human Services or the county court for the county in which the facility is located. (Section 23-06.5-17).

Advance Health Care Directive: (Section 23-06.5-17).

Health Care Power of Attorney: State specific form is part of Advance Health Care Directive. See Chapter 10 for instructions for form on CD. (Section 23-06.5-17).

Durable Power of Attorney: No state specific form. See Chapter 6 for form. (Section 30.1-30).

Trustee Residency Requirements: No provision.

Minimum Age for Grantor or Trustee: Eighteen (18). (Sections 9-02-01 & 9-02-02).

Trust-Writing Requirements: Repealed in 2007. No new requirements enacted by January, 2008.

Trustee Bond Requirements: Repealed in 2007. No new requirements enacted by January, 2008.

Trustee Pour-Over to Will: The trust must be identified in the will. The terms of the trust must be in a document other than the will and signed before or at the same time as the will. (Section 30.1-08-11).

Additional Trust Requirements: Residents should register a "Registration of Living Trust" form with the local court in their county of residence. This requirement is mandatory, although there are no penalties or consequences for failure to register. Please see proper form in Chapter 9.

Ohio

State Website: http://codes.ohio.gov/

State Law Reference: Ohio Revised Code Annotated.

Uniform Acts Adopted: Uniform Testamentary Additions to Trusts Act: (Section 2107.63). Uniform Trustees' Powers Act: (Sections 2109.39+). Uniform Gifts to Minors Act: (Sections 5814.01).

Court with Probate Jurisdiction: Court of Common Pleas.

Minimum Age for Disposing of Property by Will: 18. (Section 2107.02).

Required Number of Witnesses for Signing of Will: Two. (Section 2107.03).

Can Witnesses Be Beneficiaries?: Yes, but any gift to a beneficiary who was a witness will be void (beyond what that beneficiary would get as an intestate share) unless there were also 2 other disinterested witnesses. (Section 2107.15).

Are There Provisions for Self-Proving Wills?: No.

Are Holographic Wills Permitted?: No provision.

How Does Divorce Affect the Will?: Revokes the will as to the divorced spouse. (Section 2107.33).

How Does Marriage Affect the Will?: Does not revoke the will. (Section 2107.37).

Who Must Be Mentioned in the Will?: Children, born or adopted; surviving spouse. (Sections 2106.01 and 2107.34).

Spouse's Right to Property Regardless of Will: Generally, the surviving spouse is entitled to 1/2 of the deceased

spouse's estate if there are one or fewer children, and only 1/3 if there are two or more children. However, please refer directly to the statute as the provisions are detailed. (Section 2106.01).

Laws of Intestate Succession (Distribution If No Will): *Spouse and children of spouse surviving:* All to spouse. *Spouse and children not of spouse surviving:* If only 1 child surviving, $20,000.00 and 1/2 of balance to spouse and 1/2 of balance to children or grandchildren per stirpes. If more than 1 child surviving, $20,000.00 and 1/3 of balance to spouse and 2/3 of balance to children or grandchildren per stirpes. *Spouse, but no children or parent(s) surviving:* All to spouse. *Spouse and parent(s), but no children surviving:* All to spouse.

Children, but no spouse surviving: All to children or to their children per stirpes.

Parent(s), but no spouse or children surviving: All to parents equally or to the surviving parent.

No spouse, children, or parent(s) surviving: All to brothers and sisters equally, or their children per stirpes; or if none, 1/2 to maternal grandparents or their children and 1/2 to paternal grandparents or their children per stirpes; or if none, to the next-of-kin. (Section 2105.06).

Property Ownership: Common-law state. Tenancy-in-common and joint tenancies are recognized., Tenancy-by-the-entirety recognized if created prior to April 4, 1985. Joint tenancy must be stated in specific language "for their joint lives, remainder to the survivor of them." Joint bank account deposits are payable to any survivor. Allows beneficiary deeds and transfer-on-death vehicle titles to transfer property on death. (Sections 5302.19 and 5302.20).

State Gift, Inheritance, or Estate Taxes: No gift tax; no inheritance tax; imposes a state estate tax. (Section 5731.02).

Simplified Probate Procedures: No affidavit procedure. Simplified probate allowed for estates up to $35,000.00 ($100,000.00 if spouse is sole beneficiary). (Section 2113.03)

Living Will Form: Living Will Declaration (Section 2133-04).

Other Directives: Anatomical Gift Act (Section 2108.01+).

Living Will Effective: Two (2) physicians determine that you are in a terminal condition and your death will result without using life-sustaining procedures, including the determination that there is no reasonable possibility that you will regain the ability to make your own health care decisions. (Section 2133.03).

Living Will Witness Requirements: Sign in front of two (2) witnesses eighteen (18) years or older or a notary public. Witnesses cannot be related to you by blood, marriage, or adoption, or be your doctor or the administrator of a nursing home in which you are receiving treatment. (Section 2133.02).

Advance Health Care Directive: (Section 2133.02 is not a statutory form, but it provides suggestions for phrasing the directive.)

Health Care Power of Attorney: No state specific form. See Chapter 7 for form. Also may use Advance Health Care Directive. See Chapter 10 for instructions for form on CD. (Sections 1337.11+).

Durable Power of Attorney: No state specific form. See Chapter 6 for form. (Section 1337.09).

Trustee Residency Requirements: None. (Section 2109.21).

Minimum Age for Grantor or Trustee: Eighteen (18). (Section 3109.01).

Trust-Writing Requirements: A trust holding real estate must be in writing. (Section 1335.04).

Trustee Bond Requirements: Yes, unless not required by trust. (Section 2109.05).

Trustee Pour-Over to Will: The trust must be identified in the will. The terms of the trust must be in a document other than the will and signed before or at the same time as the will. (Section 2107.63).

Additional Trust Requirements: Upon the grantor's death, the Successor Trustee must record an affidavit regarding any real estate held by the trust. The affidavit must contain all names and address of trustees and all legal descriptions of property.

Oklahoma

State Website: http://www.lsb.state.ok.us/

State Law Reference: Oklahoma Statutes Annotated.

Uniform Acts Adopted: Uniform Testamentary Additions to Trusts Act: (Sections 84-301+). Uniform Trustees' Powers Act: (Section 60-171). Uniform Gifts to Minors Act: (Sections 58-1201+).

Court with Probate Jurisdiction: District Court.

Minimum Age for Disposing of Property by Will: 18. (Section 84-41).

Required Number of Witnesses for Signing of Will: Two. (Section 84-55).

Can Witnesses Be Beneficiaries?: Yes, if witnessed by 2 other witnesses. However, any gift under the will to a witness-beneficiary is void if it exceeds the amount that he or she would receive as an intestate share of the estate. (Sections 84-143 and 84-144).

Are There Provisions for Self-Proving Wills?: Yes. (Section 84-55).

Are Holographic Wills Permitted?: Yes. (Section 84-54).

How Does Divorce Affect the Will?: Revokes the will as to the divorced spouse. (Section 84-114).

How Does Marriage Affect the Will?: Revokes the will if a child is later born into the marriage. (Section 84-131).

Who Must Be Mentioned in the Will?: Children, born or adopted; surviving spouse. (Section 84-131).

Spouse's Right to Property Regardless of Will: Generally, the surviving spouse is entitled to 1/2 of the deceased spouse's estate if there are no children, and only 1/3 if there are children. However, please refer to the statute for details. (Section 84-44).

Laws of Intestate Succession (Distribution If No Will): *Spouse and children of spouse surviving:* If 1 child, then 1/2 to spouse and 1/2 to child or grandchildren. If deceased had more than 1 child, then 1/3 to spouse and 2/3 to children or grandchildren per stirpes.

Spouse and children not of spouse surviving: All of property acquired during the marriage by joint effort to spouse, and balance to children and spouse in equal shares.

Spouse, but no children or parent(s) surviving: 1/2 of other property to spouse and 1/3 to maternal grandparents or their children and 1/3 to paternal grandparents or their children per stirpes; or if none, to the next-of-kin.

Spouse and parent(s), but no children surviving: 1/2 of property to spouse and 1/2 to parents or surviving parent per stirpes.

Children, but no spouse surviving: All to children equally or grandchildren per stirpes.

Parent(s), but no spouse or children surviving: All to parents equally or to the surviving parent.

No spouse, children, or parent(s) surviving: All to brothers and sisters equally, or their children per stirpes; or if none, 1/2 to maternal grandparents or their children and 1/2 to paternal grandparents or their children per stirpes; or if none, to the next-of-kin. (Section 84-213).

Property Ownership: Common-law state. Tenancy-in-common, joint tenancy, and tenancy-by-the-entirety are recognized. Rights of survivorship must be stated. Joint bank account deposits are payable to any survivor. (Section 60-74).

State Gift, Inheritance, or Estate Taxes: No gift tax; no inheritance tax; imposes a state estate tax. (Section 68-803).

Simplified Probate Procedures: No affidavit procedure. Simplified probate allowed for estates up to $150,000.00. (Section 58-241).

Living Will Form: Living Will is Part 1 of Advance Directive for Health Care (Section 63-3101.4).

Other Directives: Anatomical Gift Act (Sections 63-2201+).

Living Will Effective: This Directive goes into effect once it is given to your doctor and you are unable to make your own medical decisions. In order to follow your instructions regarding life-sustaining treatment, your doctor must first consult another doctor to determine that you are persistently unconscious or suffering from a terminal condition. (Section 63-3101.3)

Living Will Witness Requirements: Sign in the presence of two (2) adult witnesses. A witness cannot be any person who would inherit from you under any existing will or by operation of law. (Section 63-3101.4).

Advance Health Care Directive: (Section 63-3101.4).

Health Care Power of Attorney: State specific form is part of Advance Health Care Directive. See Chapter 10 for instructions for form on CD. (Section 63-3101.4).

Durable Power of Attorney: State specific form. See Chapter 9. (Sections 15-1001+).

Trustee Residency Requirements: If out-of-state trustee is appointed a resident agent must also be appointed.

Minimum Age for Grantor or Trustee: Eighteen (18). (Section 15-13).

Trust-Writing Requirements: Yes. (Section 60-136).

Trustee Bond Requirements: Yes, unless not required by trust.

Trustee Pour-Over to Will: Trust must be identified in the will. Terms of the trust must be in a document other than the will and signed before or at the same time as the will. (Sections 84-301+).

Additional Trust Requirements: None.

Oregon

State Website: http://www.leg.state.or.us/ors/

State Law Reference: Oregon Revised Statutes.

Uniform Acts Adopted: Uniform Trustees' Powers Act: (Sections 128.001+). Uniform Testamentary Additions to Trusts Act: (Section 112.265). Uniform Gifts to Minors Act: (Sections 126.805+).

Court with Probate Jurisdiction: Circuit or County Court.

Minimum Age for Disposing of Property by Will: 18, however, no minimum age for married persons. (Section 112.225).

Required Number of Witnesses for Signing of Will: Two. (Section 112.235).

Can Witnesses Be Beneficiaries?: Yes. (Section 112.245).

Are There Provisions for Self-Proving Wills?: Yes. (Section 113.055).

Are Holographic Wills Permitted?: No provision.

How Does Divorce Affect the Will?: Revokes the will as to the divorced spouse. (Section 112.315).

How Does Marriage Affect the Will?: Revokes the will if the maker of the will is survived by a spouse. (Section 112.305).

Who Must Be Mentioned in the Will?: Statute contains detailed provisions regarding this matter. Please refer directly to statute text or consult an attorney if this is a critical factor. (Sections 112.405 and 114.105).

Spouse's Right to Property Regardless of Will: The surviving spouse is entitled to up to 1/4 of the deceased spouse's estate, including any property that was received under the deceased's will. Please refer directly to the statute for further details. (Section 114.105).

Laws of Intestate Succession (Distribution If No Will): *Spouse and children of spouse surviving:* All to spouse. *Spouse and children not of spouse surviving:* 1/2 to spouse and 1/2 to children or grandchildren per stirpes. *Spouse, but no children or parent(s) surviving:* All to spouse.

Spouse and parent(s), but no children surviving: All to spouse.

Children, but no spouse surviving: All to children equally or to their children per stirpes.

Parent(s), but no spouse or children surviving: All to parents equally or to the surviving parent.

No spouse, children, or parent(s) surviving: All to brothers and sisters equally, or their children per stirpes; or if none, to the next-of-kin. (Sections 112.025 to 112.045).

Property Ownership: Common-law state. Tenancy-in-common and tenancy-by-the-entirety (for real estate only) are recognized. Transfers of real estate to a husband and wife automatically creates a tenancy-by-the-entirety. Right of survivorship must be stated without using the words "joint tenancy." Joint bank account deposits are payable to any survivor unless clear evidence exists that deposit is payable only to specified survivor. (Section 93.180).

State Gift, Inheritance, or Estate Taxes: No gift tax; imposes state estate (inheritance) tax; no state estate tax. (Section 118.010).

Simplified Probate Procedures: No affidavit procedure. Simplified probate for estates with personal property up to $50,00.00 and real estate up to $90,000.00 (Sections 114.505+).

Living Will Form: Health Care Instructions serves as Living Will (Section 127.531).

Other Directives: Anatomical Gift Act (Sections 97.950 through 97.964).

Living Will Effective: Two (2) physicians agree that you have an incurable and irreversible condition that will result in death within a relatively short time, will become unconscious and, to a reasonable degree of medical certainty, will not regain consciousness, or the likely risks and burdens of treatment would outweigh the expected benefits.

Living Will Witness Requirements: Sign in the presence of two (2) adult witnesses. If you have someone sign the Declaration on your behalf, that person cannot serve as a witness. Your attending physician cannot be a witness. At least one (1) of your witnesses cannot be related to you by blood, marriage, or adoption, entitled to any portion of your estate, or be an owner, operator, or employee of your treating health care facility. (Section 127.515).

Advance Health Care Directive: (Section 127.531).

Health Care Power of Attorney: State specific form is part of Advance Health Care Directive. See Chapter 10 for instructions for form on CD. (Section 127.531).

Durable Power of Attorney: No state specific form. See Chapter 6 for form. (Section 127.005).

Trustee Residency Requirements: No provision.

Minimum Age for Grantor or Trustee: Eighteen (18). (Section 109.510).

Trust-Writing Requirements: A trust holding real estate must be in writing. (Section 93.020).

Trustee Bond Requirements: No provision.

Trustee Pour-Over to Will: The trust must be identified in the will. The terms of the trust must be in a document other than the will and signed before or at the same time as the will. (Section 112.265).

Additional Trust Requirements: None.

Pennsylvania

State Website: http://members.aol.com/StatutesPA/Index.html

State Law Reference: Pennsylvania Code.

Uniform Acts Adopted: Uniform Testamentary Additions to Trusts Act: (Sections 20-2515+). Uniform Trustees' Powers Act: (Sections 20-7131+). Uniform Gifts to Minors Act: (Sections 20-5301+).

Court with Probate Jurisdiction: Court of Common Pleas. (Section 20-102).

Minimum Age for Disposing of Property by Will: 18. (Section 20-2501).

Required Number of Witnesses for Signing of Will: Two. (Section 20-3132).

Can Witnesses Be Beneficiaries?: Yes. (Under Pennsylvania case law).

Are There Provisions for Self-Proving Wills?: Yes. (Section 20-3132.1).

Are Holographic Wills Permitted?: Yes. (Under Pennsylvania case law).

How Does Divorce Affect the Will?: Revokes the will as to divorced spouse. (Section 20-2507).

How Does Marriage Affect the Will?: Surviving spouse receives intestate share if marriage took place after will was signed, unless will gives greater share or will was expressly made in contemplation of marriage. Spouse may still be entitled to his or her statutory share under the state intestate laws. (Section 20-2507).

Who Must Be Mentioned in the Will?: Children, born or adopted; surviving spouse. (Sections 20-2203 and 20-2507).

Spouse's Right to Property Regardless of Will: The surviving spouse is entitled to 1/3 of the deceased spouse's estate. (Section 20-2203).

Laws of Intestate Succession (Distribution If No Will): *Spouse and children of spouse surviving:* $30,000.00 and 1/2 of balance to spouse and 1/2 of balance to children or grandchildren per stirpes.

Spouse and children not of spouse surviving: 1/2 to spouse and 1/2 to children or grandchildren per stirpes.

Spouse, but no children or parent(s) surviving: All to spouse.

Spouse and parent(s), but no children surviving: $30,000.00 and 1/2 of balance to spouse and 1/2 of balance to parents or surviving parent.

Children, but no spouse surviving: All to children equally or their children per stirpes.

Parent(s), but no spouse or children surviving: All to parents equally or to the surviving parent.

No spouse, children, or parent(s) surviving: All to brothers and sisters equally, or their children per stirpes; or if none, 1/2 to maternal grandparents and 1/2 to paternal grandparents; or if none, all to aunts, uncles, or their children per stirpes. (Sections 20-2102 and 20-2103).

Property Ownership: Common-law state. Tenancy-in-common and tenancy-by-the-entirety are recognized. Joint tenancy with right of survivorship only if stated. Real estate jointly-owned by spouses is presumed to be a tenancy-by-the-entirety unless stated otherwise. Joint bank account deposits are payable to any survivor. (Section 68-110).

State Gift, Inheritance, or Estate Taxes: No gift tax; imposes an inheritance tax of up to 15 percent; imposes state estate tax based on federal estate tax. (Sections 72-2101+).

Simplified Probate Procedures: No affidavit procedure. Simplified probate for estates up to $25,000.00 in personal property. (Sections 20-3102).

Living Will Form: Declaration serves as Living Will. (Section 20-5404).

Other Directives: Anatomical Gift Act (Section 20-8613).

Living Will Effective: The Declaration becomes effective when your physician receives a copy of it and determines that you are incompetent and in a terminal condition or a state of permanent unconsciousness. (Section 20-5405).

Living Will Witness Requirements: Sign in the presence of two (2) adult witnesses. If you have someone sign the Declaration on your behalf, that person cannot serve as a witness. (Section 20-5404).

Advance Health Care Directive: Referred to as Declaration. (Section 20-5404).

Health Care Power of Attorney: State specific form is part of Advance Health Care Directive. See Chapter 10 for instructions for form on CD. (Section 20-5404).

Durable Power of Attorney: State specific form. See Chapter 9. (Section 20-5601).

Trustee Residency Requirements: None.

Minimum Age for Grantor or Trustee: Eighteen (18). (Section 23-5101).

Trust-Writing Requirements: Yes. (Section 33-2).

Trustee Bond Requirements: None, unless required by trust or ordered by court. (Section 20-7111).

Trustee Pour-Over to Will: The trust must be identified in the will. The terms of the trust must be in a document other than the will and signed before or at the same time as the will. (Section 20-2515).

Additional Trust Requirements: None.

Rhode Island

State Website: http://www.rilin.state.ri.us/Statutes/Statutes.html

State Law Reference: Rhode Island General Laws.

Uniform Acts Adopted: Uniform Trustees' Powers Act: (Sections 18-4-1+). Uniform Gifts to Minors Act: (Sections 18-7-1+).

Court with Probate Jurisdiction: Probate Court. (Section 8-9-2.1+).

Minimum Age for Disposing of Property by Will: 18. (Section 33-5-2).

Required Number of Witnesses for Signing of Will: Two. (Section 33-5-5).

Can Witnesses Be Beneficiaries?: No. (Section 33-6-1).

Are There Provisions for Self-Proving Wills?: Yes. (Section 33-7-26).

Are Holographic Wills Permitted?: No provision.

How Does Divorce Affect the Will?: Revokes the will as to the former spouse. (Section 33-5-9.1).

How Does Marriage Affect the Will?: Revokes the will completely. (Section 33-5-9).

Who Must Be Mentioned in the Will?: Children, born or adopted; grandchildren (if of deceased child); surviving spouse. (Sections 33-6-23 and 33-25-2).

Spouse's Right to Property Regardless of Will: The surviving spouse is entitled to all of the deceased spouse's real estate for the rest of his or her life. (Section 33-25-2).

Laws of Intestate Succession (Distribution If No Will): *Spouse and children of spouse surviving:* Real estate: life estate to spouse and balance to children equally or grandchildren per stirpes. Personal property: 1/2 to spouse and 1/2 to children or grandchildren per stirpes.

Spouse and children not of spouse surviving: Real estate: life estate to spouse and balance to children equally or grandchildren per stirpes. Personal property: 1/2 to spouse and 1/2 to children or grandchildren per stirpes.

Spouse, but no children or parent(s) surviving: Real estate: life estate and $75,000.00 to spouse (if court approves), balance to brothers and sisters equally; or if none, 1/2 to maternal grandparents and 1/2 to paternal grandparents; or if none, to aunts and uncles equally or their children per stirpes; or if none, to the next-of-kin; or if none, to the spouse. Personal property: $50,000.00 and 1/2 of balance to spouse and 1/2 of balance to brothers and sisters equally; or if none, 1/2 to maternal grandparents and 1/2 to paternal grandparents; or if none, to aunts and uncles equally or their children per stirpes; or if none, to the next-of-kin; or if none, to the spouse.

Spouse and parent(s), but no children surviving: Real estate: life estate and $75,000.00 to spouse (if court approves), balance to parents or surviving parent. Personal property: $50,000.00 and 1/2 of balance to spouse and 1/2 of balance to parents or surviving parent.

Children, but no spouse surviving: All to children or grandchildren per stirpes.

Parent(s), but no spouse or children surviving: All to parents equally or to parent.

No spouse, children, or parent(s) surviving: All to brothers and sisters equally, or their children per stirpes; or if none, 1/2 to maternal grandparents and 1/2 to paternal grandparents; or if none, to the next-of-kin. (Sections 33-1-5, 33-1-6, and 33-1-10).

Property Ownership: Common-law state. Tenancy-in-common is presumed unless stated otherwise. Tenancy-in-common, joint tenancy, and tenancy-by-the-entirety are recognized. Joint bank account deposits are payable to any survivor. (Sections 34-3-1+).

State Gift, Inheritance, or Estate Taxes: No gift tax; no inheritance tax; imposes state estate tax. (Section 44-22-1.1).

Simplified Probate Procedures: No affidavit procedure. Simplified probate for estates up to $15,000.00 in personal property as long as no real estate is part of estate. (Section 33-24-1

Living Will Form: Declaration serves as Living Will (Section 23-4.11-3).

Other Directives: Anatomical Gift Act (Section 23-18.6+).

Living Will Effective: Your doctor must determine that your death would occur without use of life- sustaining medical care. (Section 23-4.11-3).

Living Will Witness Requirements: Sign in the presence of two (2) adult witnesses. Witnesses cannot be related to you by blood, marriage, or adoption. (Section 23-4.11-3).

Advance Health Care Directive: Referred to as Declaration. (Section 23-4.11-3).

Health Care Power of Attorney: State specific form is part of Advance Health Care Directive. See Chapter 10 for instructions for form on CD. (Sections 23-4.10+).

Durable Power of Attorney: State specific form. See Chapter 9. (Sections 18-16-1+).

Trustee Residency Requirements: No provision.

Minimum Age for Grantor or Trustee: Eighteen (18). (Section 15-12-1).

Trust-Writing Requirements: A trust holding real estate must be in writing. (Section 9-1-4).

Trustee Bond Requirements: None, unless trust requires court order. (Section 18-13-14).

Trustee Pour-Over to Will: Trust must be identified in the will. Terms of the trust must be in a document other than the will and signed before or at the same time as the will. (Sections 18-14-1+).

Additional Trust Requirements: None.

South Carolina

State Website: http://www.scstatehouse.net/

State Law Reference: Code of Laws of South Carolina Annotated.

Uniform Acts Adopted: Uniform Probate Code; (Sections 62-1-100+). Uniform Trustees' Powers Act: (Sections 62-7-701+). Uniform Testamentary Additions to Trusts Act: (Sections 62-2-510+). Uniform Gifts to Minors Act: (Sections 20-7-140+).

Court with Probate Jurisdiction: Probate Court. (Section 62-1-302).

Minimum Age for Disposing of Property by Will: 18, or if married. (Section 62-2-501).

Required Number of Witnesses for Signing of Will: Two. (Section 62-2-502).

Can Witnesses Be Beneficiaries?: Yes, if there were also 2 additional competent witnesses, otherwise witness share not to exceed intestate share. (Section 62-2-504).

Are There Provisions for Self-Proving Wills?: Yes. (Section 62-2-503).

Are Holographic Wills Permitted?: No provision.

How Does Divorce Affect the Will?: Revokes the will as to the divorced spouse. (Section 62-2-507).

How Does Marriage Affect the Will?: Does not revoke the will and spouse may still receive intestate share. (Section

62-2-301).

Who Must Be Mentioned in the Will?: Children, born or adopted; surviving spouse. (Sections 62-2-201 and 62-2-302).

Spouse's Right to Property Regardless of Will: The surviving spouse is entitled to 1/3 of the deceased spouse's estate. (Section 62-2-201).

Laws of Intestate Succession (Distribution If No Will): *Spouse and children of spouse surviving:* 1/2 to spouse and 1/2 to children or grandchildren per stirpes.

Spouse and children not of spouse surviving: 1/2 to spouse and 1/2 to children or grandchildren per stirpes.

Spouse, but no children or parent(s) surviving: All to spouse.

Spouse and parent(s), but no children surviving: All to spouse.

Children, but no spouse surviving: All to children equally or to their children per stirpes.

Parent(s), but no spouse or children surviving: All to parents equally or to the surviving parent if no brothers and sisters.

No spouse, children, or parent(s) surviving: All to brothers and sisters equally, or their children per stirpes; or if none, to lineal ancestors equally or to survivor; or if none, to aunts and uncles equally, or their children per stirpes; or if none, to the next-of-kin. (Sections 62-2-102 and 62-2-103).

Property Ownership: Common-law state. Tenancy-in-common and joint tenancy are recognized. Right of survivorship only if stated with specific language "joint tenants with right of survivorship, and not as tenants-in-common." Tenancy-by-the-entirety is not recognized. Joint bank account deposits are payable to any survivor. (Section 27-7-40).

State Gift, Inheritance, or Estate Taxes: Imposes a gift tax; no inheritance tax; imposes a state estate tax based on federal estate tax. (Section 12-16-510).

Simplified Probate Procedures: Affidavit allowed for estates up to $10,000.00 in personal property if also signed by judge. Simplified probate allowed for estates up to $10,000.00. (Sections 62-3-1201 and 62-3-1203).

Living Will Form: Declaration of a Desire for a Natural Death serves as Living Will (Section 44-77-50).

Other Directives: Anatomical Gift Act (Sections 44-43-310+).

Living Will Effective: Two (2) physicians must determine you are in a terminal condition and your death will result without using life-sustaining procedures. (Section 44-77-30).

Living Will Witness Requirements: Sign in the presence of two (2) adult witnesses and a notary public. A witness cannot be a beneficiary of your life insurance policy, your health care provider, or an employee of your health care provider. Witnesses cannot be related to you by blood, marriage, or adoption, entitled to any part of your estate, or directly financially responsible for your health care. In addition, at least one (1) witness must not be an employee of a health facility in which you are a patient. If you are a resident in a hospital or nursing facility, one of the witnesses must also be an ombudsman designated by the State Ombudsman, Office of the Governor. (Section 44-77-40).

Advance Health Care Directive: Referred to as a Declaration of a Desire for a Natural Death. (Section 44-77-50).

Health Care Power of Attorney: State specific form is part of Advance Health Care Directive. See Chapter 10 for instructions for form on CD. (Section 62-5-504).

Durable Power of Attorney: No state specific form. See Chapter 6 for form. (Section 62-5-501).

Trustee Residency Requirements: Out-of-state trustees must qualify to do business in South Carolina and if a corporate trustee, must have capital of at least $250,000.00.

Minimum Age for Grantor or Trustee. Eighteen (18). (Sections 20-7-30+).

Trust-Writing Requirements: Yes. (Section 62-7-401).

Trustee Bond Requirements: None, unless required by trust.

Trustee Pour-Over to Will: The trust must be identified in the will. The terms of the trust must be in a document other than the will and signed before or at the same time as the will. (Section 62-2-510).

Additional Trust Requirements: Upon the Grantor's death, the Successor Trustee must notify all beneficiaries of the existence of the trust.

South Dakota

State Website: http://legis.state.sd.us/statutes/

State Law Reference: South Dakota Codified Laws Annotated.

Uniform Acts Adopted: Uniform Testamentary Additions to Trusts Act: (Sections 29A-2-511+). Uniform Trustees' Powers Act: (Sections 55-1A-1+). Uniform Gifts to Minors Act: (Sections 55-10A-1+). Uniform Probate Code: (Sections 29A-1-101+).

Court with Probate Jurisdiction: Circuit Court. (Section 16-6-9).

Minimum Age for Disposing of Property by Will: 18. (Section 29A-2-501).

Required Number of Witnesses for Signing of Will: Two. (Section 29A-2-502).

Can Witnesses Be Beneficiaries?: Yes. (Section 29A-2-505).

Are There Provisions for Self-Proving Wills?: Yes. (Section 29A-2-504).

Are Holographic Wills Permitted?: Yes. (Section 29A-2-502).

How Does Divorce Affect the Will?: Revokes the will as to the former spouse. (Section 29A-2-804).

How Does Marriage Affect the Will?: Does not revoke the will, but surviving spouse is entitled to intestate share. (Section 29A-2-301).

Who Must Be Mentioned in the Will?: Surviving spouse and children born or adopted. (Sections 29A-2-202 and 29A-2-302).

Spouse's Right to Property Regardless of Will: The surviving spouse is entitled to an elective share of the deceased spouse's "augmented" estate that ranges from a "supplemental amount" for spouses married for less than 1 year, 3 percent of the "augmented" estate for spouses married from 1-2 years, and up to 50 percent for spouses married over 15 years. Please consult the statute directly for complete details. (Section 29A-2-202).

Laws of Intestate Succession (Distribution If No Will): *Spouse and children of spouse surviving:* All to spouse.

Spouse and children not of spouse surviving: $100,000.00 and 1/2 of balance to spouse, 1/2 to children or grandchildren per stirpes.

Spouse, but no children or parent(s) surviving: All to spouse.

Spouse and parent(s), but no children surviving: All to spouse.

Children, but no spouse surviving: All to children or to their children per stirpes.

Parent(s), but no spouse or children surviving: All to parents equally or to the surviving parent.

No spouse, children, or parent(s) surviving: All to brothers and sisters equally, or their children per stirpes; or if none, to the next-of-kin. (Sections 29A-2-101+).

Property Ownership: Common-law state. Tenancy-in-common and joint tenancy are recognized. Tenancy-by-the-entirety is not recognized. Joint bank account deposits are payable to any survivor. (Sections 43-2-11 to 43-2-15).

State Gift, Inheritance, or Estate Taxes: No gift tax; no inheritance tax; imposes state estate tax based on federal estate tax. (Sections 10-40A-3 and 10-40-21).

Simplified Probate Procedures: Affidavit allowed for estates up to $50,000.00 in personal property. Simplified (informal) probate allowed for all estates. (Sections 29A-301+ and 29A-3-1201+).

Living Will Form: Living Will Declaration (Section 34-12D-3).

Other Directives: Anatomical Gift Act (Sections 34-26-20 through 34-26-47).

Living Will Effective: Declaration is effective when your death will result without using life-sustaining procedures, including the determination that there is no reasonable possibility that you will regain the ability to make your own health care decisions. (Section 34-12D-5).

Living Will Witness Requirements: Sign in the presence of two (2) witnesses eighteen (18) years or older or a notary public. Although South Dakota does not have any restrictions on who can be a witness, we suggest that you not use your appointed attorney-in-fact or your health care provider. (Section 34-12D-2).

Advance Health Care Directive: Referred to as Living Will Declaration. (Section 34-12D-3).

Health Care Power of Attorney: No state specific form. See Chapter 7 for form. Also may use Advance Health Care Directive. See Chapter 10 for instructions for form on CD. (Sections 34-12C and 59-7-2.1).

Durable Power of Attorney: No state specific form. See Chapter 6 for form. (Section 59-7-9).

Trustee Residency Requirements: No provision.

Minimum Age for Grantor or Trustee: Eighteen (18). (Section 26-1-1).

Trust-Writing Requirements: A trust holding real estate must be in writing. A trust holding personal or other property may be written or oral. (Section 43-25-1).

Trustee Bond Requirements: Yes, unless not required by trust. (Section 21-22-10).

Trustee Pour-Over to Will: The trust must be identified in the will. The terms of the trust must be in a document other than the will and signed before or at the same time as the will. (Section 29A-2-511).

Additional Trust Requirements: None.

Tennessee

State Website: http://www.michie.com

State Law Reference: Tennessee Code Annotated.

Uniform Acts Adopted: Uniform Testamentary Additions to Trusts Act: (Sections 32-3-106+). Uniform Trustees' Powers Act: (Section 35-50-110). Uniform Gifts to Minors Act: (Sections 35-7-101+).

Court with Probate Jurisdiction: Probate Court. (Section 32-2-107).

Minimum Age for Disposing of Property by Will: 18. (Section 32-1-102).

Required Number of Witnesses for Signing of Will: Two. (Section 32-1-104).

Can Witnesses Be Beneficiaries?: No, unless attested by 2 disinterested witnesses. (Section 32-1-103).

Are There Provisions for Self-Proving Wills?: Yes. (Section 32-2-110).

Are Holographic Wills Permitted?: Yes. (Section 32-1-105).

How Does Divorce Affect the Will?: Revokes the will as to the divorced spouse. (Section 31-1-102).

How Does Marriage Affect the Will?: Revokes the will if a child is later born to the marriage. (Section 32-1-201).

Who Must Be Mentioned in the Will?: Children, born or adopted; surviving spouse. (Sections 31-4-101 and 32-3-103).

Spouse's Right to Property Regardless of Will: A spouse's right to property regardless of provisions in the will is dependent on length of marriage. Please consult statute directly for provisions regarding this topic. (Section 31-4-101).

Laws of Intestate Succession (Distribution If No Will): *Spouse and children of spouse surviving:* Family homestead and 1 year's support allowance and 1 child's share of estate (at least 1/3) to spouse, and balance to children equally or grandchildren per stirpes.

Spouse and children not of spouse surviving: Family homestead and 1 year's support allowance and 1 child's share of estate (at least 1/3) to spouse, and balance to children equally or grandchildren per stirpes.

Spouse, but no children or parent(s) surviving: All to spouse.

Spouse and parent(s), but no children surviving: All to spouse.

Children, but no spouse surviving: All to children equally or to their children per stirpes.

Parent(s), but no spouse or children surviving: All to parents equally or to the surviving parent.

No spouse, children, or parent(s) surviving: All to brothers and sisters equally, or their children per stirpes; or if none, 1/2 to maternal grandparents and 1/2 to paternal grandparents, or surviving grandparent; or if none, to the children of grandparents per stirpes. (Section 31-2-104).

Property Ownership: Common-law state. Tenancy-in-common and tenancy-by-the-entirety are recognized. Transfers of real estate to a husband and wife automatically creates a tenancy-by-the-entirety. Joint tenancy with right to survivorship has been abolished with regard to real estate. Joint bank account deposits are payable to any survivor. (Section 45-2-703 and 66-1-107+).

State Gift, Inheritance, or Estate Taxes: Imposes a gift tax; imposes an inheritance tax of up to 16 percent; imposes state estate tax based on federal estate tax. (Sections 67-8-102, 67-8-204, and 67-8-314).

Simplified Probate Procedures: No affidavit procedure. Simplified probate allowed for estates up to $25,000.00. (Sections 30-4-102+).

Living Will Form: Living Will (Section 32-11-105).

Other Directives: Anatomical Gift Act (Section 68-30-101+).

Living Will Effective: The Living Will becomes effective when your death will result without using life-sustaining procedures. (Section 32-11-105).

Living Will Witness Requirements: Sign in the presence of two (2) adult witnesses and a notary public. A witness cannot be a person who has claim against your estate upon your death, stands to inherit from your estate, be your doctor or an employee of your doctor, or be an owner, operator, or employee of a health care institution in which you are a patient. Witnesses also cannot be related by blood or marriage. (Section 32-11-104 and 32-11-105).

Advance Health Care Directive: Referred to as Living Will. (Section 32-11-105).

Health Care Power of Attorney: No state specific form. See Chapter 7 for form. Also may use Advance Health Care Directive. See Chapter 10 for instruction for form on CD. (Section 34-6-201).

Durable Power of Attorney: No state specific form. See Chapter 6 for form. (Section 34-6-101+).

Trustee Residency Requirements: Out-of-state trustee must qualify to do business in Tennessee. (Section 66-24-123).

Minimum Age for Grantor or Trustee: Eighteen (18). (Section 1-3-105).

Trust-Writing Requirements: A trust may be oral or written. (Section 29-2-101).

Trustee Bond Requirements: None, unless required by trust or required by court or financial institution. (Section 35-50-111).

Trustee Pour-Over to Will: The trust must be identified in the will. The terms of the trust must be in a document other than the will and signed before or at the same time as the will. (Section 32-3-106).

Additional Trust Requirements: Upon the Grantor's death, the Successor Trustee must notify all beneficiaries of the existence of the trust.

Texas

State Website: www.capitol.state.tx.us

State Law Reference: Texas Statutes and Code Annotated.

Uniform Acts Adopted: Uniform Testamentary Additions to Trusts Act: (Probate Code, Section 58A). Uniform Trustees' Powers Act: (Property, Sections 113.001+). Uniform Gifts to Minors Act: (Property, Sections 141.001+).

Court with Probate Jurisdiction: County or Probate Court. (Probate Code, Section 2)

Minimum Age for Disposing of Property by Will: 18, however no minimum age for married persons or members of the Armed Forces. (Probate Code, Section 57).

Required Number of Witnesses for Signing of Will: Two. (Probate Code, Section 59).

Can Witnesses Be Beneficiaries?: Yes, however the witness-beneficiary may not receive a bequest that exceeds the amount that he or she would have received as an intestate share of the estate. (Probate Code, Section 61).

Are There Provisions for Self-Proving Wills?: Yes. (Probate Code, Section 59).

Are Holographic Wills Permitted?: Yes. (Probate Code, Section 59).

How Does Divorce Affect the Will?: Revokes the will as to the divorced spouse. (Probate Code, Section 69).

How Does Marriage Affect the Will?: Does not revoke the will. (Probate Code, Section 63).

Who Must Be Mentioned in the Will?: Children, born or adopted. (Probate Code, Section 67).

Spouse's Right to Property Regardless of Will: Community property right to 1/2 of the deceased spouse's "community" property. (Probate Code, Section 270).

Laws of Intestate Succession (Distribution If No Will): *Spouse and children of spouse surviving:* 1/2 of community property, 1/3 life estate in separate real property, and 1/3 separate personal property to spouse; balance to children or grandchildren per stirpes.

Spouse and children not of spouse surviving: 1/2 of community property, 1/3 life estate in separate real property, and 1/3 separate personal property to spouse; balance to children or grandchildren per stirpes.

Spouse, but no children or parent(s) surviving: All community property, all separate personal property, and 1/2 separate real property to spouse; balance to brothers and sisters equally or their children per stirpes; or if none, to grandparents or their descendants; or if none, all to spouse.

Spouse and parent(s), but no children surviving: All community property, all separate personal property, and 1/2 separate real property to spouse; balance to parents (if both surviving); if only 1 parent surviving, 1/4 balance to parent and 1/4 to brothers and sisters equally, or their children per stirpes; or if none, entire 1/2 to parent.

Children, but no spouse surviving: All to children or to their children per stirpes.

Parent(s), but no spouse or children surviving: If both parents are surviving, all to parents equally; if only 1 parent surviving, 1/2 to parent and 1/2 to brothers and sisters equally, or their children per stirpes; or if none, all to parent.

No spouse, children, or parent(s) surviving: All to brothers and sisters equally, or their children per stirpes; or if none, 1/2 to maternal grandparents or their children and 1/2 to paternal grandparents or their children per stirpes. (Probate Code, Section 38).

Property Ownership: Community property state. Tenancy-in-common is recognized. Joint tenancy with right of survivorship is created only if the parties sign a separate written agreement. Tenancy-by-the-entirety is not recognized. Joint bank account deposits are payable to any survivor. (Family Code, Section 3.001+).

State Gift, Inheritance, or Estate Taxes: No gift tax; no inheritance tax; imposes state estate tax based on federal estate tax. (Tax Code, Section 211).

Simplified Probate Procedures: Affidavit allowed for intestate estates up to $50,000.00 in personal property. Simplified probate allowed for estates up to value of homestead, exempt property allowance, family allowances, last illness and burial expenses and for estates where "independent administration: is requested by the will or by all who will inherit under the will. (Probate Code, Section 137, 143, and 145).

Living Will Form: Directive to Physicians and Family or Surrogate serves as Living Will (Health and Safety Code, Section 166.033).

Other Directives: Anatomical Gift Act Texas (Health and Safety Code, Section 692).

Living Will Effective: This Directive becomes effective when your attending physician certifies in writing that you are in a terminal or irreversible condition. (Health and Safety Code, Section 166.031).

Living Will Witness Requirements: At least one (1) witness cannot be related to you by blood, marriage, or adoption, designated to make treatment decisions for you, entitled to any part of your estate, or be your doctor or an employee of your doctor. A witness cannot be an employee of a health care facility in which you are a patient, an officer, director, partner, or a business office employee of the health care facility or any part of any parent organization of the health care facility, or have a claim against your estate after you die. (Health and Safety Code, Section 166.003).

Advance Health Care Directive: Referred to as Directive to Physicians and Family or Surrogate. (Health and Safety Code, Section 166.033).

Health Care Power of Attorney: State specific form is part of Advance Health Care Directive. See Chapter 10 for instructions for form on CD. (Health and Safety Code, Section 166.033).

Durable Power of Attorney: State specific form. See Chapter 9. (Probate Code, Sections 481+).

Trustee Residency Requirements: No provision.

Minimum Age for Grantor or Trustee: Eighteen (18). (Civil Practice and Remedies, Section 129.001)

Trust-Writing Requirements: Yes. (Property, Section 112.004).

Trustee Bond Requirements: Yes, if corporate trustee. Otherwise, yes unless not required by trust. (Property, Section 113.058).

Trustee Pour-Over to Will: The trust must be identified in the will. The terms of the trust must be in a document other than the will and signed before or at the same time as the will. (Probate Code, Section 58a).

Additional Trust Requirements: None.

Utah

State Website: http://www.le.state.ut.us/

State Law Reference: Utah Code Annotated.

Uniform Acts Adopted: Uniform Probate Code: (Sections 75-1-101+). Uniform Trustees' Powers Act: (Sections 75-7-401+). Uniform Testamentary Additions to Trusts Act: (Section 75-2-511). Uniform Gifts to Minors Act: (Sections 75-5a-101+).

Court with Probate Jurisdiction: District Court.

Minimum Age for Disposing of Property by Will: 18. (Section 75-2-501).

Required Number of Witnesses for Signing of Will: Two. (Section 75-2-502).

Can Witnesses Be Beneficiaries?: Yes. (Section 75-2-505).

Are There Provisions for Self-Proving Wills?: Yes. (Section 75-2-504).

Are Holographic Wills Permitted?: Yes. (Section 75-2-502 and 503).

How Does Divorce Affect the Will?: Revokes the will as to divorced spouse. (Section 75-2-804).

How Does Marriage Affect the Will?: Does not revoke the will and spouse is entitled to intestate share. (Section 75-2-301).

Who Must Be Mentioned in the Will?: Children, born or adopted; grandchildren (if of deceased child); surviving spouse. (Sections 75-2-202 and 75-2-302).

Spouse's Right to Property Regardless of Will: The surviving spouse is entitled to 1/3 of the deceased spouse's augmented estate. (Section 75-2-202).

Laws of Intestate Succession (Distribution If No Will): *Spouse and children of spouse surviving:* All to spouse.
Spouse and children not of spouse surviving: $50,000.00 and 1/2 of balance to spouse and 1/2 to children or grandchildren per stirpes.
Spouse, but no children or parent(s) surviving: All to spouse.
Spouse and parent(s), but no children surviving: All to spouse.
Children, but no spouse surviving: All to children equally or to their children per stirpes.
Parent(s), but no spouse or children surviving: All to parents equally or to the surviving parent.
No spouse, children, or parent(s) surviving: All to brothers and sisters equally, or their children per stirpes; 1/2 to maternal grandparents or their descendants and 1/2 to paternal grandparents or their descendants per stirpes; or if none, to the next-of-kin. (Sections 75-2-102 and 75-2-103).

Property Ownership: Common-law state. Tenancy-in-common, joint tenancy and tenancy-by-entireties are recognized. Real estate is presumed to be tenancy-in-common, unless owned jointly by husband and wife (after May 5, 1997), then ownership is presumed to be joint tenancy. Joint bank account deposits are payable to any survivor. (Section 57-1-5).

State Gift, Inheritance, or Estate Taxes: No gift tax; no inheritance tax; imposes state estate tax based on federal estate tax. (Sections 59-11-103 and 59-11-104).

Simplified Probate Procedures: Affidavit allowed for estates up to $100,000.00 in personal property. Simplified probate allowed for estates up to value of homestead, exempt property allowance, family allowances, last illness and burial expenses. (Sections 75-3-1201 and 75-3-1203).

Living Will Form: Advance Health Care Directive serves as Living Will, (Section 75-2a-117).

Other Directives: Anatomical Gift Act (Section 26-28-101+).

Living Will Effective: Two (2) physicians must physically examine you and certify in writing you are in a terminal condition or persistent vegetative state. (Sections 75-2a-103 and 75-2a-109).

Living Will Witness Requirements: Sign in the presence of two (2) witnesses eighteen (18) years or older. A witness cannot be entitled to any part of your estate, be financially responsible for your medical care, be related to you by blood or marriage, be the person who signed the Declaration on your behalf, or be an employee of your health care facility. (Section 75-2a-117).

Advance Health Care Directive: (Section 75-2a-117).

Health Care Power of Attorney: State specific form is part of Advance Health Care Directive. See Chapter 10 for instructions for form on CD. (Section 75-2a-117).

Durable Power of Attorney: No state specific form. See Chapter 6 for form. (Section 75-5-501).

Trustee Residency Requirements: Out-of-state trustee must qualify to do business in Utah.

Minimum Age for Grantor or Trustee: Eighteen (18). (Section 15-2-1).

Trust-Writing Requirements: A trust holding real estate must be in writing. (Section 25-5-1).

Trustee Bond Requirements: None, unless required by trust, requested by beneficiaries, or ordered by the court. (Section 75-7-702).

Trustee Pour-Over to Will: The trust must be identified in the will. The terms of the trust must be in a document other than the will and signed before or at the same time as the will. (Section 72-2-511).

Additional Trust Requirements: None.

Vermont

State Website: http://www.leg.state.vt.us/statutes/statutes2.htm

State Law Reference: Vermont Statutes Annotated.

Uniform Acts Adopted: Uniform Testamentary Additions to Trusts Act: (Section 14-105-2329). Uniform Gifts to Minors Act: (Sections 14-115-3201+).

Court with Probate Jurisdiction: Probate Court.

Minimum Age for Disposing of Property by Will: 18. (Section 14-1-1).

Required Number of Witnesses for Signing of Will: Two (Section 14-1-5).

Can Witnesses Be Beneficiaries?: No, unless attested by 3 disinterested witnesses. (Section 14-1-10).

Are There Provisions for Self-Proving Wills?: No.

Are Holographic Wills Permitted?: No provision.

How Does Divorce Affect the Will?: Does not revoke the will. (Section 14-1-11).

How Does Marriage Affect the Will?: Does not revoke the will and spouse is entitled to intestate share of estate. (Section 14-1-11).

Who Must Be Mentioned in the Will?: Children, born or adopted; grandchildren (if of deceased child); surviving spouse. (Sections 14-45-555 and 556).

Spouse's Right to Property Regardless of Will: If there are no children or more than 1 child of the surviving spouse and the deceased, the surviving spouse is entitled to 1/3 of the deceased spouse's real estate. If there is only 1 child of the surviving spouse and the deceased, the surviving spouse is entitled to 1/2 of the deceased spouse's real estate. Please refer to the statute for instances when this effect may be barred. (Section 14-43-461).

Laws of Intestate Succession (Distribution If No Will): *Spouse and children of spouse surviving:* If 1 child surviving: 1/2 of deceased's estate to spouse; balance to child or grandchildren per stirpes. If more than 1 child surviving: 1/3 to spouse and 2/3 to children or grandchildren per stirpes.

Spouse and children not of spouse surviving: If 1 child surviving: 1/3 of deceased's estate to spouse; balance to child or grandchildren per stirpes. If more than 1 child surviving: 1/3 to spouse and 2/3 to children or grandchildren per stirpes.

Spouse, but no children or parent(s) surviving: If spouse waives the statutory share and any will provisions, then $25,000.00 and 1/2 of balance to spouse and 1/2 of balance as if surviving spouse had not survived.

Spouse and parent(s), but no children surviving: $25,000.00 and 1/2 of balance to spouse and 1/2 of balance as if surviving spouse had not survived.

Children, but no spouse surviving: All to children equally or to their children per stirpes.

Parent(s), but no spouse or children surviving: All to parents equally or to the surviving parent.

No spouse, children, or parent(s) surviving: All to brothers and sisters equally, or their children per stirpes; or if none, to the next-of-kin. (Section 14-45-551).

Property Ownership: Common-law state. Tenancy-in-common, tenancy-by-the-entirety, and joint tenancy are recognized. Real estate is presumed to be held by tenancy-in-common unless it is ownership of husband and wife, in which case, joint tenancy is presumed. Joint bank account deposits are payable to any survivor. (Section 27-1-2).

State Gift, Inheritance, or Estate Taxes: No gift tax; no inheritance tax; imposes state estate tax based on federal estate tax. (Section 32-190-7442a).

Simplified Probate Procedures: No affidavit procedure. Simplified probate allowed for estates up to $10,000.00 in personal property. (Section 14-81-1901(3)).

Living Will Form: Advance Health Care Directive serves as Living Will (Section 18-231-9700+).

Other Directives: Anatomical Gift Act (Section 18-109-5238+).

Living Will Effective: Document becomes effective if death would occur regardless of the use of life- sustaining procedures. (Section 18-231-9703).

Living Will Witness Requirements: Sign in the presence of two (2) witnesses eighteen (18) years or older. A witness cannot be entitled to any part of your estate, be your spouse, attending physician or any person acting under the direction or control of your attending physician, or any person who has a claim against your estate. (Section 18-231-9703).

Advance Health Care Directive: (Section 18-231).

Health Care Power of Attorney: No state specific form. See Chapter 7 for form. Also may use Advance Health Care Directive. See Chapter 10 for instructions for form on CD.

Durable Power of Attorney: No state-specific form. See Chapter 6 for form. (Section 14-123-3508).

Trustee Residency Requirements: If out-of-state trustee is appointed, a resident agent must also be appointed.

Minimum Age for Grantor or Trustee: Eighteen (18). (Section 1-3-173).

Trust-Writing Requirements: A trust holding real estate must be in writing; otherwise may be written or oral. (Section 27-5-303).

Trustee Bond Requirements: Yes, unless not required by trust. (Section 14-105-2301).

Trustee Pour-Over to Will: The trust must be identified in the will. The terms of the trust must be in a document other than the will and signed before or at the same time as the will. (Section 14-105-2329).

Additional Trust Requirements: None.

Virginia

State Website: http://leg1.state.va.us/

State Law Reference: Virginia Code Annotated.

Uniform Acts Adopted: Uniform Gifts to Minors Act: (Sections 31-37+).

Court with Probate Jurisdiction: Circuit Court.

Minimum Age for Disposing of Property by Will: 18. (Section 64.1-47).

Required Number of Witnesses for Signing of Will: Two. (Section 64.1-49).

Can Witnesses Be Beneficiaries?: No. (Section 64.1-51).

Are There Provisions for Self-Proving Wills?: Yes. (Section 64.1-87.1).

Are Holographic Wills Permitted?: Yes. (Section 64.1-49).

How Does Divorce Affect the Will?: Revokes the will as to divorced spouse. (Section 64.1-59).

How Does Marriage Affect the Will?: Does not revoke the will and the spouse will be entitled to his or her elective share. (Section 64.1-13).

Who Must Be Mentioned in the Will?: Children, born or adopted; grandchildren (if of deceased child); surviving spouse. (Sections 64.1-16 and 64.1-71).

Spouse's Right to Property Regardless of Will: If there are no child(ren) of the deceased, the surviving spouse is entitled to 1/2 of the deceased spouse's augmented estate. If there are any surviving child(ren) of the deceased, the surviving spouse is entitled to 1/3 of the deceased spouse's augmented estate. (Section 64.1-16).

Laws of Intestate Succession (Distribution If No Will): *Spouse and children of spouse surviving:* All to spouse. *Spouse and children not of spouse surviving:* 1/3 to spouse and 2/3 to children or grandchildren per stirpes. *Spouse, but no children or parent(s) surviving:* All to spouse. *Spouse and parent(s), but no children surviving:* All to spouse.

Children, but no spouse surviving: All to children equally or to their children per stirpes.

Parent(s), but no spouse or children surviving: All to parents equally or to the surviving parent.

No spouse, children, or parent(s) surviving: All to brothers and sisters equally, or their children per stirpes; or if none, 1/2 to maternal grandparents or their children, or maternal next-of-kin (or if none, to paternal side) and 1/2 to paternal grandparents or their children, or paternal next-of-kin (or if none, to maternal side). (Section 64.1-1).

Property Ownership: Common-law state. Joint tenancy is recognized only if right of survivorship is stated. Tenancy-in-common and tenancy-by-the-entirety are recognized. Joint bank account deposits are payable to any survivor unless clear evidence exists that deposit is payable only to specified survivor. (Sections 55-20+).

State Gift, Inheritance, or Estate Taxes: No gift tax; no inheritance tax; no state estate tax. (Sections 58.1-361 to 58.1-363).

Simplified Probate Procedures: Affidavit allowed for estates up to $15,000.00 in personal property and an additional $15,000.00 in benefits and wages. No simplified probate allowed. (Sections 64.1-123 and 64.1-132.2).

Living Will Form: Advance Medical Directive serves as Living Will (Section 54.1-2984).

Other Directives: Anatomical Gift Act (Section 32.1-8-290).

Living Will Effective: This directive becomes effective in the event that you develop a terminal condition or are in a permanent vegetative state and can no longer make your own medical decisions. (Section 54.1-2984).

Living Will Witness Requirements: Sign in the presence of two (2) witnesses eighteen (18) years or older. Witnesses cannot be related by blood or marriage. (Section 54.1-2982 and 54.1-2983).

Advance Health Care Directive: Referred to as Advance Medical Directive. (Section 54.1-2984).

Health Care Power of Attorney: State specific form is part of Advance Health Care Directive. See Chapter 10 for instructions for form on CD. (Section 54.1-2984).

Durable Power of Attorney: No state specific form. See Chapter 6 for form. (Section 54.1-3900+).

Trustee Residency Requirements: If out-of-state trustee is appointed, a resident agent must also be appointed unless trustee is a corporation authorized to do business in Virginia or is a parent, sister, or brother of decedent and has qualified to do business in Virginia. (Section 2-9-59).

Minimum Age for Grantor or Trustee: Eighteen (18). (Section 1-13-42).

Trust-Writing Requirements: A trust may be written or oral. (Section 11-2).

Trustee Bond Requirements: No provision.

Trustee Pour-Over to Will: The trust must be identified in the will. The terms of the trust must be in a document other than the will and signed before or at the same time as the will. (Section 64.1-73.1).

Additional Trust Requirements: None.

Washington

State Website: http://www.leg.wa.gov/

State Law Reference: Washington Revised Code Annotated.

Uniform Acts Adopted: Uniform Testamentary Additions to Trusts Act: (Section 11.12.250). Uniform Trustees' Powers Act: (Section 11.98.070). Uniform Gifts to Minors Act: (Sections 11.114.010+).

Court with Probate Jurisdiction: Superior Court. (Section 11.96A.040).

Minimum Age for Disposing of Property by Will: 18. (Section 11.12.010).

Required Number of Witnesses for Signing of Will: Two. (Section 11.12.020).

Can Witnesses Be Beneficiaries?: No, unless will is attested by 2 other disinterested witnesses. (Section

11.12.160).

Are There Provisions for Self-Proving Wills?: Yes. (Section 11.20.020).

Are Holographic Wills Permitted?: No provision.

How Does Divorce Affect the Will?: Revokes the will as to the divorced spouse. (Section 11.12.051).

How Does Marriage Affect the Will?: Revokes the will as to the surviving spouse. (Section 11.12.095).

Who Must Be Mentioned in the Will?: Statute contains detailed provisions regarding this matter. Please refer directly to statute text or consult an attorney if this is a critical factor. (Section 11.12.091).

Spouse's Right to Property Regardless of Will: Community property right to 1/2 of the deceased spouse's "community" property. (Under Washington case law).

Laws of Intestate Succession (Distribution If No Will): *Spouse and children of spouse surviving:* All of decedent's community property and 1/2 of decedent's separate property to spouse; 1/2 of decedent's separate property to children or grandchildren per stirpes.

Spouse and children not of spouse surviving: All of decedent's community property and 1/2 of decedent's separate property to spouse; 1/2 of decedent's separate property to children or grandchildren per stirpes.

Spouse, but no children or parent(s) surviving: All to spouse.

Spouse and parent(s), but no children surviving: All of decedent's community property and 3/4 of decedent's separate property to spouse; 1/4 of decedent's separate property to parents or surviving parent or their children.

Children, but no spouse surviving: All to children equally or to their children per stirpes.

Parent(s), but no spouse or children surviving: All to parents equally or to the surviving parent.

No spouse, children, or parent(s) surviving: All to brothers and sisters equally, or their children per stirpes; or if none, to grandparents or their children. (Section 11.04.015).

Property Ownership: Community property state. Tenancy-in-common and joint tenancy are recognized. Joint tenancy with right of survivorship is created if specifically stated. No survivorship rights in tenancy-by-the-entirety. Joint bank account deposits are payable to any survivor unless evidence exists that deposit is payable only to specified survivor, and is subject to community property rights. The beneficiary of certain accounts and/or trusts may be altered in a will, under certain circumstances. Please see the text of the statute for details. (Sections 64-28.10+ and 11.11.020).

State Gift, Inheritance, or Estate Taxes: No gift tax; no inheritance tax; imposes state estate tax. (Sections 83.100+ and 83.110A).

Simplified Probate Procedures: Affidavit allowed for estates up to $100,000.00 in personal property. Simplified probate allowed for all estates where assets exceed debts. (Sections 11.62.010+).

Living Will Form: Health Care Directive serves as Living Will (Section 70.122.030).

Other Directives: Anatomical Gift Act (Section 68.50.520+).

Living Will Effective: Declaration applies when two (2) physicians diagnose you to have a incurable or irreversible condition that will cause death in a relatively short time and you can no longer make your own medical decisions. (Section 70.122.020).

Living Will Witness Requirements: Sign in the presence of two (2) witnesses eighteen (18) years or older. A witness cannot be entitled to any part of your estate, related by blood or marriage, be your attending physician or any person acting under the direction or control of your attending physician, or be any person who has a claim against your estate. (Section 70.122.030).

Advance Health Care Directive: (Section 70.122.030).

Health Care Power of Attorney: No state specific form. See Chapter 7 for form. Also may use Advance Health Care Directive. See Chapter 10 for instructions for form on CD. (Section 11.94.010+).

Durable Power of Attorney: No state specific form. See Chapter 6 for form. (Section 11.94.010+).

Trustee Residency Requirements: No provision.

Minimum Age for Grantor or Trustee. Eighteen (18). (Section 26.28.010).

Trust-Writing Requirements: A trust holding real estate must be in writing. A trust holding personal property can be either oral or in writing. (Section 19.36.010).

Trustee Bond Requirements: No provision.

Trustee Pour-Over to Will: The trust must be identified in the will. The terms of the trust must be in a document other than the will and signed before or at the same time as the will. (Section 11.12.250).

Additional Trust Requirements: None.

West Virginia

State Website: http://www.legis.state.wv.us/

State Law Reference: West Virginia Code Annotated.

Uniform Acts Adopted: Uniform Testamentary Additions to Trusts Act: (Section 41-3-8). Uniform Gifts to Minors Act: (Sections 36-7-1+).

Court with Probate Jurisdiction: County Court. (Section 41-5-1).

Minimum Age for Disposing of Property by Will: 18. (Section 41-1-2).

Required Number of Witnesses for Signing of Will: Two. (Section 41-1-3).

Can Witnesses Be Beneficiaries?: Yes, but witness may lose bequest beyond intestate share, if any. (Section 41-2-1).

Are There Provisions for Self-Proving Wills?: Yes. (Section 41-5-15).

Are Holographic Wills Permitted?: Yes. (Section 41-1-3).

How Does Divorce Affect the Will?: Revokes the will as to former spouse. (Section 41-1-6).

How Does Marriage Affect the Will?: Revokes the will as to spouse. (Section 42-3-7).

Who Must Be Mentioned in the Will?: Children, born or adopted; grandchildren; and surviving spouse. (Sections 41-4-1, 41-4-2, and 42-3-1).

Spouse's Right to Property Regardless of Will: A surviving spouse's right to property regardless of provisions in a decedent spouse's will are dependent on length of marriage. Please consult the statute directly for provision regarding this topic. (Section 42-3-1).

Laws of Intestate Succession (Distribution If No Will): *Spouse and children of spouse surviving:* All to spouse. *Spouse and children not of spouse surviving:* 1/2 to spouse, 1/2 to deceased's children or grandchildren per stirpes. *Spouse, but no children or parent(s) surviving:* All to spouse. *Spouse and parent(s), but no children surviving:* All to spouse. *Children, but no spouse surviving:* All to children equally or to their children per stirpes. *Parent(s), but no spouse or children surviving:* All to parents equally or to the surviving parent. *No spouse, children, or parent(s) surviving:* All to brothers and sisters equally, or their children per stirpes; or if none, 1/2 to maternal grandparents or their children, or to maternal uncles, aunts, or their children, or maternal next-of-kin (or if none, to paternal side) and 1/2 to paternal grandparents or their children, or paternal uncles, aunts, or their children, or paternal next-of-kin (or if none, to maternal side). (Sections 42-1-3 and 42-1-3a).

Property Ownership: Common-law state. Tenancy-in-common, joint tenancy, and tenancy-by-the-entirety are recognized. Right of survivorship is created if stated. Joint bank account deposits are payable to any survivor. (Section 36-1-19).

State Gift, Inheritance, or Estate Taxes: No gift tax; no inheritance tax; imposes state estate tax based on federal estate tax. (Section 11-11-3).

Simplified Probate Procedures: No affidavit procedure. Simplified probate allowed for estates up to $100,000.00. (Section 44-3A-5).

Living Will Form: Living Will, (Section 16-30-4).

Other Directives: Anatomical Gift Act (Section 16-19-1+).

Living Will Effective: Your physician must certify in writing that you are in a terminal condition and your death would occur within a short period of time without the use of life-sustaining medical care. (Section 16-30-4).

Living Will Witness Requirements: Sign in the presence of two (2) adult witnesses and a notary public. A witness cannot be a person who stands to inherit from your estate, be directly financially responsible for your health care, be your attending physician, or be your health care representative or successor if you have a medical power of attorney. A witness cannot be related by blood or marriage or be the person who signed the document on your behalf. (Section 16-30-4).

Advance Health Care Directive: Referred to as Living Will. (Section 16-30-4).

Health Care Power of Attorney: State specific form is part of Advance Health Care Directive. See Chapter 10 for instructions for form on CD. (Section 16-30-4).

Durable Power of Attorney: No state specific form. See Chapter 6 for form. (Sections 39-4-1 through 39-4-7).

Trustee Residency Requirements: None.

Minimum Age for Grantor or Trustee: Eighteen (18). (Section 49-5-1).

Trust-Writing Requirements: Yes. (Section 36-1-4).

Trustee Bond Requirements: No provision.

Trustee Pour-Over to Will: The trust must be identified in the will. The terms of the trust must be in a document other than the will and signed before or at the same time as the will. (Sections 41-3-8– 41-3-11).

Additional Trust Requirements: None.

Wisconsin

State Website: http://www.legis.state.wi.us/

State Law Reference: Wisconsin Statutes Annotated.

Uniform Acts Adopted: Uniform Trustees' Powers Act: (Section 701.09). Uniform Gifts to Minors Act: (Sections 880.61+).

Court with Probate Jurisdiction: Circuit Court. (Section 851.04).

Minimum Age for Disposing of Property by Will: 18. (Section 853.01).

Required Number of Witnesses for Signing of Will: Two. (Section 853.03).

Can Witnesses Be Beneficiaries?: Yes, but a witness-beneficiary's share under the will cannot exceed that person's intestate share, if any. (Section 853.07).

Are There Provisions for Self-Proving Wills?: Yes. (Section 853.04).

Are Holographic Wills Permitted?: No provision.

Are Living Wills Recognized?: Yes, under the "Wisconsin Natural Death Act." (Sections 154.01 to 154.29).

How Does Divorce Affect the Will?: Revokes the will as to divorced spouse. (Section 853.11).

How Does Marriage Affect the Will?: Revokes the will as to the spouse if he or she is not otherwise provided for. Spouse may still be entitled to his or her statutory share under the state intestate laws. (Sections 853.11 and 853.25).

Who Must Be Mentioned in the Will?: Children, born or adopted; grandchildren (if of deceased child); surviving spouse. (Section 861.02).

Spouse's Right to Property Regardless of Will: Modified community property rights to 1/2 of the deceased spouse's "community" property. (Section 861.02).

Laws of Intestate Succession (Distribution If No Will): *Spouse and children of spouse surviving:* All to spouse. *Spouse and children not of spouse surviving:* 1/2 to spouse and 1/2 to children or grandchildren per stirpes. *Spouse, but no children or parent(s) surviving:* All to spouse. *Spouse and parent(s), but no children surviving:* All to spouse. *Children, but no spouse surviving:* All to children or to their children per stirpes. *Parent(s), but no spouse or children surviving:* All to parents equally or to the surviving parent. *No spouse, children, or parent(s) surviving:* All to brothers and sisters equally, or their children per stirpes; or if none, to grandparents or surviving grandparent; or if none, to the next-of-kin. (Section 852.01).

Property Ownership: Community property state. The Wisconsin statute, however, uses unique terminology to describe this treatment of property. Tenancy-in-common and joint tenancy are recognized (except between spouses after January 1, 1986). Ownership by spouses (created after January 1, 1986) is presumed to be community property with right of survivorship unless stated otherwise. Tenancy-by-the-entirety is not recognized. Joint bank account deposits are payable to any survivor. (Sections 700.17, 700.19, and 700.20).

State Gift, Inheritance, or Estate Taxes: Imposes a gift tax; no inheritance tax; imposes state estate tax.(Section 72.02).

Simplified Probate Procedures: Affidavit allowed for estates up to $50,000.00. Simplified probate allowed for estates up to $50,000.00 and there is a surviving spouse and/or children. (Sections 867.01 and 867.03).

Living Will Form: Declaration to Physicians serves as Living Will (Section 154-03).

Other Directives: Anatomical Gift Act (Section 157.06).

Living Will Effective: This directive becomes effective in the event that your attending physician and one (1) other physician certifies you have developed a terminal condition or are in a permanent vegetative state and can no longer make your own medical decisions. (Section 154.03).

Living Will Witness Requirements: Sign in the presence of two (2) adult witnesses. A witness cannot be a person who stands to inherit from your estate, be directly financially responsible for your health care, be your attending physician, or be an employee of your health care provider or an inpatient health care facility in which you are a patient, unless the employee is a chaplain or social worker. A witness also cannot be related by blood or marriage. (Section 154.03).

Advance Health Care Directive: Referred to as Declaration to Physicians. (Section 154.03).

Health Care Power of Attorney: No state specific form. See Chapter 7 for form. Also may use Advance Health Care Directive. See Chapter 10 for instructions for form on CD. (Section 155.05).

Durable Power of Attorney: No state specific form. See Chapter 6 for form. (Section 243.07).

Trustee Residency Requirements: Out-of-state trustee must qualify to do business in Wisconsin.

Minimum Age for Grantor or Trustee: Eighteen (18). (Section 48.02).

Trust-Writing Requirements: Yes. (Section 243.01).

Trustee Bond Requirements: Yes, unless not required by trust or ordered by court. (Section 701.16).

Trustee Pour-Over to Will: The trust must be identified in the will. The terms of the trust must be in a document other than the will and signed before or at the same time as the will. (Section 701.09).

Additional Trust Requirements: None.

Wyoming

State Website: http://legisweb.state.wy.us/

State Law Reference: Wyoming Statutes.

Uniform Acts Adopted: Uniform Trustees Powers Act: (Sections 4-10-816). Uniform Testamentary Additions to Trusts Act: (Section 2-6-102). Uniform Gifts to Minors Act: (Section 34-13-137).

Court with Probate Jurisdiction: District Court. (2-2-101).

Minimum Age for Disposing of Property by Will: 18. (Section 2-6-101 and 2-1-301).

Required Number of Witnesses for Signing of Will: Two. (Section 2-6-112).

Can Witnesses Be Beneficiaries?: No, unless attested by 2 disinterested witnesses. (Section 2-6-112).

Are There Provisions for Self-Proving Wills?: Yes. (Section 2-6-114).

Are Holographic Wills Permitted?: Yes. (Section 2-6-113).

Are Living Wills Recognized?: Yes, under the "Wyoming Living Will Act." (Sections 35-22-201+).

How Does Divorce Affect the Will?: Revokes the will as to the divorced spouse. (Section 2-6-118).

How Does Marriage Affect the Will?: Does not revoke the will. (Section 2-6-118).

Who Must Be Mentioned in the Will?: Statute contains detailed provisions regarding this matter. Please refer directly to statute text or consult an attorney if this is a critical factor. (Section 2-5-101).

Spouse's Right to Property Regardless of Will: Generally, the surviving spouse is entitled to 1/2 of the deceased spouse's estate if there are no children or if surviving spouse is parent of deceased's children; and only 1/4 if the surviving spouse is not the parent of any surviving children of the deceased. However, please refer directly to the statute as the provisions are detailed. (Section 2-5-101).

Laws of Intestate Succession (Distribution If No Will): *Spouse and children of spouse surviving:* 1/2 to spouse and 1/2 to children or grandchildren per stirpes.

Spouse and children not of spouse surviving: 1/2 to spouse and 1/2 to children or grandchildren per stirpes.

Spouse, but no children or parent(s) surviving: All to spouse.

Spouse and parent(s), but no children surviving: All to spouse.

Children, but no spouse surviving: All to children equally or to their children per stirpes.

Parent(s), but no spouse or children surviving: All to parents, brothers, and sisters equally, or to children of brothers and sisters per stirpes. *No spouse, children, or parent(s) surviving:* All to grandparents, uncles, aunts, or their children, per stirpes. (Section 2-4-101).

Property Ownership: Common-law state. Tenancy-in-common, joint tenancy, and tenancy-by-the-entirety are recognized. Right of survivorship created if stated. Joint bank account deposits are payable to any survivor. (Section 34-1-140).

State Gift, Inheritance, or Estate Taxes: No gift tax; no inheritance tax; imposes state estate tax based on federal estate tax. (Sections 39-19-101+).

Simplified Probate Procedures: Affidavit allowed for estates up to $150,000.00 in personal property. Simplified probate allowed for estates up to $150,000.00. (Sections 2-1-201 and 2-1-205).

Living Will Form: Living Will Declaration (Section 35-22-403).

Other Directives: Anatomical Gift Act (Section 35-5-102).

Living Will Effective: This Declaration becomes effective when two (2) physicians agree that you have a terminal condition from which there can be no recovery and your death is imminent. (Section 35-22-403).

Living Will Witness Requirements: Sign in the presence of two (2) witnesses eighteen (18) years or older or a notary public. Witnesses cannot be entitled to any part of your estate or financially responsible for your medical care. A witness cannot be related to you by blood or marriage or be the person who signed the Declaration on your behalf. (Section 35-22-403).

Advance Health Care Directive: (Section 35-22-403).

Health Care Power of Attorney: No state specific form. See Chapter 7 for form. Also may use Advance Health Care Directive. See Chapter 10 for instructions for form on CD. (Section 35-22-406).

Durable Power of Attorney: No state specific form. See Chapter 6 for form. (Section 3-5-101).

Trustee Residency Requirements: None.

Minimum Age for Grantor or Trustee: Eighteen (18). (Section 14-1-101).

Trust-Writing Requirements: A trust holding real estate must be in writing. (Section 1-23-105).

Trustee Bond Requirements: No provision.

Trustee Pour-Over to Will: The trust must be identified in the will. The terms of the trust must be in a document other than the will and signed before or at the same time as the will. (Section 2-6-103).

Additional Trust Requirements: None.

Glossary of Estate Planning Terms

Abatement: A reduction or complete extinguishment of a gift in a will where the estate does not have sufficient assets to make full payment.

AB Trust: A trust that gives a surviving spouse the right to the interest and principal of the trust assets for the rest of his or her life, and then the assets are distributed to the beneficiaries of the original grantor of the trust. Also known as a "marital deduction trust" or "bypass trust".

Accounts Payable: Money owed to another and due to be paid.

Accounts Receivable: Money owed from another and due to be paid.

Acknowledgment: Formal declaration before a notary public.

Ademption: The withdrawal of a gift in a will by an act of the testator that shows an intent to revoke it. For example; by giving the willed property away as a gift during his or her life.

Administration: The probate court supervised distribution of the assets of an estate of a person who died with or without a will, as long as there are probatable assets.

Administrator/Administratrix: One who is appointed to administer the estate of a deceased person who has died without a will or who has died with a will but has not named an executor. The distinction between the two titles (male and female) has largely been removed and *administrator* is proper usage for either male or female.

Advance Health Care Directive: A document outlining a person's wishes regarding health care in the event of their incapacitation. May contain a *living will*, a *health care power of attorney*, an *organ donation* form, and other documents outlining their desires. Also referred to as a *health care directive*.

Advancement: A lifetime gift made to a child by a parent, with the intent that the gift be all or a portion of what the child will be entitled to upon the parent's death.

Affidavit: A person's signed and notarized statement.

Alternate Beneficiary: A person chosen to receive a gift under a will or trust should the originally chosen beneficiary not be available or surviving.

Amend: To change or alter.

Ancestor: One from whom a person is descended.

Annuity contract: A form of investment in which the purchaser is guaranteed a certain periodic payment for life or a certain term.

Appraisal: Valuation of a piece of property, generally by a person certified to conduct such a valuation.

Assets: Any property that you own. Your assets may consist of real estate or personal property. Your personal property may consist of cash, securities, or actual tangible property.

Attestation: To sign one's name as a witness to a will.

Augmented: An augmented estate is your estate left under a will plus the value of property transferred by other means, such as joint tenancies and living trusts. The augmented estate is used to calculate the value of a spousal share of an estate in those states that use this concept.

Bank Trust Account: A type of payable-on-death account under which the main account holder retains full and unilateral control of the account until death. Same as a *Totten Trust*.

Basic Will: A simple standardized type of will.

Beneficiary: One who is named in a will to receive property; one who receives a benefit or gift, as under the terms of a trust.

Bequest: Traditionally, a gift of personal property in a will. Synonymous with *legacy*. Now, *gift* is the appropriate usage for either a gift of real estate or personal property.

Blood Relative: A person who is directly related to another through birth descent.

Bond: A document by which a bonding company guarantees to pay an amount of money if the bonded person does not carry out his or her legal duties.

Bonds: A form of investment through which a company is indebted to the holder and, generally, pays interest to the holder.

Business Interest: Ownership of any form of business, such as a sole proprietorship, partnership, corporation, or limited liability company.

Buy-out Provisions: Contractual terms contained in a business ownership agreement (such as a partnership agreement) that specify the terms under which other owners may be required or have the option to purchase (buy-out) another owner's interest in the business, often upon the death of an owner.

Bypass Trust: See *AB Trust*

Certificate of Deposit: A form of investment under which a bank issues a certificate indicating that it holds a deposit and will pay a certain rate of interest for a certain term.

Charitable Organization: A group that holds a Federal 501(c)3 "charitable organization" tax exemption status, and is able to receive tax-exempt donations.

Charitable Trust: A trust set up to give a gift or income to a charitable organization.

Children's Trust: A form of trust under which gifts to children may be held in trust beyond the child's attainment of the legal age of majority.

Clause: A separate portion of a paragraph or sentence; an article or proviso in a legal document.

Close Corporation: A corporation operated by a small number of individuals, often family members. Is often exempt from certain state laws and may operate more informally. Also referred to as a "closely-held corporation."

Codicil: A formally-signed supplement to a will that is used to alter, amend or revoke provisions in the original will.

Coercion: The application to another of either physical or moral force.

Common Law: System of law that originated in England based on general legal principles rather than legislative acts.

Common-Law Property: Property held by spouse in a common-law state. Can be jointly-held or solely-owned property. The name(s) on the title document is/are the determining factor(s). See Appendix for those states where this system of marital property applies.

Community Property: The property acquired by either spouse during marriage, other than by gift or inheritance. Each spouse owns a half-interest in the community property. See Appendix for those states in which this system of marital property applies.

Conservator: Temporary court-appointed custodian of property.

Contest: Challenge the validity of a will.

Corporation: A company formed and authorized by law to act as a single person and provided with limited liability for any shareholders, and endowed by law with the capacity of succession.

Curtesy: In ancient common law, a husband's right to all of his wife's real estate for life upon her death. Now, generally abolished in most jurisdictions and replaced with a right to a certain statutory share of a spouse's property.

Custodian: A person named to handle property left to a minor under the Uniform Gifts to Minors Act or the Uniform Transfers to Minors Act.

Death Benefits: Money, generally from either insurance policies or pension plans, that are payable to the beneficiaries of a decedent.

Deceased: No longer living; A dead person.

Decedent: One who has died.

Descend: To come from an ancestor or ancestry.

Descendant: One who is descended from another.

Descent: Inheritance by operation of law rather than by will.

Devise: Traditionally, a gift of real estate under a will. Now, *gift* is the appropriate usage for either a gift of real estate or personal property.

Disclaimer: A refusal to accept property left to a person by virtue of a will or trust.

Disinherit: prevent deliberately (as by making a will) from inheriting

Disposition: A final settlement.

Domicile: A person's principal and permanent home.

Dower: In ancient common law, a wife's right to one-third of her husband's real estate for her life upon his death. Now, generally abolished in most jurisdictions and replaced with a right to a certain *statutory share* of a spouse's property.

Durable Power of Attorney: A form of power of attorney which is still in force despite the incapacity or disability of the maker.

Employee Benefits: Money or other benefits that are payable to an employee, such as health-care insurance, travel-expense compensation, etc.

Escheat: Reversion of property to the state, if no family member is found to inherit it.

Estate: All property owned by a person.

Estate Tax: A tax imposed on property that passes to another upon death.

Execution: The formal signing of a will or other legal document.

Executor/Executrix: The person appointed in a will to carry out the testator's wishes and to administer the property.

Family Allowance: An amount that is allowed or granted to one family.

Federal Estate Tax: A percentage tax that is imposed upon the estate of a deceased person for the benefit of being able to pass the estate to others upon death. In 2008, the first $2 million dollars of a person's estate value is fully exempt from this tax, as is all estate property that passes from one spouse to another. The dollar value of the exemption is scheduled to rise to $3.5 million by 2009, and the entire estate tax is scheduled to be repealed for one year in 2010.

Fiduciary: A person with a duty of care to another. For example, a trustee has a duty of care to any beneficiary of a trust, and thus, is a *fiduciary*.

Forgery: The illegal production of something counterfeit.

Fraud: A deception deliberately practiced in order to secure unfair or unlawful gain.

Gift: A voluntary transfer of property to another without any compensation.

Gift Tax: A federal government levy on gifts made during one's lifetime. The current exemption from any gift tax in 2008 is $12,000.00. The federal gift tax is actually calculated by deducting lifetime gifts against a person's estate tax exemption amount at death.

Grantor: The person who creates a trust. Also may be referred to as a *settlor* or *trustor*.

Guardian: A person with the legal power and duty to care for another person and/or a person's property.

Guardian "of the Person:" Guardian responsible for the actual care, custody, and upbringing of a minor child.

Guardian "of the Property:" Guardian who administers the property or money left to child(ren).

Health Care Agent: A person designated under a *health care power of attorney* to make medical decisions for another person when that person is incapable of communicating their own decisions to health care providers. Also referred to as a *health care proxy*.

Health Care Directive: See *advance health care directive.*

Health Care Power of Attorney: The designation of another person to make medical decisions for another person when that person is incapable of communicating their own decisions to health care providers.

Health Care Proxy: See *health care agent.*

Heirlooms: Treasured pieces of property that have been passed down from ancestors.

Heirs: Those persons who inherit from a person by operation of law if there is no will or other document present that passes property upon death.

HIPAA: Federal law relating to the privacy of medical records. A HIPAA statement is now required for the release of any medical records to a third party. Such a statement is included in the *health care power of attorney* and the *durable* unlimited *power of attorney* (2) that are included in this book.

Holographic: A will that is entirely handwritten by the testator and unwitnessed. No longer valid in most states.

Homestead Allowance: A monetary allowance given in some states to spouses and children to insure that they are not abruptly cut off from their support by any terms of a Living Trust. See *family allowance.*

Incapacitated: Being unable to care for one's self or handle one's own financial or other affairs.

Income Property: Real estate that is held for a commercial purpose; the generation of income.

Inheritance: The receipt of property from someone who has died.

Inheritance Tax: A tax on property received that is paid by the person who has actually inherited the property.

Intestate: To die without leaving a valid will.

Intestate Distribution: A state scheme that is used to determine the distribution of the property of any person who dies without leaving a valid will or another determination of how his or her property is to be distributed upon their death.

Invalid: Not legally or factually valid.

IRA: Individual Retirement Accounts under Internal Revenue Service regulations.

Irrevocable: Impossible to retract or revoke.

Joint Tenancy: Joint ownership of property under which the surviving owner automatically owns the deceased owner's share. This is called the *right of survivorship.* May be abbreviated as JTWROS or *joint tenancy with right of survivorship.* Compare to tenancy-in-common.

Joint Tenancy with Right of Survivorship: See *joint tenancy.*

JTWROS: Joint tenancy with right of survivorship. See *joint tenancy.*

Jurisdiction: The right and power to interpret and apply the law. The territorial range of authority or control.

KEOGH: A form of retirement account.

Legacy: A gift of personal property in a will. Now, *gift* is the appropriate usage for either a gift of real estate or personal property. Synonymous with *bequest.*

Legal Age of Minority: The legal age above which a person may legally enter into contracts and otherwise act in the legal capacity of an adult.

Letters of Administration: The court order that officially appoints a person to administer the estate of another.

Letters Testamentary: The court order that officially appoints an executor named in a will as the person to administer the estate of the testator.

Liabilities: Something for which a person is liable, such as a debt.

Life Estate: Surviving spouse has the full use and enjoyment of any real estate for his or her entire life. Upon his or her death, property will pass automatically to person who has remaining share of estate. Recipient of a life estate cannot leave such property to anyone else.

Limited Liability Company: A type of business structure where the liability of a firm's owners are no more than what they have invested in the business.

Living Trust: A form of *revocable trust* which becomes irrevocable upon the death of the grantor.

Living Will: A document that can be used to state your desire that extraordinary life- support means not be used to artificially prolong your life in the event that you are stricken with a terminal illness or injury.

Loans Payable: Loans for which a person owes money to another.

Majority: The status of having reached full legal age, with attendant rights and responsibilities

Marital Property: Property which is considered owned by both spouses in a marriage, as opposed to property which is considered owned by each spouse separately. Also referred to as "community property" in those states which adhere to community property legal concepts.

Minor Child: A child who is under the legal age of majority (generally 18 or 21 years old).

Mortgage: A written statement of a debt owed for the purchase of real estate, under which the property is used as collateral.

Net Worth: A person's net value, determined by subtracting liabilities from assets.

Next of Kin: A person's closest living relative.

Notarize: To have a notary public acknowledge the signing of a document.

Notary Acknowledgment: A formal declaration made to authenticate a witness's signature to ensure legal validity.

Notary Public: A person legally empowered to witness and certify the validity of documents and to take affidavits and depositions.

Notes Payable: Money owed to another based on a promissory note and that is due to be paid.

Notes Receivable: Money owed from another based on a promissory note and that is due to be paid.

Nuncupative: An oral will, usually made during a person's last illness and later reduced to writing by another. No longer valid in most states.

Obituary: A written statement regarding a person's death, usually in a newspaper.

Partnership: A contract between two or more competent persons for joining together their money, goods, labor, or skill, or any or all of them for the purpose of carrying on a legal trade, business, or adventure.

Pass Under: Distributed under the terms of a will or clause.

Payable-on-death Account: An account, generally a bank account, for which a beneficiary is chosen who will receive the proceeds of the account upon the death of the primary account holder. See *bank trust account* or *Totten trust*.

Pension Plan: Any plan under which an employee will receive any benefits after the end of his or her employment.

Per Capita: Equally; share and share alike. For example: if a gift is made to one's descendants, *per capita*, and one has two children and two grandchildren, and one of the children dies, then the gift is divided equally between the surviving child and the two grandchildren. This amounts to one-third to the child and one-third to each grandchild.

Per Stirpes: To share by representation. For example: if a gift is made to two children, *per stirpes*, and one should die but leave two grandchildren, the deceased child's share is given to the two grandchildren in equal shares. This amounts then to one-half to the surviving child and one-fourth to each of the grandchildren.

Personal Property: Movable property, as opposed to real estate property.

Personal Representative: A person who is appointed to administer a deceased's estate. Modern usage that replaces *Executor* and/or *Administrator*.

Posthumous Child: A child born after the father's death.

Pour-over Will: A will under which a trust is the main beneficiary.

Predeceased: Died before.

Pretermitted Child: A child who is left nothing in a parent's will and there is no intent shown to disinherit. Most states then provide for the child to share in the inheritance.

Probate: The court proceeding to determine the validity of a will and, in general, the administration of the property that passes under the will and the payment of debts of the deceased person.

Promissory Note: A written promise to pay or repay a specified sum of money at a stated time or on demand.

Proprietorship: See *Sole Proprietorship*.

Proved: To have determined whether or not the document presented is actually the deceased's will.

Provision: A stipulation or qualification, especially a clause in a document or agreement.

Publication: For a will, the statement by the testator that the document that is being signed is his or her will.

Real Estate/Real Property: Land and that which is attached permanently to it, as opposed to personal property.

Relative: A person who is related by blood or marriage to another.

Residuary: The remainder of an estate after all debts, taxes, and other gifts have been distributed.

Residuary Clause: A clause in a will or trust that designates a beneficiary of the residuary of an estate.

Residue: See *residuary*.

Revocable Trust: Another name for *living trust*. Upon death, a living trust becomes irrevocable and can no longer be changed or altered in any way. In general, however, any type of trust that can be revoked by the grantor.

Revocation: The annulment of a will or other legal document, which renders it invalid. For a will, this is accomplished either by complete destruction of the original will or by executing a later will that revokes the earlier one. For other documents, generally, a written revocation is required.

Revoke: To void or annul by withdrawing, or reversing. To entirely revoke a will, it must be physically destroyed or otherwise irrevocably damaged.

Right of Survivorship: The right of a joint owner of property to automatically obtain ownership over another deceased owner's share of the property. Generally true in a joint tenancy or a tenancy-by-the-entireties.

Self-Proving Affidavit: A document that may be completed by witnesses attesting to the signing of a will by which they affirm that they did indeed witness the signing. This affidavit may then be used later in a probate proceeding to prove the signing without the necessity of calling the witnesses to testify in person at the probate court.

Separate Property: The property of a spouse in a community property or common-law state that is considered the solely-owned property of that spouse, generally property that is solely owned prior to the marriage and any property that is obtained by gift or inheritance during the marriage.

Settlor: See *Grantor*.

Shared Property: The property of a spouse in a community property or common-law state that is considered property of both spouses jointly. In community property states, this would be all property that is not separate property. In common-law property states, this would be all property that is not separate property and which is actually held in some form of joint ownership, such as tenants-in-common or as a joint tenancy.

Sibling: A brother or sister.

Signature: One's name as written by oneself. The act of signing one's name.

Signing: To affix one's signature to.

Sole Proprietorship: A business that is owned by one owner and is not a corporation or limited liability company.

Sound Mind: A legal term that refers to the testator's ability to understand what gifts you are making and who your chosen beneficiaries are.

Spouse: A marriage partner; a husband or wife.

Spouse's Share: See *statutory share*.

Spouse's Right of Election: Surviving spouse has a right to a certain share of the deceased spouse's estate. This right is regardless of any provisions in the will of the deceased spouse that may give the surviving spouse less than this "statutory" or "community" property share. Occurs in all states.

Statutory Share: In common-law states, that portion of a person's property that a spouse is entitled to by law, regardless of any provisions in a will. In community property states, a surviving spouse receives half of all of the community property, regardless of any provisions in a will.

Successor Trustee: The person who is chosen to manage and distribute trust assets upon either the incapacitation or death of the original trustee of the trust.

Supplemental Will: Will used to supplement a living trust. Not a pour-over will.

Surviving: To outlive; to outlast; as, to survive a person or an event.

Survivorship: See *right of survivorship*.

Survivorship Clause: A clause in a trust or will which provides that a beneficiary must outlive the decedent by a certain period of time in order to be considered a rightful beneficiary.

Tenancy-by-the-entirety: A form of joint tenancy (with rights of survivorship) that is only allowed for husbands and wives in certain states.

Tenancy-in-common: A form of joint ownership under which each owner owns a certain specific share of the property (perhaps one-half or another fraction). Upon the death of a co-owner, the deceased co-owner's share is passed to the heirs or beneficiaries of that co-owner, not to the other surviving co-owner(s). Compare to *joint tenancy*.

Testamentary: The expression of intent to dispose of property by will.

Testate: Having a valid will, the opposite of *intestate*.

Testator/Testratrix: A male or female who makes a will.

Totten Trust: A type of payable-on-death account at a financial institution that allows a person to name a beneficiary. Similar to a joint account, but the joint co-owner has no rights until the death of the creator of the account. Also known as a *bank trust account*.

Transfer Documents: Any documents that may be necessary to formalize the change in ownership of property, such as a deed in the case of real estate, or a title in the case of a motor vehicle.

Trust: In general, an arrangement created by one party, the *grantor*, under which property is held by another party, the *trustee*, for the benefit of yet another party, the *beneficiary*. Under a living trust, one person may initially be all three of these parties.

Trust Estate: The assets that have been transferred into a trust by a *grantor*.

Trustee: A person appointed to administer a trust. In a living trust, the trustee and the *grantor* may be the same person.

Trustor: See *Grantor*.

Uniform Gifts to Minors Act: Legislation that provides a way to transfer property to minors. Also similar is the Uniform Transfers to Minors Act.

Vacant Land: Real estate on which there are no buildings present.

Vacation House: Real estate that is owned for the purpose of being used for the owner's vacations.

Validity: The quality of having legal force or effectiveness.

Voiding: To make void or of no validity; invalidate.

Will: A formally-signed and witnessed document by which a person makes a disposition of his or her property to take effect upon his or her death.

Witness: A person who is present and sees another person sign a document.

Index

Nova Publishing Company

Small Business and Consumer Legal Books and Software

Legal Toolkit Series

Estate Planning Toolkit	ISBN 13: 978-1-892949-44		
Business Start-Up Toolkit	ISBN 13: 978-1-892949-43		
Divorce Toolkit (available March 2009)	ISBN 13: 978-1-892949-35		
Legal Forms Toolkit (available May 2009)	ISBN 13: 978-1-892949-48		
Personal Bankruptcy Toolkit (available January 2009)	ISBN 13: 978-1-892949-42		

Law Made Simple Series

Advance Health Care Directives	ISBN 13: 978-1-892949-23		
Estate Planning Simplified	ISBN 1-892949-10-5		
Living Trusts Simplified	ISBN 0-935755-51-9		
Personal Bankruptcy Simplified (4th Edition)	ISBN 1-892949-34-2		
Personal Legal Forms Simplified (3rd Edition)	ISBN 0-935755-97-7	Book w/CD	$28.95
Powers of Attorney Simplified	ISBN 13: 978-1-892949-40-0	Book w/CD	$24.95

Small Business Made Simple Series

Corporation: Small Business Start-up Kit (2nd Edition)	ISBN 1-892949-06-7	Book w/CD	$29.95
Employer Legal Forms	ISBN 13: 978-1-892949-26-4	Book w/CD	$24.95
Landlord Legal Forms	ISBN 13: 978-1-892949-24-0	Book w/CD	$24.95
Limited Liability Company: Start-up Kit (3rd Edition)	ISBN 13: 978-1-892949-37-0	Book w/CD	$29.95
Partnership: Start-up Kit (2nd Edition)	ISBN 1-892949-07-5	Book w/CD	$29.95
Real Estate Forms Simplified	ISBN 0-935755-09-1	Book w/CD	$29.95
S-Corporation: Small Business Start-up Kit (3rd Edition)	ISBN 13: 978-1-892949-36-3	Book w/CD	$29.95
Small Business Accounting Simplified (4th Edition)	ISBN 1-892949-17-2	Book only	$24.95
Small Business Bookkeeping System Simplified	ISBN 0-935755-74-8	Book only	$14.95
Small Business Legal Forms Simplified (4th Edition)	ISBN 0-935755-98-5	Book w/CD	$29.95
Small Business Payroll System Simplified	ISBN 0-935755-55-1	Book only	$14.95
Sole Proprietorship: Start-up Kit (2nd Edition)	ISBN 1-892949-08-3	Book w/CD	$29.95

Legal Self-Help Series

Divorce Yourself: The National Divorce Kit (6th Edition)	ISBN 1-892949-12-1	Book w/CD	$39.95
Incorporate Now!: The National Corporation Kit (4th Ed.)	ISBN 1-892949-00-8	Book w/CD	$28.95
Prepare Your Own Will: The National Will Kit (6th Edition)	ISBN 1-892949-15-6	Book w/CD	$29.95

National Legal Kits

Simplified Divorce Kit (2nd Edition) (3rd Edition-November 2008)	ISBN 1-892949-20-2	Book only	$19.95
Simplified Family Legal Forms Kit (2nd Edition)	ISBN 13: 978-1-892949-41-7	Bookw/CD	$19.95
Simplified Incorporation Kit	ISBN 1-892949-33-4	Book w/CD	$19.95
Simplified Limited Liability Company Kit	ISBN 1-892949-32-6	Book w/CD	$19.95
Simplified Living Will Kit (2nd Edition-November 2008)	ISBN 1-892949-22-9	Book only	$15.95
Simplified S-Corporation Kit	ISBN 1-892949-31-8	Book w/CD	$19.95
Simplified Will Kit (3rd Edition)	ISBN 1-892949-21-0	Book w/CD	$19.95

Ordering Information

Distributed by:
National Book Network
4501 Forbes Blvd. Suite 200
Lanham MD 20706

Shipping: $4.50 for first & $.75 for additionall
Phone orders with Visa/MC: (800) 462-6420
Fax orders with Visa/MC: (800) 338-4550
Internet: www.novapublishing.com
Free shipping on all internet orders (within in the U.S.)